LATIN AMERICA:
A Concise Interpretive History

SEVENTH EDITION

Latin America:
A Concise
Interpretive History

E. Bradford Burns
University of California, Los Angeles

Julie A. Charlip
Whitman College, Walla Walla

Upper Saddle River, New Jersey, 07458

Library of Congress Cataloging-in-Publication Data

BURNS, E. BRADFORD.

Latin America: a concise interpretive history / E. Bradford Burns, Julie A. Charlip.—
7th ed.
p. cm.
Includes bibliographical references and index.
ISBN 0-13-019576-6
1. Latin America—History.   2. Latin America—Social conditions.   3. Latin
America—Economic conditions.   I. Charlip, Julie A.   II. Title.

F1410.B8   2002
980—dc21   2001036189

Acquisitions Editor: *Charles Cavaliere*
Associate Editor: *Emsal Hasan*
AVP, Director of Production and Manufacturing: *Barbara Kittle*
Editorial Production/Supervision and Interior Design: *Judith Winthrop*
Cover Art Director: *Jayne Conte*
Cover Design: *Kiwi Design*
Cover Image: Pedro Figari (1861–1938) S. American, "Baile Criollo" Creole Dance, Christie's
Images, New York /Super Stock Inc.
Prepress and Manufacturing Buyer: *Tricia Kenny*
Supervisor of Production Services: *Guy Ruggiero*
Cartographers: *Carto-Graphics, Mirella Signoretto*
Copy Editor: *Cheryl S. Smith*

This book was set in 10/12 Palatino by the Composing Room
of Michigan, Inc. and was printed and bound by Courier-Stoughton
The cover was printed by Phoenix Color Corporation.

Prentice Hall   © 2002 by Pearson Education
Upper Saddle River, New Jersey 07458

Printed in the United States of America
10 9 8 7 6 5 4 3 2

ISBN 0-13-019576-6

PEARSON EDUCATION LTD., *London*
PEARSON EDUCATION AUSTRALIA PTY. Limited, *Sydney*
PEARSON EDUCATION SINGAPORE, Pte. Ltd.
PEARSON EDUCATION NORTH ASIA LTD., *Hong Kong*
PEARSON EDUCATION CANADA, LTD., *Toronto*
PEARSON EDUCACIÓN DE MEXICO, S.A. DE C.V.
PEARSON EDUCATION —Tokyo, *Japan*
PEARSON EDUCATION MALAYSIA, Pte. Ltd.
PEARSON EDUCATION, Upper Saddle River, *New Jersey*

For Professor Burns,
who believed that young people
could change the world

Contents

2

The Institutions of Empire   *29*

3

Independence   *61*

4

New Nations   *84*

5

The Emergence of the Modern State   *131*

6

New Actors on an Old Stage   *169*

7

The Past Challenged   *199*

8

From World Wars to Cold War   *226*

9

The Revolutionary Option   *255*

10

Modern Problems   *286*

11

The Enigma Remains   *313*

List of Maps

Preface

I was fortunate to have the opportunity to train with E. Bradford Burns at the University of California, Los Angeles. I was among the last of his graduate students: He signed my dissertation in August 1995 and died that December. I have missed him terribly, especially as I have taught this text and wished that we could continue our long talks and often heated debates about Latin America. Prentice Hall's invitation to revise the book was simultaneously flattering and daunting. It is an honor to try to carry on the Burns tradition, but it also seems presumptuous to rewrite one's mentor. I was aided in the task, however, by Professor Burns's own sage advice to me years ago: "It is the job of each generation of scholars to revise the previous generation." I am taking him at his word.

This book remains a landmark in the teaching of Latin American history. It is a narrative that weaves the history of an entire region into a coherent story that emphasizes both common themes and regional and national specificity; it thus breaks away from the old tradition of marching through the separate stories of various countries in the region. Most importantly, the narrative is grounded in Professor Burns's sharp, succinct analysis of the central dynamic of Latin American history: the enigma of "poor people inhabiting rich lands" because the region's elites have "tended to confuse their own well-being and desires with those of the nation at large." I find that analysis to be as on target today as it was in 1972, when the first edition of this text was published.

When it first appeared, the textbook also was the first to adopt the perspective of dependency theory, which came to dominate the debate about Latin American development until the 1990s. It has become quite fashionable at the end of the millennium to dismiss the dependency school, laughing at its naiveté. But as Robert A. Packenham argues in *The Dependency Movement: Scholarship and Politics in Development Studies*, "reports of the death of the dependency movement are premature." Packenham describes the 1991 World Congress of the International Political Science Association meeting in Buenos Aires, at which dependency authors restated their supposedly dated views to enthusiastic applause and even a standing ovation. Indeed, it can be argued that Latin America is more dependent than ever before.

There have been many critiques of dependency theory, from within the wide-ranging dependentista camp itself, between classical Marxists and dependentistas, and between modernization advocates and dependency theorists. Some of the more simplistic versions of dependency theory did seem to reduce Latin American relations to an "us" and "them" dynamic, ignoring the role of Latin American elites. At times the elites were seen as mere lackeys of the developed countries, rather than a dominant class with its own agenda within Latin America. Dependency theorists who predicted that no real change could take place within the structure of Latin American economies were confronted by examples such as Brazil, which combined the state, the private sector, and foreign interests in an extensive process of industrialization and changed from a primary-product exporter to a regional power in manufacturing. Some dependentistas, Burns among them, advocated a virtual withdrawal from the world market and a return to a more simple life, in which domestic goods would suffice.

Many of those debates do indeed seem outmoded today. Certainly solutions that called for near autarky seem unrealistic amid today's relentless onslaught of globalization. Nonetheless, the basic description provided by dependency theory still holds true: The mere equation of growth with development is erroneous. The rise in gross national product, if it is not redistributed, benefits only a tiny percentage of the population. Latin America still suffers from the world's most inequitable distribution of wealth, a condition that has only worsened in the past two decades. And changes in Latin America's economy are still conditioned by the drive and direction of the more industrialized world, albeit with the full cooperation and at times initiation of regional elites. Because those conditions still hold true, the use of dependency in this text remains instructive.

Much of the theoretical community has moved on to contemplate ideas of post-modernism, discourse, and the subaltern. At their worst, some of these approaches have fastened on the uses of language at the risk of ignoring the very real material conditions that exist in Latin America. At their best, these approaches have helped us to think about the multivariant roles people play, of shifting class and power positions, and the ways in which gender, race, and ethnicity have interacted with class. In many ways, Professor Burns's work presaged these developments, especially in his emphasis on the ways in which the "folk" struggled to maintain their cultures and resist the imposition of the elite vision—or as scholars may put it today, the ways in which the subaltern struggled against the dominant discourse. What is most important is not to worry so much about the labels, but keep a keen eye on what we are describing.

While I have retained the general dependentista description, I have, however, revised the text quite extensively, updating it with more recent research and adding my own interpretation of the history. I am grateful to Thomas Whigham for helping me reconsider the case of Paraguay, which had been featured as a prime example of autonomous development. Newer scholarship questions the benefits to the majority of the Paraguayan model and casts doubts on Dr. Francia as a "folk" caudillo. Rather than detail these changes, I have simply opted to remove Paraguay from the discussion. I also have endeavored to weave women's roles throughout the text, rather than relegating them to one chapter. In addition to updating the material, I have rearranged it to suit my own idiosyncratic view of the logic of the narrative, following the way I have taught the material for the past eight years. I have added several primary documents to each chapter to strengthen the voice of Latin Americans in the telling of their history. Most importantly, I have tried to preserve Professor Burns's voice, while blending it with my own.

Acknowledgments

I owe a debt of thanks to those who have advised me on this project, especially Thomas Holloway, Steven Topik, Hector Lindo Fuentes, James Green, and Enrique Ochoa. I am thankful to Whitman College for a Louis B. Perry Summer Research Scholarship, which enabled me to hire Valarie Hamm and Mollie Lewis, who helped me enormously in the review of new scholarship on Latin America. Most of all I thank my husband, Charly Bloomquist, and my daughter, Delaney, who put up with my long hours of work and provided me with love and support.

Julie A. Charlip
Walla Walla, Washington

LATIN AMERICA:
A Concise Interpretive History

1

The Origins of a Multiracial Society

Asians, Europeans, and Africans all met on the vast and varied stage of the New World. Representatives of the three regions arrived at different times and for different reasons. They mixed, mingled, and married. From their contributions emerged the unique panorama of Latin American society.

The Land

Although historians study people through time, the historian cannot neglect location, the habitat of those people. Geography is destiny until one has the technology to surmount it. Geographic attributes have contributed to Latin America's economic organization and created challenges for settlement and state building.

Contemporary Latin America is a huge region of a continent and a half, stretching 7,000 miles southward from the Río Grande to Cape Horn, varying widely in its geographic and human composition. Geopolitically the region encompasses eighteen Spanish-speaking republics, French-speaking Haiti, and Portuguese-speaking Brazil, a total of approximately 8 million square miles, and a rapidly growing population exceeding 495 million. In recent

Latin America: the outstanding geographic features.

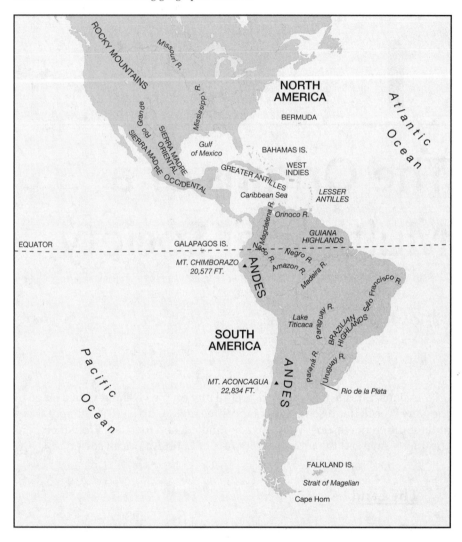

years, the region's population growth has slowed, from more than 2 percent to 1.5 percent, more in line with the world average of 1.4 percent. Half of that population is either Brazilian or Mexican. Despite concerns in the more developed world about Latin American population growth, the region is relatively underpopulated, with the exception of overcrowded El Salvador and Haiti. More than twice the size of Europe, the area contains less population than Europe. It occupies 19 percent of the world's land but contains only 7 percent of the world's population.

Despite its phenomenal physical size, its growing population, and its resources, the region remains underdeveloped, its potential unfulfilled. For half a millennium, the great majority of the people remained poor, and the record for the past century points to increasing poverty among ever larger numbers. This reality calls for an explanation as well as a reversal. History, more than geography, suggests explanations for these grim trends.

Most of Latin America lies within the tropics. In fact, only one country, Uruguay, has no territory in the tropics. South America reaches its widest point, 3,200 miles, just a few degrees south of the equator, unlike North America, which narrows rapidly as it approaches the equator. However, the cold

Population Density of Latin America and Selected European Countries, 2000

COUNTRY	LAND AREA (in square kilometers)	POPULATION	DENSITY
Netherlands	33,889	15,892,237	469
Belgium	30,230	10,241,506	339
El Salvador	20,720	6,122,515	295
Haiti	27,560	6,867,995	249
United Kingdom	241,590	59,511,464	246
Germany	349,223	82,797,408	237
Italy	294,020	57,634,327	196
Dominican Republic	48,380	8,442,533	174
Poland	304,465	38,646,023	127
Denmark	42,394	5,336,394	126
Hungary	92,340	10,138,844	110
France	545,630	59,329,691	109
Cuba	110,860	11,141,997	101
Austria	82,738	8,131,111	98
Costa Rica	50,660	3,710,558	73
Honduras	111,890	6,249,598	56
Mexico	1,923,040	100,349,766	52
Ecuador	276,840	12,920,092	47
Nicaragua	120,254	4,812,569	40
Colombia	1,038,700	39,685,655	38
Panama	75,990	2,808,268	37
Venezuela	882,050	23,542,649	27
Guatemala	108,430	12,639,939	24
Peru	1,280,000	27,012,899	21
Brazil	8,456,510	172,860,370	20
Chile	748,800	15,153,797	20
Uruguay	173,620	3,334,074	19
Paraguay	397,300	5,585,828	14
Argentina	2,736,690	36,955,182	14
Bolivia	1,084,390	8,152,620	8

Source: Data drawn from *The World Factbook 2000,* Washington, D.C.: Central Intelligence Agency, 2000.

Pacific Ocean currents refresh much of the west coast of Latin America, and the altitudes of the mountains and highlands offer a wide range of temperatures that belie the latitude. For centuries, and certainly long before the Europeans arrived, many of the region's most advanced civilizations flourished in the mountain plateaus and valleys. Today many of Latin America's largest cities are in the mountains or on mountain plateaus: Mexico City, Guatemala City, Bogotá, Quito, La Paz, and São Paulo, to mention only a few. Much of Latin America's population, particularly in Middle America and along the west coast of South America, concentrates in the highland areas.

In Mexico and Central America, the highlands create a rugged backbone that runs through the center of most of the countries, leaving coastal plains on either side. Part of that mountain system emerges in the Greater Antilles to shape the geography of the major Caribbean islands. In South America, unlike Middle America, the mountains closely rim the Pacific coast, while the highlands skirt much of the Atlantic coast, making penetration into the flatter interior of the continent difficult. The Andes predominate. The world's longest continuous mountain barrier, it runs 4,000 miles down the west coast and fluctuates in width between 100 and 400 miles. Aconcagua, the highest mountain in the hemisphere, rises to a majestic 22,834 feet along the Chilean–Argentine frontier. The formidable Andes have been a severe obstacle to exploration and settlement of the South American interior from the west. Along the east coast, the older Guiana and Brazilian Highlands average 2,600 feet in altitude and rarely reach 9,000 feet. Running southward from the Caribbean and frequently fronting on the ocean, they disappear in the extreme south of Brazil. Like the Andes, they too have inhibited penetration of the interior. The largest cities on the Atlantic side are all on the coast or, like São Paulo, within a very short distance of the ocean. In contrast to the west coast, the east boasts of some extraordinary natural harbors.

Four major river networks, the Magdalena, Orinoco, Amazon, and La Plata, flow into the Caribbean or Atlantic, providing an access into the interior missing on the west coast. The Amazon ranks as one of the world's most impressive river systems. Aptly referred to in Portuguese as the "river-sea," it is the largest river in volume in the world. Its volume exceeds that of the Mississippi by fourteen times. In places it is impossible to see from shore to shore, and over a good part of its course the river averages 100 feet in depth. Running eastward from its source 18,000 feet up in the Andes, it is joined from both the north and south by more than 200 tributaries. Together this imposing river and its tributaries provide 25,000 miles of navigable water.

Farther to the south, the Plata network flows through some of the world's richest soil, the Pampas, a vast flat area shared by Argentina, Uruguay, and Brazil. The river system includes the Uruguay, Paraguay, and Paraná rivers, but it gets its name from the Río de la Plata, a 180-mile-long estuary separating Uruguay and the Argentine province of Buenos Aires. The system drains a basin of more than 1.5 million square miles. Shallow in depth, it still provides a vital communication and transportation link between the Atlantic coast and the southern interior of the continent.

No single country better illustrates the kaleidoscopic variety of Latin American geography than Chile, that long, lean land clinging to the Pacific shore for 2,600 miles. One of the world's bleakest and most forbidding deserts in the north gives way to rugged mountains with forests and alpine pastures. The Central Valley combines a Mediterranean climate with fertile plains, the heartland of Chile's agriculture and population. Moving southward, the traveler encounters dense, mixed forests; heavy rainfall, and a cold climate, warning of the glaciers and rugged coasts that lie beyond. Snow permanently covers much of Tierra del Fuego.

While Chile offers a dazzling array of extremes, many of the other nations offer just as much variety. Latin Americans have always been aware of the significance of their environment. Visiting the harsh, arid interior of northeastern Brazil for the first time, Euclydes da Cunha marveled in his *Rebellion in the Backlands* (*Os Sertöes*, 1902) at how the land had shaped a different people and created a civilization that contrasted sharply with that of the coast:

> Here was an absolute and radical break between the coastal cities and the clay huts of the interior, one that so disturbed the rhythm of our evolutionary development and which was so deplorable a stumbling block to national unity. They were in a strange country now, with other customs, other scenes, a different kind of people. Another language even, spoken with an original and picturesque drawl. They had, precisely, the feelings of going to war in another land. They felt that they were outside Brazil.

Across the continent in Peru, novelist Ciro Alegría depicted life in the tropical rain forest dominated by the presence of a great river, the upper reaches of the Amazon. One of the characters of his novel *The Golden Serpent* (*La Serpente de Oro*, 1935) gazes at the Amazon's tributary and exclaims, "The river, yes, the river. I never thought of it. It is so large, so masterful, and it has made all this, hasn't it?"

Latin American films, too, often assign nature the role of a major protagonist. Certainly in the Argentine classic *Prisoners of the Earth* (*Prisioneros de la Tierra*, 1939), the forests and rivers of the northeast overpower the outsider. Nature even forces the local people to bend before her rather than conquer her. A schoolteacher exiled by a military dictatorship to the geographically remote and rugged Chilean south in the Chilean film *The Frontier* (*La Frontera*, 1991) quickly learns that the ocean, mountains, and elements dominate and shape the lives of the inhabitants. Nature thus enforces some characteristics on the people of Latin America. The towering Andes, the vast Amazon, the unbroken Pampas, the lush rain forests provide an impressive setting for an equally powerful human drama.

The Indian

The continents of Asia, Europe, and Africa contributed to the peopling of the Western Hemisphere, and subsequently, a greater racial mixing has resulted there than in any other part of the world. From Asia came the first migrants in various waves between 20,000 and 40,000 years ago. Anthropologists generally believe that they crossed from one continent to the other at the Bering Strait in pursuit of game animals. Hunger propelled them. Moving slowly southward, they dispersed throughout North and South America. Over the millennia, at an uneven rate, some advanced through hunting and fishing cultures to take up agriculture. At the same time they fragmented into many linguistic (up to 2,200 different languages) and cultural groups, although they maintained certain general physical features in common: straight black hair, dark eyes, copper-colored skin, and short stature.

The Indian societies can best be understood by grouping them as nonsedentary, semi-sedentary, and sedentary societies. Nonsedentary societies, found mostly in what is now the northern Mexico frontier, the Argentine pampas, and the interior of Brazil, were gathering and hunting groups that followed a seasonal cycle of moving through a delimited territory in search of food. In semisedentary societies, hunting was still important, but they had also developed slash-and-burn agriculture, shifting sites within their region to accommodate this technique. They populated much of Latin America and were often found on the fringes of fully sedentary peoples. Fully sedentary peoples had settled communities based on intensive agriculture, with enough surplus to support a hierarchical society with specialized classes. They were found in central Mexico, Guatemala, Ecuador, Peru, and Bolivia.

Varied as the early American cultures were, a majority of them shared enough traits to permit a few generalizations. The family or clan units served as the basic social organization. All displayed a profound faith in supernatural forces that they believed shaped, influenced, and guided their lives. For that reason, the *shamans*, those intimate with the supernatural, played important roles in the indigenous societies. They provided the contact between the mortal and the immortal, between the human and the spirit. In most rituals and celebrations, the participants danced, sang, beat drums, shook rattles, and possibly played flutes. Common to the oral literature of most of the groups were stories of the cultural hero, the ancestor who taught the early members of the tribe their way of life, and the prankster whose exploits aroused both mirth and admiration. In the more complex and highly stratified societies, there was a differentiation between the more extensive landholdings of the nobility and that of the commoners. But in all indigenous societies, land was provided to everyone on the basis of membership in the community. Game roamed and ate off the land. Further, the land furnished fruits, berries, nuts, and roots. Tilling the soil produced other foods—corn and potatoes, for example. Many artifacts, instruments, and implements were similar from Alaska to Cape Horn. For example, spears, bows and arrows, and clubs were the common weapons of warfare or for the hunt. Although these similarities are significant, the differences among the many cultures were enormous and impressive. By the end of the fifteenth century, between 15 million and 100 million people inhabited the Western Hemisphere. Scholars still heatedly debate the figures, and one can find forceful arguments favoring each extreme.

Mistaking the New World for Asia, Christopher Columbus called the inhabitants he met "Indians," a name that has remained to cause endless confusion. Exploration later indicated that the "Indians" of the New World belonged to a large number of cultural groups of which the most important were the Aztecs and Mayas of Mexico and Central America; the Carib of the Caribbean area; the Chibcha of Columbia; the Inca of Ecuador, Peru, and Bolivia; the Araucanian of Chile; the Guaraní of Paraguay; and the Tupí of Brazil. Of these, the Aztec, Maya, and Inca exemplify the most complex cultural achievements, with fully sedentary and imperial societies.

Two distinct periods, the Classic and the Late, mark the history of Mayan civilization. During the Classic period, from the fourth to the tenth centuries, the Mayas lived in Guatemala; then they suddenly migrated to Yucatán, beginning the Late period, which lasted until the Spanish conquest. The exodus baffles anthropologists, who most often suggest that the exhaustion of the soil in Guatemala limited the corn harvests and forced the Mayas to move in order to survive. Corn provided the basis for the Mayan civilization. The Mayan account of creation revolves around corn. The gods "began to talk about the creation and the making of our first mother and father; of yellow corn and of white corn they made their flesh; of cornmeal dough they made the arms and the legs of man," relates the *Popul Vuh*, the sacred book of the Mayas. All human activity, all religion centered on the planting, growing, and harvesting of corn.

The Mayas dug an extensive network of canals and water-control ditches, which made intensive agriculture possible. These efficient agricultural methods produced corn surpluses and hence the leisure for a large priestly class to dedicate its talents to religion and scientific study. Extraordinary intellectual achievements resulted. The Mayas progressed from the pictograph to the ideograph and thus invented a type of writing, the only Indians in the hemisphere to do so. Sophisticated in mathematics, they invented the zero and devised numeration by position. Astute observers of the heavens, they applied their mathematical skills to astronomy. Their careful studies of the heavens enabled them to predict eclipses, follow the path of the planet Venus, and prepare a calendar more accurate than that used in Europe. As the ruins of Copán, Tikal, Palenque, Chichén Itzá, Mayapán, and Uxmal testify, the Mayas built magnificent temples. One of the most striking features of that architecture is its extremely elaborate carving and sculpture.

To the west of the Mayas, another native civilization, the Aztecs, expanded and flourished in the fifteenth century. The Aztecs had migrated from the north in the early thirteenth century into the central valley of Mexico, where they conquered several prosperous and highly advanced city-states. In 1325, they founded Tenochtitlán, their island capital. They made effective use of their lake location through development of a highly productive system of agriculture including *chinampas*, or floating gardens. From their religious and political center they radiated outward to absorb other cultures until they controlled all of Central Mexico. Constant conquests gave prominence to the warriors, and, not surprisingly, the god of war and the sun predominated among the multiple divinities. To propitiate him, as well as other gods, required human sacrifices on a grand scale. The Aztecs devised the pictograph, an accurate calendar, an impressive architecture, and an elaborate and effective system of government.

Largest, oldest, and best organized of the Indian civilizations was the Incan, which flowered in the harsh environment of the Andes. By the early sixteenth century, the empire extended in all directions from Cuzco, regarded as the center of the universe. It stretched nearly 3,000 miles from Ecuador into Chile, and its maximum width measured 400 miles. Few empires have been more rigidly regimented or more highly centralized, a real miracle when one realizes that it was run without the benefit—or hindrance—of written accounts or records. The only accounting system was the *quipu*, cords upon which knots were made to indicate specific mathematical units. (Some scholars now claim the Incas wove some sort of code into the threads.) The highly effective government rapidly assimilated newly conquered peoples into the empire. Entire populations were moved around the empire when security suggested the wisdom of such relocations. Every subject was required to speak Quechua, the language of the court. In weaving, pottery, medicine, and agriculture, the achievements of the Incans were magnificent. Challenged by a stingy soil, they developed systems of drainage, terracing, and irrigation and learned the value of fertilizing their fields. They produced impressive food surpluses, stored by the state for lean years.

Many differences separated these three high Indian civilizations, but at the same time some impressive similarities existed. Society was highly structured. The hierarchy of nobles, priests, warriors, artisans, farmers, and slaves was ordinarily inflexible, although occasionally some mobility did occur. At the pinnacle of that hierarchy stood the omnipotent emperor, the object of the greatest respect and veneration. The sixteenth-century chronicler Cieza de León, in his own charming style, illustrated the awe in which the people held the Inca: "Thus the kings were so feared that, when they traveled over the provinces, and permitted a piece of the cloth to be raised which hung round their litter, so as to allow their vassals to behold them, there was such an outcry that the birds fell from the upper air where they were flying, insomuch that they could be caught in men's hands. All men so feared the king, that they did not dare to speak evil of his shadow." Little or no distinction existed between civil and religious authority, so that for all intents and purposes church and state were one. The Incan and Aztec emperors both were regarded as representatives of the sun on earth and thus as deities, a position probably held by the rulers of the Mayan city-states as well.

Royal judges impartially administered the laws of the empires and apparently enjoyed a reputation for fairness. The sixteenth-century chroniclers who saw the judicial systems functioning invariably praised them. Cieza de León, for one, noted, "It was felt to be certain that those who did evil would receive punishment without fail and that neither prayers nor bribes would avert it." These civilizations rested on a firm rural base. Cities were rare, although a few existed with populations exceeding 100,000. They were centers of commerce, government, and religion. Eyewitness accounts as well as the ruins that remain leave no doubt that some of the cities were well-organized and contained impressive architecture. The sixteenth-century chronicles reveal that the cities astonished the first Spaniards who saw them. Bernal Díaz del Castillo, who accompanied Hernando Cortés into Tenochtitlán in 1519, gasped, "And when we saw all those cities and villages built in the water, and other great towns on dry land, and that straight and level causeway leading to Mexico [City], we were astounded. These great towns and cities and buildings rising from the water, all made of stone, seemed like an enchanted vision from the tale of Amadis. Indeed, some of our soldiers asked whether it was not a dream!" The productivity of the land made possible an opulent court life and complex religious ceremonies.

The vast majority of the population worked in agriculture. The farmers grew corn, beans, squash, pumpkins, manioc root, and potatoes, as well as other crops. Communal lands were cultivated for the benefit of the state, religion, and community. The state thoroughly organized and directed the rural labor force. Advanced as these Indian civilizations were, however, not one developed the use of iron or used the wheel, since they lacked draft animals to pull wheeled vehicles. However, the Indians had learned to work gold, silver, copper, tin, and bronze. Artifacts that have survived in those metals testify to fine skills.

There is some disagreement among scholars about the roles that women played in these societies. In both the Inca and Aztec worlds, women primarily bore responsibility for domestic duties. In the Aztec world, that included the ritual sweeping that was related to religious practices. Women also sold goods in the markets (where they often had supervisory positions), were cloth makers and embroiderers, and served as midwives. But strong evidence points to narrowly circumscribed roles, particularly in terms of sexuality. Mothers instructed their daughters, "Do not deliver yourself to anyone, because if merely by that you cease being a virgin, if you become a woman, you will be lost, because then you will never be under the protection of someone who truly loves you." In Inca society, women took care of the home, but also worked in agriculture. Their work tended to be seen not as private service for husbands but as a continuation of household and community. Some scholars contend that these separate roles were clearly unequal, while others contend that they were different but equally valued. However strong or equal women's position may have been at an earlier time in Aztec and Inca society, it appears that their roles diminished as the societies became more militant and the role of warriors became exalted.

The spectacular achievements of these advanced farming cultures contrast sharply with the more elementary evolution of the gathering, hunting, and fishing cultures and the intermediate farming cultures among the Latin American Indians. The Tupí tribes, the single most important native element contributing to the early formation of Brazil, illustrate the status of the many intermediate farming cultures found throughout Latin America.

The Tupí tribes tended to be very loosely organized. The small, temporary villages, often surrounded by a crude wooden stockade, were, when possible, located along a river bank. The Indians lived communally in large thatched huts in which they strung their hammocks in extended family or lineage groups of as many as one hundred persons. Most of the tribes had at least a nominal chief, although some seemed to recognize a leader only in time of war and a few seemed to have no concept of a leader. More often than not, the *shaman,* or medicine man, was the most important and powerful tribal figure. He communed with the spirits, proffered advice, and prescribed medicines. The religions abounded with good and evil spirits.

The men spent considerable time preparing for and participating in tribal wars. They hunted monkeys, tapirs, armadillos, and birds. They also fished, trapping the fish with funnel-shaped baskets, poisoning the water and collecting the fish, or shooting the fish with arrows. They cleared away the forest to plant crops. Nearly every year during the dry season, the men cut down trees, bushes, and vines, waited until they had dried, and then burned them, a method used throughout Latin America, then as well as now. The burning destroyed the thin humus and the soil was quickly exhausted. Hence, it was constantly necessary to clear new land, and eventually the village moved in order to be near virgin soil. In general (although not exclusively), the women took change of planting and harvesting crops and of collecting and preparing the food. Manioc was the principal cultivated crop. Maize, beans, yams, peppers, squash, sweet potatoes, tobacco, pineapples, and occasionally cotton were the other cultivated crops. Forest fruits were collected.

To the first Europeans who observed them, these Indians seemed to live an idyllic life. The tropics required little or no clothing. Generally nude, the Tupí developed the art of body ornamentation and painted elaborate and ornate geometric designs on themselves. Into their noses, lips, and ears they inserted stone and wooden artifacts. Feathers from the colorful forest birds provided an additional decorative touch. Their appearance prompted the Europeans to think of them as innocent children of nature. The first chronicler of Brazil, Pero Vaz de Caminha, marveled to the king of Portugal, "Sire, the innocence of Adam himself was not greater than these people's." In the beginning, the Europeans overlooked the grim affinity of the Indians for fighting and for at least ceremonial cannibalism to emphasize their inclinations to dance and sing. More extensive contact with the Indians caused later chroniclers to tell quite a different tale, one in which the Indians emerged as wicked villains, brutes who desperately needed the civilizing hand of Europe.

The European romantics who thought they saw a utopia in Indian life obviously exaggerated. The Indians by no means had led the perfect life. Misunderstanding, if not outright ignorance, has always characterized outsiders' perceptions of the Indians. Even today it remains difficult to pull back the veil of myth to glimpse reality. It appears that much of indigenous society, especially outside the great empires, was quite egalitarian, with community responsibility emphasized over competition. The Indians adapted well to their environments, whether in the difficult craggy Andes or the lush tropics, although it would be easy to idealize their relationship with the land and management of resources. Far too often since the conquest, images of Indians have erred at either extreme—the savage or the noble savage—rather than showing their humanity.

The European

As the sixteenth century approached, Europe was on the eve of a commercial revolution. Merchants dreamed of breaking the Arab and Italian monopolies of trade with Asia, thereby sharing the lucrative profits from the spices, precious stones, pearls, dyes, silks, tapestries, porcelains, and rugs coveted by wealthy Europeans. Portugal led the quest for those new trade routes.

Like the neighboring kingdoms in Spain, Portugal had been the crossroads of many peoples—Iberians, Celts, Phoenicians, Greeks, Carthaginians, Romans, Visigoths, and Moslems—and had blended their cultures together. The last of the many invaders of the peninsula, the Moslems, had begun their conquest of Iberia in 711. The Christians initiated their crusade to reconquer the peninsula in 732 at the Battle of Tours and intermittently continued it until Granada fell in 1492.

Portugal, to assert its independence, had to free itself both of Moslem control and Castilian claims. In 1139, Afonso Henriques of the House of Burgundy for the first time used the title "King of Portugal," a title officially recognized four decades later by the Pope, then arbiter of such matters. The new state struggled to expel the Moslems and finally succeeded in driving their remaining armies from the Algarve, the far south, in 1250. Neighboring Castile, deeply involved in its own campaign against the Moors, reluctantly recognized the existence of Portugal. The task of consolidating the new state fell to King Denis, whose long reign, bridging the thirteenth and fourteenth centuries, marked the emergence of Europe's first modern national state.

Portugal became for a time Europe's foremost sea power. Its location, on the westernmost tip of continental Europe, was well suited for that role. Most of the sparse population, less than a million in the fifteenth century, inhabited the coastal area. They faced the great, gray, open sea and nearby Africa. At peace at home and with no imminent foreign threats to prepare for, Portugal could turn its attention outward. The Portuguese initiated their overseas expansion in Africa in 1415 with the conquest of strategic Ceuta, guardian of the opening to the Mediterranean. They were motivated primarily by commercial reasons, as all classes of society were dazzled by the vision of a Lisbon made rich as the entrepôt of Asian merchandise. In a society dominated by the Roman Catholic Church, religious motives for expansion also played at least a superficially important role. The Portuguese hoped to defeat the enemies of their faith in Africa and to carry the word of God to the continent.

The first to appreciate fully that the ocean was not a barrier but a vast highway of commerce was Prince Henry (1394–1460), known as "the Navigator" to English writers, although he was a confirmed landlubber. Listening to the expert advice of his day, he defined Portugal's policy of exploration: systematic voyages outward, each based on the intelligence collected from the former voyager and each traveling beyond its predecessor. The improvements in geographic, astronomical, and navigational knowledge that characterized a century of accelerating seaborne activity facilitated the task. In 1488, Bartolomeu Dias rounded the Cape of Good Hope and pointed the way to a water route to India.

News from Christopher Columbus that he had reached India by sailing west in 1492 momentarily disturbed the Portuguese, who were on the verge of reaching the Orient by circumnavigating Africa. Unlike Portugal, Spain had earned little reputation for maritime prowess. In the last quarter of the fifteenth century, some Spanish expeditions plied the African coast, and one of them laid Spanish claims to the Canary Islands. Most Spanish energy, however, had been expended internally on the struggle against the Moors and on the effort of unification. The marriage of Isabel of Castile to Ferdinand of Aragón in 1469 forged the major link in Spanish unity. Thereafter, first the external and then the internal policies of Castile and Aragón harmonized. Those two monarchs increased the power of the crown by humbling both the nobility and the municipal governments. Equating religious with political unification, they expelled those Jews and Moors who refused to embrace the Roman Catholic faith. The infamous Inquisition sternly enforced religious conformity. When Isabel died in 1504, Ferdinand ruled as king of Aragón and regent of Castile.

While the two monarchs were unifying Spain, they accelerated the struggle to expel the Moors. In 1492, Granada, the last Moorish domain on the Iberian Peninsula, fell. Providentially, in that same year, Columbus opened a new horizon for the Spaniards. The energy, talent, and drive that previously had gone into the reconquest, that holy and political campaign allying cross and sword for eight centuries, were invested immediately in overseas expansion. The Spaniards carried with them many of the ideas—religious intolerance and fervor, suspicion of foreigners—as well as many of the institutions—vice-royalty, *encomienda*—developed during the long reconquest. On all levels, then, the Spaniards regarded their conquests in the Americas as the logical extension of reconquests on the Iberian peninsula.

The return of Columbus from his first voyage intensified rivalry between Spain and Portugal, both of which sought to guard their own sea lanes and prohibit the incursion of the other. War threatened until diplomacy triumphed. At Tordesillas in 1494, representatives of the two monarchs agreed to divide the world. An imaginary line running pole to pole 370 leagues west of the Cape Verde Islands gave Portugal everything discovered for 180 degrees east and Spain everything for 180 degrees west. With the exception of an interest in the Philippines, Spain concentrated its attention on the Western Hemisphere. Within the half of the world reserved for Portugal, Vasco da Gama discovered the long-sought water route to India. His protracted voyage in 1497–99 joined East and West by sea for the first time. Subsequent voyages by Columbus in 1493–96, 1498–1500, and 1502–04, suggested the extent of the lands he had discovered but proved that in fact he had not reached India. Portugal, at least for the moment, monopolized the only sea lanes to India, and that monopoly promised to enrich the realm. The cargo that Vasco da Gama brought back to Lisbon repaid sixty times over the original cost of the expedition. For the time being, the Portuguese maritime routes were proving to be far more lucrative than those of the Spaniards. The kings of Portugal became rich merchants and the Portuguese turned to the sea as never before. Pedro Alvares Cabral received command of the fleet being prepared to follow up the exploit of da Gama. While sailing to India in 1500, the fleet veered off course and Cabral discovered and claimed Brazil, which later was found to fall within the half of the world the Tordesillas treaty had allocated to Portugal. Along the coasts of South America, Africa, and Asia, the Portuguese eagerly established their commercial—not colonial—empire. The Chief Cosmographer of the Realm boasted, "The Portuguese discovered new islands, new lands, new seas, new people; and what is more, new sky and new stars." It was a glorious age for Portugal, and one of the great epic poets of all times, Luís de Camoes, composed *The Lusiads* to commemorate the achievements.

The discovery of the Americas was an accident, the unforeseen byproduct of an Iberian search for new maritime routes and desire for direct trade with the East. At first, the discovery did not seem particularly rewarding. The

Western Hemisphere loomed as an undesirable barrier to a direct water route to Asia. Furthermore, the native inhabitants displayed scant interest in trading with the Iberian merchants.

Confrontation and Conquest

The discoveries of Columbus and Cabral brought the Iberians face to face with the peoples of the New World. The confrontation puzzled each side and awoke a great deal of mutual curiosity.

Because commerce had motivated the oceanic explorations that resulted in the discoveries, the Iberians hoped to trade with the inhabitants they encountered. The peoples of the simple societies of the Caribbean and along the coast of eastern South America showed scant inclination for such commercial intercourse. In fact, they had little to offer the Iberians and required even less from them. The Portuguese soon found along the coast rich stands of brazilwood, a wood that gave the newly discovered land its name and furnished an excellent red dye much in demand by the new European textile industries. The crown established a monopoly over its exploitation and eagerly sold rights to merchants. Fernão de Noronha, the first to buy the contract, dispatched ships in 1503 to fetch the dyewood. The ship captains bartered with the Indians, exchanging trinkets for the brazilwood they cut. A lucrative trade in the wood developed during the sixteenth century. In addition to its limited economic role, Brazil served strategically for many decades as the guardian of the western flank of the prized trade route to Asia. So long as Portugal held a monopoly over that seaborne trade, Brazil received only minimal attention.

On the other hand, for three decades after Columbus's discovery, Spain searched the eastern coast of the New World for a westward passage, a route other European states began to seek as well. Columbus made three long voyages touching the largest Caribbean islands and coasting along the shores of northern South America and Central America. In 1513, Juan Ponce de León reconnoitered the coast of Florida and that same year Vasco Nuñez de Balboa marching across Panama came upon the Pacific Ocean, which he promptly claimed for his monarch. The desire to get to that ocean by some water route intensified.

At the same time the Spaniards began to settle some of the major Caribbean islands. On his second voyage Columbus transported men and supplies to establish the first such colony. On the northern coast of Hispaniola, he marked out a grid pattern for a town, set up a municipal government, divided up the land among the colonists, and assigned Indians to each settler to work their land. He thereby established a pattern of colonization faithfully imitated in the succeeding decades wherever the Spaniards went in the New World. Many of the new arrivals searched hopefully for gold, and the islands yielded enough to excite speculations about even greater discoveries. Others turned to agriculture. The monarchs encouraged the migration of artisans and farmers to the New World. In his instructions to one governor departing for the Indies in 1513, the Spanish king ordered him to take "farmers so that they may attempt to plant the soil." Similar orders were repeated frequently. Sugar cane was planted as early as 1493. By 1520, it was a profitable industry with at least twenty-eight sugar mills operating on Hispaniola. Domestic animals imported onto the islands multiplied rapidly. Ships returning to Spain carried sugar and hides. The monarch and merchants of Spain sought to encourage such trade. In 1503, Ferdinand sanctioned the establishment of the Casa de Contratación in Seville to oversee the commerce between Spain and the New World. Nonetheless, much of the agricultural production in Spanish America, at least during the first century and a half, went to feed the colonists and to provide supplies for conquest, expansion, and further settlement.

The Spanish pattern of exploration and settlement changed after 1521, a year marking the circumnavigation of the globe by Ferdinand Magellan and the conquest of central Mexico by Hernando Cortés. The long voyage, begun by Magellan in 1519 but concluded by Juan Sebastian del Cano in 1521 after Magellan was killed by natives in the Philippine Islands, proved at last the possibility of reaching Asia by sailing west. The expedition had found the way around the barrier of North and South America, but it also had proven that the westward passage was longer and more difficult than the African route used by the Portuguese. At the same time Spain realized it did not need the route to India. Conquered Mexico revealed that the New World held far more wealth in the form of the coveted gold and silver than the Spaniards could hope to reap from trade with Asia. Spanish opinion changed from deprecating the New World as an obstacle to the East to considering it a rich treasure chest. No longer considered simply a way station on the route to Asia, America became the center of Spanish attention.

History provides few epics of conquest more remarkable than Cortés's sweep through Mexico. His capture of the opulent Aztec empire initiated a period of conquest during which Spain defeated the major Indian nations and made their inhabitants subject to the Castilian monarch. Generally these conquests were private undertakings, the result of contract, known as a *capitulación*, signed between the monarch and the aspiring conquistador, who was given the title of *adelantado*. Those contracts introduced European capitalism, as it had taken shape by the early sixteenth century, into the Americas. The adelantados by no means wandered around the Americas unchecked by the monarchs. Royal officials accompanied all the private expeditions to ensure respect for the crown's interests and fulfillment of the capitulación.

Diverse motives propelled the adelantados. By subjugating new peoples to the crown, they hoped to win royal titles, positions, and wealth. By introducing heathens to Christianity, they sought to assure God's favor now as

Spanish explorer Hernando Cortés in a suit of armor. (Library of Congress.)

well as guarantee for themselves a fitting place in the life hereafter. As Bernal Díaz, chronicler of the conquest of Mexico, commented, "We came here to serve God, and also to get rich." Conquest, exploration, and settlement offered opportunities for some marginal or impoverished men to ascend socially and economically. The enterprises required risks whose rewards could be substantial. Some adelantados earned fortunes and repaid their investors.

They leaped from obscurity to fame. History, for example, treats generously the once impoverished and minor noble, Hernando Cortés, and the illegitimate and modestly prepared Francisco Pizarro. However, most adelantados failed.

The conquest of large empires by a relatively few Spaniards proved to be surprisingly easy. Steel, the crossbow, and effective military tactics—a contrast to the ritualized warfare of many Indian groups—facilitated the European victories. Gunpowder startled the Indians, and the Europeans' horses provided a great tactical advantage, serving as the tanks of the conquest. Most importantly, the Spaniards found the Indians divided among themselves. In the Aztec region, subjugated communities provided thousands of indigenous warriors who gladly joined with the Spaniards to defeat their Indian enemies. Indeed, indigenous communities at times skillfully manipulated the Spanish into attacking traditional indigenous enemies. In the Incan empire, rivalry between two claimants to the crown had already split the empire, facilitating European conquest.

The introduction of European diseases also decimated the ranks of the Indians, who lacked immunity to them. In the regions of great pre-Columbian civilizations in both Mexico and Peru, population declined more than 90 percent during the first century after contact with the Europeans, falling from approximately 35 million to less than 2 million. No group remained untouched by the ravages of the new diseases. In some local areas entire populations, including whole culture groups, were completely obliterated. For these reasons, Spanish conquest spread rapidly after Cortés's victory. Central America fell to the Spaniards by 1525. Yucatán put up a bitter resistance, and the coastal portions of the peninsula surrendered to the invaders in 1545. Between 1513 and 1543, the Spaniards explored and claimed the territory in North America between the Carolinas and Oregon. In fact, two-thirds of the territory of the continental United States was at one time claimed by Spain. By the time George Washington was inaugurated as president, Spain had established colonies over a far greater area—ranging from San Francisco to Santa Fe to San Antonio to St. Augustine—than that encompassed by the original thirteen states.

Spain expanded just as prodigiously in South America. Once again the adelantados knew little or nothing of the lands they invaded. Inspired by the success of Cortés and excited by rumors of a wealthy kingdom along the west coast of South America, Francisco Pizarro sailed south from Panama to initiate Spanish conquest of that continent. Only on his third attempt, in 1531–32, did he succeed in penetrating the Incan heartland, and it was still not until 1535 that Pizarro completed his conquest of the Incan empire. The wealth he encountered surpassed that which Cortés had found in Mexico. From Peru, other expeditions fanned out into South America: Sebastian de Benalcázar seized Ecuador in 1533, Pedro de Valdivia conquered the central valley of Chile in 1540–41, and Gonzalo Pizarro crossed the Andes to explore the upper Amazon in 1539. From that expedition Francisco de Orellana and a small band of men floated down the Amazon, reaching the Atlantic Ocean in 1542.

Spanish attention in South America focused on Peru, and most of the other explorations, conquests, and settlements of South America radiated from that center. Two exceptions, the Caribbean coast and the Plata, illustrate how areas with no visible sources of immediate wealth failed to hold the crown's attention. Charles V granted a large section of the Venezuelan coast to the Welsers of Augsburg in 1528 in return for financial aid, but that banking house failed to colonize it successfully, and in 1546 the grant was rescinded. Several small settlements were made along the Colombian coast, and in 1536 Gonzalo Jiménez de Quesada set out to conquer the Chibcha Indians in the mountainous interior, and he brought the highly civilized Indian kingdom within the Spanish empire. The Río de la Plata attracted some interest first as a possible westward passage to the Orient and later as a possible route to the mines of Peru. Pedro de Mendoza searched in 1535–36 to open such a route, and the early settlements in the Platine basin date from his efforts. Finding no evidence of wealth, the Spanish ignored the estuary, guarding it only to prevent outsiders from attempting to penetrate the interior and threaten the mines.

Spanish claims to the New World expanded with amazing rapidity. Within half a century after Columbus's discovery, Spanish adelantados had explored and conquered or claimed the territory from approximately 40 degrees north —Oregon, Colorado, and the Carolinas—to 40 degrees south—mid-Chile and Argentina—with the exception of the Brazilian coast. Spanish settlers had colonized in scattered nuclei an impressive share of that territory. Reflecting the Spanish preference for urban living, by 1550 the settlers had already founded all of Latin America's major cities: Havana, 1519; Mexico City, 1521; Quito, 1534; Lima, 1535; Buenos Aires, 1536 (refounded in 1580); Asunción, 1537; Bogotá, 1538; and Santiago, 1541. The Spaniards built Mexico City and Bogotá where Indian cities had long existed, not an uncommon practice. The rich silver and gold mines of Mexico, Colombia, and Peru stimulated the economy, but the economy enjoyed a sounder base than that. Although gold and silver were preferred exports, agriculture provided the basis for exploration, expansion, and trade. Wherever the Spaniards settled they introduced domesticated animals and new crops. Stock raising turned once unproductive lands into profitable grazing areas, and the introduction of the plow made it possible to exploit land unmanageable under the hoe culture of the Indians. The crown encouraged agriculture by sending seeds, plants, animals, tools, and technical experts to the New World.

The opening of mines, the establishment of agriculture, and the trade between the Iberian motherlands and their American colonies did not go unnoticed in other Western European capitals. The commercial successes of

Spain and Portugal whetted the already hungry appetites of the English, Dutch, and French. Brazil attracted both the French and Dutch. The French operated a colony near Rio de Janeiro between 1555 and 1567. The Dutch enjoyed far greater success. They controlled as much as one-third of Brazil for a time in the seventeenth century (1630–54). From their thriving capital of Recife, they shipped convoys of sugar to European markets. The Brazilian expulsion of the Dutch from the Northeast prompted the renewed attention of the Dutch to the Caribbean. Between 1595 and 1620, the English, French, and Dutch attempted to establish colonies in the Guianas. The Dutch were the most successful, but the other two nations also eventually succeeded. In 1624 the English colonized some small islands in the Lesser Antilles, while between 1630 and 1640 the Dutch expanded into the Caribbean. By the mid-seventeenth century the French had established their Caribbean presence with settlements in Martinique and Guadeloupe.

The late European arrivals hoped to disrupt Spanish trade, but primarily their interest lay in furnishing European goods to the entire Middle America region and in growing tropical products for export. Usually tobacco supplied the first cash crop. After the expulsion of the Dutch from Brazil, attention focused on sugar production. Sugar sold well and profitably in the Old World. The Europeans introduced new production techniques, and their efficiency soon threatened markets once dominated by Portuguese America, thus depressing Brazil's sugar trade. Confronted with the problems of labor, the new European colonizers quickly imported Africans to work the plantations. A few white masters oversaw the work of armies of African slaves.

Before the end of the seventeenth century, Spain lost its monopoly in the Caribbean. The European governments employed a variety of colonial policies in the area, but their objectives were one: to work the colonies profitably for the metropolis (see "A Glossary of Concepts and Terms"). Land patterns, such as plantations, were similar; labor patterns, such as the use of slaves, were also alike.

European influence on the New World and its inhabitants was immediately visible. The Europeans tried to transplant their social, economic, and political institutions across the ocean and found they would have to adapt them to successfully control the indigenous population. They required the Indians to swear allegiance to a new king, worship a new God, speak a new language, and alter their work habits. In the process of exploitation, the Europeans denigrated indigenous culture and destroyed indigenous social organization, forcing the Indians into the role of subservient workers. Their labor they were forced to give, but their loyalty they held in reserve. The gulf between the master and the laborer has seldom been bridged in Latin America. In general, and despite ceaseless and heavy pressures, the Indians opted to retain, so far as possible, their distinctive, original cultural patterns. To an amazing degree at the beginning of the twenty-first century, which is to say after five centuries of oppression, they still keep much of their culture in the highlands of Chiapas (Southern Mexico) and Guatemala and throughout the vast Andean region.

In the confrontation of the New and Old Worlds, the Americas also influenced the course of events in Europe. The abundance of gold and silver shipped from Mexico, Peru, and Brazil caused prices to rise in Europe and helped to finance industrialization. Iberian merchants introduced into Europe new products: tobacco, rubber, cacao, and cotton; new plants: potatoes and corn, two of the four most important food crops of the world; and drugs: quinine, coca used in cocaine and novocaine, curare used in anesthetics, datura used in pain relievers, and cascara used in laxatives. The potato alone helped to transform Europe, providing an abundance of food from Ireland to Russia that facilitated both urbanization and industrialization. Corn transformed animal husbandry by supplying the food to promote its astonishing increase. Both of those cheap, abundant, and relatively reliable crops contributed to the rise of European capitalism and the modern state.

The Americas also forced upon European scholars new geographic, botanical, and zoological information, much of which contradicted the classical writers. As one result, scholars questioned hoary concepts. These contradictions came at about the same time Copernicus published his heliocentric theory (1543) and thus helped to usher in the age of modern science. The vast extension of empire in the New World strengthened the European monarchs, who derived wealth and thus independence from their overseas domains and generally exercised greater power overseas than at home. Such great empires required innovation and revision of governmental institutions. The struggles over boundaries in the New World agitated the European courts and more than once threw European diplomacy into a crisis. Art, music, and literature sooner or later expressed Indian themes. It has been estimated that nearly 50,000 Indian words were incorporated into Spanish, Portuguese, English, and French. The New World was not simply the passive recipient of European civilization; rather, it modified and changed Europe's civilization and contributed to the development of the Old World.

To adapt to their new environment, the European settlers depended heavily on the Indians and learned much from the conquered. The Indians showed the Europeans the best methods for hunting and fishing, the value of the drugs the forests offered, the quickest way to clear the lands, and how to cultivate the crops of the New World. When necessary, the Europeans adopted the light boats skillfully navigated by the Indians on the inland waters and copied the methods used by the Indians to build simple, serviceable structures. As a concession to the tropics, the Europeans adopted the Indian hammock—as did the navies of the world. One early arrival to Brazil noted his delight with the hammock in these words: "Would you believe that man could sleep suspended in a net in the air like a bunch of hanging grapes? Here this is the common thing. I slept on a mattress but my doctor advised me to sleep in a net. I tried it, and I will never again be able to sleep in a bed, so comfortable is the rest one gets in the net." In truth, the Europeans everywhere in the hemisphere depended heavily on the Indians during the early decades of settlement in order to accommodate the novel conditions. Thomas Turner, an Englishman who lived in Brazil for two years at the end of the sixteenth century, summed up that dependence of Spaniard and Portuguese alike in his observation. "The Indian is a fish in the sea and a fox in the woods, and without them a Christian is neither for pleasure or profit fit for life or living."

During the early decades of conquest and colonization more European males than females arrived in the New World. Thirty women were allowed on Columbus's third voyage in 1498, and in 1527 the crown licensed brothels in Puerto Rico and Santo Domingo "because there is need for it in order to avoid worse harm." As late as the 1540s in Peru there was one Spanish woman for every seven or eight men. In the later conquests, Spanish women sometimes participated alongside the men. Doña Isabel de Guevara participated in the conquest of the region of La Plata in the 1530s. In seeking an *encomienda* years later, doña Isabel recounted, "The men became so weak that all the tasks fell on the poor women, washing the clothes as well as nursing the men, preparing them the little food there was, keeping them clean, standing guard, patrolling the fires, loading the crossbows when the Indians came sometimes to do battle, even firing the cannon, and arousing the soldiers who were capable of fighting, shouting the alarm through the camp, acting as sergeants and putting the soldiers in order. . . . [O]ur contributions were such that if it had not been for us, all would have perished; and were it not for the men's reputation, I could truthfully write you much more and give them as the witnesses."

The paucity of Spanish women led the men to turn to indigenous women. From the beginning, the conquerors regarded Indian women as part of the conquest, and rape was common. Indigenous men would frequently hide the women from the Spaniards in the Caribbean islands. Other indigenous groups gave women to the Spaniards to cement alliances. The conquest of women is in many ways a metaphor for the conquest of the New World itself—the conquest of virgin territory. The most famous example of Spanish conquest of indigenous women is the story of Malintzin, known by the Spanish as doña Marina or Malinche, a term that has come to mean traitor. Malintzin was a Mayan Indian who had been sold into slavery before she was given as a gift to Hernando Cortés. Because she could speak Nahuatl, the language of the Aztecs, she became Cortés's translator. She bore Cortés a son, but within a few years he married her off to one of his men, Juan de Jaramillo.

Concubinage and casual intercourse were common, but so was marriage between Europeans and Indians. Intermarriage was permitted by the Spanish monarch in 1501 and often encouraged for reasons of state, as in

Brazil during the years that Pombal directed the Portuguese Empire (1750–77). As a result there appeared almost at once a "new race," the *mestizo,* a blend of European and Indian. The mestizos accelerated the amalgamation of two cultures.

Some Indians saw opportunities in the new Iberian-dominated economy and quickly joined in. Many commoners saw the Spaniards as new lords who were little different than previous indigenous masters. However, many more Indians did not want to forego communal life to work for the Europeans. When the Spaniards and Portuguese failed to persuade the Indians of the merits of laboring to turn the wheels of European capitalism, they applied coercion. They forced the natives to paddle their canoes; to guide them through the interior; to plant, tend, and harvest their sugar, wheat, tobacco, and cotton; to guard their cattle and sheep; to mine their gold and silver; and to wait upon them in their homes. Passively or actively the Indians resisted.

When the Indians proved inadequate, reluctant, or rebellious, or where their numbers were insufficient (particularly in the Caribbean and Brazil), the colonists began to look elsewhere for their labor supply. Their attention turned to Africa, where the Portuguese were already involved in the slave trade.

The African

Africa, the second largest continent, offers extremes of contrasts: mountains and savannas, deserts and jungles. Three impressive river networks, the Nile, the Congo, and the Zambesi, add to the variety. The relatively small population contributes further to the diversity. Divided into hundreds of tribes, African cultures range from the primitive to the sophisticated, with many developing highly complex societies. The base of the social structure was the family. Many of the societies were rigidly hierarchical. The political units varied from village tribes to extensive empires. The economy was agricultural, but many artistic and mechanical skills were well developed: woodcarving, bronzework, basketry, goldsmithing, weaving, and ironworking. One early European visitor to the Gambia Coast marveled. "The blacksmiths make all sorts of tools and instruments for tillage, etc. as also weapons and armor, being indifferent skillful at hardening of iron, and whetting it on common stones." Trade was carried on in organized markets. Indeed, commerce was well developed on local and regional levels and in some instances reached transcontinental proportions.

Repeated invasions by the Phoenicians, Greeks, Romans, and Arabs brought foreigners to Africa as early as 100 B.C.E. The fall of Ceuta in 1415 C.E. heralded new European incursions. Africa's commercial potential—gold, ivory, cotton, and spices—attracted the Europeans, who soon enough discovered that the Africans themselves were the continent's most valuable export. Between 1441 and 1443, the Portuguese began to transport Africans to Europe for sale. The intercontinental slave trade initiated and for centuries carried on by Europeans marks one of the most inhumane chapters of world history.

From the very beginning, some Africans from the Iberian Peninsula participated in the exploration and conquest of the Americas. It is believed that the first African slaves reached the New World as early as 1502. Later, the slave trade, carried on with the sanction of the Iberian monarchs, transported large numbers of slaves directly from Africa to the New World. Probably the first shipments of slaves arrived in Cuba in 1512 and in Brazil in 1538, and they continued until Brazil abolished its slave trade in 1850 and Spain finally terminated the slave trade to Cuba in 1866. As the American colonies grew, accommodated themselves to European demands, and developed plantation economies, the rhythm of slave importation accelerated. A majority of the 3 million slaves sold into Spanish America and the 5 million sold into Brazil over a period of approximately three centuries came from the west coast of Africa between the Ivory Coast and South Africa, a stretch of territory exceeding 3,000 miles. These numbers do not reflect the millions of Africans killed in the process of transportation and "seasoning," a genocide of dismal proportions. Africans could be found in all parts of Latin America and formed a large part of the population. They quickly became and remained the major workforce in the Caribbean and Brazil. Their presence dominated the plantations that they worked, and their influence spread quickly to the "big house," where African women served as cooks, wet nurses, and companions of the woman of the house, while black children romped with white children.

Male slaves outnumbered females by a ratio of almost two to one. The plantation owners preferred men and paid more for them because they considered them better field hands and hence more profitable. But the women worked hard, too. Indeed, traditionally they were regarded more as laborers than mothers. Their owners discouraged large-scale reproduction as uneconomical. Thus, the Latin American slave system was seldom self-sustaining and required constant replacement through the slave trade. African influence also permeated the cities where they worked as domestic servants, peddlers, mechanics, and artisans. In the sixteenth century, blacks outnumbered whites in Lima, Mexico City, and Salvador da Bahia, the three principal cities of the Western Hemisphere. The sex ratio among slaves seems to have been more equal in the cities, where women played particularly active roles as domestic servants, street vendors, prostitutes, and mistresses. The urban records seem to indicate that more freedwomen than freedmen existed. The city apparently offered the African woman more opportunity to change her status, partly because of her skills as vendor and her appeal as prostitute and mistress, partly because her sale price was lower than a man's, and partly because of her economic acumen.

Handicapped by the removal of all their possessions when taken into captivity, the Africans, uprooted and brutalized, still contributed handsomely to the formation of a unique civilization in the New World. First and foremost were the Africans themselves: their strength, skill, and intelligence. They utilized their former skills, and their intelligence permitted them to master new ones quickly. In fact, they soon exercised—and in some cases perfected—all the trades and crafts of the Europeans. Visitors to the Caribbean and Brazil remarked on the diversity of skills mastered and practiced by the Africans. They were masons, carpenters, smiths, lithographers, sculptors, artists, locksmiths, cabinetmakers, jewelers, and cobblers. Around the plantations and in the cities, these craftspeople, artisans, and mechanics became an indispensable ingredient in New World society.

Herdsmen in Africa, they mounted horses to become cowboys in the New World. They followed the cattle into the Brazilian hinterlands and helped to occupy the rich Platine pampas. In these as well as other ways they participated in the conquest and settlement of the interior. In Brazil, after the discovery of gold, the Africans were transported into Minas Gerais to mine the gold that created the Luso-Brazilian prosperity of the eighteenth century. From the plantations and mines, they helped to transport the raw products of the land to the ports, where other Africans loaded the wealth of Latin America into ships that carried it to the markets of Europe. The slaves were even expected to defend the system that exploited them. In doing so, they sacrificed their blood to protect the Luso-Spanish empires at Havana, San Juan, Cartagena, Recife, Salvador, Rio de Janeiro, and elsewhere. The first black historian of Brazil, Manuel Querino (1851–1923), reviewed the great contributions of the Africans in these words:

> Whoever takes a look at the history of this country will verify the value and contribution of the Negro to the defense of national territory, to agriculture, to mining, to the exploitation of the interior, to the movement for independence, to family life and to the development of the nation through the many and varied tasks he performed. Upon his well-muscled back rested the social, cultural, and material development. . . . The black is still the principal producer of the nation's wealth, but many are the contributions of that long suffering and persecuted race which has left imperishable proofs of its singular valor. History in all its justice has to respect and praise the valuable services which the black has given to this nation for more than three centuries. In truth it was the black who developed Brazil.

The Africans possessed a leadership talent that the slave system never fully tapped. It became evident when the runaway slaves organized their own communities, known variously as *palenques* or *cumbes* in Spanish America and *quilombos* in Brazil, or when slaves revolted against their masters. The most famous quilombo, Palmares, located in Alagoas, lasted roughly from 1630 to 1697; it included as many as 5,000 African slaves, from different African regions, speaking different languages, but all united in the community. There were six attempts to conquer Palmares between 1680 and 1686, and the final assault was won only after a bitterly fought 44-day siege. The threat of slaves running away, however, was not as frightening to the slave owners as the threat of uprisings. Slave revolts occurred in Mexico in 1537, 1546, 1570, 1608, 1609, 1611, 1612, and 1670. One viceroy informed his monarch that the slaves in New Spain sought "to buy their liberty with the lives of their masters." Most of the documented slave revolts in Brazil took place in the early nineteenth century. Between 1807 and 1835, there were nine revolts or attempted revolts. In addition, many slaves rebelled through forms of resistance in their daily lives. Many women practiced abortion to avoid bringing children into such a horrible life.

Mixing with both European and Indian, the Africans contributed their blood to the increasing racial mixture of the New World. Mulattos, the cross of white and black, and myriad other interracial types resulting from the combination of the mixed descendants of white, black, and Indian appeared immediately after the introduction of the African slaves. Illustrative of the extent of the mixture of white and black was the population of Salvador da Bahia at the end of the colonial period. In 1803, the city boasted of a population of approximately 100,000, of which 40,000 were black, 30,000 white, and another 30,000 mulatto. Most Brazilians, in fact, could claim at least some African ancestry.

It would be difficult to think of any activity concerned with the formation and development of society in Latin America in which Africans did not participate. They helped to smooth away the asceticism of churchgoing by enlivening some of the religious festivals. They drew the festivals out into the streets and enhanced them with folkplays, dances, and music. Much of their contribution was rooted in the syncretism by which they sought to fuse their own beliefs with those of the Roman Catholic Church. They did, in fact, develop a syncretized religion, still very visible in Cuba (*santería*), Haiti (*vudún*), and Brazil (*candomblé*). Wherever the Africans went in the New World, they modified the culinary and dietary habits of those around them. Many of the rice and bean dishes so common in Latin America have African origins. Yams, okra, cola nuts, and palm oil are but a few of the contributions of the African cooks. The Africans introduced thousands of words into the Spanish and Portuguese languages and helped to soften the pronunciation of both. Their proverbs, riddles, tales, and myths mixed with those of Europeans and Indians to form the richly varied folklore of Latin America. The music, whether classical or popular, bears the imprint of African melodies. The Africans continued to sing the songs they remembered from their homelands, and to accompany themselves they introduced a wide range of percussion instruments. With the music went dances. The samba, frevo, and merengue descend from African imports.

The forced migration of Africans to the New World completed the ethnic triptych of Asian, European, and African. Each contributed to the formation of a unique civilization representing a blend of the three. Overlaying that civilization were powerful institutions imported from the Iberian Peninsula and adapted to local circumstances.

Aztecs Lament the Fall of Tenochtitlán

Many years after the conquest, Spanish priests taught Aztec nobles how to write their native Nahuatl language using a Roman alphabet. The Spaniards asked the Aztecs to tell their history and traditions. Among the materials to emerge was poetry, including this poem lamenting the fall of the Aztec empire.

Broken spears lie in the roads;
we have torn our hair in grief.
The houses are roofless now, and their walls
are red with blood.

Worms are swarming in the streets and plazas,
and the walls are splattered with gore.
The water has turned red, as if it were dyed,
and when we drink it,
it has the taste of brine.

We have pounded our hands in despair
against the adobe walls,
for our inheritance, our city, is lost and dead.
The shields of our warriors were its defense,
but they could not save it.

Source: *The Broken Spears: The Aztec Account of the Conquest of Mexico*, Miguel Leon-Portilla, ed. © 1962, 1990 by Miguel Leon-Portilla. Expanded and Updated Edition © 1992 by Miguel Leon-Portilla. Reprinted by permission of Beacon Press, Boston.

Cortes is Awed by Tenochtitlán

Hernando Cortés wrote a series of letters to the Spanish king, Charles V, to inform him about the new lands that Cortés aimed to conquer in his name. In this letter, Cortés describes with amazement the market of the Aztec capital, Tenochtitlán.

The city has many open squares in which markets are continuously held and the general business of buying and selling proceeds. One square in particular is twice as big as that of

Salamanca and completely surrounded by arcades where there are daily more than 60,000 folk buying and selling. Every kind of merchandise such as may be met with in every land is for sale there, whether of food or victuals, or ornaments of gold and silver or lead, brass, copper, tin, precious stones, bones, shells, snails and feathers; limestone for building is likewise sold there, stone both rough and polished, bricks burnt and unburnt, wood of all kinds and in all stages of preparation. There is a street of game where they sell all manner of birds that are to be found in their country. . . . They also sell rabbits, hares, deer and small dogs which they breed specially for eating. There is a street of herb-sellers where there are all manner of roots and medicinal plants that are found in the land. There are houses as it were of apoth-ecaries where they sell medicines made from these herbs, both for drinking and for use as ointments and salves. There are barbers' shops where you may have your hair washed and cut. There are other shops where you may obtain food and drink. There are street porters such as we have in Spain to carry packages. There is a great quantity of wood, charcoal, braziers made of clay and mats of all sorts, some for beds and others more finely woven for seats, still others for furnishing halls and private apartments. All kinds of vegetables may be found there. . . . There are many different sorts of fruits including cherries and plums very similar to those found in Spain. They sell honey obtained from bees, as also the honeycomb and that obtained from maize plants which are as sweet as sugar canes. . . . All kinds of cotton thread in various colors may be bought in skeins, very much in the same way as in the great silk exchange of Granada. . . . They have colors for paint-ing as good quality as any in Spain, and of as pure shades as may be found anywhere. There are leathers of deer both skinned and in their natural state. . . . A great deal of chinaware is sold of very good quality and including earthen jars of all sizes for holding liquids, pitchers, pots, tiles, and an infinite variety of earthenware all made of very special clay and almost all decorated or painted in some way. Maize is sold both as grain and in the form of bread. . . . Pastries made from game and fish pies may be seen on sale, and there are large quantities of fresh and salt water fish both in their natural state and cooked and ready for eating. Eggs from fowl, geese and the other birds . . . may be had, and likewise omelettes ready made. There is nothing to be found in all the land which is not sold in these markets.

Second Letter from Hernando Cortés to Emperor Charles V
Sent October 30, 1520

Source: *Hernando Cortés, Five Letters of Cortés to the Emperor, 1519–1526,* J. Bayard Morris, tran. (N.Y.: W. W. Norton and Co., 1962), 87–89. Copyright © 1969 by J. Bayard Morris. Used by permission of W. W. Norton & Company, Inc.

Equiano: A Slave En Route to the New World

Most African slaves in the New World were not taught to read or write, and we've come to know about their conditions via the observations of others. Olaudah Equiano, a slave from Nigeria, was among the few who learned to write. In this excerpt of his life story, Equiano tells of his enslavement.

The first object which saluted my eyes when I arrived on the coast was the sea, and a slave ship which was then riding at anchor and waiting for its cargo. These filled me with astonishment, which was soon converted into terror when I was carried on board. I was immediately handled and tossed up to see if I were sound by some of the crew, and I was now persuaded that I had gotten into a world of bad spirits and that they were going to kill me. Their complexions too differing so much from ours, their long hair and the language they spoke (which was very different from any I had every heard) united to confirm me in this belief. Indeed, such were the horrors of my views and fears at that moment that, if ten thousand worlds had been my own, I would have freely parted with them all to have exchanged my condition with that of the meanest slave in my own country. . . .

I was soon put down under the decks, and there I received such a salutation to my nostrils as I had never experienced in my life: so that with the loathsomeness of the stench and crying together, I became so sick and low that I was not able to eat, nor had I the least desire to taste anything. I now wished for the last friend, death, to relieve me; but soon, to my grief, two of the white men offered me eatables, and on my refusing to eat, one of them held me fast by the hands and laid me across the windlass, and tied my feet while the other flogged me severely. I had never experienced anything like this before, and although not being used to the water, . . . nevertheless could I have got over the nettings I would have jumped over the side.

The story of Olaudah Equiano, a slave from Nigeria

Source: *Equiano's Travels: His Autobiography,* Paul Edwards, ed. (Oxford: Heinemann International, 1989), 25–26. Reprinted by permission of Heinemann Educational.

2

The Institutions of Empire

The American domains of the Iberian crowns furnished great wealth for Spain and Portugal. The discovery of fabulous deposits of silver in Spanish America provided the reward the Spanish crown coveted. For its part, Portuguese Brazil proved by the mid-sixteenth century that a plantation economy distant from Europe could still be lucrative. Sugar profits more than made up for high transportation costs.

The Iberian monarchs managed to keep control of these vast, distant, and wealthy territories for more than 300 years. To do so, they relied on familiar institutions exported from the European peninsula: the power of the crown and the Church, topping a hierarchical society resting on a base of patriarchal family and servile labor. From the imperial point of view, the Iberians succeeded brilliantly. They converted millions to Christianity and incorporated most of them within the two empires; they explored, conquered, and settled millions of square miles; they produced an incalculable wealth. Of course, they did so within a political and economic framework that subordinated the well-being of the colonies to the demands of the Europeans.

Economy

The Iberians had not set off on voyages of conquest and settlement. They had sought a much more modest goal: trade. Their encounter with the New World rather than China or India forced a drastic change of plans.

The Americas at first frustrated the Iberians. The Indians of the Caribbean and the Brazilian coast, the first known to the Europeans, showed no inclination for or interest in transoceanic trade. The Portuguese contented themselves for three decades with exporting the brazilwood found growing close to the coast. The Spaniards lacked even that product to stimulate commerce in the Caribbean.

With little trade in sight, the Iberians focused on the search for a single item: gold. It offered three attractive advantages: easy shipment, imperishability, and high value. The Portuguese encountered little of it among the Brazilian Indians. The first Spaniards, however, came into limited but tantalizing contact with the prized metal almost at once, as the Indians displayed some golden ornaments. The Indians also spoke of gold on various Caribbean islands, causing the Spaniards to begin a search for deposits at once. In 1494, they discovered gold on the south side of Hispaniola (later the Dominican Republic). Other discoveries followed. Between 1501 and 1519 the Caribbean produced approximately 8 million pesos of gold.

The principal source of gold in Spanish America was New Granada (Colombia), which, by 1600, had exported more than 4 million ounces of gold. Most of that gold came from placer deposits worked by slave labor. Production of gold in New Granada grew steadily, with eighteenth-century production nearly tripling that of the sixteenth. In total, it supplied the motherland with about 30 million ounces of gold.

Gold discoveries in Brazil came late in the colonial period. The hardy *bandeirantes* (explorers) found gold for the first time in 1695 in the interior of Minas Gerais; other rich strikes occurred in 1721 in Mato Grosso and in 1726 in Goiás. Such discoveries were incentives to open the vast southern interior of Brazil to settlement. Each discovery precipitated a wild rush of humanity to find fortune. Each ship arriving at Brazil's shores brought Portuguese and other foreigners destined for the mines. From every city and hamlet, from the coast as well as the interior, whites, blacks, Indians, mulattos, and mestizos descended on the gold region. Rich and poor, young and old, men and women, none of whom had the slightest knowledge of prospecting techniques, scurried to find fortune. The boom not only caused a notable population growth in eighteenth-century Brazil but also caused a population shift from the older sugar-producing region of the Northeast to the newly opened regions of the Southeast. Gold production mounted there until 1760, when a decline set in. During the eighteenth century, Brazil produced 32 million ounces of gold, a majority of the world's gold supply.

Most of Spain's wealth, however, came not from gold but from silver, discovered after the conquest of Mexico and Peru. Spaniards discovered silver in Mexico at Taxco in 1534 and Zacatecas in 1546. Other strikes followed at Guanajuato (1550) and San Luis Potosí (1592). But the biggest find was in 1545 at Potosí, a remote area in mountainous Upper Peru (later Bolivia), where the Spaniards opened one of the richest silver mines the world was ever to see. In the sixteenth century, Mexico shipped more than 35 million pesos worth of precious metals to Spain. It became Spanish America's leading producer toward the end of the seventeenth century, and, in fact, over the course of the entire colonial period, the Viceroyalty of New Spain produced half of the New World's mineral wealth. During the course of the colonial period, some 100,000 tons of silver were produced in colonial Latin America.

The Iberian crowns maintained a lively interest in all mining operations and carefully collected their *quinto,* or one-fifth, of the precious metals mined in Peru. They employed large bureaucracies to oversee the mining of the metals and the collection of the quinto. The Spanish monarchs encouraged the use of the latest mining techniques, employing European mining engineers when necessary. In the mid-sixteenth century, the Spaniards adopted the amalgamation process of separating silver from ore by means of quicksilver (mercury), a far more efficient process than smelting.

Mining brought prosperity. Silver constituted at least 70 percent of Mexican exports for most of the colonial period. Mining provided the wealth that paid for European imports, and its profits were reinvested in local industry. Cities grew up wherever precious metals appeared, and some of them became major urban centers. Potosí, with 160,000 inhabitants in 1670, was the largest city in the New World. Farming and livestock raising followed the miners to supply food demands. The search for precious metals encouraged exploration, so mining became a major means of opening the interior of Latin America to European settlement. It filled the royal treasuries, providing funds that could be leveraged to finance Spanish interests in Europe.

Many emphasize the negative aspects of mining. Some scholars contend that the flow of gold and silver sparked serious inflation both in Europe and in the Americas. Others argue that only a residue of the wealth remained in the New World. One Bolivian lamented that all Bolivia got from centuries of silver mining at Potosí was a hole in the ground. The wealth slipped not only through local fingers but eventually through those of the Iberians as well. The gold and silver only paused in the motherlands before falling into the hands of the northern Europeans, particularly the English, who sold manufactured goods to Portugal and Spain. The Brazilians mused, wryly but with some truth, that Brazilian gold mined by African slaves financed the English industrial revolution. Certainly mining contributed to the well-established pattern of wealth flowing from the Americas to the Iberian peninsula and then on to Northern Europe, which industrialized while the Iberian empires rusticated.

Mining exemplified the region's dependence on exports. The crowns were hungry for gold and silver, but more than that, they were hungry for wealth. In areas without gold and silver, Iberians and their descendants searched for other exportable goods. They sent to Iberia—and on to Europe— the rich purplish-blue dye made from the indigo plant and the deep red dye, cochineal, made from the insects feeding on nopal cactuses. The hides of New World cattle at first made fine leather goods, and when England industrialized, provided the thick bands that connected machinery. Cacao beans fed the new desire for chocolate, sweetened by New World sugar. Success depended on the resources provided by geography, and by perhaps the greatest wealth of the colonies—labor to produce the goods.

In the search for a workable labor system, Spaniards first looked to their own traditions. Seeing the conquest of the New World as a continuation of their reconquest of the Iberian Peninsula, they transferred an institution that had served in the Reconquista—the *encomienda,* or entrustment. Once used for the control and exploitation of the Moors, the adelantados employed it in the Americas to Christianize and exploit the Indians. The institution required the Spanish *encomendero* to instruct the Indians entrusted to him in Christianity and European civilization and to defend and protect them. In return he could demand tribute and labor from the Indians.

The crown hesitated to approve the transfer of the encomienda to the Caribbean. After all, the monarchs had just unified Spain and were in the process of strengthening their powers in the peninsula. They were reluctant therefore to nourish in the New World a class of encomenderos who could impose their will between the monarchs and their new Indian subjects. It smacked too much of feudalism for royal tastes. In accordance with her desires to centralize authority in the crown, Isabel ordered in 1501 that the governor of the Indies free the Indians from the encomiendas. When that experiment resulted in the flight of Indians from plantations and their refusal to work for the Spaniards, the queen changed her mind. By royal *cédula,* or edict, in 1503 she legalized and institutionalized the encomienda in the New World. The cédula expressed concern over the welfare of the Indian subjects and admonished the Spaniards to treat them well, but it also sanctioned a labor system that would permit many abuses.

The encomienda system spread rapidly and was most effective among sedentary Indian populations accustomed to participating in indigenous draft rotary labor systems that built and maintained communal structures and provided labor for indigenous nobility. Such systems had existed among the Aztecs (*coatequitl*) and the Inca (*mita*). In many regions, indigenous people continued to live in their own villages, sending a portion of workers to labor on Spanish lands. However, increasing contact with Spaniards exposed the Indians to European diseases for which they had no immunities, including smallpox, typhus, measles, and influenza, which proved lethal. Between 1519 and 1650, about 85 percent of the Indian population of Middle America was wiped out. Other areas of the Americas suffered proportional decreases.

While the encomenderos were primarily concerned with the economic aspects of the encomienda, the Catholic monarchs were also concerned with the encomenderos' responsibility to Christianize, civilize, and protect the Indians. At great expense, the monarchs dispatched priests to convert the indigenous peoples, a task that was extremely difficult. Not only did they have to master the Indian languages, win the Indians' confidence, and persuade them to embrace Catholicism, but they also had to fight against the planters and miners who feared religious interference with their all-important labor system. Alarmed by the declining numbers and abuse of their charges, a few clergymen raised their voices to defend their neophytes, to protest the practices of the colonists, and to prod the royal conscience. In their anger and concern, they took the Indians' case directly to the monarchs, to whom they vividly reported the mistreatment of their American subjects.

Those prods to King Ferdinand's conscience, coupled with his own political misgivings about the increasing power of the encomendero class, prompted him to control the encomiendas. In 1512, he promulgated the Laws of Burgos, the first general code for the government and instruction of the Indians. It called for the fair, humane treatment of the Indians. The policy as pronounced in Madrid sounded fine, but royal officers in the Indies found it difficult to translate theory into practice. They faced the protests, threats, and power of the angry encomenderos who needed Indian labor.

Cortés immediately and successfully transplanted the encomienda to Mexico, where he liberally divided the Indians among his followers. For himself, he allotted an encomienda of 100,000 Indians. The others were considerably smaller. Although royal officials in Santo Domingo approved his action, the crown by 1519 was reluctant to see the encomienda spread. In 1520, Charles V abolished the institution. By then, however, it was too firmly entrenched in the New World to be summarily eradicated. The encomenderos refused to acknowledge the abolition, and royal officials did not enforce the law.

The encomenderos actively pressed their case before the monarch. They dispatched their own representatives to Madrid to emphasize the "barbarian" nature of the Indians, their indolence and ignorance. Without coercion, they emphasized, the Indians simply would not work. Their labors here on earth, the argument ran, amounted to small compensation for the eternal salvation offered by the Roman Catholic faith to which the Europeans introduced them. Further, they pointed out, the civilizing hand of Europe taught the natives how to better care for and feed themselves. In the final analysis, the encomenderos regarded their charges as a just reward for their participation in conquest or for some service rendered the crown. They adamantly refused to do the menial labor themselves; the encomienda provided the means to get work done. Their powerful lobby at court persuaded Charles to modify his position.

Religious pressure mounted. Bartolomé de las Casas, a Dominican missionary and later bishop, spoke most persuasively in defense of the Indians. Indignant, he returned to Spain from the Caribbean in 1515 to plead the cause of the Indians before Ferdinand. For the next half-century he pressed their case. He reported Spanish abuses and portrayed the Indians not as savages but as innocents in need of protection. Las Casas sternly reminded the monarch that the Pope had granted him territory in the New World solely for the purpose of converting the heathen. Thus, he argued, Spain had no right to use the natives for secular goals. Foremost among those who opposed Las Casas was Juan Ginés de Sepúlveda, who relied heavily on Aristotelian theory for his arguments. Because of the intellectual superiority of the Europeans, Sepúlveda reasoned, the Indians should be subjected to them in a kind of natural servitude, which would permit the Indians to improve themselves by observing a better example of virtue, devotion, and industry. Las Casas won the debates, and Pope Paul III supported his cause with a bull in 1537 declaring the Indians fully capable of receiving the faith of Christ—that is, that they possessed souls and should not be deprived of their liberty and property.

Charles then promulgated the New Laws in 1542, which forbid the enslavement of the Indians, their compulsory personal service, the granting of new encomiendas, and the inheritance of encomiendas. More positively, they declared the Indians to be free persons, vassals of the crown, and possessed of their own free will. The colonists protested vehemently. Rebellion threatened Mexico; in Peru encomenderos rose up to defy the law. Once again under extreme pressure, the monarch modified some of the laws and revoked others. But from this point in the mid-sixteenth century, the institution waned, though continuing for some time in parts of the sprawling American empire. Its decline, however, had less to do with religious concern and more to do with practical matters. The pressures of increasing Spanish immigration to the Americas and declining Indian population created limits to the awarding of new encomiendas. As a result, the state exerted even greater control over the declining Indian population.

Replacing the encomienda as the major labor institution in Spanish America was the *repartimiento*, the temporary allotment of Indian workers for a given task. Significantly, under this institution royal authorities controlled and parceled out the Indians. The Spanish colonist in need of laborers applied to a royal official explaining both the work to be done and the time it would take and requesting a specific number of Indians to do it. In theory, the crown officials looked after the welfare of the Indians to ensure fair payment and satisfactory working conditions; in practice, abuse of the repartimiento system abounded. Planters and miners constantly badgered royal officials to bend the system to better fit local needs. The institution flourished in the last half of the sixteenth century and in the first half of the seventeenth. In addition to furnishing an agricultural labor force, the repartimiento system also provided the major share of the workers for the mines in South America. In the Viceroyalty of Peru, the Spaniards developed the *mita* into a particularly burdensome form of repartimiento in Potosí. All adult male Indians of the Peruvian Andes were subject to serve in the mita for one year out of every seven. Far from his home, the Indian miner worked under the most dangerous conditions and earned a wage that did not suffice for half of his own and his family's expenses. Members of the family had to work in order to make up the difference.

As in Spanish America, the landowners in Brazil relied in part (at least in the sixteenth century along the coast and for several more centuries in the interior and in the north) on the Indians as a source of labor. Some employed Indian labor from the *aldeias*, the villages. The crown and the religious orders tried to concentrate the nomadic Indians into villages, first organized and administered by the religious orders, but after 1757 administered by the crown. Protected within the village, the Indians were introduced to Christianity and European civilization. In return, they gave a portion of their labor to the Church and state. This part of the aldeia system resembled the encomienda. In addition, planters could apply to the aldeia administrators for paid Indian workers to perform a specific task for a specified period of time. In this respect, the aldeia system approximated the repartimiento. The aldeia system included only a small percentage of the Brazilian Indians. The rest the planters hunted to enslave, always explaining to questioning church or crown officials that they had captured their Indian slaves in a "just" war.

After their arrival in 1549, the Jesuits spoke out to protect the Indians. In the sixteenth and seventeenth centuries, three notable Jesuits, Manuel da Nóbrega, José de Anchieta, and Antoñio Vieira, who had influence both in Brazil and at court, vigorously defended the Indians. They reminded the Portuguese monarch of his obligations. On the other hand, the planters sent their own representatives to court to present their point of view. The high death rate among the Indians exposed to European demands and diseases, their retreat into the interior, their amalgamation into the new Brazilian society through miscegenation, and the increasing importation of Africans to supply the growing labor needs of the colony did more to solve the complex question of Indian–European relations than did all the altruistic but impractical or ignored legislation of the Portuguese kings.

By the mid-sixteenth century there were virtually no Indians left in the West Indies, and in Brazil most Indians had died or fled to the interior. Where there was the possibility of a lucrative export product, miners and landowners imported African slaves to replace the indigenous workforce. The Africans offered the added benefit of immunity to European diseases because they had long been in contact with Europeans. By the end of the sixteenth century, Africa furnished most of the productive labor in Brazil and the West Indies. By the time the slave trade ended (1821–24 in most places, 1850 in Cuba, and 1860 in Brazil) 8 million slaves had been sold into Latin America: 3 million went to Spanish America and 5 million to Brazil. Brazil alone received nearly 40 percent of the Atlantic slave trade, six times more than the United States.

In the highland areas of Spanish America, however, settled indigenous populations survived, and landowners continued to seek ways to control their labor. Growing agricultural and export demands and a limited population base intensified competition among the landowners for workers, prompting them to devise a new method of ensuring a more dependable labor system: contracting the Indians as wage laborers. As early as 1546 at the mines of Zacatecas, Indians were paid wages to lure them to the relatively remote northern region. Wage labor systems spread beyond mining areas as the repartimiento system became more cumbersome, breaking down under favoritism and bribery.

The crown approved the creation of a large wage-earning class as a progressive step. To the monarch it seemed to verify the assimilation and Europeanization of the Indians. However, employers wanted to keep the wages low and keep the workforce from moving on in search of better jobs. Some tried to convert contract wage labor into debt peonage, tying the Indians and their descendants to the landowner by debt. The *hacendados* made deceptively friendly loans to the Indians, who were to repay with their labor. However, the wages paid for such labor often did not suffice to liquidate the debt, and fathers passed their debts on to sons. But the very labor scarcity that prompted debt peonage also provided the Indians with some maneuverability in their relations with the landowners. When possible, the workers gravitated toward employers who promised better salaries or working conditions. Many workers had no qualms about accepting a loan from one employer, then moving on to another. Without a strong military or police force, fleeing workers were virtually impossible to catch—especially as long as they could flee to unoccupied lands.

Initially, land was abundant and Spaniards were most concerned about acquiring the labor to work it for them. However, competition for land intensified as more Spaniards immigrated to the New World, the indigenous population recovered from the initial decline after conquest, and lucrative markets developed both abroad and in the colonies for agricultural products. Ownership of land became a basis for wealth and prestige and conveyed power. From the beginning the adelantados distributed land among their followers as a reward for services rendered. The officers received large shares of land as well as grants of Indians, while the common men received smaller shares of land but usually were not granted any Indians.

In 1532, Martim Afonso founded the first permanent settlement in Brazil at São Vicente, near present-day Santos, and distributed the land with a lavish hand to his followers. In his generosity he established a pattern of land distribution quite contrary to the prevailing custom in Portugal. Since 1375, the Portuguese kings had sparingly parceled out the *sesmaria*, the traditional land grants, so that no one person received more than could be effectively cultivated. Aware of the immensity of the territory in front of him, Martim Afonso ignored such a precaution. As a consequence, the good coastal land was quickly divided into immense sugar plantations, and not many more decades elapsed before the huge sesmarias in the interior for cattle ranches put much of the backlands under claims as well.

Over the generations many of the original grants of land grew to gigantic proportions. The more astute landowners bought out their neighbors or simply encroached upon other lands. The declining Indian population freed more and more land, which the Iberians rapidly grabbed up as their awareness of its value increased. A series of legal devices favored the Spaniard in acquiring land: the *congregación, denuncia,* and *composición.* The congregación concentrated the Indians in villages and thereby opened land for seizure; the denuncia required the Indians to show legal claim and title to their property—a legality for which their ancient laws had not prepared them—and failure to do so meant that the land could be seized; the composición was a means of claiming land through legal surveys, a concept once again for which the Indians had little preparation. By these, as well as other means, the Spanish landowners steadily pushed the remaining Indians up the mountainsides and onto arid soils, in short, into the marginal lands.

For their part, the Portuguese monarchs, critical of the inefficiency of the large *fazendas,* most of whose land lay fallow and hence unproductive, belatedly tried to reverse the course already well underway in Brazil. Repeatedly, promulgated decrees tried to limit the size of the estates. One of the viceroys late in the eighteenth century, the Marquis of Lavradio, complained bitterly that the huge estates, poorly managed and often only partially cultivated, retarded the development of Brazil. He pointed to the unused fields held by their owners as symbols of prestige, while at the same time he noted that farmers petitioned him for land to till. Some of the regions imported food that they were perfectly capable of producing themselves. Nonetheless, the *latifundia* that originated at the birth of the colony remained as dominant a characteristic of Brazil as it did of Spanish America.

Some of the haciendas and fazendas achieved princely proportions. There were instances of haciendas in Mexico exceeding 1 million acres. In Brazil the ranch of Diaz d'Avila by all accounts surpassed most European states in size. Begun in the late sixteenth century in northern Bahia, it centered on the São Francisco River and extended far into the interior. The huge estates were worlds in themselves.

The Luso-Brazilians quickly developed the prototype of the plantation economy, thanks to the ready and profitable market they found in Europe for sugar, a crop that grew exceedingly well along the coast. By 1550, Pernambuco, the richest and most important of the sixteenth-century captaincies, produced enough sugar in its fifty mills to load forty or fifty ships annually

for Europe. The Brazilian sugar plantations flourished during the last half of
the sixteenth and first half of the seventeenth centuries, as the mills busily
ground the cane into sugar for the international market. The economic pattern of a single crop for international trade was fastened onto Brazil early. In
Spanish America, for many years the haciendas produced only for local markets. One of their chief responsibilities was to feed the mining towns. Only as
the eighteenth century neared did the haciendas enter into international trade
on a scale comparable to that of the Brazilian plantations.

The type of life exemplified by the hacienda or fazenda often has been
termed feudal, a term that carries a strong emotional overtone connoting exploitation. Certainly the classical feudalism of medieval society did not appear in the New World. Weak though his power might have been in some of
the remoter areas, the king never relinquished the prerogatives of sovereignty
to the landlords. Royal law prevailed. Nor does the self-sufficient manorial
system properly describe the large estates, because for all their self-sufficiency they were closely tied by their major cash crop to the capitalistic economy. Perhaps the *patrimonialism* defined by Max Weber comes closest to describing the system. Under patrimonialism, the landowner exerts authority
over his followers as one aspect of his property ownership. Those who live
on his land fall under his control. He uses armed force arbitrarily to enforce
his authority within the bounds of his estate. With such authority, he admin-
isters his estate in a highly personal manner according to his own whims and
without any set table of organization. Finally he controls all trade between his
estate and the outside world. Through that trade, he participates in the capitalistic marketplace.

The plantations, ranches, and mines provided a rich and varied source
of income for the Iberian monarchs, capitalists, and merchants. Sugar, tobacco, cacao, indigo, woods, cotton, gold, silver, diamonds, and hides were
some of the natural products the American colonies offered to the Old World.
The Iberian Peninsula depended on the New World for its prosperity. Both
Lisbon and Madrid relied heavily on its raw products for their foreign trade.
For example, for many years the products of Brazil constituted approximately
two-thirds of Portugal's export trade.

Iberian settlers searched for any means of making money, but they were
restricted by more than geographical constraints. They were also subject to
the desires of European markets, and restricted by Iberian controls over trade.
Often just one or a small number of products sold abroad dictated the course
of colonial prosperity. If a product sold well, an entire region prospered; if not,
stagnation and misery engulfed that region. External demand dictated colonial well-being. The colonies had no control over their own economic destiny.
Nor did the Iberians ever achieve notable efficiency in the exploitation of
those natural products with which a generous nature endowed their lands.
With little competition and cheap labor, there was no incentive to overcome

old-fashioned, inefficient methods. The case of sugar is an excellent example. The Portuguese held almost a monopoly on sugar production for well over a century. Between 1650 and 1715, the Dutch, English, and French increased production of sugar in the Caribbean, employing efficient organization, new equipment, and their extensive financial resources and enjoying a geographic position closer to the European markets. As a result, the sugar economies of Portugal's European rivals prospered, while the economy of the traditional producer languished. With quick and large profits as its goal, the economy of Latin America was largely speculative and hence subject to wide variations. The patrimonial system of land and labor contributed to economic fluctuations and inefficiency. In sum, the economy of Latin America was not geared to its own best interests but to the making of immediate profits for the Iberian metropolises and for a small, New World planter-trader elite, almost exclusively of European origin.

The Iberian monarchs and merchants enjoyed the wealth that streamed in from colonies, unconcerned that much of it was spent to buy goods from other European countries. Meanwhile, during the seventeenth century, England began to industrialize, to experiment with commercial innovations, and to expand its trade. The English were pioneering a new path to economic prosperity that the Iberians showed slight interest in following.

Government

Spain and Portugal ruled their American empires for more than three centuries, a remarkable longevity that places them among the great imperial powers of all time. They owed that success to quite different concepts of imperial organization. The Spanish colonial administration was relatively well organized; the hierarchical ranks, well defined; and the chain of command, easy to recognize. The Portuguese empire was loosely organized, the institutions more transitory. The two monarchies used different colonial systems partly because of their own histories, and partly because of the material conditions they encountered.

The concept of government markedly differed from those discussed in contemporary courses on political theory. Few of the political subtleties we must reckon with today had yet developed. Neither division of power nor distinction between branches of government existed. Church and state were closely linked, and although secular and ecclesiastical officials bickered, the two institutions buttressed each other, together preserving order and stability.

The monarch was the State. He ruled by divine right, serving as the supreme earthly patriarch in the well-established hierarchy of God, King, and Father. The mystique and tradition of the monarchy gave the institution such force that no one questioned the king's right to rule or refused his loyalty to the crown. The monarch possessed all power, and from the throne all power emanated.

The great distance between the Iberian Peninsula and the New World and the slowness of communication and travel worked to confer considerable local autonomy on officials in the New World. In practice it meant that the kings could only hope to dictate the broad outlines of policy, leaving much of the interpretation and implementation to colonial and local officials. *Obedezco pero no cumplo* ("I obey but I do not fulfill") became the accepted way for New World officials to manifest their loyalty to the Spanish crown while bending the laws to suit local situations. The philosophy of acknowledging the king's authority without enforcing his will—as common in Brazil as in Spanish America—accounts, at least in part, for the longevity of the empires. It permitted a certain flexibility in the laws that could accommodate many interests, the monarch's as well as the colonist's. As the third governor-general of Brazil, Mem de Sa, confided to the king, "This land ought not and cannot be ruled by the laws and customs of Portugal; if Your Highness was not quick to pardon, it would be difficult to colonize Brazil."

To keep their royal officials and their subjects in check, the Iberian monarchs sent officials of unquestioned loyalty to the New World. At best they suspected that the colonies increased in everyone "the spirit of ambition and the relaxation of virtues." For that reason they hesitated to appoint many Americans to the highest colonial posts. They frankly suspected their loyalty. But as the empires matured, Americans increasingly held influential ecclesiastical, military, and political positions. Despite royal frowns, Iberian officials married into distinguished American families, providing a link between the local and Iberian elite. The crown's check on these officials was the *visita*, an on-the-spot investigation to which all subordinates could be subjected. And at the end of all terms of office, each administrator could expect a *residencia*, a judicial inquiry into his public behavior.

Considering the size of the American colonies, the scant number of small and scattered garrisons, and the handful of royal officials, almost all of whom resided in the most populous cities, the extent of metropolitan control over the American colonies was nothing short of remarkable. It must be concluded then that the crowns maintained their authority and control principally through the power of legitimacy or hegemony. The Americans accepted the system, rarely questioned it, and seldom challenged it. Popular uprisings, mostly motivated by economic discontent, broke out periodically, but the populace reacted to specific grievances rather than adhering to any philosophical current advocating change. For their part, the American elites, feeling they had more to gain through cooperation with the metropolises, lent their considerable authority to the maintenance of the imperial system.

Brazil emerged as Portugal's most valuable overseas possession. Still, until the royal house of Braganza moved its court from Lisbon to Rio de Janeiro in 1807, Brazil was governed by no special laws or institutions that would have distinguished it as a separate, distinct, or privileged entity within the larger empire. In 1532–34, in order to colonize Brazil without reaching into the royal coffers, the Portuguese monarch had distributed Brazil in the form of large captaincies to twelve donataries who were to enjoy broad powers in return for colonizing the American domains. By 1548, John III reversed that decision and began to reassert his authority. In 1549, a central government under a governor-general began to bring some order. In 1646, the king elevated Brazil to the status of a principality, and thereafter the heir to the throne was known as the Prince of Brazil. After 1720, all the chiefs of government of Brazil bore the title of viceroy. Brazil was in effect a viceroyalty thereafter. Finally, Prince-Regent John raised Brazil to a kingdom in 1815, putting it, at least in theory, on an equal footing with Portugal.

Portugal was well into the sixteenth century before the rulers made any distinction between home and overseas affairs. Never did the crown authorize a special body to handle exclusively Brazilian matters. A variety of administrative organs that exercised a combination of consultative, executive, judicial, and fiscal functions assisted the king in ruling his domains. One of the most important was the Overseas Council *(Conselho Ultramarino)* created by John IV in 1642. It was the evolutionary result of considerable experience. The president, secretary, and three councilors of the Overseas Council usually had served in the colonies. The council divided itself into standing committees to treat the various military, administrative, judicial, and ecclesiastical matters. As its primary duty, it advised the king.

Other governmental organs continued to have dual metropolitan and colonial responsibilities. A Treasury Council *(Conselho da Fazenda)* administered public finances and the treasury. A Board of Conscience and Religious Orders *(Mesa de Consciência e Ordens)* established in 1532 advised the Crown on Indian matters. Finally a Casa da Suplicação served as a supreme court for many colonial judicial disputes.

A royal secretary or secretary of state, who after 1736 bore the title of Minister of Navy and Overseas, also assisted the monarchs in their imperial rule. These ministers became increasingly important in the last half of the eighteenth century. The ministers, as well as other close advisers to the crown, were selected because of loyal and often meritorious service and enjoyed unqualified royal confidence.

In Brazil, representatives of the royal government administered the colony. At the apex stood the governor-general, after 1720 called the viceroy. His effectiveness depended largely on his own strengths and weaknesses. Those viceroys who were vigorous exerted considerable influence over the colony. Those who were weak found themselves almost unable to control the capital city and their powers eroded by ambitious bishops and subordinate bureaucrats.

Salvador da Bahia, a splendid port, served as the first seat of the central government of Brazil. Prompted by foreign threat to the south of the colony, in 1763 the seat of the viceroyalty moved southward to Río de Janeiro. Foreign threats to the northeastern sugar coast ended after the defeat and expulsion of the Dutch in 1654. However, by the end of the seventeenth century, Portuguese America faced a growing threat from the Spanish in the Plata region. In 1680, the Portuguese had founded the settlement of Colônia do Sacramento on the left bank of the Río de la Plata, across from Buenos Aires. The Spanish challenge to Portuguese claims to the region caused a century and a half of intense rivalry and frequent warfare along the Plata.

The governors-general and later the viceroys depended on a growing bureaucracy to carry out their primary functions of administering the colony, overseeing its military preparedness, dispensing the king's justice, and enforcing taxes. Of greatest importance was the High Court (*Relação*), the first of which was established in Bahia in 1609 under the presidency of the governor-general. A second was established in Rio de Janeiro in 1751. These courts primarily had judicial responsibilities: They functioned as the highest law tribunals in Brazil, from which there was limited appeal to the Casa de Suplicação in Lisbon. They reviewed the conduct of all officials at the end of their terms of office. Secondarily they served as consultative and administrative organs. When the governor-general absented himself from the capital, the highest member of the court usually governed in his place. The governor-general often requested the advice of the legally trained judges on a host of judicial and administrative matters. Tax questions and the supervision of the treasury were the responsibility of another bureau, the Board of Revenue (*Junta do Fazenda*).

The nation we know today as Brazil was divided during most of the colonial period into two states. The state of Brazil was by far the more important of the two, but another, very impoverished colony existed in the far north, the state of Maranhão. The northern state never developed the vitality of the southern one, and depended heavily on Lisbon. The king appointed a governor-general and a chief justice after the state was established in 1621. Slow growth and a scanty population negated the need for a high court and none was ever authorized. In 1751, the capital was transferred from São Luis to Belém, a smaller although an increasingly more active port that for some time had been the effective center of the state. In recognition of the growing importance of the Amazon, the king created in 1755 the Captaincy of São José do Rio Negro (the present-day Amazonas), subordinate to the Captaincy of Pará.

Captaincies were the principal territorial subdivisions of the two states. Representatives and appointees of the king, the governors or captains-general of those captaincies carried out the same responsibilities on a regional level as the governor-general or viceroy did on a broader scale. Here, as in so many instances, theory and practice diverged. Distance, the varying effectiveness of personalities, intrigue, and vagueness of the law often meant that the governor-general was only first among equals and sometimes unable to exert any authority in the captaincies. In truth, the governor-general and his later successor, the viceroy, never exercised the same degree of control or authority as their counterparts in Spanish America.

The municipal government was the one with which most Brazilians came into contact and the only one in which they participated to any degree. Governing much more than the town and its environs, the municipality extended into the countryside. In sparsely settled Brazil, the municipalities contained hundreds, often thousands, of square miles.

The most important institution of local government was the *senado da câmara,* the municipal council. A restricted suffrage of the *homens bons,* the propertied class, elected two justices of the peace, three aldermen, and a procurator to office every three years. At first the presiding officer was selected by the other councilmen, but by the end of the seventeenth century, the crown was appointing a presiding officer in the most important towns and cities. The duties of the council varied. Meeting twice weekly, it meted out local justice, handled routine municipal business and local administration, and passed the necessary laws and regulations. The procurator executed those laws. In cooperation with the church, the senado helped to oversee local charities. The municipality enjoyed its own source of income: rents from city property, license fees for tradesmen, taxes on certain foodstuffs, charges for diverse services such as the verification of weights and measures, and fines. On occasions, the senados and governors engaged in power struggles. The senado of São Luís during the seventeenth century was particularly ambitious. So often did it summon the governor to appear before it that the king in 1677 ordered it to desist forthwith, reminding the councilors that the governor represented the crown and could not be ordered around. To protect their interests, the larger cities maintained a representative at the court in Lisbon as a sort of lobbyist.

The senado frequently served as the first arena for the struggles between the *mazombos,* the whites born in Brazil, and the *reinóis,* the whites born in Portugal. Portuguese officials, occupying all levels of government except the municipal, enforced the law of the empire; their point of view was global. The mazombos sitting on the municipal councils cared only for the local scene; their vision was Brazilian. They wanted to enforce those aspects of the laws beneficial to them, to their community, and, to a lesser extent, to Brazil. These different perspectives gave rise to repeated clashes in which the mazombos did not always give ground to the renóis. In times of crises, the senado da câmara amplified its membership to become a *conselho geral,* a general council. At those times, local military, judicial, and ecclesiastical authorities as well as representatives of the people met to discuss the emergency at hand.

A second influential institution of local government was the regional militia. In its ranks, the region's principal figure of prestige and power, usually the largest landowner, bore the rank of *capitão-mor,* equivalent to colonel. The majority of them seem to have been born in the colony. In the absence of regularly constituted governmental officials in the hinterlands, the capitães-mor performed a variety of administrative and judicial tasks. Their power varied widely and, as in so many cases, depended mainly on their own abilities and strengths, since the distant government could do little to help or hinder them. They often became the local strongmen or *caudilhos*, the precursors of the later *coroneis*, who controlled rural Brazil.

Unlike the Portuguese monarchs, the Spanish established separate bodies in Spain to administer the colonies. The first was the Casa de Contratación, founded in 1521, which served to regulate and develop commerce with the New World. The second, the Council of the Indies *(Consejo de las Indias)*, established in 1524, advised the king on all American affairs. It prepared most of the laws for governing the Americas, saw that the laws were executed, and then sat as a high court to judge cases involving the fracture or interpretation of the laws. Ecclesiastical matters fell within its jurisdiction as well.

The viceroy served as the king's principal representative in the New World. Columbus bore the title of viceroy of any new lands he might discover when he left Spain in 1492. The crown appointed Antonio de Mendoza, a member of one of Spain's foremost families and a trusted diplomat of Charles V, as the first Viceroy of New Spain. Amid great pomp, he arrived in Mexico City in 1535 and immediately tried to restrict the authority of the adelantados and encomenderos while he strengthened and centralized the king's power in the New World. By the time he left Mexico in 1551, he had imposed law and order, humbled the landowning class, and exalted the royal powers. In short, he consolidated the conquest of New Spain. Peru became the second viceroyalty. The first viceroy arrived in 1543 to find chaos, rivalries, and civil war disrupting Spanish South America. Not until the able administration of the fifth viceroy, Francisco de Toledo (1569–81), was the king's authority firmly imposed on his unruly South American subjects. Like Mendoza, Toledo's major achievement was the consolidation of Spanish rule.

Numerous accounts testify to the splendor and prestige surrounding the viceroys and their New World courts. They were the "shadows of the king," and many accustomed themselves to royal treatment in their American domains. For example, in his lively history of Potosí written during the early decades of the eighteenth century, Bartolomé Arzáns de Orsúa y Vela provided posterity with a vivid view of a viceregal visit to that extremely important silver-mining center in 1716. Priests, nobles, and representatives of one of the labor guilds met Viceroy don Fray Diego Morcillo Rubio de Auñón outside the city to escort him into Potosí, whose principal streets and plazas opulently displayed banners and bunting of silk, damask, and satin. Passing beneath silver-encrusted triumphal arches especially constructed for the visit, the official party approached the awaiting municipal dignitaries who stood expectantly beneath "a canopy of very rich pearl-colored cloth lined with silk." A short musical concert began, while Urbanity and Generosity (represented by two children) recited elegant verses expressive of the city's gratitude for the honor of the visit. The viceroy then accepted as gifts golden spurs and a richly decorated Chilean horse with silver stirrups. On the fine steed the viceroy, accompanied by a growing crowd of elaborately dressed worthies, marched to the principal church richly outfitted with hangings of satin, velvet, silk tapestries, and damasks and paintings of landscapes and portraits—a magnificence, the historian assured his readers, only the local women "all with their beauty, fine clothing, coiffures, jewels, and pearls" surpassed. The priests and representatives of the city's religious communities awaited His Excellency on the steps to conduct him into the service. Hours later, exiting from the lavish religious pageantry, the viceroy reviewed the troops smartly drawn up in an adjacent plaza. Finally, he retired to a local aristocrat's home "so richly and appropriately adorned so spacious and magnificent that it was worthy of lodging our king and lord Philip V himself."

More than a description of a visit, the account identifies which persons—and more importantly the institutions they represented—enjoyed prestige. The viceroy greeted the local elite, the city officials, the clergy, and the military. Significantly, at least some labor (guild) representatives participated in the elaborate rituals. Thus, the arrangements surrounding the hospitality accorded the viceroy in Potosí detail accurately the composition of the local ruling hierarchy in colonial Spanish America and preserve a glimpse into their relations with a distant monarch and his immediate representative.

The *audiencia* was the highest royal court and consultative council in the New World. In some instances it also prepared legislation. The Spanish audiencias had much in common with the Portuguese relação. The first audiencias were established in Santo Domingo in 1511; Mexico City, 1527; Panama City, 1535; Lima, 1542; and Guatemala, 1543. In the eighteenth century, fourteen such bodies functioned. The number of *oidores,* or judges, sitting on the audiencia varied. In the sixteenth century, their number fluctuated between three and four, but later it expanded to as many as fifteen. Because the tenure of the oidores exceeded that of the viceroy and overlapped each other, the oidores provided a continuity to royal administration.

Captaincies-general were the major subdivisions of the viceroyalties. Theoretically the captains-general were subordinate to the viceroys, but in practice they communicated directly with Madrid and paid only the most formal homage to the viceroys. Ranking beneath them were the governors, *corregidores,* and *alcaldes mayores* who administered the municipalities and other territorial divisions. Within their localities, these minor officials possessed executive and judicial authority as well as some limited legislative powers.

Municipal government, known as the *cabildo,* provided the major opportunity for the creole, the American-born white, to hold office and to exercise some political power during the early colonial period. By the middle of the eighteenth century, the creoles also held all but the highest government offices. As in Brazil, the town council governed not only the town itself but also the surrounding countryside, thus in some instances exercising power

The viceroyalties in Latin America at the end of the eighteenth century.

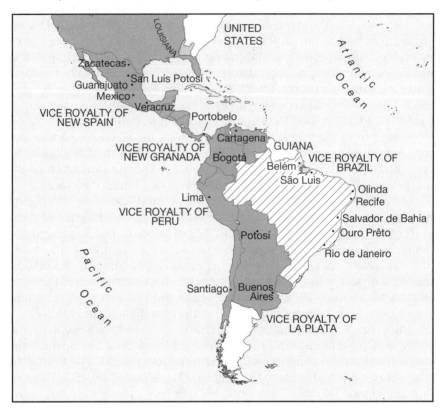

over vast areas. Property-owning citizens at first elected the *regidores*, the town councilmen, although later increasing numbers purchased or inherited the office.

Parallel to the creole cabildos were indigenous cabildos; in some regions they disappeared relatively quickly, merging into the creole cabildos. In other regions, they lasted until independence. Especially in the early years, the Spaniards relied on indigenous leadership to collect tribute or organize the workforce for public works. In essence, royal administration of the colonies rested on a handful of royal officials who oversaw Spanish settlers, and later creoles, and indigenous who actually produced the wealth.

For much of the colonial period, Spanish America was divided only into two viceroyalties—the Viceroyalty of Mexico, which included all of modern Central America, and the Viceroyalty of Peru, including all of Spanish South America. However, as the late colonial period saw the reorientation of trade to the Atlantic Coast and the rising importance of the port at Buenos Aires, the Crown created two new viceroyalties—New Granada, including modern Colombia, Venezuela and Ecuador, and La Plata, including parts of modern Chile, Argentina, Bolivia, and Uruguay.

The new viceroyalties signal the importance of trade in shaping government entities. From the earliest colonial days, merchants constituted a small but important class. They united into *consulados* and obtained formidable privileges and prerogatives. The crown authorized the first such trade association for Mexico in 1592; the merchants of Lima received permission for one in 1613. Thereafter, the consulado spread to other parts of Spain's American empire, a significant indicator of increasing trade with the metropolis. Together with the consulados in Seville and Cadiz they exercised a monopoly over the trade and commerce of Spanish America.

The Church

The presence of twelve friars accompanying Columbus on his second voyage to the New World and of six Jesuits in the retinue of Brazil's first governor-general, Tome de Sousa, signified yet another intention of the Iberian monarchs. They resolved to Christianize the Indians, a resolution they took seriously. Columbus's instructions stated, "the King and Queen, having more regard for the augmentation of the faith than for any other utility, desire nothing other than to augment the Christian religion and to bring divine worship to many simple nations." The immense task of evangelizing millions of Indians involved more than simple conversion. By Christianizing the Indians, the priests would also be Europeanizing them: teaching the trades, manners, customs, languages, and habits of the Spanish and Portuguese.

Conversion was essential not only to give the Indians the true faith and eternal salvation but also to make them loyal subjects to Their Most Catholic Majesties. To be Portuguese or Spanish was to be Roman Catholic. Religion served as a proto-nationalism as the Catholic monarchs used faith as a measure of citizenship, starting with the expulsion of Jews and Moslems.

Most Spaniards embraced the Catholic faith unquestioningly and defended it devotedly. Iberians were born, reared, married, and buried Catholics. The Church touched every aspect of their lives. The monarchs defended the faith within their realms, in return for which the Pope conferred royal patronage upon the crown by bulls to the Spanish monarchs in 1501 and 1508 and to the Portuguese monarchs temporarily in 1515 and permanently in 1551. That royal patronage permitted the Iberian monarchs to exercise power over the Church in their empires in all but purely spiritual matters. They collected the tithe and decided how it should be spent, appointed (and at times recalled) the bishops, priests, and other ecclesiastical officials, authorized the construction of new churches, determined the boundaries of the bishoprics, and approved and transmitted papal messages—or refused to. The royal patronage meant that the state dominated the Church, but conversely, it allowed the Church to pervade the state. If the king and his ministers had a final say in church matters, it is equally true that clerics often occupied the top administrative posts in governments. Churchmen often served as ministers, captains-general, viceroys, and even regents. Cardinal Henry, after all, ruled the Portuguese empire in the sixteenth century.

As the priests attended to conversions, clerical organization and hierarchy, transferred from the Old World to the New, followed the European model. The Spanish crown authorized the first bishoprics in 1511, two in Hispaniola and one in Puerto Rico. By 1600, there were five archbishoprics and twenty-seven bishoprics in Spanish America, numbers that jumped to ten and thirty-eight respectively before the end of the colonial period. The Portuguese crown erected the Bishopric of Brazil in 1551, and in 1676 approved the creation of the Archbishopric of Brazil with its see in Salvador. Two new bishoprics, Rio de Janeiro and Pernambuco, were established at the same time. By the end of the eighteenth century there were four others.

Initially, the Church depended on priests who belonged to the regular clergy, that is, the religious orders, as contrasted with the secular clergy, who served as priests in the growing number of churches. In turn, the priests relied on the tradition of the Indians. A religious people, the indigenous did not need to be convinced of the existence of deities. Indigenous people were polytheistic and accustomed to adding the gods of conquerors to their pantheon of gods. After all, the god of the conqueror must clearly be stronger; the Aztec symbol for conquest was the burning temple. A more difficult problem was Catholic insistence on monotheism, and the proliferation of Latin American saints days can be attributed to the linking of Catholic saints with local deities.

Sedentary Indians were usually incorporated into encomiendas and their spiritual needs attended to by the priest hired by the encomendero. While it is questionable how much of the doctrine was actually understood and accepted by the Indians, they were at least nominally Christians. The apparent success with sedentary groups prompted prelates to gather the nomadic natives into villages, the aldeias in Brazil and the *reducciones* in Spanish America, where they could more easily be instructed, Christianized, and protected under a watchful eye. The village system permitted the maximum use of the few regular clergy: usually one or two brothers administered each village. Each village centered on a church, built of course by the indigenous converts themselves. Around it were a school, living quarters, and warehouses. The ringing of church bells awoke the neophytes each day, summoning them to mass. Afterward, singing hymns along the way, they marched outside the village to cultivate the fields. The brothers taught reading, writing, and the mastering of useful trades. Indian sculptors, painters, masons, carpenters, bakers, and locksmiths, among others, were soon practicing their trades. Many of the villages achieved a high degree of self-sufficiency, and most raised some commercial crops, such as tobacco, sugar, or wheat, for sale to outside markets. Large cattle herds tended by the neophytes provided hides and meat for sale. Although the brothers administered the church through various Indians whom they appointed to office and invested with the customary symbols of that office, the churchmen in the final analysis rigidly controlled the lives of their charges. It was not a simple figure of speech when they spoke of the Indians as "their children," for that was exactly how they regarded them. Their subjects did not always view the priests as kind fathers, however, as abundant letters of protest to the king indicate. Indians complained that priests beat them and seduced their wives.

In the late colonial period, priests founded missions on the fringes of the colonies, most notably in the northern reaches of California and Texas, and the southern Amazon region. In these regions, priests brought the scattered Indians into the safety of a community behind walls. The mission system minimized Indian revolts and warfare and helped to hold distant frontiers against foreign claims and intrusions. The missions freed the small number of soldiers on the fringes to pay less attention to Indian threats and more to encroachments from other colonial powers. The appearance of a standing army, along with locally formed militias, was a phenomenon of the late colonial period. Until then, there were no professional soldiers in Latin America—even the infamous conquistadores were at best soldiers of fortune.

Of major importance to the social and religious lives of the colonists were the lay brotherhoods, voluntary associations of the faithful. They built handsome churches, merrily celebrated the feast days of patron saints, and dutifully maintained charitable institutions such as hospitals and orphanages. Indeed, works of charity, education, and social assistance composed some of the noblest chapters of the history of the Roman Catholic Church in the New World.

The Church also offered women an alternative to family life, a choice they did not always make voluntarily. Patriarchs sometimes placed their daughters in convents to guard their virginity or to prevent marriage. A marriage could mean a huge dowry of land, property, or capital, which the father preferred to pass on intact to a son. On the other hand, widows often retired to a convent from which they administered their wealth, estates, and property. A religious life by no means meant one dominated exclusively by prayer and meditation. Nor were nunneries necessarily dreary houses of silence, service, and abnegation. Through the religious orders, women operated schools, hospitals, and orphanages. In some convents, the nuns, attended by their servants, entertained, read secular literature, played musical instruments, sang, prepared epicurean delights, and enjoyed a lively and comfortable life.

The Church maintained a careful vigil over its flock. Nonetheless, some examples of moral corruption among the clergy provided bawdy gossip for colonial ears. Alleged backsliders—especially Jewish converts, the New Christians—could expect to account for themselves before the Inquisition. Philip

A weathered cathedral in Havana, Cuba. (Library of Congress.)

II authorized the establishment of the Holy Office in Spanish America in 1569, and it began to operate in Lima in 1570; in Mexico City in 1571; and in Cartagena in 1610. Significantly he exempted the Indians from the jurisdiction of the Inquisition "because of their ignorance and their weak minds." The Inquisition served more of a political than religious end in its vigilant efforts to purge and purify society in order to make it unified and loyal. The considerable power of the Inquisition lasted until the last half of the eighteenth century, when the winds of the Enlightenment blew across the Iberian Peninsula, causing the flames of the Holy Tribunal to flicker. As an institution it was never established in Brazil, but it operated there through the bishops and three visitations from Inquisitors. In general, the hand of the Inquisition rested lightly on Brazil.

Perhaps the relations between Church and state were not always perfect examples of harmony but they were sufficiently tranquil to allow the Church to grow wealthy in the New World. Tithes, the sale of papal indulgences, and parochial fees provided a small share of the Church's income. The legacy furnished the principal source of wealth. In their wills, the affluent were expected to leave at least part of their wealth to the Mother Church. Over the decades the Church accumulated vast estates, quickly becoming the largest landowner in the New World. Financial transactions, such as fees and interest rates on loans, further filled ecclesiastical coffers.

The Church wealth was by no means evenly distributed. In cities such as Lima, Salvador da Bahia, Ouro Prêto, Quito, Antigua, and Mexico City, ostentatiously imposing churches crowded one another, while "shocking poverty" characterized hundreds of humble parish churches dotting the countryside. While some of the higher clergy lived on incomes surpassing those of many of the sovereign princes of Germany, impoverished clerics administered to the needs of the faithful in remote villages.

The wealth reinforced the conservative inclinations of the Iberian Church. After the initial phase of evangelizing, it too exploited the Indians, as well as the African slaves, to till Church lands or to erect larger and more opulent edifices. To the masses it preached resignation. If God had made them poor, it would be a sin to question why. Poverty was to have its reward in the next life. It was not from the masses that the Church drew its leadership. Generally the sons of the wealthy and/or noble became bishops and archbishops, positions in the New World dominated by the European-born. Thus, the highest ranks of the clergy, like those in the military and civil service, were associated with and filled by the elite. In wealth, power, prestige, and monopoly of education, the Roman Catholic Church by the end of the eighteenth century ranked as an omnipotent institution in the Western Hemisphere. Its influence weighed heavily, not only in the social and religious life of the community, but in politics and economics as well.

Society and Culture

At the base of society was the patriarchal family, sanctified by religion and serving as a model for the organization of society and policy. The male head of the family dominated the household and its businesses. In rural Brazil, that included plantation, slaves, and tenants. While males of the household liberally expanded the basic family unit through their sexual escapades to include hosts of mestizo and mulatto children, the Iberian woman was expected to live a pure life of seclusion. Ideal models were set for the behavior of the women of the patriarch's family, who were destined either for matrimony or religious orders. They were to remain virgins until their marriage and to live separated from all men except their fathers, husbands, and sons. A high value was placed on their duties as wives and mothers, and control over their sexuality was essential to guarantee that the Iberian elites remained of pure blood. Although women of other economic strata could not follow such an elitist model, they were certainly influenced by it. Profoundly Christian and emphatically patriarchal, these family units set the social tone and pattern for the entire colony. The traditional godparent relationship *(com-*

padrio in Brazil, *compadrazgo* in Spanish America) further reinforced the family structure. The strongest of the families formed a landed aristocracy, which in the colonial period dominated the senados and cabildos, and later, in the imperial period, the newly independent national governments.

Women served an important role in Iberian acculturation. They taught indigenous children, as well as their own, and instructed their household staffs in Spanish and Portuguese, in religion, and ways of life. While elite Iberian and creole women were expected to stay mostly in the home, lower-class women of necessity participated in many occupations: bakers, healers (*curanderas*), midwives, seamstresses, potters, candle makers, innkeepers, and landladies. Some women were even slave sellers and speculators in real estate.

Legally, women were treated as minors, looked after first by their fathers and then their husbands, who were also the legal guardians of their children. However, upon the father's death, widows inherited half of the father's wealth, and male and female children equally divided the other half. Widows were frequently executors of men's wills and guardians of their children. Their freedom often resulted in great societal pressure for them to remarry. Sometimes the women would choose instead to retreat to convents as *beatas*, holy women, though not technically nuns.

Much of the culture of the colonial period came from the Church. While the Church censored books, it also educated Americans and fostered most of the serious scholarship in the New World. In the sixteenth century, some sensitive intellectual church members wrote excellent studies of the very Indian cultures they were helping to eradicate. In order to facilitate the mastery of the Indian tongues, and thus to speed up the process of Christianization, the friars compiled dictionaries and grammars of the many Indian languages. Because church members composed a large share of the educated of the colonies, it was from their ranks that most of the teachers came. The Church exercised a virtual monopoly over education. Monasteries housed the first schools and taught reading, writing, arithmetic, and Catholic doctrine. Contrary to the attitude of the Portuguese crown, the Spanish monarch encouraged the founding of universities in the New World, granting the first charters in 1551 to the University of Mexico and the University of San Marcos in Lima. The clergy occupied most of the chairs. Before Harvard opened its doors in 1636, a dozen Spanish-American universities, drawing on medieval Spanish models, offered a wide variety of courses in law, medicine, theology, and the arts, most of them taught in Latin. The universities made one major concession to the New World: They taught theological students Indian languages for their future benefit and effectiveness.

One of the most remarkable intellectuals of the colonial period was a nun, Sor Juana Inés de la Cruz (1651–95), whose talent earned her fame in New Spain during her lifetime and whose complex and brilliant poetry ensured her an exalted place in literature. Her works, expressing ideas far advanced for her own time, reveal a complex personality. For one thing, she argued that women were as intelligent as men, a conclusion her own life amply illustrated. She also advocated education for women. The Church once reprimanded her and suggested she apply her intelligence to study of the Holy Scriptures. Yet the Church also expressed a certain pride in her brilliance, and for many years she enjoyed her status as a favorite in the viceregal court and among Mexican intellectuals (all male).

The Spanish and Portuguese occupied the top tier of the social hierarchy in the New World. Below them came their descendants, of pure Iberian blood but born in the colonies—the creoles of Spanish America and mazombos of Brazil. Together they constituted a small minority, precariously balanced above the darker masses. Most confusing for society was the mixture of peoples—mestizos of mixed Iberian and indigenous blood, mulattos of mixed European and African ancestry. They pushed for inclusion in a society that linked race and class. At the base of society was the mass of darker people—Indians, Africans and mixtures of the two. They far outnumbered the elites, but they had none of their privileges.

Cracks in the Empire

At the core of Spanish and Portuguese expansion was interest in trade and belief in economic doctrines known as *mercantilism*. Mercantilism rationalized that colonies existed to enrich the mother countries; consequently, any Iberian policies sprang from the determination that the American colonies would strengthen Portugal and Spain. The possession of bullion distinguished a successful mercantilist program, but those precious metals enriched the Iberian treasuries only momentarily.

Spanish mercantilist policies rigorously controlled trade with the New World. All commerce fell under the direction of the Casa de Contratación, aided by the *consulados*. The Casa authorized Cádiz and Seville as the only Spanish ports to trade with Spanish America, and Vera Cruz and Portobelo as their American counterparts. Under the protective guns of the royal navy, two fleets sailed each year, one to Vera Cruz, the other to Portobelo. These two fleets returned bearing the products of Spanish Middle and South America. Despite the restrictions, contraband still flourished—to which the slow but constant growth of Buenos Aires testified. The English, French, and Dutch were only too eager to enter the markets of the New World, and at times European wars and diplomacy forced the Spaniards to legalize some aspect of that contraband trade. A later device to eliminate contraband trade was the formation in Spain of monopolistic companies with exclusive rights in the New World. The crown itself exercised monopolies including salt, pepper, quicksilver, and gunpowder.

The great wealth of the colonies was squandered by the Habsburg kings of Spain. When the Bourbon royal family took the throne in the eighteenth century, they found a bankrupt monarchy. Changes were needed, and particularly under Charles III (1759–88), Spain reformed its imperial structure, with the goal of increasing administrative efficiency, political control, and profits. The power of the Council of the Indies waned as the ministers of the king took over many of its former duties. In the eighteenth century, the chief responsibility for the government of Spanish America rested in the hands of the Minister of the Indies. The Casa de Contratación also felt the weight of Bourbon reforms. The king's ministers absorbed so many of its powers that it became useless and was abolished in 1790.

The most radical innovation was the establishment of the intendancy system, an administrative unit used by the Bourbons in France and copied by their relatives in Spain. The intendants, royal officials of Spanish birth, with extensive judicial, administrative, and financial powers, supplanted the numerous governors, corregidores, and alcaldes mayores in the hope that a more efficient and uniform administration would increase the king's revenue and end bureaucratic abuses and corruption. In financial affairs, the intendants reported directly to the crown. In religious, judicial, and administrative matters, they were subject to the viceroy and were to respect his military prerogatives. In 1764, Cuba became the first intendancy, and by 1790 the system extended to all the Spanish American colonies.

The new system infuriated the creoles, who were accustomed to holding all but the highest government offices. Now they were displaced by a new layer of Iberian personnel. And although the complicated Habsburg tax structure was simplified and reduced, the new intendants saw that the taxes were indeed collected, filling imperial coffers at creole expense.

As another reform measure, Charles III in the 1760s created a colonial militia with creole officers in order defend the increasingly important distant fringes of the empire. The granting of military commissions to the creoles afforded them a new prestige. Usually the high ranks were reserved for—or bought by—wealthy members of the local aristocracy. Hence, a close identification developed between high military rank and the upper class. Further, the creole officers enjoyed a most practical advantage, the *fuero militar*, a special military privilege, that exempted them from civil law. In effect, it established the military as a special class above the law, the effects of which would be increasingly disruptive for Latin American society.

The Bourbon kings infused a more liberal economic spirit into the empire. They hoped to strengthen Spain by liberalizing trade, expanding agriculture, and reviving mining. They dispatched European engineers and mining technicians to the New World to encourage the latest mining techniques, even authorizing establishment of a College of Mining in Mexico.

In the eighteenth century, Cádiz lost its old commercial monopoly when the king permitted other Spanish ports to trade with the Americas. The fleet system gradually disappeared. After 1740, Spanish ships commonly rounded

Cape Horn to trade with Peru and slowly abandoned the old isthmian trade route. In the 1770s Charles lifted the restrictions on intercolonial commerce.

Portuguese mercantilism was never as effective as that of its neighbor, particularly before 1750. Attempts were made sporadically to organize annual fleets to and from Brazil protected by men-of-war, but the highly decentralized Portuguese trade patterns and a shortage of merchant and war ships caused difficulties. Between the mid-seventeenth and mid-eighteenth centuries, the crown partially succeeded in instituting a fleet system for the protection of Brazilian shipping. Still, it never functioned as well as the Spanish convoys. Economic companies fared little better. The crown licensed four. In general they were unpopular with the residents of Brazil and the merchants, both in Portugal and Brazil. The Brazilians criticized them for abusing their monopolies and raising prices with impunity. The merchants disapproved of the monopolies, which eliminated them from much trade, and accused the companies of charging outlandish freight rates. All sides bombarded the companies with charges of inefficiency. Crown monopolies—such as brazilwood, salt, tobacco, slaves, and diamonds—flourished.

Royal control over Brazil tightened during the eighteenth century. The plantations produced their major crops for export, demand dictated incomes, and incomes regulated production. While Lisbon encouraged the capitalist trends toward higher production, it continued to prevent direct trade with European markets, much to the increasing frustration of the Brazilian elites. Their desire to enter the capitalist marketplace of the North Atlantic and the imperial, mercantilist, and monopolistic policies of the Portuguese crown charted a course of conflict that prompted the exercise of greater royal control.

The absolutist tendencies noticeable during the reign of John V (ruled 1706–50), were realized under the Marquis of Pombal, who ruled through the weak Joseph I (ruled 1750–77). Pombal hoped to strengthen his economically moribund country through fuller utilization of its colonies. To better exploit Brazil, he centralized its government. He incorporated the state of Maranhão into Brazil in 1772. He dissolved the remaining hereditary captaincies, with one minor exception, and brought them under direct royal control. To fortify royal authority, Pombal expelled the Jesuits from the empire in 1759. He accused the order of challenging the secular government and of interposing itself between the king and his Indian subjects. Some 600 Jesuits were forced to leave Brazil. (In 1767, Charles III followed suit, expelling some 2,200 Jesuits from Spanish America.) Pombal strengthened the government's hand in both the education and care of the Indians. For good or for bad, he ended the isolation enforced on them by the church-controlled aldeias. By requiring Indians to speak Portuguese, dress like Europeans, and adopt trades and crafts, and by encouraging whites to intermarry with them, he tried to bring them within the Luso-Brazilian community. Finally, he tried to restrict the independence of municipal governments.

To the end of the colonial period, the metropolises feared their American colonies might relax their efforts to grow the crops, to raise the herds, or to mine the minerals Europe demanded. Royal officials also kept sharp eyes peeled for any unnecessary diversification of the American economies. They forbid Brazil or Spanish America to produce anything that the Iberian nations already produced or could furnish. With few exceptions the colonies were not encouraged to manufacture. The motherlands wanted to supply all the needed manufactured goods and earn for themselves the profits for doing so.

Officials in the metropolis never deviated from the idea that the colony existed to serve the motherland. However, by the last half of the eighteenth century, Latin American elites began to question their role in the imperial relationship. They concluded that their own best interests were not being served by Iberian mercantilism. Just as the Spanish elites considered only their own well-being, however, the creole elites remained unconcerned with the needs of the majority of Latin Americans.

In sum, the colonial period in Latin America was formative, with greater significance than for the North American colonies. It began a century earlier, and by 1550 every major city in the region had been founded. While the Spaniards had transplanted institutions from the old world to the new, they were forced to modify them to fit local circumstances, frequently building on the indigenous structures. During 300 years of imperial rule, patterns emerged that would resonate throughout the modern period: It was a hierarchical society, led by a small white elite that dominated poor, darker masses. Political, economic, and social power was in the hands of a few, buttressed by the validation of a hierarchical church. The economy was characterized by large landholdings and low-paid workers, with a dependence on exports, making the region disproportionately affected by foreign affairs. And it would be foreign affairs that would impel the colonies to become nations.

An Early Feminist Statement

Sor Juana Inés de la Cruz (1651–95) has become a heroic example of early feminism. A favorite of the wife of Mexico's viceroy, she was brought to the court, where her beauty and wit won her many admirers. Instead of marrying, she chose to enter the convent at eighteen, where she devoted her life to poetry and scientific experiments. She was chided by her superiors for her unseemly interest in worldly matters, and she eventually gave up writing and devoted herself to penance and nursing the sick.

> Silly, you men—so very adept
> at wrongly faulting womankind,
> not seeing you're alone to blame
> for faults you plant in woman's mind.
>   After you've won by urgent plea
> the right to tarnish her good name,
> you still expect her to behave—
> *you*, that coaxed her into shame.
>   You batter her resistance down
> and then, all righteousness, proclaim
> that feminine frivolity,
> not your persistence, is to blame.
>   When it comes to bravely posturing,
> your witlessness must take the prize:
> you're the child that makes a bogeyman,
> and then recoils in fear and cries.
>   Presumptuous beyond belief,
> you'd have the woman you pursue
> be Thais when you're courting her,
> Lucretia once she falls to you.
>   For plain default of common sense,
> could any action be so queer
> as oneself to cloud the mirror
> then complain that it's not clear?
>   Whether you're favored or disdained,
> nothing can leave you satisfied.
> You whimper if you're turned away,
> you sneer if you've been gratified.
>   With you, no woman can hope to score;
> whichever way, she's bound to lose;
> spurning you, she's ungrateful;
> succumbing, you call her lewd.
>   Your folly is always the same:
> you apply a single rule
> to the one you accuse of looseness
> and the one you brand as cruel.

What happy mean could there be
for the woman who catches your eye,
if, unresponsive, she offends,
yet whose complaisance you decry?

Still, whether it's torment or anger—
and both ways you've yourselves to blame—
God bless the woman who won't have you,
no matter how loud you complain.

It's your persistent entreaties
that change her from timid to bold.
Having made her thereby naughty,
you would have her good as gold.

So where does the greater guilt lie
for a passion that should not be:
with the man who pleads out of baseness
or the woman debased by his plea?

Or which is more to be blamed—
though both will have cause for chagrin:
the woman who sins for money
or the man who pays money to sin?

So why are you men all so stunned
at the thought you're all guilty alike?
Either like them for what you've made them
or make of them what you can like.

If you'd give up pursuing them,
you'd discover, without a doubt,
you've a stronger case to make
against those who seek you out.

I well know what powerful arms
you wield in pressing for evil:
your arrogance is allied
with the world, the flesh, and the devil!

Source: Sor Juana Inés de la Cruz, *A Sor Juana Anthology*, Alan S. Trueblood, trans. (Cambridge, MA: Harvard University Press, 1988), 110–13. Reprinted by permission of the publisher Harvard University Press, Copyright © 1988 by the President and Fellows of Harvard College.

An Indian Cabildo Writes to the Crown, 1554

The relatively small number of Spaniards in the colonies could not possibly have ruled the extensive territories and guaranteed the labor and tribute of the indigenous without the help of traditional indigenous leaders. The Spanish refashioned the local governments into Spanish-style cabildos and used these

indigenous cabildos to pass on their orders. The cabildo
members quickly learned to appeal to higher-ups when local
burdens seemed excessive or their autonomy was threatened.
They believed that the king did not necessarily know what
abuses were committed locally in his name, and they frequently
petitioned the crown. It is unlikely, however, that anyone on the
Council of the Indies read these documents, written in Nahuatl
using the Roman alphabet. Many of these documents have been
collected and translated by James Lockhart, who pioneered the
use of Nahuatl documents to understand colonial Latin America.

> Our much revered ruler:
> We Mexica and Tenochca bow down to you and kiss your
> precious hands and feet, you our ruler and prince who guard over
> things for our lord Jesus Christ there in old Spain and here in New
> Spain; we set before you our weeping, tears, and great concern,
> for well we know that you greatly love us your poor vassals who
> are citizens here in New Spain, as it is called.
> Your benevolence appears in the very good orders with
> which you and your precious father our great emperor have
> defended us. If your orders for us had been carried out, we would
> have had no concern and would have lived in great happiness.
> We think that it is because of our failings that your orders have
> been fruitless, which greatly increases our concern, so that it is not
> for nothing that we put before you our weeping, tears and
> concerns.
> Listen, our much revered ruler and prince; although you
> have sent many orders here to benefit us your poor vassals, those
> who serve you and exercise your rulership here in New Spain do
> not carry them out, which causes us great suffering and loss of
> possessions and property, now and in the past. And although it is
> very piteous and worrisome, we merely set our weeping and tears
> before our god and ruler God our Lord so that he will remedy it
> when he wishes.
> There is another great affliction of ours which now newly
> concerns us, with which we cry out to you, our precious prince,
> for now in the year 1554 the rule and governorship that our
> fathers and grandfathers bequeathed us was going to be taken
> from us and given to the Spaniards. And oh king, it would have
> been carried out if our fathers the friars of San Francisco had not
> supported us; they would have made us all their slaves. And
> those who wish to do this are making every effort to carry it out;
> we think that they will indeed impose their will on us if you and
> your precious father do not defend us. Two alcaldes mayores were
> appointed, one to serve in Mexico City and the other in Tlatelolco,
> and they were to be in charge of the governorship, justice and
> town council business. When we heard of the order we brought

complaint before your representative don Luis de Velasco the viceroy, and the friars of San Francisco also spoke to him on our behalf. Then he gave orders that the two should not be called alcaldes mayores but only protectors, and he instructed them that their only duty would be to save us from any Spaniard, mestizo, Black or mulatto molesting us in the marketplace, on the roads, in the canals, or in our homes; he instructed them to be on the watch day and night that no one molest us. We greatly approve this order of your viceroy, for we need it very much, and we implore you to order them to take great care with their task, for the Spaniards, mestizos, Blacks and mulattos do greatly molest us. We also implore you that no one take our government and jurisdiction from us. If it is thought we do not know how to rule, govern, and do true justice, let such laws be made for us as are necessary so that we can perform our duties properly, and if we do not observe them let us be punished. Let the right to rule which belongs to those who will follow us not be taken from them.

And if it is thought that we do not love the ruler and king of Castile, to put your mind to rest we here take oath as rulers, all of us who govern your city of Mexico; we who write this letter swear and take oath as rulers before God and St. Mary and all the saints and before you our ruler that we will always love, obey, and revere the ruler and king of Castile until the end of the world. And we want this oath to hold for those who are born after us, and so that this our statement and rulers' oath will be valid we set down here are names and signatures.

Done here in Mexico City on December 19, 1554.

Your poor vassals who kiss your precious hands and feet.

Don Esteban de Guzmán, judge. Don Pedro de Motecuçoma. Don Diego de Mendoza, alcalde. Francisco de San Pablo, alcalde. Don Pedro de la Cruz, regidor. Don Luis de Paz, regidor. Bartolomé de San Juan, regidor. Don Baltasar Tlillancalqui, regidor. Diego Tezcacoacatl, regidor. Martín Cano, regidor. Martín Coçotecatl, regidor. Francisco Jiménez, regidor. Martín Tlamacicatl, regidor.

Source: From a set of translations of Nahuatl documents used in UCLA classes by James Lockhart. Reprinted by permission.

3

Independence

During the long colonial period, the psychology of the Latin Americans, particularly the elite, changed significantly. A feeling of inferiority before the Iberian-born gave way to a feeling of equality and then superiority. At the same time, nativism, a devotion to one's locality, matured into feelings of nationalism, a group consciousness attributing supreme value to the land of one's birth and pledging unswerving dedication to it. These changing attitudes resulted partly from the Latin Americans' greater appreciation of and pride in the regions where they were born and raised, and partly from a fuller understanding that their own interests could be better served if they, not distant monarchs, made the fundamental economic and political decisions. Inspired by the North American example and encouraged by the changes wrought in Napoleonic Europe, they declared their independence in order to realize their potential and chart their own future. In all cases, except in Haiti and during the early stages of the Mexican revolution, the creole and mazombo elites directed the movements toward independence, broke the ties with the former mother countries, and exercised the powers once reserved for the Iberians. The major historical questions for consideration during this period encompassing the end of the eighteenth century and the opening of the nineteenth are why the Latin Americans pursued independence, how they achieved it, and what they intended to do with it. Who benefited and who lost as a result of the political change from colony to nation? And finally, why did independence affirm rather than change the basic patterns of society?

A Changing Mentality Begets New Attitudes and Action

Before the end of the first century of Iberian colonization, the inhabitants of the New World began to reflect on themselves, their surroundings, and their relations to the rest of the world. They spoke and wrote for the first time in introspective terms. Juan de Cárdenas, although born in Spain, testified in his *Problemas y Secretas Maravillosos de las Indias* (The Marvellous Problems and Secrets of the Indies), published in 1591, that in Mexico the creole surpasses the peninsular (the Iberian) in wit and intelligence. Evincing a strong devotion to New Spain, Bernardo de Balbuena penned his *La Grandeza Mexicana* (The Grandeur of Mexico) in 1604 in praise of all things Mexican. He implied that for beauty, interest, and charm, life in Mexico City equaled—or surpassed—that in most Spanish cities. In 1618, Ambrósio Fernandes Brandão made the first attempt to define or interpret Brazil in his *Diálogos das Grandezas do Brasil* (Dialogues of the Greatness of Brazil). In doing so, he exhibited his devotion to the colony, chiding those Portuguese who came to Brazil solely to exploit it and return wealthy to the peninsula. Poets, historians, and essayists reflected on the natural beauty of a generous nature. They took up with renewed vigor the theme extolled in the early sixteenth century that the New World was an earthly paradise. A climax of sorts was reached in the early nineteenth century when the Brazilian poet Francisco de São Carlos depicted paradise in his long poem *A Assunção* in terms that made it sound strikingly similar to Brazil.

Concentrating ever more earnestly on themselves and their surroundings, the elite in the New World searched for ways of improving their conditions. The intensification of that search coincided with the sweep of the Enlightenment across Latin America. As manifested in that part of the world, the Enlightenment became primarily a search for and then promotion of useful knowledge, a selective search. The Latin American intellectuals drew from the enlightened ideologies those practical examples that best suited their goals. Principal attention focused on science, economics, commerce, agriculture, and education. Political matters received secondary attention and religion, at least for the time being, little at all. The American intellectuals carefully read the foremost European thinkers in order to extract ideas and examples. Nor did they neglect ideas emanating from the United States, whose declaration of and struggle for independence and the resultant federal republic fascinated the Ibero-American elite.

The pressures of the British and French on the Iberian monarchs for greater trade with their American empires, burgeoning European contraband in the Americas, and the more liberal commercial code promulgated by Spain in 1778 brought Latin America into ever closer contact with Europe and with European ideas. Foreigners visited the Americas, many of them on scientific missions. Representatives of the American elite traveled more frequently in Europe during the eighteenth century. American students went to Iberian universities and at times to French and English universities.

Once admitted, the new ideas from abroad diffused rapidly throughout the colonies. The universities of Spanish America, of which twenty-three existed at the opening of the nineteenth century, contributed to their spread. Professors and students alike challenged the hoary theories of Aristotle and the scholastic traditions. Other centers in Spanish America for the diffusion of the latest European knowledge were the Economic Societies of the Friends of the Country (Sociedades Económicas de Amigos del País), which had developed in Spain and spread to the New World by the 1780s. In general the societies showed a strong tendency to emphasize the natural and physical sciences, agriculture, commerce, and education, as well as to give some attention to political and social questions. Portuguese America had not a single university, but its counterpart of the Spanish economic societies was the literary and scientific academies, of which there were six, all established between 1724 and 1794 in either Salvador or Rio de Janeiro. Each had a short but apparently active life. The printing presses in Spanish America—Lisbon rigidly prohibited the setting up of a press in its American possessions—contributed significantly to spreading ideas. Among their many publications numbered several outstanding newspapers, all fonts of enlightened ideas and nativism. Their pages were replete with references to, quotations from, and translations of the major authors of the European Enlightenment.

The privileged classes in the New World desired most to reform commerce and trade. The American merchants and planters chafed under monopolies and restrictions. To the extent that the eighteenth-century reforms further increased the economic and political powers of the Iberian monarchs, the Americans did not welcome them. Closer supervision from Lisbon and Madrid exacerbated the tensions between the colonies and the metropolises.

Physiocrat doctrine—the ideas that wealth derived from nature (agriculture and mining) and multiplied under minimal governmental direction—gained support among Brazilian intellectuals. They spoke out in favor of reducing or abolishing taxes and duties and soon were advocating a greater freedom of trade. From Bahia, João Rodrigues de Brito boldly called for full liberty for the Brazilian farmers to grow whatever crops they wanted, to construct whatever works or factories were necessary for the good of their crops, to sell in any place, by any means, and through whatever agent they wished to choose without heavy taxes or burdensome bureaucracy, to sell to the highest bidder, and to sell their products at any time when it best suited them.

Similar complaints and demands reverberated throughout the Spanish-American empire. Chileans wanted to break down their economic isolation.

Reflecting on the potential wealth of Chile and the lingering poverty of its inhabitants, José de Cos Iriberri, a contemporary of the Bahian Rodrigues de Brito, concluded, "Crops cannot yield wealth unless they are produced in quantity and obtain a good price; and for this they need sound methods of cultivation, large consumption, and access to foreign markets." Manuel de Salas agreed and insisted that free trade was the natural means to wealth. And Anselmo de La Cruz asked a question being heard with greater frequency throughout the colonies: "What better method could be adopted to develop the agriculture, industry, and trade of our kingdom than to allow it to export its natural products to all the nations of the world without exception?"

As the American colonies grew in population and activity, and as Spain became increasingly involved in European wars in the eighteenth century, breaches appeared in the mercantilistic walls that Spain had carefully constructed around its American empire. British merchants audaciously assailed those walls and when and where possible widened the breaches. For their part, the Spanish Bourbons tried hard to introduce economic reforms that would reinforce Spain's monopolistic economic control. They authorized and encouraged a series of monopolistic companies. Doubtless, the Guipúzcoa Company best illustrates the effects of these monopolies and certainly the protests they elicited from a jealous native merchant class.

By the end of the seventeenth century, Venezuela exported a variety of natural products, most important of which were tobacco, cacao, and salt, to Spain, Spanish America, and some foreign islands in the Caribbean. This trade expanded to England, France, and the North American colonies during the early years of the eighteenth century. Commerce enjoyed a reputation as an honest and respectable profession in that Spanish colony. A small, prosperous, and increasingly influential merchant class emerged. The liberator of northern South America, Simón Bolívar, descended from one of the most successful of these native merchant families. The creation of the Guipúzcoa Company in 1728 to ensure that Venezuela traded within the imperial markets and to eliminate commercial intercourse with foreigners evoked sharp protest from the merchants, who readily foresaw the impending injury to their welfare. They complained that the company infringed on their interests, threatened their economic well-being, shut off their profitable trade with other Europeans, and failed to supply all their needs. Spain, after all, they quickly pointed out, could not absorb all of Venezuela's agricultural exports, whereas an eager market in the West Indies and northern Europe offered to buy them. Finally, exasperated with the monopoly and discouraged from expecting any results from their complaints, the merchants fostered an armed revolt against the company in 1749, a revolt that took Spain four years to quell. The struggle against the company was both armed and verbal, and it fostered a hostile feeling toward the crown, which was committed to supporting the unpopular company. The friction between the local merchants, businesspeople, landowners, and population on the one hand and the Guipúzcoa Company and crown on the other continued throughout the rest of the century. The merchants' belief that freer trade would fatten their profits was more than satisfactorily proven when Spain, after 1779, entered the war against England with the consequent interruption caused by the English fleet in the trade between Venezuela and Spain. The merchants took immediate advantage of the situation to trade directly and openly with the English islands in the Caribbean. Their profits soared.

Two new institutions soon organized the protests and activities of the disaffected Venezuelans. The Consulado de Caracas, established in 1793, brought together merchants and plantation owners, and it soon became a focal point for local dissatisfaction and agitation. Then in 1797 the merchants formed a militia company to protect the coast from foreign attack. That responsibility intensified their nativism, or, at that stage, patriotism. Nurtured by such local institutions, the complaints against the monopoly, burdensome taxes, and restrictions mounted in direct proportion to the increasing popularity of the idea of free trade. As one merchant expressed it, "Commerce ought to be as free as air." One of the results of these intensifying complaints was the series of armed uprisings in 1795, 1797, and 1799. Great Britain continued to encourage these and other protests against Spain's system of commercial monopoly. Clearly English interests coincided with those of the creole elite, who thought in terms of free trade.

Economic dissatisfaction extended beyond the narrow confines of the colonial elite. Many popular elements protested the burdensome taxes and expressed hope for improvements. Popular songs at the end of the eighteenth century expressed those economic protests:

All our rights
We see usurped
And with taxes and tributes
We are bent down
If anyone wants to know
Why I go shirtless
It's because the taxes
Of the king denude me
With much enthusiasm
The Intendents aid the Tyrant
To drink the blood
Of the American people

In fact, a wider segment of the population probably understood and appreciated the economic motivations for independence more than they did the political ones. Popular antitax demonstrations rocked many cities in both Spanish and Portuguese America in the eighteenth century. Oppressive economic conditions helped to spark two potentially serious popular uprisings, the Tupac Amaru Revolt in Peru in 1780 and the Comunero Revolt in New

Granada (Colombia) in 1781, and to foment the Bahian Conspiracy in Brazil in 1798.

Taking the name Tupac Amaru II and considering himself the rightful heir to the Incan throne, the mestizo José Gabriel Condorcanqui Noguera led a revolt—mainly of Indians, but at least in the beginning with the support of mestizos as well as some creoles—that broke out in November 1780, to protest the most distressing abuses of the Spanish colonial system. Excessive taxation, economic exploitation, and forced labor constituted some of the bitterest complaints of the followers of the Incan pretender. Much blood flowed before a well-armed militia checked the Indians, captured their leader, and suppressed the revolt in 1781.

Protesting an increase in taxes and burdensome monopolies, creoles and mestizos in New Granada rose up to nullify unpopular Spanish laws. The revolt spread spontaneously through New Granada in 1781. Faced with the growing success of the rebels, the Spanish authorities capitulated to their demands for economic reforms. However, once the communeros dispersed, satisfied with their apparent success, the viceroy abrogated former agreements and arrested the leaders, who were executed in 1782 and 1783.

Across the continent in Bahia, another popular conspiracy, this one against the Portuguese metropolis, came to a head in 1798. It exemplified the diffusion of the ideas of the Enlightenment among the masses, which, in this case, thought in terms of economic, social, and political reforms, even of independence. The conspirators were from the popular classes: soldiers, artisans, mechanics, workers, and so large a number of tailors that the movement sometimes bears the title of the "Conspiracy of the Tailors." All were young (under thirty years old), and all were mulattos. The conspirators spoke in vague but eloquent terms of free trade, which they felt would bring prosperity to their port, and of equality for all men without distinctions of race or color. They denounced excessive taxation and oppressive restrictions.

Dissatisfaction thus pervaded many classes. Its increase during the eighteenth century coincided with many reforms enacted by the Iberian crowns. Perhaps this situation further substantiates the conclusion of the historian Crane Brinton that revolutions stem from hope, not despair, from the promise of progress rather than from continuous oppression. The Latin Americans came to realize that in order to effect the reforms they desired, they themselves would have to wield political power.

The enlightenment of the elite (and to a much lesser degree of a small portion of the masses); the growing feeling of nativism, which indicated a greater self-confidence on the part of the Latin Americans and certainly a psychological change that diminished former feelings of inferiority; concern among the Latin Americans with the mighty potential of their region coupled with frustration because the potential went unrealized; resentment of the overseas metropolitan exploitation of the colonies; and growing complaints of excessive taxes, restrictions, and monopolies all widened the gap between the colonials and the Iberians. The resentment was noticeable on the highest level, between the creoles and mazombos on the one hand and the peninsulares and reinóis on the other. Creole families owned most of the rural estates, provided nearly all parish priests, and dominated the lower reaches of imperial government, particularly as secretaries and petty administrators. As the colonial viceroys brought fewer people with them, creoles filled out their entourages. The creoles not only dominated the cabildos, but they also held the majority in the audiencias.

However, creoles were denied the highest positions, which remained in the hands of the Iberian born. Of the 170 viceroys, only four were creoles—and they were the sons of Spanish officials. Of the 602 captains-general, governors, and presidents in Spanish America, only fourteen had been creoles; of the 606 bishops and archbishops, 105 were born in the New World. Such preference aroused bitter resentment among the creoles. The gap was made greater by the appointment of the intendants, all peninsulars, who formed a new layer of political power between the creoles and the crown. As Bolívar stated in 1815, "The hatred that the Peninsular has inspired in us is greater than the ocean which separates us." The Iberian suspicion of the New World elite in effect questioned both their ability and loyalty. One high Portuguese official remarked of Brazil, "That country increases in everyone the spirit of ambition and the relaxation of virtues." A distinguished Chilean, advising the king that all would be better served if the crown would make use of the creoles, concluded, "The status of the creoles has thus become an enigma: they are neither foreigners nor nationals . . . and are honorable but hopeless, loyal but disinherited." Further, the New World inhabitants resented the flow of wealth into the pockets of the peninsulares and reinóis who came to the Americas to exploit the wealth and return to Iberia to spend their hastily gained riches. By the end of the colonial period, most of the merchants who dominated foreign trade were still peninsulars. A visitador to New Spain, José de Gálvez, expressed to the crown an oft-repeated creole grievance: "Spaniards not only don't allow us to share the government of our country, but they carry away all our money."

Obviously the points of view of the Iberian and the American varied. The first came to the New World with a metropolitan outlook. He saw the empire as a unit and catered to the well-being of the metropolis. The latter had a regional bias. His prestige, power, and wealth rested on his lands. His political base was the municipal government, whose limited authority and responsibility reinforced his parochial outlook. In short, he thought mainly in terms of his region and ignored the wider imperial views.

During the last half of the eighteenth century, a new position, once again of local significance, was opened to the Latin Americans when the crowns created the colonial militias. The obligation to defend the colonies from foreign attack intensified nativism. Further, the high militia ranks conferred new prestige on creoles and mazombos alike and encouraged their ambitions.

They awaited with growing impatience an opportunity to improve their status. The Napoleonic wars provided that opportunity.

Napoleon rocked the foundations of both Iberian monarchies. In 1807, his armies crossed Spain, invaded Portugal, and captured Lisbon. The Portuguese Braganzas, however, did not fall prisoner to the conquering French armies. Prince-Regent John packed the government aboard a fleet and under the protecting guns of English men-of-war sailed from Lisbon for Rio de Janeiro just as the French reached the outskirts of the capital. The transfer of a European crown to one of its colonies was unique. The Braganzas were the only European royalty to visit their possessions in the New World during the colonial period. They set up their court among the surprised but delighted Brazilians and ruled the empire from Rio de Janeiro for thirteen years.

After seizing control of the Portuguese metropolis, Napoleon immediately turned his attention to Spain. He swept first Charles IV and then Ferdinand VII off the Spanish throne in order to crown his brother Joseph king. The Spaniards detested the Bonaparte puppet and renewed allegiance to Ferdinand, a prisoner in France. Rising up against Napoleon, they created a series of juntas to govern the empire in the name of the captive king. Spanish-Americans reacted with equal repugnance to the usurper. Various juntas appeared in the New World to govern in Ferdinand's name. In effect, this step toward self-government constituted an irreparable break with Spain. By abducting the king, Napoleon had broken the major link between Spain and the Americas. The break once made was widened by the many grievances of the Latin Americans against the metropolis.

Most of Latin America achieved its independence during a period of two decades, between the proud declaration of Haiti's independence in 1804 and the Spanish defeat at Ayacucho in 1824. Nearly 20 million inhabitants of Latin America severed their allegiance to France or to the Iberian monarchs. Every class and condition of people in Latin America participated at one time or another, at one place or another, in the protracted movement. Three distinct types of independence movement developed: the slave uprising in Haiti, the popular revolt in Mexico, and the elitist defiance in most of the rest of Latin America.

The Slaves Declare Haiti's Independence

Saint Domingue, the western third of the island of Hispaniola, witnessed the only completely successful slave rebellion in the New World. Long, bloody, devastating, it expelled or killed the white masters, terminated French rule, and left the former slaves free to govern themselves.

Sugar profits soared in the eighteenth century as the French planters exploited the good soil of the island, adopted the latest techniques for growing and grinding the cane, and imported ever larger numbers of African slaves to work the land and to process the crop. The motherland smiled with satisfaction on its rich Caribbean treasure. A multiracial society had developed, a divided society, which by 1789 counted 40,000 whites and half a million blacks with approximately 25,000 mulattos. The Code Noir, promulgated in 1685, regulated slavery. Theoretically it provided some protection to the black slave, facilitated manumission, and admitted the freed slave to full rights in society. In reality, the European code but slightly ameliorated the slave's dreadful state. In general, slavery on the lucrative plantations was harsh. To meet the demand for sugar, the plantation owner callously overworked his slaves, and to reduce overhead he frequently underfed them. An astonishingly high death rate testified to the brutality of the system.

The distant French revolutionary cry of "Liberty, equality, fraternity" echoed in the Caribbean in 1789. Each segment of the tense colony interpreted it differently. The white planters demanded and received from the Paris National Assembly a large measure of local autonomy. Then the Assembly extended the vote to all free persons, a move favoring the mulattos. The planters' demand for the repeal of that law precipitated a struggle between them and the mulattos. Then on August 22, 1791, the slaves demanding their own liberty rebelled in northern Saint Domingue. More than 100,000 arose under the leadership of the educated slave Toussaint L'Ouverture, son of African slave parents. In pursuit of his goal of liberating his fellow slaves, he fought for the following decade against, depending on the time and circumstances, the French, British, Spaniards, and various mulatto groups. Victory rewarded his extraordinary leadership and the courage of the slaves. By 1801, L'Ouverture commanded the entire island of Hispaniola.

Meanwhile, the chaos of the French revolution had yielded to the control of Napoleon, who took power in 1799. In 1801, Napoleon resolved to intervene to return the island to its former role as a profitable sugar producer. A huge army invaded Saint Domingue and the French induced L'Ouverture to a meeting only to seize him treacherously. Imprisoned in Europe, he died in 1803. His two lieutenants, Jean-Jacques Dessalines and Henri Christophe, took up the leadership. A combination of the slaves' strength and yellow fever defeated the massive French effort. On January 1, 1804, Dessalines proclaimed the independence of the western part of Hispaniola, giving it the name of Haiti. Haiti emerged as the second independent nation of the Western Hemisphere, the first in Latin America. For the exploited slaves of the New World, it represented hope; among the hemisphere's plantation owners, it inspired a chilling fear.

The African-born Dessalines acclaimed himself Emperor Jacques I in October of 1804. His brief reign collapsed two years later when mulattos who had risen up against his regime ambushed and killed him. The nation split. Christophe, an illiterate, Caribbean-born black, ruled the north; he crowned himself King Henri I in 1811. Alexandre Pétion, a mulatto educated in Paris, governed the south as president until his death in 1818. Paralyzed by a stroke and confronted with rebellion in 1820, King Henri committed suicide. These deaths paved the way for the reunification of Haiti. Jean-Pierre Boyer, the French-educated mulatto who succeeded Pétion, not only united the north and south but also subdued the eastern two-thirds of Hispaniola (later to be known as the Dominican Republic) and by early 1822 brought the entire island under his control in Port-au-Prince, the capital.

An Unsuccessful Popular Revolution in Mexico

Taking advantage of the political vacuum in Spain in 1808, the creoles of New Spain maneuvered to form a local junta to govern the viceroyalty, a move calculated to shift political power from the Spaniards to the Mexican elite. Alarmed by the maneuvering, the peninsulars feared the loss of their traditional, preferred positions. They acted swiftly to form their own junta and thus shoved the creoles aside. The creoles plotted to seize power and enlisted the help of Father Miguel Hidalgo, the parish priest of the small town of Dolores. In September 1810, the peninsulars discovered the plan and jailed the leaders. The wife of one leader, Josefa Ortiz de Dominguez, got word to Hidalgo, who on September 16, 1810, rang the church bells to summon the mostly mestizo and indigenous parishioners.

Well educated, indeed, profoundly influenced by the Enlightenment, Hidalgo professed advanced social ideas. He believed that the Church had a social mission to perform and a duty to improve the lot of the downtrodden Indians. Personally he bore numerous grievances against peninsulars and the Spanish government—he had been educated by the Jesuits until their expulsion in 1767, and had been investigated by the Inquisition on charges of mismanaging funds while rector of the College of San Nicolás Obispo in Valladolid.

When his parishioners gathered, Hidalgo exhorted them to rise up and reclaim the land stolen from them 300 years before: "Long live Ferdinand VII! Long live America! Down with bad government! Death to the Spaniards!" Hidalgo's words fell on fertile ground. The town of Dolores was a mere ten miles from Guanajuato, making it dependent on the mining economy. In 1809, an unusually dry summer had decreased maize production, ruining many small farmers. Food prices had quadrupled, and miners couldn't feed the mules needed in mining, leading to layoffs of mine workers.

Hidalgo had unleashed new forces. Unlike the creoles who simply wanted to substitute themselves for the peninsulars in power, the mestizo and Indian masses desired far-reaching social and economic changes. There were 600 people gathered in Dolores; as they marched toward Guanajuato, the numbers swelled to 25,000. At Guanajuato, the intendant, local militia, peninsulares, and some creoles barricaded themselves in the granary, leaving the city defenseless. The lower classes of Guanajuato joined the insurgents and burned and pillaged the city. By the time the mob reached Mexico City, it numbered 60,000 to 80,000, and in their rampage they made no distinction between creole and peninsular. With energies released after three centuries of repression, the Indians and mestizos struck out at all they hated. The creoles became as frightened as the peninsulars, and the two rival factions united before the threat from the masses.

Hidalgo did little to discipline the people under him. Indeed, his control of them proved minimal. His ideas were disorganized, vague, at times contradictory. While voicing his loyalty to Ferdinand, he denounced the abuses of the viceregal government—later he declared Mexico free and independent. He threatened the peninsulars with death; he abolished slavery. Poised before Mexico City, he hesitated, then ordered a withdrawal, an action that cost him much of the allegiance of the masses. The Spanish army regained its confidence and struck out in pursuit of the ragtag rebels. It captured Hidalgo and tried him before a nine-member panel that included six creoles. In mid-1811, ten months after the Grito de Dolores, Hidalgo's call to arms, a firing squad executed him. His severed head was mounted on the wall of the granary at Guanajuato, a clear warning to others.

Nonetheless, Hidalgo's banner was taken up by another parish priest, José María Morelos. Morelos came from a poor mestizo family and worked as a mule driver; through great personal effort he became a priest, always assigned to the poorest, backwoods parishes, where poor indios and mestizos labored. He had joined Hidalgo's movement, but after Hidalgo's death determined that undisciplined hordes were not the answer. He trimmed the forces, organized them into a more disciplined force, and tried to appeal to the creoles while still carrying Hidalgo's banner of social reform. He defined his program: establish the independence of Mexico; create a republican government in which the Mexican people would participate with the exclusion of the formerly wealthy, nobility, and entrenched officeholders; abolish slavery; affirm the equality of all people; terminate the special privileges of the Church as well as the compulsory tithe; and partition the large estates so that all farmers could own land. At Chilpancingo, he declared that Mexico's sovereignty resided in the people, who could alter the government according to their will. He called forth pride in the Mexican—not the Spanish—past. His program contained the seeds of a real social, economic, and political revolution and thereby repulsed peninsular and creole alike. He ably led his small, disciplined army in central Mexico for more than four years. In 1815, the Spaniards captured and executed him. The royalists immediately gained the ascendancy in Mexico and dashed the hopes of the mestizos and Indians for social and economic changes. New Spain returned momentarily to its colonial slumbers.

When independence was won in Mexico, it was under conservative leadership, a reaction to the restored king's turn to liberalism. After Napoleon's defeat at Waterloo, Ferdinand was freed from his French prison and restored to the Spanish throne in 1814. He was faced with a liberal constitution adopted in his absence. He intended to continue ruling as an absolute monarch, but a revolt in 1820 forced the king to adhere to the constitution. The peninsulars and creoles in New Spain rejected Spanish liberalism just as they earlier had turned away from Mexican liberalism. In their reaction to the events in Spain, they decided to free themselves and chart their own destiny. The ecclesiastical hierarchy, fearful of the loss of property and of secular restrictions if the liberals in control of Spain had their way, converted to the independence movement, buttressing it with the Church's prestige and power. The peninsulars and creoles selected a pompous creole army officer, Augustín de Iturbide, who had fought against Hidalgo and Morelos, first as their instrument to effect independence and then as their emperor. The most conservative forces of New Spain ushered in Mexican independence in 1821. They advocated neither social nor economic changes. They sought to preserve—or enhance if possible—their privileges. The only innovation was political: A creole emperor replaced the Spanish king, which was symbolic of the wider replacement of the peninsulars by the creoles in government. The events harmonized little with the concepts of Hidalgo and Morelos, but suited creole desires. The Mexican struggle for independence began as a major social, economic, and political revolution but ended as a conservative coup d'etat. The only immediate victors were the creole elite.

Elitist Revolts

The triumph of the Mexican creole elite paralleled similar victories in other parts of Latin America where the local aristocrats, occasionally in alliance with some peninsulars, took advantage of the disgust with Iberian rule, the changing events in Europe, the example of the United States of America, and the desires for reform, to declare the independence of their locality and assume power. The actual consummation of independence in Latin America only affected a minority of the area's inhabitants. The masses, composed primarily of Indians, blacks, mestizos, and mulattos, played an ambiguous role, at times fighting for their Iberian leaders and at other times filling the ranks of the American armies. Their loyalty often depended on a variety of local factors as well as the abilities, promises, and persuasiveness of rival generals. The masses gained little. At best there were vague and contradictory promises of change that might have improved their lot.

The issues at stake revolved mainly around control of the government and trade policies and as such affected almost exclusively the local aristocracy. The successful urban merchants and rural planters stood to gain the most from independence. The landed gentry enjoyed considerable power and social prestige because of their huge estates and their influence over local government. They identified more closely with local conditions than with either of the distant Iberian metropolises. They favored independence in order to expand their own power and to assure a greater freedom of access to international markets. Conservative by nature, they advocated few structural reforms. An influential Brazilian journalist of the period summed up their viewpoint when he pleaded, "Let us have no excesses. We want a constitution, not a revolution."

The cities brought together the planters to discuss their common problems and aspirations, while at the same time within the cities a small but vocal class of free persons appeared, neither plantation owners nor slaves nor peasants, an unstable class eager to improve its status. Most influential of the urban dwellers were the merchants, who saw in independence an opportunity to better control their own destiny and hence to increase trade and business. The cities had previously been focal points of discontent and agitation. In them, the waves of nativism crested. Frequently the municipal councils served as the forum of debate and the instrument for action by which the cause of independence advanced.

Representatives of the privileged classes led the hastily recruited American armies, whose ranks of patriots as well as adventurers expanded or contracted depending on the forcefulness of the generals and their successes in battle. The wars for independence in South America—in many areas, protracted, bloody, devastating—have been reduced largely to a chronicle of the exploits and brilliance of a handful of able generals: Simón Bolívar, Bernardo O'Higgins, José de San Martín, and Antonio José de Sucre, to cite those most often mentioned. The narrative and glorification of the biographies of single elitist leaders evolved into a marked characteristic of Latin American historiography. In Brazil, the Visconde de Pôrto Alegre once announced, "To know the biographies of all the outstanding men of a period is to know the history of those times." The Peruvian historian Francisco García Calderón later echoed that observation: "The history of the South American Republics may be reduced to the biographies of their representative men." Such an outlook obviously eliminated the study of the actions and thoughts of the common people. Increasingly, attention focused on the exploits of two extraordinary representatives of the creole elite, General José de San Martín of Argentina and General Simón Bolívar of Venezuela, who between them led courageous armies through a grand pincers movement that defeated the Spaniards in South America.

In 1810, the movements for independence began simultaneously in opposite ends of South America, Venezuela, and Argentina. The Argentine movement went practically unchecked, while in the north the Venezuelans battled heroically, although not always victoriously. The struggle for Spanish America's independence fell into three rather well-defined periods: the initial thrust and expansion of the movement between 1810 and 1814; the faltering of the patriotic armies and the resurgence of royalist domination, from 1814 to 1816; and the consummation of independence between 1817 and 1826. The

South American liberator Simon Bolivar (7/24/1783–12/17/1830). (Library of Congress.)

actual fighting was limited to a few areas, principally Mexico and Venezuela. In large sections of Latin America—Central America, Paraguay, Argentina, and Brazil—no major battles occurred.

In both Venezuela and Argentina some leaders understood that their declarations would be meaningless and their aspirations thwarted so long as a Spanish army remained anywhere on the South American continent. For that reason they expanded their struggle from the regional to the continental stage. From Argentina, the army of San Martín crossed the Andes to contribute in 1817 to Chile's struggle against the Spaniards and then in 1820 invaded Peru, stronghold of Spanish royalism. In the north, Bolívar's army moved back and forth between Venezuela and Colombia before penetrating southward into Ecuador, Peru, and Bolivia. Although the independence of Spanish South America was virtually guaranteed by Sucre's decisive victory at Ayacucho in late 1824, the wars of liberation really only ended in early 1826 when the Spanish garrison occupying Callao, Peru's principal port, surrendered. Long before then, the new nations of Latin America had declared their independence. In most cases either a specially assembled congress or a local assembly—always dominated by the creoles—issued the declaration.

Most of the fighting forces of independence were composed of the darker masses, who were given vague promises about changes in their status with independence. And a few of those who fought in the ranks were women. Evangelista Tamayo fought with Bolívar's forces; and numerous women disguised themselves as men to join the fighting. Bolívar praised the efforts of women, albeit in stereotypical terms: "even the fair sex, the delights of humankind, our amazons, have fought against the tyrant of San Carlos." Most women did not serve as soldiers, but they worked as nurses in field hospitals, kept the home front functioning, and used assumptions of female innocence to serve as messengers and spies, using their voluminous skirts as a cover for smuggling. The most famous of these women was Policarpa Salavarrieta of Colombia, known as La Pola, who was eventually captured and executed. As the crowd watched in the main plaza of Bogotá, La Pola exclaimed, "Although I am a woman and young, I have more than enough courage to suffer this death and a thousand more."

The prolonged struggle for independence had some social and economic consequences for the new nations. Class and color lines blurred slightly. None of the newly independent nations continued the legal disabilities once restricting mestizos. In spite of some creole desires, it was impossible. In Mexico, for example, the clergy no longer kept the minute records of caste in their parochial books. In fact, some mestizo army officers quickly rose to power in the new nations. Mentally they tended to identify with the creoles. In a few areas, the governments abolished slavery or began the process of gradual emancipation. Contacts with Europe north of the Pyrenees multiplied, with the resultant influx of new ideas. Economically the revolutions brought disaster to many areas. Normal trade and communication routes were interrupted; mines were flooded and equipment destroyed; herds of livestock were slaughtered, confiscated, or dispersed; currency manipulation, depreciation, inflation, the flight of capital, forced loans, confiscation of property, and capricious taxation brought financial ruin; and part of the workforce was scattered, maimed, or killed. On the other hand, the ports of Latin America opened to the world and trade policies liberalized, although these changes were not without their disadvantages. Iberian mercantilist policies were abandoned, but in the new order, Great Britain came to exercise the economic hegemony once held by Spain and Portugal. The complex taxation system of the colonial past gave way to a reliance on customs duties as the principal source of national income.

Portuguese America achieved its independence during the same tumultuous years. Like its republican neighbors, Argentina and Paraguay, Brazil entered into nationhood almost bloodlessly, and following the trend evident in Spanish America; the mazombos clamored for the positions of the reinóis, although their ascendancy was more gradual than that of the creoles. The difference lay in the way Brazil achieved its independence.

Under the guidance of John VI, Brazil's position within the Portuguese empire improved rapidly. He opened the ports to world trade, authorized and encouraged industry, and raised Brazil's status to that of a kingdom, the equal of Portugal itself. Rio de Janeiro changed from a quiet viceregal capital to the thriving center of a far-flung world empire. The psychological impact on Brazilians was momentous. Foreigners who knew Brazil during the first decade of the monarch's residence there commented on the beneficial effect the presence of the crown exercised on the spirit of Brazilians. Ignacio José de Macedo typified the optimism of his fellow Brazilians when he predicted, "The unexpected transference of the Monarchy brought a brilliant dawn to these dark horizons, as spectacular as that on the day of its discovery. The new day of regeneration, an omen of brighter destinies, will bring long centuries of prosperity and glory."

When the royal court returned to Lisbon in 1821, after thirteen years of residence in Brazil, John left behind the Braganza heir, Prince Pedro, as regent. The young prince took up his duties with enthusiasm, only to find himself caught between two powerful and opposing forces. On the one side, the newly convened parliament, the Côrtes, in Lisbon, annoyed with and jealous of the importance Brazil had assumed within the empire during the previous decade and a half, sought to reduce Brazil to its previous colonial subservience; on the other, Brazilian patriots thought in terms of national independence. As the Côrtes made obvious its intent to strip Brazil of previous privileges as well as to restrict the authority of its prince-regent, Pedro listened more attentively to the mazombo views. He appointed the learned and nationalistic mazombo José Bonifácio de Andrada e Silva to his cabinet, the first Brazilian to hold such a high post. Bonifácio was instrumental in persuading Pedro to defy the humiliating orders of the Côrtes and to heed mazombo opinion, which refused to allow Lisbon to dictate policies for Brazil. Princess Leopoldina, although Austrian by birth, had dedicated her energies and devotion to Brazil after she arrived in Rio de Janeiro in 1817 to marry Pedro. She too urged him to defy Portugal. She wrote him as he traveled to São Paulo in September 1822: "Brazil under your guidance will be a great country. Brazil wants you as its monarch. . . . Pedro, this is the most important moment of your life. . . . You have the support of all Brazil." On September 7, 1822, convinced of the strength of Brazilian nationalism, Pedro declared the independence of Latin America's largest nation, and several months later in a splendid ceremony he was crowned "Constitutional Emperor and Perpetual Defender of Brazil."

The evolutionary course upon which Brazil embarked provided a stability and unity that no other former viceroyalty of the New World could boast. Contrary to the contractual political experiences of Spanish America, an unbroken patriarchal continuity, hereditary governance, flowed in Brazil. Similar to the experiences of Spanish America, nonetheless, Brazilian independence affected and benefited only the elite. Like the elites everywhere, the Brazilians rushed to embrace foreign ideas and to continue, even to deepen, the colonial dependency on exports. To a surprising degree, continuity more than change characterized the independence period.

Micaela Bastidas Puyucahua Advises Her Husband, Túpac Amaru

Among the uprisings to threaten the Spanish empire in the late colonial period was the movement led in Peru by a mestizo, José Gabriel Condorcanqui Noguera, who took the name Túpac Amaru. He appealed to Indians, mestizos, and creoles by stressing to each the burdens that colonialism imposed on their communities. The revolt began in November 1780 and was suppressed in January 1781. Condorcanqui's chief aide was his wife, Micaela Bastidas Puyucahua. In this letter, she shows the strong role that she played in the ill-fated uprising. When the revolt was finally suppressed, Micaela was sentenced to have her tongue cut out and to be strangled in front of her husband.

Dear Chepe:
You are causing me grief and sorrow. While you saunter through the villages, even very carelessly delaying two days in Yauri, our soldiers rightly grow tired and are leaving for their homes.

I do not have any patience left to endure all this. I am capable of giving myself up to the enemy and letting them take my life, because I see how lightly you view this grave matter that threatens the lives of all. We are in the midst of enemies and we have no security. And for your sake all my sons are in danger, as well as all our people.

I have warned you sufficient times against dallying in those villages where there is nothing to be done. But you continue to saunter without considering that the soldiers lack food supplies even though they are given money; and their pay will run out soon. Then they will all depart, leaving us helpless, and we will pay with our lives because they (as you must have learned) only follow self-interest and want to get all they can out of us. Now the soldiers are already beginning to desert . . . ; the soldiers are terrified and seek to flee, fearing the punishment that might befall them. Thus we will lose all the people I have gathered and prepared for the descent on Cuzco, and the Cuzco forces will unite with the troops from Lima who have already been on the march against us for many days.

I must caution you about all this, though it pains me. But if you wish to ruin us, you can just sleep. You were so careless that you walked alone through the streets of the town of Yauri, and even went to the extreme of climbing the church tower, when you should not commit such extreme actions under the present conditions. These actions only dishonor and even defame you and do you little justice.

I believed that you were occupied day and night in arranging these affairs, instead of showing an unconcern that robs me of my life. I am only a shadow of myself and beside myself with anxiety, and so I beg you to get on with this business.

You made me a promise, but from now on I shall not place any faith in your promises, for you did not keep your word.

I do not care about my own life, only about those of our poor family, who need all my help. Thus, if the enemy comes from Paruro, as I suggested in my last letter, I am prepared to march out to meet them with our forces, leaving Fernando in a designated place, for the Indians are not capable of moving by themselves in these perilous times.

I gave you plenty of warnings to march on Cuzco immediately, but you took them all lightly, allowing the enemy sufficient time to prepare, as they have done, placing cannon on Picchu mountain, plus other trickery so dangerous that you are no longer in a position to attack them. God keep you many years.

Tungasuca, December 6, 1780.

I must also tell you that the Indians of Quispicanchi are worn out and weary from serving so long as guards. Well, God must want me to suffer for my sins.

Your wife.

After I finished this letter, a messenger arrived with the news that the enemy from Paruro are in Archos. I shall march out to meet them though it cost me my life.

Source: June E. Hahner, ed., *Women in Latin American History: Their Lives and Views*, revised edition (Los Angeles: UCLA Latin American Center Publications, 1980), pp. 36–37. Reprinted with permission of The Regents of the University of California.

Simón Bolívar: The Jamaica Letter

Simón Bolívar is regarded as the father of Latin American independence. Born in Caracas, Venezuela, he was a member of the Caracas junta that rose up against Spanish rule. After the king was restored and independence forces were defeated, he went into exile in Jamaica. He returned to Latin America in 1816, where he successfully led the independence movement in what became Colombia, Venezuela, Ecuador, and Peru. In the Jamaica letter, he responds to a query about the independence movement by describing its causes and possible future.

Kingston, Jamaica, September 6, 1815

My dear Sir:

I hasten to reply to the letter of the 29th ultimo which you had the honor of sending me and which I received with the greatest satisfaction.

Sensible though I am of the interest you desire to take in the fate of my country, and of your commiseration with her for the tortures she has suffered from the time of her discovery until the present at the hands of her destroyers, the Spaniards, I am no less sensible of the obligation which your solicitous inquiries about the principal objects of American policy place upon me. . . . Every conjecture relative to America's future is, I feel, pure speculation. When mankind was in its infancy, steeped in uncertainty, ignorance and error, was it possible to foresee what system it would adopt for its preservation? Who could venture to say that a certain nation would be a republic or a monarchy; this nation great, that nation small? To my way of thinking, such is our situation. We are a young people. We inhabit a world apart, separated by broad seas. We are young in the ways of almost all the arts and sciences, although, in a certain manner, we are old in the ways of civilized society. I look upon the present state of America as similar to that of Rome after its fall. Each part of Rome adopted a political system conforming to its interest and situation or was led by the individual ambitions of certain chiefs, dynasties, or associations. But this important difference exists: those dispersed parts later reestablished their ancient nations, subject to the changes imposed by circumstances or events. But we scarcely retain a vestige of what once was; we are, moreover, neither Indian nor European, but a species midway between the legitimate proprietors of this country and the Spanish usurpers. In short, though American by birth we derive our rights from Europe, and we have to assert these rights against the rights of the natives, and at the same time we must defend ourselves against the invaders. . . .

The role of the inhabitants of the American hemisphere has for centuries been purely passive. Politically they were non-existent. We are still in a position lower than slavery, and therefore it is more difficult for us to rise to the enjoyment of freedom. . . . States are slaves because of either the nature or the misuse of their constitution; a people is therefore enslaved when the government, by its nature or its vices, infringes on and usurps the rights of the citizen or subject. Applying these principles, we find that America was denied not only its freedom but even an active and effective tyranny. . . .

We have been harassed by a conduct which has not only deprived us of our rights but has kept us in a sort of permanent infancy with regard to public affairs. If we could at least have managed our domestic affairs and our internal administration, we could have acquainted ourselves with the processes and mechanics of public affairs. We should also have enjoyed a personal consideration, thereby commanding a certain unconscious respect from the people, which is so necessary to preserve amidst revolutions. That is why I say we have even been deprived of an active tyranny, since we have not been permitted to exercise its functions.

Americans today, and perhaps to a greater extent than ever before, who live within the Spanish system occupy a position in society no better than that of serfs destined for labor, or at best they have no more status than that of mere consumers. Yet even this status is surrounded with galling restrictions, such as being forbidden to grow European crops, or to store products which are royal monopolies, or to establish factories of a type the Peninsula itself does not possess. To this add the exclusive trading privileges, even in articles of prime necessity, and the barriers between American provinces, designed to prevent all exchange of trade, traffic, and understanding. In short, do you wish to know what our future held?—simply the cultivation of the fields of indigo, grain, coffee, sugar cane, cacao, and cotton; cattle raising on the broad plains; hunting wild game in the jungles; digging in the earth to mine its gold—but even these limitations could never satisfy the greed of Spain.

So negative was our existence that I can find nothing comparable in any other civilized society, examine as I may the entire history of time and the politics of all nations. Is it not an outrage and a violation of human rights to expect a land so splendidly endowed, so vast, rich, and populous, to remain merely passive?

As I have just explained, we were cut off and, as it were, removed from the world in relation to the science of government and administration of the state. We were never viceroys or governors, save in the rarest of instances; seldom archbishops and bishops; diplomats never; as military men, only subordinate;

as nobles, without royal privileges. In brief, we were neither
magistrates nor financiers and seldom merchants—all in flagrant
contradiction to our institutions.

Emperor Charles V made a pact with the discoverers,
conquerors, and settlers of America, and this, as Guerra puts it,
is our social contract. The monarchs of Spain made a solemn
agreement with them, to be carried out on their own account and
at their own risk, expressly prohibiting them from drawing on the
royal treasury. In return, they were made the lords of the land,
entitled to organize the public administration and act as the
court of last appeal, together with many other exemptions and
privileges that are too numerous to mention. The King committed
himself never to alienate the American provinces, inasmuch as
he had no jurisdiction but that of sovereign domain. Thus, for
themselves and their descendants, the *conquistadores* possessed
what were tantamount to feudal holdings. Yet there are explicit
laws respecting employment in civil, ecclesiastical, and tax-raising
establishments. These laws favor, almost exclusively, the natives
of the country who are of Spanish extraction. Thus, by an outright
violation of the laws and the existing agreements, those born in
America have been despoiled of the constitutional rights as
embodied in the code. . . .

Events in Costa Firme have proved that institutions which
are wholly representative are not suited to our character, customs,
and present knowledge. . . .As long as our countrymen do not
acquire the abilities and political virtues that distinguish our
brothers of the north, wholly popular systems, far from working
to our advantage, will, I greatly fear, bring about our downfall.
Unfortunately, these traits, to the degree in which they are
required, do not appear to be within our reach. On the contrary,
we are dominated by the vices that one learns under the rule of a
nation like Spain, which has only distinguished itself in ferocity,
ambition, vindictiveness and greed.

It is harder, Montesquieu has written, to release a nation
from servitude than to enslave a free nation. . . . Despite the
convictions of history, South Americans have made efforts to
obtain liberal, even perfect, institutions, doubtless out of that
instinct to aspire to the greatest possible happiness, which,
common to all men, is bound to follow in civil societies founded
on the principles of justice, liberty, and equality. But are we
capable of maintaining in proper balance the difficult charge of a
republic? Is it conceivable that a newly emancipated people can
soar to the heights of liberty, and, unlike Icarus, neither have its
wings melt nor fall into an abyss? Such a marvel is inconceivable
and without precedent. There is no reasonable probability to
bolster our hopes. . . .

The American provinces are fighting for their freedom, and
they will ultimately succeed. Some provinces as a matter of course

will form federal and some central republics; the larger ones will inevitably establish monarchies, some of which will fare so badly· that they will disintegrate in either present or future revolutions. To consolidate a great monarchy will be no easy task, but it will be utterly impossible to consolidate a great republic.

It is a grandiose idea to think of consolidating the New World into a single nation, united by pacts into a single bond. It is reasoned that, as these parts have a common origin, language, customs, and religion, they ought to have a single government to permit the newly formed states to unite in a confederation. But this is not possible. Actually, America is separated by climatic differences, geographic diversity, conflicting interests, and dissimilar characteristics. . . .

Among the popular and representative systems, I do not favor the federal system. It is over-perfect, and it demands political virtues and talents far superior to our own. For the same reason I reject a monarchy that is part aristocracy and part democracy, although with such a government England has achieved much fortune and splendor. Since it is not possible for us to select the most perfect and complete form of government, let us avoid falling into demagogic anarchy or monocratic tyranny. These opposite extremes would only wreck us on similar reefs of misfortune and dishonor; hence, we must seek a mean between them. I say: Do not adopt the best system of government, but the one that is most likely to succeed. . . .

Surely, unity is what we need to complete our work of regeneration. The division among us, nevertheless, is nothing extraordinary, for it is characteristic of civil wars to form two parties, *conservatives* and *reformers*. The former are commonly the more numerous, because the weight of habit induces obedience to established powers; the latter are always fewer in number although more vocal and learned. Thus, the physical mass of the one is counterbalanced by the moral force of the other; the contest is prolonged, and the results are uncertain. Fortunately, in our case, the mass has followed the learned.

I shall tell you with what we must provide ourselves in order to expel the Spaniards and to found a free government. It is *union*, obviously; but such union will come about through sensible planning and well-directed actions rather than by divine magic. America stands together because it is abandoned by all other nations. It is isolated in the center of the world. It has no diplomatic relations, nor does it receive any military assistance; instead, America is attacked by Spain, which has more military supplies than any we can possibly acquire through furtive means.

When success is not assured, when the state is weak, and when results are distantly seen, all men hesitate; opinion is divided, passions rage, and the enemy fans these passions in order to win an easy victory because of them. As soon as we are strong and under the guidance of a liberal nation which will lend us her protection, we will achieve accord in cultivating the virtues and talents that lead to glory. Then will we march majestically toward that great prosperity for which South America is destined. Then will those sciences and arts which, born in the East, have enlightened Europe, wing their way to a free Colombia, which will cordially bid them welcome.

Such, Sir, are the thoughts and observations that I have the honor to submit to you, so that you may accept or reject them according to their merit. I beg you to understand that I have expounded them because I do not wish to appear discourteous and not because I consider myself competent to enlighten you concerning these matters.

I am, Sir . . .   Simón Bolívar

Source: *Selected Writings of Bolívar,* compiled by Vicente Lecuna, Harold A. Bierck Jr., ed. (N.Y.: Bolivarian Society of Venezuela, 1951), 103–22.

4

New Nations

Most of Latin America had gained independence by the end of the first quarter of the nineteenth century. The protracted struggle elevated to power a small, privileged elite who, with few exceptions, had enjoyed many benefits from the Spanish and Portuguese colonial systems and reaped even greater rewards during the early decades of nationhood. The independence of the new nations proved almost at once to be nominal, since the ruling elites became culturally dependent on France and economically subservient to Great Britain. The impetus to build a nation-state came from "above." In the apt judgment of Cuban independence leader José Martí, the elites created "theoretical republics." They tended to confuse their own well-being and desires with those of the nation at large, an erroneous identification because they represented less than 5 percent of the total population. That minority set the course upon which Latin America has continued to the present.

In any examination of the decades immediately following independence, fundamental questions arise: How do people create new governments and what types of government should they forge? How does economic poverty influence the exercise of sovereignty? Should past social patterns be abandoned or enhanced? These and other questions challenged the new nations and their citizens.

The Transfer and Legitimization of Power

Who would govern and how they would govern were fundamental questions facing the newly independent Latin Americans. They were questions previously unasked. For centuries all authority and power had been concentrated in the Iberian kings, who ruled the New World in accordance with an ancient body of laws and customs and by "divine right." For nearly three centuries the inhabitants of the New World had accepted their rule. The monarchies provided their own hereditary continuity. The declarations of independence created a novel political vacuum. Latin Americans experienced anguish, bloodshed, and chaos in their uncertain and contradictory efforts to fill this vacuum.

Brazil alone easily resolved the questions, mainly because of the presence of the royal family in Portuguese America. On hand to lend legitimacy to the rapid, peaceful political transition of Brazil from viceroyalty to kingdom to empire were first King John VI and then his son, Prince Pedro, heir to the throne, who severed the ties between Portugal and Brazil and wore the new imperial crown. The mazombo elite supported the concept of royal rule and thereby avoided the acrimonious debates between republicans and monarchists that split much of Spanish America. Obviously facilitating their decision was the convenient presence of a sympathetic prince, a Braganza who had declared Brazil's independence. By his birth and inheritance as well as through the concurrence of the Brazilian elite, Pedro's position and power were at once legitimate. As a Braganza, he inherited his authority. Historical precedent strengthened his position. The throne legitimately occupied by a Braganza proved to be the perfect unifier of the new and immense empire.

Although there was a genuine consensus as to *who* would rule, the question remained open as to *how* he should rule. The emperor and the elite agreed that there should be a constitution, but the contents and limits of that projected document sparked a debate that generated the first major crisis in the Brazilian empire. Elections were held for an assembly that would exercise both constituent and legislative functions. The group that convened on May 3, 1823, composed of lawyers, judges, priests, military officers, doctors, landowners, and public officials, clearly represented the privileged classes of the realm. They came from the ranks of the old landed aristocracy and the new urban elite, two groups that remained interlinked. Almost at once, the legislature and the executive clashed, each suspicious that the other infringed on its prerogatives. Furthermore, the legislators manifested rabid anti-Portuguese sentiments and thus by implication a hostility to the young emperor born in Lisbon. Convinced that the assembly not only lacked discipline but also scattered the seeds of revolution, Pedro dissolved it.

Despite the dissolution, Pedro intended to keep his word and rule under a constitution. He appointed a committee of ten Brazilians to write the document and then submitted it to the municipal councils throughout Brazil

The last Brazilian Emperor Dom Pedro II de Alcantara. (Library of Congress.)

for their ratification. After most of them signified their approval, Pedro promulgated the new constitution on March 25, 1824. It provided for a highly centralized government with a vigorous executive. Although power was divided among four branches—executive, legislative, judiciary, and moderative—the lion's share rested in the hands of the emperor. Assisted by a Council of State and a ministry, the emperor exercised the functions of chief executive, a function enhanced by the novel moderative power, which made him responsible for the maintenance of the independence of the nation as well as the equilibrium and harmony of the other powers and the twenty provinces. The emperor was given and expected to use broad powers to ensure harmony in a far-flung empire whose wide geographic and human diversity challenged the existence of the state. In the last analysis, the crown was the one pervasive, national institution that could and did represent all Brazilians. The General Assembly was divided into a senate, whose members were appointed by the emperor for life, and a chamber of deputies periodically and indirectly elected by a highly restricted suffrage. The constitution afforded broad individual freedom and equality before the law. Proof of the viability of the constitution lay in its longevity: it lasted sixty-five years, until the monarchy fell in 1889. It has proven to be Brazil's most durable constitution and one of Latin America's longest lived.

The Brazilians gradually took control of their own government. At first, Pedro disappointed them by surrounding himself with Portuguese advisers, ministers, and prelates. The Brazilians had their independence but were tacitly barred from exercising the highest offices in their own empire. The mazombos accused the young emperor of paying more attention to affairs in the former metropolis than to those of the new empire. As the Brazilians demanded access to the highest offices of their land, the currents of anti-Portuguese sentiments swelled. Pedro's failure to understand those nationalistic sentiments and to appoint Brazilians to top positions was a primary cause of the discontent leading to his abdication in 1831. After his departure for Europe, members of the elite with their roots firmly in the plantation economy replaced the Portuguese-born who monopolized the high posts of the First Empire. In 1840, when Pedro II ascended the throne, a Brazilian—for the adolescent emperor had been born and raised in the New World—even occupied that exalted position. Thus, the mazombo ascendency was much more gradual than the creole. It began in 1808 when the royal court arrived in Rio de Janeiro and reached its climax in 1840 when a Brazilian-born emperor took the scepter.

Unlike Brazil, Spanish America experienced a difficult transfer and legitimation of power. The political vacuum stirred winds of disorder and ambition that blew forcefully for many decades. The question of what form the new governments should take absorbed considerable energy and aroused heated debates, particularly over the issues of federalism versus centralism and a republic versus a monarchy. Monarchy harmonized with the past and with the hierarchical, aristocratic structure of Spanish-American society. However, a desire to repudiate at least the outward symbols of the Spanish past, an infatuation with the political doctrines of the Enlightenment, and the successful example of the United States strengthened the arguments of the partisans for a republic. Only in Mexico did the monarchists carry the day, but, unable to persuade a European prince to accept the new Mexican scepter, the creoles crowned one of their own, Augustín de Iturbide, whose brief reign lasted from May of 1822 until February of 1823. Still, since Mexico at that time included the territory from Oregon to Panama, it meant that together with Brazil, a majority of Latin America in late 1822 and early 1823 fell under monarchical sway.

Iturbide's reign was not a happy one, largely because he was trying to satisfy conflicting groups with the scant resources of an economy hard hit by the independence wars. To reassure the merchants and capitalists, he cut taxes, which led to a decline in the revenue needed to maintain the army. To pay the army, which was crucial to uphold a government that had not yet achieved hegemony, he issued paper money, which led to inflation. He then took foreign loans, which the government could not repay, and demanded forced loans from the elites and from the Church, alienating his strongest supporters. With growing political unrest, Iturbide closed Congress, which alienated his political allies. The final straw came when there were no funds to fight the Spanish royalist troops still holding out at the fortress of Veracruz. Iturbide responded to the complaints of the Mexican force's commander, Antonio López de Santa Anna, by firing him. Santa Anna then led a coup against Iturbide. The army banished Iturbide in early 1823, abolished the empire, and helped to establish a liberal, federal republic. With that, the principle of republicanism triumphed, at least as an ideal, throughout Spanish America. Nonetheless, some would continue to argue the case for monarchy, and, in fact, Mexico experimented with it once again in the 1860s.

The debate over the merits of centralism and federalism lasted much longer than the struggle between monarchy and republic. A reaction against the previous Spanish centralism, a host of local rivalries, and the apparent successful example of North American federalism combined to persuade many Latin American leaders to experiment with federalism. The tendency of most people to identify with their immediate region, the *patria chica* or small country, added impetus to the federalist movement. The experiments at best were unsuccessful, but in the case of Mexico and the United Provinces of Central America, they were a disaster that led to partial or total dismemberment of the nation.

The question of who should govern posed yet another problem for the new states to solve. The immediate answer was to turn the reins of authority over to independence heroes, and therefore the first chiefs of state in many lands were the very men who had declared and fought for the independence of these nations. The Latin Americans found it more difficult to select successors to the independence heroes, most of whom were turned out of office as their popularity faded and people found that war heroes did not necessarily make great statesmen. Efforts to fill presidential chairs unleashed bitter power struggles among various factions of the elite, struggles conducive to despotism.

The contending factions all too often sought simply to seize, hold, and

The Age of Anarchy in Mexico: Heads of State, 1822–55

1822–23	Emperor Agustín de Iturbide
1824–29	Guadalupe Victoria (Felix Fernández)
1829	Vicente Guerrero
1829	José María Bocanegra (Interim)
1829	Pedro Vélez, Luis Quintanar, Lucas Alamán (Triumvirate)
1830–32	Anastasio Bustamante
1832	Melchor Múzquiz (Interim)
1832–33	Manuel Gómez Pedraza
1833–35	Antonio López de Santa Anna
1835–36	Miguel Barragán
1836–37	José Justo Corro
1837–39	Anastasio Bustamante (Acting)
1839	Antonio López de Santa Anna (Acting)
1839	Nicolás Bravo
1839–41	Anastasio Bustamante (Acting)
1841	Javíer Echeverría
1841–42	Antonio López de Santa Anna (Acting)
1842	Anastasio Bustamante (Acting)
1842–43	Nicolás Bravo
1842	Anastasio Bustamante (Acting)
1843	Antonio López de Santa Anna (Acting)
1843–44	Valentín Canalizo
1844	Antonio López de Santa Anna (Acting)
1844–46	José Joaquín Herrera
1846	Mariano Paredes y Arrillaga
1846	Nicolás Bravo (Acting)
1846	Mariano Salas
1846–47	Valentín Gómez Farías (Acting)
1847	Antonio López de Santa Anna (Acting)
1847	Pedro María Anaya
1847–48	Manuel de la Peña y Peña
1847	Antonio López de Santa Anna (Acting)
1848–51	José Joaquín Herrera (Interim)
1851–53	Mariano Arista
1853	Juan Bautista Ceballos (Interim)
1853	Manuel María Lombardini
1853–55	Antonio López de Santa Anna (Acting)
1855	Martín Carréra

Source: http://www.mexconnect.com/mex_/history/presidents.html

exercise power for its own sake and its own reward. Only secondarily did the leaders cloak their power with some cloth of legality, a cloth usually of exotic and impractical fabric. During the early decades of independence, elections seldom were held and even more rarely were honest. Consequently the various factions resorted to violence as the path to power. Once in office, they usually exerted more violence to maintain that power.

A political map of contemporary Latin America.

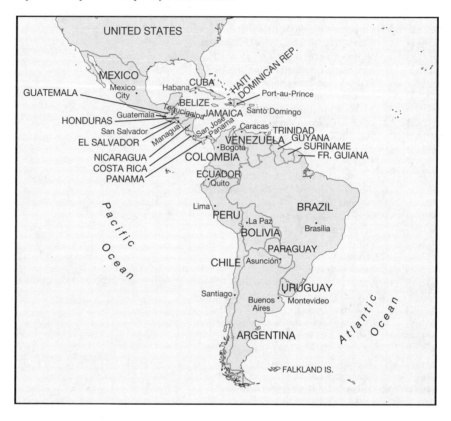

As the question of who was going to rule was never properly answered in most of the republics during the first decades after independence—at best satisfactory *ad hoc* solutions were provided—so too did the problem of how the nations should be governed remain largely unsolved. Almost without exception the elites, imbued with a long legalistic tradition, desired a written constitution, even though in most cases the document proved to be more theoretical than practical. The elite and their political representatives espoused an idealism, thanks to their flirtation with the Enlightenment, far removed from local realities. In their compulsive writing and rewriting of their constitutions, they repeatedly eschewed local experience to import the latest ideas from abroad. Apparently the more novel the idea the better, so long as it originated in one of the nations they regarded as progressive. The most popular models for the many nineteenth-century Latin American constitutions were the North American and French constitutions as well as the Spanish Constitution of 1812, considered in the early nineteenth century as a splendid example of liberal thought.

The Latin Americans promulgated and abandoned constitutions with numbing regularity. It has been estimated that in the century and a half after independence, they wrote between 180 and 190 of them, a large percentage of which were adopted during the chaotic period before 1850. Venezuela holds the record with 22 constitutions since 1811. The four major Latin American nations have a somewhat more stable constitutional record. Brazil's constitution, promulgated in 1824, lasted until 1889. After several attempts, Chile adopted a constitution in 1833 that remained in force until 1925. Argentina's Constitution of 1853 survived until 1949 but was put into force again in 1956. Mexico promulgated a constitution in 1857 that remained the basic document until 1917.

Generally the constitutions invested the chief executive with paramount powers so that both in theory and practice he exercised far greater authority than the other branches of government, which were invariably subservient to his will. In that respect, the Latin Americans reverted to their experience of the past. The presidents played the omnipotent role of past kings. Chile and Brazil experimented with parliamentary government. By the mid-nineteenth century, all the Latin American governments shared at least three general characteristics: strong executives, a high degree of centralization, and restricted suffrage—the vote invariably was limited to literate and/or propertied males. With a few notable exceptions, the new governments were by, of, and for the elite. The masses generally stood as silent witnesses to political events.

The Tense Societies

Tension characterized the early governments from independence to at least the mid-nineteenth century. The new governments felt threatened by internal challenges, aggression from their neighbors, and the possibility of European reconquest. There was the psychological insecurity of those uncertain of their new positions of power, of those pressing for class fluidity—the restive commercial class and educated mestizos—and of those apprehensive about political change and its implications for the future. The mounting tensions between those imposing Europeanization and those favoring the folk culture of the past often erupted into violence.

From the start, the fear existed that Spain or Portugal, alone or in union with other European governments, might try to recapture the former colonies in the New World. The conservative monarchies of Russia, Austria, and Prussia formed the Holy Alliance, which numbered among its goals the eradication of representative government in Europe and the prevention of its spread to areas where it was previously unknown. The Alliance boldly intervened in a number of European states to dampen the fires of liberalism. At one time, it seemed possible that the Holy Alliance might help Spain in an effort to reassert its authority over its former American colonies. The possibility alarmed their rival, England—concerned with Latin American markets—as well as the United States—concerned with Russian settlement advancing down the western coast of North America. The English urged the United States to join in a statement discouraging foreign colonization of the Americas. Instead, an independent-minded President James Monroe in 1823 issued what became known as the Monroe Doctrine, which declared that the Americas were no longer open to European colonization and that the United States would regard any intervention of a European power in the Americas as an unfriendly act against the United States. Most Latin American elites welcomed the possibility of help from their northern neighbors as they took their first shaky steps as new nations. However, they found the doctrine to be empty rhetoric; the United States did not come to the aid of Latin American countries until the end of the nineteenth century.

Latin American fears of European intervention were not unfounded. Several European governments did physically intervene in the new republics. Spain invaded Mexico and Central America in 1829 and 1832. During the 1860s, Spain made war on Peru, seizing one of its guano-producing islands, and bombarded the Chilean port of Valparaíso. During that same decade, the Dominican Republic, a sad spectacle of chaos, invited Isabel II to accept the return of a contrite nation to the Spanish fold. Spain reasserted its authority in 1861, but the insular nation proved so unruly and expensive that Spain withdrew in 1865, leaving the Dominican Republic independent once again, the unique example of a former colony that voluntarily returned to its colonial status. France and Great Britain also intervened in the New World. The French occupied Veracruz, Mexico, in 1838 to force Mexico to pay alleged debts; and they blockaded Buenos Aires in 1838–40 and again in 1845–48, this time in conjunction with the British, to discipline Argentine dictator Juan Manuel de Rosas. The Argentine adventures proved to be far less successful than the Mexican one. The most brazen European intervention occurred in Mexico during the 1860s. Responding to the grandiose schemes of Napoleon III, a French army in 1862 marched into central Mexico to set the hapless Maximilian of Austria on a shaky throne. The French remained until their withdrawal in 1866, tired of fighting the troops commanded by Benito Juárez, chastised by an unhappy United States government, and increasingly concerned about competition in Europe as Otto von Bismarck unified Germany. These examples show that Latin American anxieties over European intervention were well founded. The threat and reality of foreign invasion increased local tensions as well as diverted resources and energy that could have been invested more profitably in national development.

To diminish the threat of invasion from the former mother countries as well as from other European states, the new nations sought international recognition of their independent status. The European governments hesitated to extend a hand of friendship before the former mother countries did so. Portugal, due to a family pact among the Braganzas, who occupied the thrones both in Lisbon and Rio de Janiero, extended the promptest recognition, accorded to Brazil in 1825. France delayed its recognition of Haitian independence, declared in 1804, until 1825. Spanish recognition was tardiest and most complicated. The death of Ferdinand VII in 1833 ended unrealistic Spanish intransigence and opened the way for negotiations with the former colonies. In 1836, Spain and Mexico agreed "to forget forever the past differences and dissensions which unfortunately have interrupted for so long a period the friendship and harmony between two peoples." Spain then recognized Mexico, and gradually over the decades extended similar recognition to the other republics, the last being Honduras in 1894.

Unlike the European nations, the United States felt no need to consider the feelings of the Iberian monarchs before acting, although other considerations—the desire to obtain Florida from Spain, for example—delayed recognition. In 1822, the process began when the Department of State recognized Argentina, Gran Colombia, and Mexico, followed in 1823 by the recognition of Chile, and in 1824 of Brazil and Central America. The United States maintained a high degree of interest in Latin America. Of the ten legations provided for by the Department of State's budget in 1824, five were in Latin America. By 1821, commerce with the southern neighbors already accounted for more than 13 percent of U.S. trade. Although formal recognition might have made the new states feel somewhat more secure, it did not in and of itself eliminate foreign threats or even deter interventions.

The threats were by no means all external. The national unity of the new states proved to be extremely fragile, and the forces that shattered it more often than not were internal. Geography provided one major obstacle to unity and the creation of the nation-state. Vast tracts of nearly empty expanse, impenetrable jungles, mountain barriers, and lonely deserts separated and isolated population pockets among which communication was tardy and difficult and transportation often nonexistent or at best hazardous and slow. The rainy season halted all communication and transportation in many regions. Such poor communications and transportation complicated the exchange of goods, services, and ideas on a national basis. It was easier and cheaper to ship a ton of goods from Guayaquil, Ecuador, to New York City via the Straits of Magellan than to send it 200 miles overland to the capital, Quito. Rio de Janiero could import flour and wheat more economically from England than from Argentina. Likewise the inhabitants of northern Brazil found it easier to import from Europe than to buy the same product from southern Brazil, despite the fact that sailing vessels connected Brazil's littoral population nuclei.

Most of the population lived within easy reach of the coast. To penetrate the interior, the Brazilians relied on inland waterways, in some areas generously supplied by the Amazon and Plata networks, or cattle trails. A journey from Rio de Janiero to Cuiabá, capital of the interior province of Mato Grosso, took eight months in the 1820s. The situation was comparable in Spanish America. The trip from Veracruz, Mexico's principal port, to Mexico City, a distance of slightly less than 300 miles over the nation's best and most used highway, took about four days of arduous travel when Frances Calderón de la Barca made the journey under the most favorable conditions in 1839. She described the road as "infamous, a succession of holes and rocks." In the 1820s a journey from Buenos Aires to Mendoza, approximately 950 miles inland at the foothills of the Andes, took a month by ox cart or two weeks by carriage, although a government courier in an emergency could make the trip in five days on horseback.

Distance, difficult geography, slow communication and transportation, and local rivalries, in part spurred by isolation, encouraged the growth of a regionalism hostile to national unity. Experiments with federalism intensified that regionalism. With the exception of Brazil, the former viceroyalties engendered few feelings of unity among their widely dispersed residents, who tended to give their loyalty to their local communities and regions, the *patria chica*, as opposed to the abstract notion of the nation. As a result, soon after independence the former territories of the Spanish viceroyalties disintegrated. None splintered more than the Viceroyalty of New Spain. In 1823, Central America, the former Kingdom of Guatemala, seceded. In turn, in 1838–39, the United Provinces of Central America broke into five republics. Texas left the Mexican union in 1836, and after the war of 1846–48 the United States won California, Arizona, and New Mexico. Gran Colombia failed to maintain the former unity of the Viceroyalty of New Granada: Venezuela left the union in 1829 and Ecuador followed the next year. Chile and Bolivia felt no loyalty to Lima, and consequently the Viceroyalty of Peru disbanded even before the independence period was over. In a similar fashion, Paraguay, Uruguay, and part of Bolivia denied the authority of Buenos Aires, thus spelling the end of the Viceroyalty of La Plata. By 1840, the four monolithic Spanish viceroyalties had split, giving rise to all of the Spanish-speaking republics of the New World except Cuba, which remained a Spanish colony until 1898, and Panama, which split from Colombia in 1903. In both cases, the new nations' fate was tied to the emergence of a new, aggressive North American imperialism in the late nineteenth and early twentieth centuries.

None of the eighteen new nations had clearly defined frontiers with its neighbors, a problem destined to cause war, bloodshed, and ill will. In some cases, commercial rivalries added to the difficulties. Further, the rapid multiplication of new states raised hemispheric trade barriers, which in turn complicated and intensified those rivalries. In short, former colonial regional rivalries took on a nationalistic tone after independence. The resultant suspicion and distrust among the eighteen states accelerated the tensions felt within the new societies. On occasion, these tensions gave rise to war, as neighbor fought neighbor in the hope of gaining a trade advantage, greater security, or additional territory.

Argentina and Brazil struggled in the Cisplatine War (1825–28) over possession of Uruguay and in an exhausted stalemate agreed to make the disputed territory independent; Chile attacked Peru and Bolivia in 1836 to prevent the federation of the two neighbors, and during the War of the Pacific (1879–83) the three fought for possession of the nitrate deposits of the Atacama Desert. Chile won and expanded northward at the expense of both Peru and Bolivia. The Dominican Republic battled Haiti in 1844 to regain its independence; westward expansion brought the United States into conflict with Mexico, 1846–48; and throughout the nineteenth century the five Central American republics challenged each other repeatedly on the battlefield. This catalog of conflicts is only representative, not inclusive. The major conflict of the century pitted tiny, landlocked Paraguay against the Triple Alliance—Argentina, Brazil, and Uruguay—in a clash of imperialistic pretensions in the strategic La Plata basin, one phase in a continuing struggle to maintain the balance of power there. It took the allies five years, 1865–70, to subdue plucky Paraguay. That war solved two difficult problems that had troubled the region since independence: First, it definitively opened the Plata River network to international commerce and travel, a major concern of Brazil, which wanted to use the rivers to communicate with several of its interior provinces. Second, it freed the small states of Uruguay and Paraguay from further direct intervention from Argentina and Brazil, which came to understand the importance of the independence of the two small Platine states as buffer zones. The two large nations might try to sway one or both of the small nations to its side, but neither Brazil nor Argentina physically intervened again.

Relations between the new states and the Roman Catholic Church created tensions of another sort. The Church was the one colonial institution to survive independence, and it enjoyed the support of the people. In addition, due to efficient organization, able administration, and the generosity of the pious, the Church continued to amass riches. At the end of the eighteenth century, the Church controlled as much as 80 percent of the land in some provinces of New Spain. That, however, constituted only part of the Church's wealth. Lucas Alamán, a devout Catholic, leader of the clerical party in Mexico during the early nineteenth century, and one of Mexico's most respected historians of the time, showed that although rural estates and urban properties of the Church accounted for half the total value of the nation's real estate, the Church's real wealth accrued from mortgages and the impressive sums of interest collected.

Church power came not just from its wealth. The clergy, one of the best-educated segments of society, enjoyed such tremendous prestige, particularly among the masses, that a mere suggestion from them often carried the weight of a command. The clerics regularly entered politics, held high offices in the new governments, or endorsed political candidates. The clergy exerted its influence within the educational system; in almost all of the new countries they monopolized education from the primary school through the university. Further, the uneducated masses had more contact with the Church than with officials of the new state. In addition to Sunday services, people looked to the priests for all the most important events of their lives: baptism of their babies, marriage ceremonies, last rites, and finally burial in a church graveyard. The Church wielded great influence not only in the spiritual lives of the new nations but also in economics, politics, society, and intellectual pursuits.

Criticism of the Church centered not on religion itself but rather on the secular power and influence of the institution and its servants. Leaders of the independence movements and their early successors offered to Catholicism recognition of its traditional position and privileges. The new constitutions respected the status of the Church. But many of the leaders of the new states quickly became apprehensive of the overwhelming power wielded by the privileged Church, which was far better organized, more efficient, and better financed than the state, and enjoyed a traditional relationship with the people that the state had yet to forge. Fledgling leaders believed that the independence of the new states could not be guaranteed if they did not exercise some temporal control over the Church. For that reason, the Latin American chiefs of state claimed the right to exercise national patronage as heirs of the former royal patronage. The Pope in turn announced that the patronage had reverted back to the papacy, its original source, with the declarations of independence. In their open sympathy with the Spanish monarchy the popes antagonized the Latin American governments. In 1824, Pope Leo XII issued an encyclical to archbishops and bishops in America to support Ferdinand VII. This confirmed to Latin American leaders that the Vatican was in league with the Holy Alliance. The new governments in turn expelled a number of ranking clerics who refused to swear allegiance to the new state.

Out of consideration for the feelings of Madrid, the Vatican for a long time refused to recognize the new American states, much to the chagrin of their governments, which were fearful that the discontent of the American Catholics with their isolation might endanger independence. Rome began to change its attitude toward the Latin American states in 1826, when the Pope announced his willingness to receive American representatives strictly as ecclesiastical delegates, in no way implying political recognition. The next year the Roman pontiff began to approve candidates presented by the American governments. With the death of Ferdinand VII in 1833, the Pope no longer felt any Spanish constraints on his policy in the New World. In 1835, the Vatican recognized New Granada (Colombia) and the following year accredited to Bogotá the first papal nuncio. The recognition of New Granada signified the end both of the problem over political recognition and of Spanish influence over the Vatican's diplomacy in and relations with Spanish America. However, other questions remained unsolved, and for the remainder of the century the difficulties between Church and state centered on such questions as lay teaching, secularization of the cemeteries, civil marriage, the establishment of a civil register for births, marriages, and deaths, ownership of religious property, and patronage.

The religious questions rigidly separated the adherents to the two strongest political currents of nineteenth-century Latin America, liberal and conservative. While the views of liberals and conservatives varied on many issues from nation to nation, and even region to region, they were steadfast in their views of the Church. The conservatives invariably favored the status quo, supporting the Church's spiritual and temporal powers, privileges, and prestige. Just as invariably, the liberals challenged the temporal powers of the Church. They uncompromisingly demanded that the state exercise patronage and thus temporal control.

The disputants often failed to settle their differences by compromise or conciliation. Then, armies took to the field to settle them. Mexico, in particular, suffered from the conflict over the question of the proper place of the Church within the new states. The early constitutions established Roman Catholicism as the state Church but endorsed the principle of national patronage. The liberals campaigned to reduce the privileges of the Church, and in 1833, during the brief tenure of Valentín Gómez Farías as chief of state, enacted reforms to secularize the California missions and to confiscate their funds, to secularize public education, to abolish compulsory tithes, to give members of religious orders the option of retracting their vows, and to strengthen the principle of national patronage. Santa Anna removed Gómez Farías from power in 1834 and annulled these reforms. Under the succeeding conservative governments, the Church regained its privileged status. During this time, Mexico expended much of its energy and resources against the rebels in Texas, to thwart French intervention, and to attempt to halt or deflect the expansion of the United States into the northern provinces. The attendant bankruptcy and disappointments paved the way to power for a new generation of liberals, the most prominent of whom was Benito Juárez, a full-blooded Indian. Never deviating from his liberal principles, he held the liberals together during a decade and a half of stress. In the Plan of Ayutla issued in 1854, the liberals called for the overthrow of Santa Anna and a new constitution. They came to power the following year but were repeatedly challenged. Of all the issues at stake, the religious question predominated.

The liberals initiated their religious reforms in 1855 with the Ley Juárez, which restricted the privileges of military and ecclesiastical courts by abolishing the *fueros*, their jurisdiction in purely civil cases. In 1856, the Ley Lerdo required all corporations to sell their lands; the intention of this law was to divest the Church of all its property not strictly devoted to religious purposes. The well-intentioned law had several unfortunate consequences for Mexico. In the first place, the Church lands were more often than not the most efficiently run and productive and hence a major contributor to the national economy. Further, income from these lands supported a wide variety of essential charities. The requirement that all corporations sell their lands included the Indian *ejidos,* so therefore the liberals contributed to divesting the Indian communities of their lands, a brutal blow to folk societies and a major impetus to the spread of capitalism and privilege. The *hacendados,* owners of the large estates, found as a result of the enforcement of the Ley Lerdo considerable new land on the markets that they snatched up to add to their already considerable holdings. The new constitution promulgated in 1857 incorporated both the Ley Juárez and the Ley Lerdo and went on to nullify compulsory observance of religious vows and to secularize education. The conservatives and the Church denounced the new laws and constitution. Pope Pius declared, "We raise our Pontifical voice in apostolic liberty . . . to condemn, to reprove, and to declare null and void the said decrees and everything else that the civil authority has done in scorn of ecclesiastical authority and of this Holy See." The clergy and military united to defend their privileges and attacked the liberals, initiating the bloody War of the Reform, 1858–61. The bold challenge to the liberal government unleashed an avalanche of anticlerical laws upon the Church: the nationalization of cemeteries, civil marriage, abolition of tithes, nationalization of all real property of the Church, separation of Church and state, suppression of all monasteries, and the prohibition of novitiates in nunneries.

Defeated on the battlefields, the conservatives resolved to seek foreign intervention rather than accept the triumph of Juárez. Their desires coincided with the ambitions of Napoleon III, who intervened in 1862 supposedly to force Mexico to pay its debts. At the invitation of the conservatives, Napoleon helped reinstitute monarchy by naming Austrian Archduke Maximilian to the throne. Maximilian arrived in 1864, and much to the annoyance of the conservatives, he turned out to have liberal views; he accepted the religious reforms. To oppose the French intervention and monarchical restoration, the liberals took up arms again. Napoleon found it necessary to commit 34,000 regular troops to support the unsteady throne of Maximilian. Even so, the monarchy never extended its authority over more than a fraction of Mexican territory and never enjoyed the support of more than a minority of the Mexican population. The French withdrawal in 1866 condemned the monarchy to immediate extinction. The next year the liberal army captured and shot Maximilian. Juárez returned to Mexico City and the herculean task of rebuilding a ravaged Mexico. The Church had lost considerable wealth, prestige, and power during its prolonged struggle with the state, but the battles were by no means over. They flared up later and extended well into the twentieth century.

Mexico represents an extreme in the Church–state struggles that added much to the tensions of nineteenth-century Latin America. Although such bitter warfare did not characterize all of the hemisphere, no new nation entirely escaped the conflict. The struggle over patronage and to reduce the Church's powers continued throughout the nineteenth century.

Economic Stagnation

A major paradox has always characterized Latin America: the potential richness of the land and the abject poverty of the majority of the people who work it. The contrast between what could be and what is confounds all careful observers. Luís dos Santos Vilhena, a Portuguese professor of Greek who resided twelve years in Salvador da Bahia at the end of the eighteenth century, posed the sad question about Brazil: "Why is a country so fecund in natural products, so rich in potential, so vast in extent, still inhabited by such a small number of settlers, most of them poor, and many of them half-starved?" He answered his own question frankly, putting the blame for underdevelopment on slave labor, the latifundia, and inefficient or obsolete agricultural methods. At the same time, Chilean intellectual José de Cos Iriberri asked an identical question: "Who would imagine that in the midst of the lavishness and splendor of nature the population would be so scanty and that most of it would be groaning under the oppressive yoke of poverty, misery and the vices which are their inevitable consequences?" He blamed the sad economic condition of Chile on the unequal distribution of the land, which favored a few large landowners but condemned most of the population to the role of overworked, underpaid, landless peons. What they said about Brazil and Chile could be applied to all of Latin America. All economic discussions of Latin America must begin with an understanding of land-ownership and land-use patterns.

Independence proved no panacea for Latin America's economic ills. The trend established during the colonial period to subordinate the economy to Europe's needs continued unaltered. During the nineteenth century, Latin America's economy remained locked into commercial capitalism, more dependent than ever on foreign markets for local prosperity. Meanwhile, Europe and the United States had industrialized and moved into yet another phase of international capitalism—financial—in which financiers owned and managed the assets of large, industrial empires.

During the first half of the century, Europe and the United States entered a period of rapid population growth and accelerated industrialization and urbanization. They demanded raw products: food for the urban centers and materials for the factories. In turn, they sought markets in which to sell growing industrial surpluses. Latin America exported the raw materials required in Europe, and to a lesser extent the United States, and imported the manufactured goods pouring in from distant factories. Latin America's exports depended on and responded to foreign requirements. In catering to the caprices of an unpredictable market, the Latin Americans encouraged the growth of a reflex economy, little different, except perhaps more disadvantageous, than the previous colonial economy. External factors, over which the Latin Americans had little or no influence, determined whether the economies prospered or vegetated. The economic cycle of boom and bust repeatedly reoccurred in all regions of Latin America, condemning most of the area to the periphery of international capitalism.

Between 1800 and 1850, world trade tripled, and Latin America participated in that growth. After recovering from the wars of independence, it shipped ever greater amounts of agricultural produce abroad. While two or three ships a year had handled trade between Chile and England in the 1815–20 period, more than 300 carried Chilean exports to England in 1847. The value of exports leaving Buenos Aires nearly tripled from 1825 to 1850.

Improving international transportation put Europe and the United States into closer contact with Latin America. Faster sailing vessels and the introduction of the steamship, which was being used successfully in North Atlantic crossings in the 1830s, were responsible. The steamships appeared in the waters of Brazil in 1819 and of Chile in 1822. By 1839, a steamship line connected Rio de Janiero with the northern provinces of the empire. A dramatic event in 1843 impressed the Brazilians with the importance of the steamship for their future development. In that year the puffing and chugging *Guapiassú* churned the waters of the Amazon for the first time. The steamship journeyed from Belém to Manaus, 900 miles upstream, in nine days and returned in half the time, a remarkable record considering that sailing vessels had required two or three months to ascend and a month to descend.

In 1840, the British chartered the Royal Mail Steam Packet Company to provide regular twice-monthly steamship service to the entire Caribbean area. That same year, the Pacific Steam Navigation Company initiated steamship service along the western coast of South America. For the Atlantic coast, the Royal Mail Steam Packet from England to Brazil began service in 1851. The English inaugurated direct steam service to the Río de la Plata soon thereafter. At the same time, the United States expanded its international steamship service, which reached Latin America in 1847 with the foundation of the Pacific Mail Company. These improved communication and transportation systems further meshed the economies of Latin America with those of the United States and Europe and most particularly with that of Great Britain.

Great Britain quickly replaced the two Iberian kingdoms as the dominant economic force in Latin America and held that primacy throughout the nineteenth century. Foreign Secretary George Canning mused in 1824, "Spanish America is free, and if we do not mismanage our affairs sadly, she is English." As soon as Portugal and Spain fell to Napoleon, eager British merchants began to move in large numbers into Latin America to capture the markets they had so long craved. The British immediately sold more to Latin America than anyone else and in some cases almost monopolized the imports into certain countries. British firms handled the lion's share of Latin America's foreign trade, and British bottoms carried much of it to distant ports. The English government maintained men-of-war in Latin American waters to protect British commerce, to safeguard the rights of Englishmen, and on occasion to transport specie. London supplied most of the loans and investments to the new nations. Already by 1822, four Latin American loans had been floated, in 1824 five more were, and the following year saw an additional five. In the years immediately after independence, British investors readily subscribed to joint-stock companies being formed in Latin America, particularly the mining companies—almost all of which failed.

By 1850, foreigners had invested a limited amount of capital, most of which was British. The most successful investments were in trading firms. The Europeans largely invested their capital to facilitate the production and export of the products they needed most. Thus, they used their capital to shape the Latin American economy to suit their needs, not those of the Latin Americans.

The British government successfully wrested from the Latin Americans agreements and treaties favorable to its merchants, traders, and bankers. Brazil's experience was classic. The new empire provided the English merchants and manufacturers with their most lucrative Latin American market. Exports to Brazil in 1825 equaled those sold to the rest of South America and Mexico combined and totaled half those sent to the United States. Naturally the British wanted to keep their Brazilian market. In exchange for arranging Portugal's recognition of Brazilian independence in 1825, London exacted a highly advantageous commercial treaty from Pedro I. It limited the duty placed on English imports to 15 percent and bound Brazil not to concede a lower tariff to any other nation. The treaty thereby assured British manufacturers domination over the Brazilian market and postponed any Brazilian efforts to industrialize.

Captivated by foreign political ideologies that bore little relevance to local conditions, the Latin American elite also showed a penchant for economic doctrines more suitable to an industrializing Europe than to an underdeveloped New World. Adam Smith mesmerized many Latin American intellectuals, who embraced free trade as a solution to their nations' economic problems. Of course, Smith was writing about England in 1776, at a time when the country enjoyed the natural protection of being the world's only industrialized power. But, in the words of Mexico's *El Observador* in 1830, the country needed "absolute and general freedom of commerce" to promote prosperity. In reaction to the former mercantilism they had deplored, the Latin Americans adopted policies of economic liberalism that they associated with the triumph of the Enlightenment but that bore no relation to the requirements of Latin America. Consistently modest tariffs deprived the new governments of sorely needed incomes and facilitated the flood of European manufactured articles inundating the New World, to the detriment of local industrialization. Mexico, for example, opened its ports in 1821 to all foreign goods at a uniform tariff of 25 percent ad valorem. Artisan manufacturing immediately declined. A petition to the national government in 1822 from Guadalajara for protection blamed the liberal tariff for putting 2,000 artisans in that city alone out of work. Free trade never contributed to the economic development of Latin America, although liberals and conservatives alike maintained—and still maintain—a fatal attraction to a theory that has failed to serve them well in practice. They refused to draw from history the lessons it could teach them.

Latin America's early economic woes cannot be blamed exclusively on the flirtations of the intellectuals with European ideologies. The destruction wrought by the wars of independence in many parts of the hemisphere and unsettled conditions during the early decades of the national period inhibited economic growth. The chronic political instability so characteristic of most of the new countries did not provide the proper climate for development. Politics rather than economics absorbed most of the attention and energy of the new nations. At the same time the quality of public administration deteriorated. Many trained public administrators departed with the defeated Spanish armies or returned to Lisbon with John's court. Recruitment seldom was based on talent; rather, positions in the civil service came as a political reward, and the frequent changes of government hindered the training of a new professional civil service. The national treasuries lay bare. Public financing was precarious and the fiscal irresponsibility of the governments notorious.

Legal changes in the labor system further disturbed the precarious Latin American economies. The government abolished Indian tribute (in theory, if not always in practice) and slowly freed the slaves. Central America and Chile ended slavery in 1823; Bolivia, in 1826; Mexico, 1829; Uruguay, 1830; Colombia, 1851; Ecuador and Argentina, 1853; and Peru and Venezuela, 1854. Brazil forbade further importations of African slaves after 1850. As usual, however, the resourceful landowners found a variety of ways of observing the letter of the law while changing but slightly the patterns of labor employment. They developed systems of apprenticeship and debt peonage to that end.

Labor in many regions remained in short supply. Because the greatest profits came from the export sector, the workers were often shifted to producing exportable crops, leaving an inadequate force to grow subsistence crops. Labor allocations tended to reinforce the patterns of Latin America's deepening dependency. Furthermore, subsistence farmers were expected not only to grow and market cheap food products but also to sell their labor—cheaply—to local landowners, particularly during periods of maximum labor demand such as planting and harvesting. That double exploitation enriched the rural elite, while leaving much of the rural masses as poor as ever.

Mining and manufacturing suffered the most during the decades after independence. With some mines flooded and machinery destroyed during the fighting, the labor system in flux, and investments lacking, the production of the once-fabled mines plummeted. The decline continued steadily in Mexico and Peru until midcentury. The Bolivian mines did not revive until around 1875. Industry fared no better. The availability of cheap European manufactured goods reversed the industrial advances made during the final decades of Iberian rule, decimated the handicraft industries, and put local artisans out of work.

After the initial shock and decline, agriculture recovered and improved. The markets of Europe and the United States readily absorbed many of the agrarian products, and their sale provided the basis for any prosperity in the decades before 1850. At midcentury, the overwhelming majority of Latin Americans lived in the countryside. Fully 90 percent of Mexico's 8 million inhabitants, for example, were rural. Social indicators for that population were dismal but not unusual: Literacy reached only 10 percent, life expectancy barely twenty-four years.

Most large estates survived intact from the turmoil of the independence period. In fact, many multiplied in size during those turbulent years. In northern Mexico, the Sanchez Navarro family, by a combination of astute business practices and shrewd political maneuvering, managed to preserve everything it had amassed during the colonial period. The power base the family chiefs had built in the state of Coahuila enabled them to expand significantly during the early decades of Mexican independence. Their landholdings reached a maximum between 1840 and 1848, consisting of seventeen haciendas that encompassed more than 16 million acres, the largest latifundio ever to have existed in Mexico. In Argentina, the Anchorena family, wealthy merchants in Buenos Aires, began to invest in ranches in 1818. Four decades later, they boasted of being the largest landowners in the country with 1.6 million prime, amply watered acres. Indeed, the times proved to be exceptionally propitious for the landlords to extend their holdings. The governments put the lands of the Church, Indian communities, and public domain on the market. From the old ejidos, the new governments authorized small plots for subsistence, while hacendados and fazendeiros added to their already large landholdings. By 1830 in Argentina, approximately 21 million acres of public land had been acquired by 500 individuals. The elites acquired land at a rapid pace, but they often failed to exploit it efficiently.

In the national period, as in the colonial past, the economy was still based on primary products; land retained its primary importance as the principal source of wealth, which led to prestige and power. The landed gentry immediately took control of the new governments. The chiefs of state owned large agricultural estates or were intimately connected with the landowning class. Representatives of that privileged class filled the legislatures. As far as that goes, the voting requirements of property ownership and/or literacy almost restricted the franchise to that class. The courts represented them—from the ranks of the elite came the lawyers and judges—and usually decided cases in their favor. Not surprisingly then, the governments supported debt peonage to ensure an adequate and docile labor force for the expanding estates—though with limited police forces, they found the laws difficult to enforce. The burgeoning foreign trade that had eluded the landed aristocracy during the colonial period beckoned after independence, and the elite ruled for its own benefit, disregarding the larger and more fundamental well-being of the nation as a whole.

The rapid consolidation of large but often inefficient estates raised serious social and economic questions, which were occasionally addressed although more often ignored. In Mexico shortly after independence, Francisco Severo Maldonado, for one, warned that national prosperity required widespread land ownership. He advocated the establishment of a bank to buy land from those who owned large, unused parcels and to sell it "at the lowest possible price" to those without land. One observer of Brazil's economy, Sebastião Ferreira Soares, concluded in 1860 that if Brazil's economy were to develop, it would require that uncultivated land be put in the hands of people who would work it. An editorial in the Buenos Aires newspaper *El Río de la Plata*, September 1, 1869, lamented, "The huge fortunes have the unfortunate tendency to grow even larger, and their owners possess vast tracts of land which lie fallow and abandoned. Their greed for land does not equal their ability to use it intelligently or actively."

One inevitable result of agrarian mismanagement was the increase in the price of basic foodstuffs. In 1856, the leading newspaper of Brazil's vast Northeast, *Diário de Pernambuco,* sharply condemned large landholdings as a barrier to development. Their owners withheld land from use or cultivated the land inefficiently, resulting in scarce and expensive foodstuffs. Better use of the land, the newspaper editorialized, would provide more and cheaper food for local markets as well as more exports. At the same time in the southern province of Rio de Janiero, a region undergoing a boom in coffee production for export, Ferreira Soares came to similar conclusions about the distortion of the economy through land misuse and export orientation. He observed with alarm the rapid extension of the export sector accompanied by declining production of food for internal consumption, a trend he documented with convincing statistical evidence. He noted that foods that had been exported from Rio de Janeiro as late as 1850 were being imported a decade later. Prices of basic foodstuffs—beans, corn, flour—rose accordingly. By withholding most of their acreage from cultivation, the large landowners caused the spiraling costs of foodstuffs, deprived the rural inhabitants of steady employment, and consequently encouraged the unemployed or underemployed to migrate to the cities, where no jobs awaited them. While the elite few became wealthy from coffee exports, the majority suffered loss of land and employment and much resultant misery. In short, the emphasis on export crops abused the land to the detriment of Brazil's majority.

In order to better understand the Latin American economy, i
while to examine the large estate and something of its operation. The
a patriarchal chief, ruled family, servants, slaves, tenant farmers, sharecrop-
pers, peasants, and even neighbors—unless they were large estate owners like
himself—with absolute authority. The vastness of the estate, its isolation from
the seat of government, the relative weakness of local bureaucrats, and the
propensity of the government to side with the landed class all strengthened
the landlord's power. Furthermore, the estate chaplain and local parish priest
orbited around him like satellites, lending the prestige of the Catholic Church
to augment his authority. From the comfort and security of his house, because
naturally the "big house" was the focal point of the estate's activity, the patriarch administered his holdings, listened to petitions from his subordinates,
dispensed justice, and in general held court. These large, strong, and sometimes well-furnished houses sat in the midst of barns, stables, carriage houses,
warehouses, workshops, granaries, sheds, and a chapel. In the lowland plantations the slave quarters stood nearby; in the highlands the Indian peons lived
in small villages on the estate. The estate contained fields for growing the commercial crop as well as food for the residents, orchards, pastures for pack animals, cattle, and sheep, and forests for firewood. Still, only a fraction of the
extensive estates was put to use. As far as possible, the estates were self-con-
tained. The patriarch and part of his family visited the nearest town and the
nation's capital from time to time to purchase from the outside world a few
luxury items for themselves and to savor the conviviality and pleasures of urban life. The wealthiest landlords maintained city homes. Often they or a
member of their families served in the local municipal government.

Foreign visitors to Latin America in the nineteenth century have left us
vivid accounts of the large estates. After having been a guest in numerous
Mexican country homes in the early 1840s, Frances Calderón de la Barca gen-
eralized:

> As for the interior of these haciendas, they are all pretty much alike so far as
> we have seen; a great stone building, which is neither farm nor countryhouse
> (according to our notions), but has a character peculiar to itself—solid enough
> to stand a siege, with floors of painted brick, large deal tables, wooden
> benches, painted chairs, and whitewashed walls; one or two painted or iron
> bedsteads, only put up when wanted; numberless empty rooms; kitchen and
> outhouses; the courtyard a great square, round which stand the house for
> boiling sugar, whose furnaces blaze day and night; the house, with machinery
> for extracting the juice from the cane, the refining rooms, the places where it
> is dried, etc., all on a large scale. If the hacienda is, as here, a coffee plantation
> also, then there is a great mill for separating the beans from the chaff, and
> sometimes also there are buildings where they make brandy. Here there are
> 400 men employed exclusive of boys, 100 horses, and a number of mules.
> The property is generally very extensive, containing the fields of sugar cane,
> plains for the cattle, and the pretty plantations of coffee, so green and spring-

like, this one containing upwards of 50,000 young plants, all fresh and vigorous, besides a great deal of uncultivated ground, abandoned to the deer and hares and quails, of which there are great abundance.

Huge plantations dominated the Brazilian countryside as well. To all appearances, the fazendas remained the same in structure and operation as they had for hundreds of years. One observant traveler, Daniel F. Kidder, visited a fazenda at Jaraguá in the interior of São Paulo at midcentury. The estate belonged to an enterprising woman who resided most of the year in the city of São Paulo. The variety of the products grown on the fazenda impressed Kidder: sugar cane, manioc, cotton, rice and coffee. He was even more impressed by the customs of the plantation houses and of his hosts:

> Our social entertainments at Jaraguá were of no ordinary grade. Any person looking in upon the throng of human beings that filled the house when we were all gathered together, would have been at a loss to appreciate the force of a common remark of Brazilians respecting their country, viz that its greatest misfortune is a want of population. Leaving travelers and naturalists out of the question, and also the swarm of servants, waiters, and children—each of whom, whether white, black, or mulatto, seemed emulous of making a due share of noise—there were present half a dozen ladies, relatives of the Donna, who had come up from the city to enjoy the occasion. Among the gentlemen were three sons of the Donna, her son-in-law, a doctor of laws, and her chaplain, who was also a professor in the law university, and a doctor in theology. With such an interesting company the time allotted to our stay could hardly fail to be agreeably spent. . . . It is a pleasure to say, that I observed none of that seclusion and excessive restraint which some writers have set down as characteristic of Brazilian females. True, the younger members of the company seldom ventured beyond the utterance of Sim Senhor, Não Senhor, and the like; but ample amends for their bashfulness were made by the extreme sociability of Donna Gertrudes. She voluntarily detailed to me an account of her vast business concerns, showed me in person her agricultural and mineral treasures, and seemed to take the greatest satisfaction in imparting the results of her experience on all subjects.

The ownership and management of estates by women was probably not all that uncommon. Carl Scherzer encountered a female rancher in mid-nineteenth century Nicaragua: "I met with an elderly lady, the owner of an estate in Segovia, who had been to Granada with a large quantity of [hides] for sale, and was now returning with a heavy purse and twenty-one beasts lightened of their burden."

Lower-class women always had been required to work and therefore did not comply with the elite ideal of the secluded woman who remained in the house. The wars of independence had created opportunities for women on both sides of the struggle to step outside their traditional bounds. However, no constitution of the new nations recognized these contributions with full citizenship, and society and government tended to take the patriarchal family as its model. This model would be challenged to some extent by the emergence of greater market relations and greater commercialization of land and labor. As men sought work away from traditional landholdings, women became the heads of households.

The elite tended to romanticize the large estate, one useful means of enhancing their ideology. No one better idealized the mid-nineteenth century hacienda than Jorge Isaacs in his highly acclaimed novel *Maria* (1867). The author provided a wealth of detail about a patriarchal estate in the Cauca Valley of Colombia, from which emerged his concept of the exemplary hacienda. Orderly, hierarchical, harmonious, the novel's well-run estate centered on the comfortable "big house" and patriarchal authority, which extended from the doting family to the devoted slaves. "Father" always knew best in that patrilineal setting. The novel's extreme popularity arose mainly from the ideal but tragic romance it depicted, although it must also have come from its appealing portrait of the idyllic country life where people and nature intertwined, where social roles were well defined and unquestionably accepted, where the values of human relationships took precedence over business and ambition, and where alienation apparently was unknown. Such patriarchal estates symbolized the model society to many Latin American writers, who frequently used them as backdrops for their stories. This vision complemented a system that doubtless seemed less perfect to the *campesinos* than it did to the elites.

A Lingering Legacy of the Enlightenment

The ideas propagated by the Enlightenment lingered throughout the nineteenth century in Latin America. Because they shaped official attitudes and institutions of the new nations and pervaded the thinking of a large number of the ruling class, the elites, they exerted a profound influence on the lives of all Latin Americans no matter how humble.

The Enlightenment bequeathed to Latin America a complex legacy. An inherent and obvious danger resided in the fact that most of the ideas the Latin Americans associated with the Enlightenment originated in Europe north of the Pyrenees and thus reflected experiences alien to those of Indo-Ibero-Afro-America. Political ideas associated with the Enlightenment encouraged the urge for independence and nationhood. Affirming that each people should enjoy its own right to self-government, the Enlightenment prescribed the form and content of those governments. The notion that each people should enjoy the fruits of its own resources and labor was another powerful concept, which convinced the Latin Americans to deregulate commerce, experiment with free trade, and to embrace the practice of comparative advantage, whereby they willingly entered a commercial relationship to sell agrarian and mineral products and to purchase manufactured goods. They professed an attachment to experimentation, which dictated the adoption of European technology, increasingly regarded as the explanation for Northern European prosperity. Education—European education, because the elites wanted to duplicate European society in the New World—was emphatically regarded as the portal through which any nation or person must pass to achieve happiness, success, and wealth. Latin American faith in the redeeming virtues of a European education remained unshakable. Obviously the Latin Americans ignored other aspects of the many-sided Enlightenment.

Although the precise political labels adopted by the elites in the nineteenth century varied, they tended to group themselves under the headings of Liberals and Conservatives. Those labels confused rather than clarified because the elites had much more in common than in opposition. They tended to gravitate toward what (in the broadest terms of the Enlightenment) was considered to be liberal for the early nineteenth century: a written constitution, which defined the office of the chief executive, who shared power with a legislature and judiciary; a limitation if not outright abolition of trade restrictions; public education; and formal equality before the law.

The ideology of progress that emerged from the elites' flirtation with the Enlightenment was nowhere better expressed than by Argentina's Generation of 1837, an exceptionally articulate group of liberal intellectuals. Their ideas and actions reached far beyond the Argentine frontiers to shape much of the thinking of modern Latin America. Impressive unity and urgency were achieved by those intellectuals because they believed they faced a powerful alternative to their preferences in the figure of the popular caudillo Juan Manuel de Rosas, who dominated Argentina from 1829 until 1852. The Generation of 1837 regarded their conflict with Rosas as a struggle between "civilization" and "barbarism," a dialectic repeatedly invoked by intellectuals throughout the century. In defining civilization, the Generation of 1837 identified the Argentina they intended to create, and in fact did create, as a copy of Europe.

Associated with the port of Buenos Aires, the intellectuals looked with horror on the rest of the nation as a vast desert in need of the civilizing hand of Europe. Buenos Aires would serve, according to their blueprint, as a funnel through which European culture would pass on its civilizing mission to redeem the countryside—if it was redeemable. Many of the elite finally concluded it was not and advocated European immigration as the best means to "save" their country. They aspired to govern Argentina by means of a highly restrictive democracy. Esteban Echeverría summed up that aspiration in his influential *Dogma Socialista* (1838): Men of reason should govern rationally to avoid the despotism of the masses. Domingo Faustino Sarmiento forcefully set forth the dialectic in his *Civilization and Barbarism* (1845): The conflict was between the progress of the Europeanized city versus the ignorance, barbarism, and primitivism of the countryside. The best-known Argentine novel of that century, *Amalia* (1855), further propagated the attitudes of the Generation of 1837. The author, José Mármol, characterized Rosas as a tyrant, the representative of rural barbarity. An open racism pervaded the novel: The persecuted elite of the capital was white, thus of pure European lineage and obviously "civilized"; the supporters of Rosas were a cruel collection of "mongrels," mulatto and mestizo, equated with inferiority and barbarism. *Amalia,* like *Civilization and Barbarism* and *Dogma Socialista,* represented the outlook of a generation instrumental in the shaping of Argentina in the nineteenth century. Indeed, two participants in that movement, Bartolomé Mitre and Sarmiento, served successively as presidents of Argentina (1862–68 and 1868–74) during crucial years in the formation of that nation.

The ideology of progress pursued by the dominant elites extolled a type of liberty and democracy sanctioning individualism, competition, and the unchecked pursuit of profit. That ideology tended to be abstract, exclusive, and dependent on authority. The elites spoke constantly of "progress," perhaps the most sacred word in their political vocabulary. It defied facile definition. Later generations of scholars substituted the word "modernization," but that replacement did little to clarify the concept. Both words, used interchangeably hereafter, implied an admiration for the latest ideas, modes, inventions, and styles of Europe and the United States and a desire to adopt—rarely to adapt—them. The elites believed that "to progress" meant to recreate their nations as closely as possible in the shape of their European and North American models. Believing that they would benefit from such a recreation, they assumed by extension that their nations would benefit as well. They always identified (and confused) class well-being with national welfare.

The economic system that the elites obviously associated with progress was capitalism. It could not be otherwise when their primary models were England, France, and the United States. The constitutions, laws, and political practices they put into effect complemented the penetration and growth of capitalism. They abandoned the protective but restrictive neocapitalism and mercantilism of the Iberian empires to try their fortunes with the dominant capitalist nations of the century. In nineteenth-century practice, the landowners produced their crops on as large a scale as possible for sale in an external market from which they expected a satisfactory profit. Foreign exploitation of natural resources was approved by politicians, who hoped that some residue of the wealth created would enrich them. The wealth from the countryside and mines—shared increasingly with middlemen in the ports—also brought landowners and politicians prestige, and the combination of both conferred power. The growing merchant class, dependent first on the flow of primary products from the countryside and mines and secondly on the ability of the landed gentry and political leaders to afford costly European imports, exhibited scant inclination to challenge a system that also benefited them.

Progress was always measurable in quantitative terms—at least according to the elite, politicians, and scholars. It could be measured in the number of miles of railroad tracks or telegraph lines built, no matter where they went or what ends they served. The expansion of port facilities was equated with development, as were rising exports. Capital cities vied for the coveted title of "The Paris of Latin America," and to the extent that they approximated their model, historians classified them as "cultured," "civilized," or "progres-sive." The arrival of increasing numbers of European immigrants signified the continuation and acceleration of the progress cherished by the elites, because the newcomers brought with them tastes and skills their American counterparts lacked or only knew secondhand.

Nineteenth-century historians chose the "progress" of Latin America as a major theme for their studies. A city that adopted the outward manifestations of Europe was to be praised, while an Indian village that remained loyal to its indigenous past was categorized as "primitive." Any Latin American politician who spoke with the rhetoric of the Enlightenment emerged in the history books as a statesman, but a political leader who appealed to local customs and the American past either was ignored by the scholars or castigated as a "barbarian." The historical dichotomy became as simplistic as it was universal. Latin American historiography, with only occasional but noteworthy exceptions, lauds the liberal laws and constitutions despite the fact that they obviously spoke to a small minority and more often than not were used as a means to intensify the concentration of political and economic power.

Competitive social intercourse demanded by the ideology of progress obviously favored the strong, wealthy, and resourceful minority over the huge but weakened majority. In fact, the values the elites placed on abstract liberties and democracy conflicted with the values and experiences of most of the population, who understood little of European theories and nothing of the European experiences that gave rise to them. Their own experiences were rooted in the New World, and they drew from a past of interdependence, cooperation, and solidarity that was contrary to the theories of individualism and competition. Not prepared for the values imposed by the elites, the masses could not hope to gain much from them. In fact, they did not. Liberty and democracy as they took form in nineteenth-century Latin America quickly became a superficial rationale excusing or disguising the exploitation of the many by the few. As one Argentine historian, Hector Inigo Carrera, graphically expressed it, "Liberalism promised a theoretical garden of happiness which historically became a jungle of poverty."

The masses often repudiated the values imposed on them and attempted to express their own. What distinguished the folk was their adherence to ideas and values formulated by the American experience over centuries. Because the folk drew cautiously and slowly from European sources, carefully mediating those outside influences, they did not embrace the values and ideology emanating from Europe—and later the United States—with the same enthusiasm and rapidity that generally characterized the welcome extended by the elite, wealthy, and aspiring middle class.

Folk culture, a common way of life shared by ordinary people, was based on common language, heritage, beliefs, and means of facing daily life. It instilled a feeling of unity, loyalty, and tradition within the folk, more intuitive than codified, although folk wisdom, poetry, and tales gave insight into them. Throughout much of that century, the common folk cultures bound people together into intradependent, intimate, and largely self-sufficient folk societies (organized groups of individuals characterized by a folk culture), with a well-defined moral order in which each person knew both his or her own role and his or her interrelationship with other individuals. The folk held more to fixed laws of behavior and human existence. A unity of feeling and action accompanied a sense of harmony with the environment to satisfy inner needs. Education within those folk societies emphasized the individual's relationship to the group and inculcated in children a moral behavior honored by the community. Education provided continuity by passing on and maintaining tradition.

The incentives to work and to trade originated in subsistence economies that depended on cooperative arrangements, leading to the development of strong tradition, moral dictates, community obligations, and kinship relations. In those cultures, economic decisions were closely intertwined with social considerations. The system worked sufficiently well to provide the folk with employment, food, housing, and community spirit. Lifestyles were simple; hardships were common; the disadvantages were obvious, at least to the outsider. Such lifestyles repulsed the Europeanized elites of the cities. Indeed, the behavior of the folk could be neither understood nor explained within the framework of Western thought. It did not evolve exclusively from the Iberian experience, nor did it acknowledge the influence of the liberal ideology of the Enlightenment or the French Revolution. Within their own experience, however, the folk societies seem to have provided adequately for their members.

In the face of the elites' Europeanized "official" culture, one function that Latin American folk culture assumed, consciously or not, was protest. Folk values readily reveal the limited "universality" of the official culture. To comprehend this, one can juxtapose official rhetoric, such as "Equality before the law," with popular proverbs such as "The rich man eats, while the poor man works." The limits of official culture can be understood in the lifestyles of at least that part of the masses that refused to accept the "universal" values. Large numbers of Indian groups tenaciously held and still hold their own beliefs and culture in the face of strong pressure from the official culture. Their own manner of dress is a direct challenge to the official consumer ideology that each person must dress differently, own a variety of clothes, and change styles frequently. Throughout Latin America viable folk cultures existed— and still exist—that either challenged the official cultures, or adapted to it, or evolved parallel, albeit subordinate, to it.

In making any assessments of the success or failure of folk cultures and especially of liberal "progress," one confronts a major semantic confusion: the equating of growth with development. The failure to distinguish between these two concepts creates innumerable difficulties. They are quite distinct. *Growth* indicates simply and only numerical accumulation, and in no way indicates how it occurred, who, if anyone, it benefited, or, for that matter, what grew. Latin America in the nineteenth century grew wealthier through exports, but the wealth increasingly concentrated into fewer hands. One could argue convincingly that such growth was detrimental. *Development,* on the other hand, signifies the maximum use of a nation's potential for the greatest benefit of the largest number of inhabitants. Development can imply or include growth, although it is conceivable that a nation can develop without growing. Involved in these assessments are considerations of quantity (statistical matters rather easily resolved) and of quality of life (more subjective and consequently more controversial). Questions of development inevitably address the sage advice of Adam Smith in his *The Wealth of Nations:* "No society can surely be flourishing and happy, of which the far greater part of the members are poor and miserable."

Caudillos

The violence, tension, and economic uncertainties during and after the struggles for independence gave rise to the rule of the *caudillo,* or strong leader. The caudillos were an assorted lot. Some were popinjays who sported splendiferous uniforms and adopted sonorous titles; others lived ascetic lives, hidden from public view and attired in somber suits. All radiated mystique and charisma. They rose in the vacuum of power left by the departure of Spanish authority. Most originally were military leaders who were the only ones capable of maintaining order in a society that had become armed and militarized in the wars. They ruled by virtue of their personal authority, not by institutional legitimacy. The majority of the caudillos faithfully represented the elites and thus at least paid lip service to the ideology of progress. Those caudillos often spouted language drawn from the ideologues of the Enlightenment.

Advocating a selective Europeanization while cautious not to disturb well-established institutions, they enjoyed the support of the elites. In truth, these caudillos offered a continuation of the patterns of the past: large landed estates, debt-labor systems, export-oriented economies, and highly centralized political power. All power, all authority emanated from the caudillo; he played, in short, the role of the "king." In practice, however, he exercised more control over his "subjects" than the Spanish monarchs ever dared. The caudillos shared power with no one. As one remarked, "I neither want nor like ministers who think. I want only ministers who can write, because the only one who can think am I, and the only one who does think am I." Neither convictions nor principles necessarily guided the caudillo. He favored expediency, an ideological irresponsibility in which his will and whim were supreme. To rule, the caudillo employed force with impunity. Nor did his measures stop with imprisonment, confiscation, or exile. He could and did impose the death penalty as he saw fit. The general lack of restraints on his power permitted him to tax and spend as he pleased, a situation conducive to financial abuse, if not outright dishonesty.

To balance the picture, it should be noted that many of the "elite" caudillos bestowed some benefits on the nations they governed. Those disturbed by the chaos of the early decades of independence welcomed the order and stability characteristic of *caudillismo.* The early caudillos unified some of the nations, and there can be no doubt that their great strength in several notable cases prevented a national disintegration. Later caudillos liked to cast themselves as modernizers and in that role bequeathed material improvements to the nations they governed. They built roads and imposing government buildings, lay railroad tracks, strung telegraph wires, and renovated ports. They even built schools with the intention of propagating their own virtues in them. Their favorite project was to rebuild the centers of the capital cities in accord with the latest European architectural dictates, an outward manifestation of modernization that brought great satisfaction to the elites, who could thus fancy their nations as thoroughly up to date.

Although the caudillos did not have to concern themselves with public opinion—for all intents and purposes it did not exist—they did seek the support of at least three groups, individually or in combination, to buttress their personal power: the rural aristocracy, the Roman Catholic Church, and the army. The early caudillos were more often than not members of or related to the rural landowning class, men notable for their desire to preserve their class' prestige, wealth, and power and for their opposition to land reform, extension of the suffrage, and popular government. The caudillos usually represented their interests. Despite the fact that they ruled from the capital cities (although they might spend long periods of time on their estates), they tended to suppress the influence of the more liberal urban elements. The Church as an institution was a conservative force suspicious of reforms and usually in open conflict with the liberals. Church leaders, with a few notable exceptions, rallied to endorse any caudillo who respected and protected Church interests and property.

The army, the only truly national institution, immediately emerged as a political force. Its strength revealed the weakness of the political institutions. In many countries it was the dominant political force and has so remained. Because few of the republics developed satisfactory means to select or alter governments, palace coups—in which the military always had a role—became the customary means for effecting political shifts throughout the nineteenth century. The military then exercised the dual role of guaranteeing order on one hand and changing governments on the other. No caudillo or president would willfully alienate the military. Consequently officers enjoyed generous salaries and rapid promotions. The Latin American armies became and have remained top-heavy with brass. Thus, armies not only retarded the growth of democracy through their political meddling, but also slowed down economic growth by absorbing a lion's share of the national budgets. They spent the capital needed for investment. On the average, prior to 1850, the military received more than 50 percent of the national budgets. Mexico provides one of the most shocking examples: Between 1821 and 1845 the military budget exceeded the total income of the government on fourteen occasions. Caudillos often arose from the ranks of the army; thus they understood and commanded the major institution for maintaining order and power. Chile was the first, and for a long time the only, Spanish-speaking nation to restrict the army to its proper role of defending the nation from foreign attack. After 1831 and until the civil war of 1891, the army kept out of Chilean politics. Few other nations could boast of a similarly well-behaved military.

A few caudillos, however, championed the lifestyles and needs of the dispossessed majority and can be considered "popular" or "folk" caudillos. A highly complex group, they shared some of the characteristics of the elite caudillos, but two major distinctions marked them as unique. They refused to accept unconditionally the elites' ideology of progress, exhibiting a preference for the American experience with its Indo-Afro-Iberian ingredients and consequently greater suspicion of the post-Enlightenment European model. Further, they claimed to serve the folk rather than the elite.

The folk expected their leader to represent and strengthen their unity, personify their values, and increase their harmony; in short, to be as one with the people he led. Their caudillo recognized and understood the folk's distinctive way of life and acted in harmony with it. In the eyes of the people, he inculcated the local, regional, or national values—traditional values—with which most of the people felt comfortable. He was a natural, charismatic leader of the majority, who found in him an adviser, a guide, a protector, a patriarch in whom they entrusted their interests. They surrendered power to him; he incarnated authority. In his discussion of leadership and folk, José Carlos Mariátegui ascribed to the leader the roles of "interpreter and trustee." Mariátegui concluded, "His policy is no longer determined by his personal judgment but by a group of collective interests and requirements." The leader seemingly arose from and blended with his physical and human environment. Thus identified with America, he contrasted sharply with the Europeanized leaders imposed by the elites.

Juan Bautista Alberdi, probably more than anyone else in the nineteenth century, studied the psychology of the relationship of popular caudillos with the masses, and he concluded that the people regarded a popular caudillo as "guardian of their traditions," the defender of their way of life. He insisted that such leaders constituted "the will of the popular masses . . . the immediate organ and arm of the people . . . the caudillos are democracy." If the folk obeyed unreservedly those popular leaders, the caudillos in turn bore the obligation to protect and to provide for the welfare of the people. The ruled and ruler were responsible to and for each other, a personal relationship challenged in the nineteenth century by the more impersonal capitalist concept that a growing gross national product would best provide for all. The popularity of those caudillos is undeniable. Their governments rested on a base of folk culture, drew support and inspiration from the folk, and expressed, however vaguely, their style. Under the leadership of such caudillos, the masses apparently felt far more identification with government than they ever did under the imported political solutions advocated by the intellectuals and the elite. On many occasions the folk displayed support of their caudillos by fighting tenaciously to protect them from the Europeanized elites or foreign invaders. Few in number at the national level, the folk or populist caudillos had disappeared by 1870. But during the first half of the nineteenth century, these few leaders showed the possibility of a different kind of leadership and development.

One of the most controversial folk caudillos was Juan Manuel de Rosas, who enjoyed the support of the Argentine gauchos from 1829 until his exile in 1852. He appeared in Argentine history at the exact moment that Argentina, submerged in anarchy, threatened to split apart. The old viceroyalty of La Plata had disintegrated in the early nineteenth century and Argentina itself dissolved into squabbling regions. Sharpest was the rivalry between Buenos Aires, the port and province growing prosperous through trade with Europe, and the interior provinces, impoverished and wracked by civil wars.

Buenos Aires elites advocated a centralized government—which it fully expected to dominate—while the interior provinces favored a federalized one that would prevent the hegemony of the port. The bitter struggle between Buenos Aires and the interior delayed Argentine unification until Rosas strode onto the political stage. He had lived and worked in *gaucho* country before being elected governor of Buenos Aires in 1829, and he judiciously pursued the federalist idea of a pastoral economy, based on the simple premise that whatever complemented the life of the interior's cattle herding people benefited society. Understandably, the cattle breeders and the hide and meat producers supported Rosas because his economic inclinations favored them. Indeed, he was one of them—he owned extensive estancias, and his cousins were the Anchorenas, the largest landowners in Argentina. In his full exercise of political control, however, the caudillo acted as a centralist. Suspicious of Europe, he defied on occasion both England and France, deflecting their economic penetration of Argentina. The Argentine masses were convinced that he had their interests at heart and governed for their benefit. It would appear that the gauchos enjoyed an access to land, freedom of movement, greater economic alternatives, and better living conditions during the Rosas period than at any time afterward. To stimulate occupation of the land, Rosas initiated a program in 1840 to distribute land to soldiers. Nonetheless, there was no large-scale redistribution of land under Rosas, and vagrancy laws were initiated toward the end of his rule. But the masses—both the rural gauchos and urban blacks and mulattos—demonstrated their identification with and loyalty to Rosas by their willingness to fight for him for nearly a quarter of a century. Their caudillo suffered defeat and exile only when the elites enlisted the Brazilian and Uruguayan armies to unite with them to overthrow him. Defeated at the Battle of Monte Caseros, Rosas left Argentina for a European exile. The fall of Rosas in 1852 opened the door to the promulgation of a liberal constitution, the growth of capitalism, a flurry of land speculation, and the commercial expansion of the cattle industry on an unprecedented scale. Argentina merged with the capitalist world and intensified its dependency in the process.

An intriguing example of the caudillos who preferred local models to imported ones is Rafael Carrera, who governed Guatemala from 1839 until his death in 1865. At least half Indian, Carrera negated many of the Enlightenment reforms applied by previous liberal governments and ruled at least in part for the benefit of the Indians, the vast majority of the Guatemalans. The elites regarded him as a barbarian; the Indians exalted him as their savior.

Carrera led the Indian revolt of 1838–39. Among the many changes that popular rebellion represented was the refusal of the Indians to countenance any further exploitation and destruction through Europeanization. They wished to be left alone by the elites of Guatemala City so that they could live unmolested according to the dictates of their own culture. They rejected Europeanizing education, culture, economy, and laws that would integrate them into a capitalist economy centered in Europe. They chose instead to withdraw, to isolate themselves; and withdrawal was, and remains, a common reaction of the Indians to the Europeans. But, in regions where the elites depended on those Indians for labor and taxes, withdrawal signified rebellion. Carrera understood the Indian position, he sympathized with their desires, and he rose to power on their strength. As Carrera wrote in his memoirs, "When attempts are made suddenly to attack and change the customs of the people, it provokes in them such emotion that, no matter how sound the intention of those who seek to change their traditional ways and institutions, they rise in protest."

During the generation in which Rafael Carrera dominated Guatemala, he respected the native cultures, protected the Indians as much as was possible, and sought to incorporate them into his government. His modest successes in those efforts assume greater significance when compared to the disastrous conditions suffered by the Indian majority during the decades of liberal, Europeanized governments that preceded and followed the Carrera period. That popular caudillo, totally unschooled in foreign theories, was a practical man who knew Guatemala and its peoples well. He had traveled and lived in many parts of the nation, always among the humble folk whom he understood. He learned from and drew upon his Guatemalan experiences, a marked contrast to the elites seduced by European experiences and theories. Carrera appreciated the Indians' opposition to the Europeanization process imposed by the liberals. He regarded it as his principal duty to allow "the people to return to their customs, their habits, and their particular manner of living." The government, he affirmed, had the obligation of representing the majority of the people and of offering "a living example of virtue, equity, prudence, and justice." Those principles seem to have guided much of his long administration.

While Carrera repudiated the radical ideas of the liberals, he never rejected change. He believed it must come slowly and within the particular social context, a change acceptable to the people and not forced on them. The president held that the art of governing well sprang from the "formation of a government of the people and for the people." Accordingly, the government officially abandoned the liberals' goal to incorporate the Indians into Western civilization. One even could argue that under Carrera the government was "Indianized." Indians and particularly mestizos, all of relatively humble classes, participated directly in the government, holding, in addition to the presidency of course, such exalted offices as the vice-presidency, the heads of ministries, governorships, and high military ranks. The army became nearly an Indian institution. The Carrera government was unique to Latin America for encouraging the political ascendency of the once-conquered race. Significantly the "white" political monopoly was broken, and never again could the minute white aristocracy alone govern Guatemala.

To lift some of the economic burden from the impoverished majority, President Carrera reduced taxes on foodstuffs and abolished the head tax. Further, he excused the Indians from contributing to the loans the government levied from time to time to meet fiscal emergencies. By removing many of the taxes on the Indians, which were paid in the official currency circulating in Europeanized Guatemala, the government lessened the need for the indigenous population to enter the monetary economy, thus reducing the pressure on them to work on the estates. The Indians, then, could devote that time and energy to their own agricultural and community needs.

Of all the efforts made on behalf of the Indians, none surpassed those affecting the protection of Indian lands, the return of land to Indian communities, and the settlement of land disputes in their favor. The government declared in 1845 that all who worked unclaimed lands should receive them. What was even more unusual, it enforced the decree. It was decided in 1848 and again in the following year that all pueblos without ejidos were to be granted them without cost, and, if population exceeded available lands, then lands elsewhere were to be made available to any persons who voluntarily decided to move to take advantage of them. In 1851, Carrera decreed that "the Indians are not to be dispossessed of their communal lands on any pretext of selling them," a decree strengthened a few months later by prohibiting the divestment of any pueblos of their lands for any reason. Carrera thus spoke forcefully and effectively to the most pressing problem of Latin America: the overconcentration of land in the hands of the elite and the need for the rural masses to have land to cultivate. Those decades witnessed increasing agrarian diversification. The intent was not so much to increase exports as to ensure a plentiful supply of food in the marketplace at prices the people could afford. From the evidence at hand it would seem that the quality of life for the Indian majority improved during the Carrera years. The characteristics marking the Carrera experience as unique in Indo-America are the respect the government extended to Indian cultures and the reluctance to push the Indian population into Europeanizing themselves.

The Indian victory under Carrera proved to be as transitory as the gauchos' under Rosas. The death of Carrera in 1865 reinvigorated the elites' effort to wield power, and they succeeded under the leadership of another and different type of caudillo, Justo Rufino Barrios (1873–85). Positivist in orientation, President Barrios duly emphasized order and material progress. Under the liberal reforms of the Barrios period, capitalism made its definitive entry into Guatemala, which meant large-scale exportation of coffee with all the attendant consequences for the agrarian economy. The government rushed to import foreign technicians, ideas, and manufactured goods. It did not hesitate to contract foreign loans to pay for the Europeanization. The improvement of roads from the highland plantations to the ports and then the construction of the much-desired railroads first to the Pacific and later to the Atlantic accelerated coffee production and integrated Guatemala into the world market system more closely than ever.

Spiraling coffee production for export had several long-range, negative consequences. For one thing, it diminished the amount of land, labor, and capital available to produce food for local consumption. Wheat harvests especially declined. Monoculture again became a dominant characteristic of the economy. To create the necessary workforce on the coffee *fincas,* the Indians were forced, under a burdensome system called *mandamientos* (not dissimilar to the old *repartimientos),* to become wage laborers. Meanwhile the government did not hesitate to concede to private landowners many lands on which the Indians had lived and worked for generations. By a variety of means, the large estates encroached on the Indians' communal lands. As a consequence the economic and social position of the Indian majority declined.

During the period when Carrera governed Guatemala, Bolivia, another overwhelmingly Indian country, witnessed the singular leadership of its own popular caudillo, Manuel Belzú. He played an extremely complex role combining the forces of populism, nationalism, and revolution in ways that would not be used again in Latin America for more than half a century. He built an effective power base of campesino and urban-artisan support, which brought him to the presidency in 1848 and sustained him until he peacefully left the presidential palace in 1855. As dispossessed and impoverished as their counterparts throughout Latin America, the artisans and campesinos rallied to Belzú probably because his novel rhetoric spoke directly to their needs and certainly because of a series of wildly popular actions he took. He encouraged the organization of the first modest labor unions, ended some free-trade practices, terminated some odious monopolies, abolished slavery, permitted the landless Indians to take over lands they worked for the latifundista elite, and praised the Indian past. Often vague, frequently unsuccessful, his varied programs nonetheless won popular support. To his credit, Belzú seemed to have understood the basic problems bedeviling Bolivia: foreign penetration and manipulation of the economy and the alienation of the Indians' land.

Under the intriguing title "To Civilize Oneself in Order to Die of Hunger," a series of articles in a weekly La Paz newspaper in 1852 highlighted a vigorous campaign denouncing free trade and favoring protectionism. The paper argued that free trade deprived Bolivian workers of jobs while enriching foreigners and importers. It advocated "protectionism" as a means to promote local industry and thereby to benefit the working class, goals that had the obvious support of the president. Indeed, free trade bore some responsibility for the nation's poor agricultural performance. A chronic imbalance of trade between 1825 and 1846 had cost Bolivia nearly $15 million pesos, much of which was spent to import food the country was perfectly capable of producing. La Paz, for example, imported beef, mutton, and potatoes, among other foods. The local producers might deserve protection from cheaper imports, but protective tariffs alone would not necessarily raise the efficiency of the notoriously inefficient latifundios.

Although taking no legal steps to reform the land structures, Belzú never opposed the Indian occupation of their former community lands. Landlords, fearful of the restive Indian masses, found it prudent to move to the safer confines of the cities, thus abandoning their estates, which the Indians promptly occupied. Two major consequences of the de facto land reforms were the greater supplies of food entering the marketplaces and the drop in food prices. Belzú further delighted the campesinos by relieving them of some taxes.

If rhetoric were the measure of government, Belzú's administration stood as revolutionary. These examples from his public speeches serve as a yardstick:

> Comrades, an insensitive throng of aristocrats has become arbiter of your wealth and your destiny; they exploit you ceaselessly and you do not observe it; they cheat you constantly and you don't sense it; they accumulate huge fortunes with your labor and blood and you are unaware of it. They divide the land, honors, jobs and privileges among themselves, leaving you only

with misery, disgrace, and work, and you keep quiet. How long will you sleep? Wake up once and for all! The time has come to ask the aristocrats to show their titles and to investigate the basis for private property. Aren't you equal to other Bolivians? Aren't all people equal? Why do only a few enjoy the conditions of intellectual, moral and material development and not all of you?

Companions, private property is the principal source of most offenses and crimes in Bolivia; it is the cause of the permanent struggle among Bolivians; it is the basis of our present selfishness eternally condemned by universal morals. No more property! No more property owners! No more inheritances! Down with the aristocrats! Land for everyone; enough of the exploitation of man. . . . Aren't you also Bolivians? Haven't you been born to equality in this privileged land?

For the great mass of dispossessed campesinos, Belzú's heady words did not fall on idle ears. Some seized the estates. Where the landlords resisted, the followers of Belzú attacked and defeated them.

The identification of the folk with President Belzú and vice versa established the harmony and integration between caudillo and people that conferred sweeping power on the former. The president cultivated that identification. From the balcony of the presidential palace, Belzú assured his listeners, "I am one of you, poor and humble, a disinherited son of the people. For that reason, the aristocrats and the rich hate me and are ashamed to be under my authority." The president frequently reminded his followers that all power originated in the people who had conferred it on him. He simply acted on behalf of the people and their interests. Belzú correctly claimed that new elements of order and stability supported his government: "The popular masses have made themselves heard and played their role spontaneously; they have put down rebellions and fought for the constitutional government. The rise to power of this formidable force is a social reality of undeniable transcendence."

In the last analysis, Belzú was too Europeanized to feel comfortable for long as a folk caudillo, for he insisted on codifying his government within the confines of a Europeanized constitution. His political reforms and Constitution of 1851 reduced the presidential term to a specific period and prohibited reelection. Elections in 1855, classified by one Bolivian historian as "the cleanest ever held," brought a constitutional end to the Belzú presidency, awarding the office to the president's preferred candidate—his illegitimate son, Jorge Córdoba—a man unequal to the tumultuous task. In August of 1855, at the height of his power, Belzú stepped down, unwilling to follow the well-established precedent of *continuismo*, turned over the presidency to his elected successor, and temporarily left Bolivia. To the Indian masses he remained their "tata Belzú," friend and protector, whose short, unique government had benefited them.

The Indians had every reason to be apprehensive of the electoral process in which they had played no role. With Belzú in Europe, the old elites quickly seized power. At the same time, they took possession of their former lands and returned the campesinos to subservience. In the years that followed, the Indians often revolted with cries of "Viva Belzú!" on their lips, but as the elites became increasingly integrated into international trade and consequently strengthened, they were not about to repeat the previous political errors that had permitted a popular caudillo to govern. When, for example, the Huaichu Indians of Lake Titicaca rebelled in 1869 to regain communal lands, President Mariano Melgarejo dispatched the army to massacre them.

The populist caudillos constitute an intriguing chapter in nineteenth-century Latin American history. They appeared and disappeared within a sixty-year period. Yet, in 1850, three folk caudillos ruled at the same time: Carrera, Belzú, and Rosas. Two of those nations had large Indian populations with well-defined cultures, while the Argentine gauchos boasted an equally well-defined folk culture. The popular caudillos identified with the majority and vice versa. In all three cases, foreign investments were comparatively low or practically nonexistent; the governments and majority expressed strong views against foreigners and shunned foreign influences. At the same time, land became available for the majority and pressures on the peasants diminished. Subsistence agriculture dominated export agriculture. More food was available for popular consumption. Although those folk governments obviously appealed to large elements of society that customarily had been neglected, we cannot lose sight of the fact that they were few in number and had disappeared by 1870. The elites succeeded in imposing their will on the folk and on Latin America. Nonetheless, those few folk governments serve as useful reminders of possible alternatives to the Europeanized governments that the elites imposed. If, indeed, the people enjoyed a more satisfactory quality of life under the folk caudillos, those governments then suggest possible roads to development that were denigrated or ignored after 1870.

The continuity between the thirty years after independence and the colonial period is remarkable. Economic changes were few. Agriculture and the large estate retained their prominence, and the new nations became as subservient to British economic policies as they once had been to those of Spain and Portugal. The wars of independence had shaken and weakened some of the foundation stones of society, but the edifice stood pretty much intact. A small, privileged elite ruled over muted although sometimes restless masses. Less than one in ten Latin Americans could read and less than one in twenty earned enough to live in even modest comfort. Land remained the principal source of wealth, prestige, and power, and a few owned much of the land.

There were also, however, some significant changes. The first and most obvious was the transmission of power from the Iberians to the creole and mazombo elites. Political power no longer emanated from Europe; it had a local source. The second was the emergence of the military in Spanish America as an important political institution destined to play a decisive role in Latin

American history. The military was the elite's only guarantee of order, and initially it provided prestigious employment for some sons of the rich as well as a means of upward mobility for ambitious plebeians. Early in the national period, the liberals challenged the status of the military, thus alienating the officers and driving them into the welcoming embrace of the conservatives. The remarkable early stability of both Brazil and Chile can be explained in part by the close identification and harmony between conservatives and the military.

Mexico, perhaps more than any other Latin American country, epitomized the problems faced by the new nations in the early nineteenth century. Leaders tried to unite a huge geographical area, separated by mountains, deserts, forests and jungles. After its initial experiment with monarchy, Mexico was riven by competing Liberal and Conservative factions. The country suffered repeated invasions—by Spain in 1829, France in 1838, and the United States in 1846. Intense local regionalism and splits between folk and elite cultures led to internal dissent—Texas in 1836, the Caste War of the Yucatán in 1847. In the struggle for power, the presidency changed hands thirty-six times from 1833 to 1855, for an average term of seven and a half months. The only stability was provided by Antonio López de Santa Anna, an independence hero who became a caudillo and served as president eleven times.

Domingo F. Sarmiento, *Civilization and Barbarism*

Domingo Faustino Sarmiento (1811–88) was among the foremost
liberal reformers and authors of the nineteenth century. He was a
tireless opponent of the caudillo Juan Manuel de Rosas, a follow-
er of Horace Mann who advocated for widespread education,
and served as president of Argentina from 1868 to 1874. In his
most famous work, *Facundo o la civilización y barbarie,* he articu-
lates the liberal, elite preference for an urban, Europeanized way
of life.

    The people who inhabit these extensive districts belong to
two different races, the Spanish and the native; the combinations
of which form a series of imperceptible gradations. The pure
Spanish race predominates in the rural districts of Cordova and
San Luis, where it is common to met young shepherdesses fair
and rosy, and as beautiful as the belles of a capital could wish to
be. In Santiago del Estero, the bulk of the rural population still
speaks the Quichua dialect, which plainly shows its Indian origin.
The country people of Corrientes use a very pretty Spanish
dialect. . . . The Andalusian soldier may still be recognized in the
rural districts of Buenos Ayres; and in the city foreign surnames
are the most numerous. The negro race, by this time nearly extinct
(except in Buenos Ayres), has left, in its zambos and mulattos, a
link which connects civilized man with the denizen of the woods.
This race mostly inhabiting cities, has a tendency to become
civilized, and possesses talent and the finest instincts of progress.
    With these reservations, a homogenous whole has resulted
from the fusion of the three above-named families. It is
characterized by love of idleness and incapacity for industry,
except when education and the exigencies of a social position
succeed in spurring it out of its customary pace. To a great extent,
this unfortunate result is owing to the incorporation of the native
tribes, effected by the process of colonization. The American
aborigines live in idleness, and show themselves incapable, even
under compulsion, of hard and protracted labor. This suggested
the idea of introducing negroes into America, which has produced
such fatal results. But the Spanish race has not shown itself more
energetic than the aborigines, when it has been left to its own
instincts in the wilds of America. Pity and shame are excited by
the comparison of one of the German or Scotch colonies in the
southern part of Buenos Ayres and some towns of the interior of
the Argentine Republic; in the former the cottages are painted,
the front-yards always neatly kept and adorned with flowers and
pretty shrubs; the furniture simple but complete; copper or tin
utensils always bright and clean; nicely curtained beds; and the

occupants of the dwelling are always industriously at work. Some such families have retired to enjoy the conveniences of city life, with great fortunes gained by their previous labors in milking their cows, and making butter and cheese. The town inhabited by natives of the country presents a picture entirely the reverse. There, dirty and ragged children live, with a menagerie of dogs; there, men lie about in utter idleness; neglect and poverty prevail everywhere; a table and some baskets are the only furniture of wretched huts remarkable for their general aspect of barbarism and carelessness. . . .

Upon the boundless expanse above described stand scattered here and there fourteen cities, each the capital of a province. The obvious method of arranging their names would be to classify them according to their geographical position. . . . But this manner of enumerating the Argentine towns has no connection with any of the social results which I have in view. A classification adapted to my purpose must originate in the ways of life pursued by the country people, for it is this which determines their character and spirit. . . .

All the Argentine provinces, except San Juan and Mendoza, depend on the products of pastoral life; Tucuman avails itself of agriculture also, and Buenos Ayres, besides raising millions of cattle and sheep, devotes itself to the numerous and diversified occupations of civilized life.

The Argentine cities, like almost all the cities of South America, have an appearance of regularity. Their streets are laid out at right angles, and their population scattered over a wide surface, except in Cordova, which occupies a narrow and confined position, and presents all the appearance of a European city, the resemblance being increased by the multitude of towers and domes attached to its numerous and magnificent churches. All civilization, whether native, Spanish, or European, centers in the cities, where are to be found the manufactories, the shops, the schools and colleges, and other characteristics of civilized nations. Elegance of style, articles of luxury, dress-coats, and frock-coats, with other European garments, occupy their appropriate place in these towns. I mention these small matters designedly. It is sometimes the case that the only city of a pastoral province is its capital, and occasionally the land is uncultivated up to its very streets. The encircling desert besets such cities at a greater or less distance, and bears heavily upon them, and they are thus small oases of civilization surrounded by an untilled plain, hundreds of square miles in extent, the surface of which is but rarely interrupted by any settlement of consequence.

The cities of Buenos Ayres and Cordova have succeeded better than the others in establishing about them subordinate towns to serve as new foci of civilization and municipal interests; a fact which deserves notice. The inhabitants of the city wear the European dress, live in a civilized manner, and possess laws, ideas of progress, means of instruction, some municipal organization, regular forms of government, etc. Beyond the precincts of the city everything assumes a new aspect; the country people wear a different dress, which I will call South American, as it is common to all districts; their habits of life are different, their wants peculiar and limited. The people composing these two distinct forms of society do not seem to belong to the same nation. Moreover, the countryman, far from attempting to imitate the customs of the city, rejects with disdain its luxury and refinement; and, it is unsafe for the costume of the city people, their coats, their cloaks, their saddles, or anything European, to show themselves in the country. Everything civilized which the city contains is blockaded there, proscribed beyond its limits; and any one who should dare to appear in the rural districts in a frock-coat, for example, or mounted on an English saddle, would bring ridicule and brutal assaults upon himself.

The whole remaining population inhabit the open country, which, whether wooded or destitute of the large plants, is generally level, and almost everywhere occupied by pastures, in some places of such abundance and excellence, that the grass of an artificial meadow would not surpass them. Mendoza and especially San Juan are exceptions to this general absence of tilled fields, the people here depending chiefly on the products of agriculture. Everywhere else, pasturage being plenty, the means of subsistence of the inhabitants—for we cannot call it their occupation—is stock-raising. Pastoral life reminds us of the Asiatic plains, which imagination covers with Kalmuck, Cossack or Arab tents. The primitive life of nations—a life essentially barbarous and unprogressive—the life of Abraham, which is that of the Bedouin of to-day, prevails in the Argentine plains, although modified in a peculiar manner by civilization. The Arab tribe which wanders through the wilds of Asia, is united under the rule of one of its elders or of a warrior chief; society exists, although not fixed in any determined locality. Its religious opinions, immemorial traditions, unchanging customs, and its sentiments of respect for the aged, make altogether a code of laws and a form of government which preserves morality, as it is there understood, as well as order and the association of the tribe. But progress is impossible, because there can be no progress without permanent possession of the soil, or without cities, which are the means of developing the capacity of man for the processes of industry, and which enable him to extend his acquisitions. . . .

Before 1810, two distinct, rival, and incompatible forms of society, two differing kinds of civilization existed in the Argentine Republic: one being Spanish, European, and cultivated, the other barbarous, American, and almost wholly of native growth. The revolution [1810] which occurred in the cities acted only as the cause, the impulse, which set these two distinct forms of national existence face to face, and gave occasion for a contest between them, to be ended, after lasting many years, by the absorption of one into the other.

I have pointed out the normal form of association, or want of association, of the country people, a form worse, a thousand times, than that of the nomad tribe. I have described the artificial associations formed in idleness, and the sources of fame among the gauchos—bravery, daring, violence, and opposition to regular law, to the civil law, that is, of the city. These phenomena of social organization existed in 1810, and still exist, modified in many points, slowly changing in others, and yet untouched in several more. These foci, about which were gathered the brave, ignorant, free, and unemployed peasantry, were found by thousands through the country. The revolution of 1810 carried everywhere commotion and the sound of arms. Public life, previously wanting in this Arabico-Roman society, made its appearance in all the taverns, and the revolutionary movement finally brought about provincial, warlike associations, called *montoneras,* legitimate offspring of the tavern and the field, hostile to the city and to the army of revolutionary patriots. As events succeed each other, we shall see the provincial montoneras headed by their chiefs; the final triumph, in Facundo Quiroga, of the country over the cities throughout the land; and by their subjugation in spirit, government, and civilization, the final formation of the central consolidated despotic government of the landed proprietor, Don Juan Manuel Rosas, who applied the knife of the gaucho to the culture of Buenos Ayres, and destroyed the work of centuries— of civilization, law, and liberty. . . .

Thus elevated, and hitherto flattered by fortune, Buenos Ayres set about making a constitution for itself and the Republic, just as it had undertaken to liberate itself and all South America: that is, eagerly, uncompromisingly, and without regard to obstacles. Rivadavia was the personification of this poetical, utopian spirit which prevailed. He therefore continued the work of Las Heras upon the large scale necessary for a great American State—a republic. He brought over from Europe men of learning for the press and for the professor's chair, colonies for the deserts, ships for the rivers, freedom for all creeds, credit and the national bank to encourage trade, and all the great social theories of the day for the formation of government. In a word, he brought a second Europe, which was to be established in America, and to accomplish in ten years what elsewhere had required centuries. Nor was this project altogether chimerical; all his administrative creations still exist, except those which the barbarism of Rosas found in its way. Freedom of conscience, advocated by the chief clergy of Buenos Ayres, has not been repressed; the European population is scattered on farms throughout the country, and takes arms of its own accord to resist the only obstacle in the way of the wealth offered by the soil. The rivers only need to be freed from governmental restrictions to become navigable, and the national bank, then firmly established, has saved the people from the poverty to which the tyrant would have brought them. And, above all, however fanciful and impracticable that great system of government may have been, it was at least easy and endurable for the people; and, notwithstanding the assertions of misinformed men, Rivadavia never shed a drop of blood, nor destroyed the property of any one; but voluntarily descended from the Presidency to poverty and exile. Rosas, by whom he was so calumniated, might easily have been drowned in the blood of his won victims, and the forty millions of dollars from the national treasury, with the fifty millions from private fortunes which were consumed in ten years of the long war provoked by his brutalities, would have been employed by the *"fool*—the *dreamer,* Rivadavia,"* in building canals, cities, and useful public buildings. Then let this man, who died for his country, have the glory of representing the highest aspirations of European civilization, and leave to his adversaries that of displaying South American barbarism in its most odious light. For Rosas and Rivadavia are the two extremes of the Argentine Republic, connecting it with savages through the pampas, and with Europe through the river La Plata. . . .

Ah! when will an impartial history of the Argentine Republic be written? And when will its people be able, without fear of a tyrant, to read the terrible drama of the revolution,— the well-intentioned and brilliant, but chimerical government of Rivadavia; the power and brutal deeds of Facundo Quiroga; and the administration of Rosas, the great tyrant of the nineteenth century, who unconsciously revived the spirit of the Middle Ages, and the doctrine of equality armed with the knife of Danton and Robespierre. . . . If we lack an intelligent population, let the people of Europe once feel that there is a permanent peace and freedom in our country, and multitudes of emigrants would find their way to a land where success is sure. No, we are not the lowest among Americans. Something is to result from this chaos; either something surpassing the government of the United States of North America, or something a thousand times worse than that of Russia,—the Dark Ages returned, or political institutions, superior to any yet known.

Source: Domingo F. Sarmiento, *Life in the Argentine Republic in the Days of the Tyrants: Or Civilization and Barbarism* (N.Y.: Hafner, n.d.), 10–15, 54–55, 126–27, 246–47. Reprinted with permission of The Free Press, a Division of Simon & Schuster, Inc., from *Life in the Argentine Republic in the Days of the Tyrants, or Civilization and Barbarism* by Domingo F. Sarmiento. Translated by Mrs. Horace Mann (New York: The Free Press, 1970).

El Gaucho Martín Fierro

José Fernández (1834–86) reclaimed the image of the gaucho
with his epic poem Martín Fierro, published in 1872 and 1879.
Contrary to Sarmiento's views of the gaucho as barbarian, Fernández gives us the honest man, soul of Argentina, put upon by
the corrupt forces of government and business.

I am a gaucho, and take this from me
as my tongue explains to you:
for me the earth is a small place
and it could well be bigger—
the snake does not bite me
nor the sun burn my brow.

I was born as a fish is born
at the bottom of the sea;
no one can take from me
what I was given by God—
what I brought into the world
I shall take from the world with me.

It is my glory to live as free
as a bird in the sky:
I make no nest on this ground
where there's so much to be suffered,
and no one will follow me when I take flight again. . . .

Let whoever may be listening
to the tale of my sorrows—
know that I never fight nor kill
except when it has to be done,
and that only injustice threw me
into so much adversity.

And listen to the story told
by a gaucho who's hunted by the law;
who's been a father and husband
hard-working and willing—
and in spite of that, people take him
to be a criminal. . . .

In my part of the land, at one time,
I had children, cattle, and a wife;
but my sufferings began,

they pushed me out to the frontier—
and when I got back, what was I to find!
a ruin, and nothing more. . . .

You couldn't call that service
nor defending the frontier,
it was more like a nest of rats
where the strongest one plays the cat—
it was like gambling with a loaded dice.

Everything here works the wrong way round,
soldiers turned into laborer
and go round the settlements
out on loan for work—
they join them up again to fight
when the Indian robbers break in.

In this merry-go-round, I've seen
many officers who owned land,
with plenty of work-hands
and herds of cattle and sheep—
I may not be educated
but I've seen some ugly deals. . . .

I was returning after three years
of suffering so much for nothing,
a deserter, naked and penniless,
in search of a better life—
and like an armadillo
I headed straight for my den.

I found not a trace of my cabin—
there was only the empty shell.
Christ! if that wasn't a sight
to bring sorrow to your heart. . . .
I swore at that moment
to be as pitiless as a wild beast. . . .

I mounted, and trusting to God,
I made for another district—
because a gaucho they call a vagrant
can have no place of his own,
and so he lives from one trouble to the next
lamenting what he has lost.

He's always on the run,
always poor and hounded,

he has neither a hole nor a nest
as if there were a curse on him,
because being a gaucho . . . curse it,
being a gaucho is a crime.

Source: José Fernández, *The Gaucho Martín Fierro*, bilingual edition. English
version by Catherine E. Ward. (N.Y.: State University of New York Press, 1967), 9,
11, 23, 63, 77, 101. Reprinted by prmission of the State University of New York
Press © 1967, State University of New York. All rights reserved.

5

The Emergence of the Modern State

By the mid-nineteenth century, the chaos of the early independence years had given way to the emergence of a new political stability and economic prosperity. Foreign threats had diminished; the republican principle had triumphed everywhere but in Brazil; and centralized government had been gradually accepted. Nationalism became a better-defined force as more and more citizens in the various states expressed greater pride in their homeland, appreciated its uniqueness, and sought its progress. Feuding elites realized that they would profit most from stable governments that would encourage foreign investment and trade. Positivist ideology dominated governmental circles and complemented foreign investment and capitalist expansion. However, while elites overcame many of their earlier divisions to concentrate on the national project of "progress," large numbers of the population felt marginalized and threatened by the changes. They responded with protests and at times violence.

While political change and instability had marked the first half of the nineteenth century, economic and social innovations as well as political stability characterized the last half. An accelerating prosperity—at least for the favored classes—encouraged material growth and attracted a wave of immigrants, particularly to Argentina, Brazil, and Chile. The combination of stability and prosperity helped to accelerate three trends: industrialization, urbanization, and modernization, which in turn threatened to alter some of the established patterns inherited from the colonial past.

But to understand the successes, failures, and challenges of the last half of the nineteenth century, the historian must question the type of economic growth that occurred and who benefited from it.

Political Stability

The conflict among elites that characterized the early national period gave way to agreement on a new economic project: the large-scale export of primary products and the import of foreign capital and manufactured goods, accompanied by limited industrialization. This new economic order required political order, for without political stability, foreigners would not invest in Latin America.

With civil disorder on the wane, the chiefs of state consolidated and extended their authority. They governed supremely with few if any checks from the congresses and the courts, which they customarily dominated. In some cases, they selected their own successors, who were assured of impressive electoral victories. Nonetheless, a greater respect for legal forms prevailed, and some caudillos even appeared to be more legally conscious and circumspect than their predecessors. At any rate, they paid more lip service to constitutional formalities and some even showed an occasional indication of heeding the constitution. In somber frock coats, representatives of the elite discussed and debated the political issues of the day.

The term "elite" can be hard to define. First, one must recognize that no single elite existed in any of the Latin American nations. Rather, a plurality of elites combined in various ways to dominate each nation. At best, elite is a shorthand expression signifying those in social, economic, and political control. Because of their economic power, wealth, prestige, knowledge of Europe and the ideas originating there, skills, influence, and importance, the small but varied groups of elites one way or another exerted authority over a society whose formal institutions were of European inspiration. They made the major decisions affecting the economic and political life of their nations.

The earlier political division between conservative and liberal prevailed. The liberals often flirted with federalist schemes, maintained a theoretical interest in the rights of man, demanded an end to the Church's temporal powers, embraced laissez-faire economic doctrine, and professed a willingness to experiment with new ideas and methods. The conservatives, on the other hand, lauded centralism, defended a hierarchical society, approved the privileges and prerogatives of the Church, and felt more comfortable with a controlled or regulated economic system. However, neither political division expressed any desire to tamper with the major land, labor, and social systems. Nor did either party become seriously concerned with extending the suffrage.

Consequently, on many fundamental issues the two major political divisions harmonized rather than diverged. In Brazil, the Visconde de Albuquerque wryly remarked, "There is nothing quite so much like a Conservative as a Liberal in office." More distinctive than party labels were the personalities. The individual, rather than a vague catalog of political ideas, attracted or repelled support. The politician as a man, as a leader, exercised far more strength than the more abstract institution, the party.

Two countries were unusual in achieving political stability early in the century: Brazil and Chile. Brazil had enjoyed stability during the First Empire (1822–31); but during the regency established after the abdication of Pedro I, regional forces threatened the empire. One province after another, from the far north to the far south, rebelled against the government in Rio de Janeiro. To save national unity, the Brazilians proclaimed the young Pedro II emperor in 1840, four years before he was legally of age to ascend the throne. As expected, the monarchy, the only truly effective national institution in Brazil, provided the ideal instrument to impose unity on the disintegrating nation. Brazil's nearly disastrous experiment with federalism ended when Pedro II reimposed a high degree of centralism on the nation. In 1847, the emperor created the post of President of the Council of Ministers, and a type of parliamentary system developed. The emperor saw to it that the two political parties, Liberals and Conservatives, alternated in power.

The fall of a Liberal ministry in 1868 divided the political history of the Second Empire. The Liberals blamed the heavy hand of the emperor for their loss of power, in their opinion nothing short of a coup d'etat. As a result, the next year the Liberals issued a reform manifesto. If enacted, their federalist program would have weakened the government in Rio de Janeiro. At the same time, the Federal Republican Party emerged, and in a December 1870 manifesto denounced the monarchy and called for a federal republic. By 1870, significant structural change had been proposed, including the abolition of slavery, substitution of a republic for a monarchy and federalism for centralism, and the expansion of the political base.

The foundations of the monarchy slowly weakened. In the early 1870s, a church–crown conflict alienated conservatives allied with the church. The dispute began when the Bishop of Olinda carried out a papal order, unapproved by the emperor, to expel Masons from the lay brotherhoods of the Roman Catholic Church. Pedro II ordered the bishop to remove the penalty. His refusal to comply directly challenged the emperor. The government arrested and jailed the churchman along with another bishop, and the royal courts found both guilty of disobeying civil law. The situation worsened in 1888 with the manumission of the slaves without any compensation to the owners, causing an·important sector of the landowning class to abandon the emperor. Emancipation had been brought about largely by urban groups who did not identify closely with the monarchy, which they felt did not represent their interests. They viewed the aging emperor as a symbol of the past, anathema to the modernization they preached. It was among these urban groups that republican doctrine spread. That doctrine, as well as the urban mentality, also pervaded the army officer corps. Pedro had ignored the military officers, an increasingly restless group in the 1880s. In them, the disgruntled clergy, landowners, and urban dwellers, as well as the coffee planters, found their instrument for political change. The republican cause won many military converts, particularly among the junior officers who equated a republic with progress and modernization. The fate of the monarchy was sealed when the principal military leader, Marshal Deodoro da Fonseca, switched his allegiance and proclaimed himself in favor of a republic. Under his leadership on November 15, 1889, the army overthrew the monarchy and declared Brazil to be a republic. The old emperor abdicated and, like his father before him, sailed into European exile. The transition was bloodless. A new constitution, presidential, federal, democratic, and republican, was promulgated on February 24, 1891.

Chile reached stability even earlier. By 1830, a small and powerful landowning class had consolidated quickly in the relatively small geographic area of central Chile, hemmed in by the arid Atacama Desert to the north and unconquered Mapuche Indians to the south. From the ranks of the relatively homogenous conservative elites emerged one of Chile's most skillful leaders of the nineteenth century, Diego Portales. Through his force and efficiency, he imposed conservative rule in 1830, and it lasted until 1861. Although he never served as president, he held various ministerial portfolios and ruled behind the scenes until his assassination in 1837. Portales was concerned with power, discipline, stability, and order, not social or economic reforms. In sharp contrast to the rest of Spanish America, he succeeded in subordinating the army to a civilian government, thereby removing the military from nineteenth-century politics. He also framed the Constitution of 1833, which lasted until 1925.

Presidential mandates in Chile lasted five years and could be renewed for an additional five. Three conservative leaders each held the office for ten years, enforcing the remarkable stability imposed by Portales. Manuel Montt, who served from 1851 to 1861, accepted a moderate, José Joaquín Pérez, to succeed him. The thirty years, 1861–91, were a period of liberal rule tempered by conservative opposition, in direct contrast to the preceding three decades. The major reforms enacted by the liberals indicated the direction and degree of change they advocated: private liberty of worship in houses and schools, the establishment of cemeteries for non-Catholics, the abolition of the privileged Church courts, civil marriage, freedom of the press, no reelection of the president, a modification of the electoral reform law to substitute a literacy test for property qualifications, greater autonomy for municipal governments, and the power of congress to override a presidential veto. As is obvious, none of these altered the power structure in Chile, none attempted to shift the social and economic imbalance of the country. Chile's record of stability and order encouraged economic prosperity and material progress.

Argentina and Mexico experienced far greater difficulty than Chile and

Brazil in their search for political stability. After Rosas fell in 1852, the city and province of Buenos Aires refused to adhere to the new Argentine union, fearful that they would have to surrender too much power. The old struggle between the port and the provinces continued until 1862, when the prestigious and powerful governor of Buenos Aires, Bartolomé Mitre, was able to impose his will on the entire nation. His force and ability reunited the nation. A succession of strong and able presidents, each of whom served for six years, followed him. These presidents wielded almost total power. In 1880 the thorny question of the city and province of Buenos Aires was finally solved. New legislation separated the city from the province, federalized the city, and declared it the national capital, a role it had previously played. The rich province then went on its own way with a new capital, La Plata. Meanwhile, the nation was investing the energy once given to political struggles into economic growth. In 1879–80, General Julio Roca led a war that became known as Conquest of the Desert, although it really constituted the conquest of the Araucanian Indians. With the invention of the repeating rifle, the Argentines were able to finally succeed in overpowering the nonsedentary Indians who had daunted their Spanish forefathers by using the same pattern of annihilation carried out on the United States plains. For his efforts, Roca went on to become president.

Mexico's search for stability was one of the most difficult in Latin America, complicated by questions of federalism and the position of the Church in the new nation. The bloodshed and drama that began in 1810 lasted well over half a century and exhausted the nation. Finally a mestizo strongman, Porfirio Díaz, who had risen through the military ranks to become general and in the process had fought against Santa Anna, the French, and Maximilian, brought peace to Mexico in 1876—an iron peace, as it turned out. For the next thirty-four years, he imposed a conservative, centralized government on Mexico while ruling under the liberal, federal Constitution of 1857. His government brought order and stability to a degree unknown since the colonial period. The strength and political longevity of Díaz rested on the powerful supporting alliance he created. The Church, the army, foreign capitalists, and the great landowners found it beneficial to back his regime, and they reaped substantial material rewards for their allegiance. On the other hand, the wily Díaz manipulated them at will for his own ends; for example, he promoted potential rivals to positions that required they relocate, undermining any chance of building a local power base. Under his guidance, Mexico made outstanding material progress and witnessed a prosperity surpassing the best years of colonial mining. The supporting alliance that Díaz formed proved to be the most effective combination of forces to promote political stability. To varying degrees the chiefs of states of other nations made use of similar combinations to buttress their power. The two key groups obviously were the army and the landowners.

In country after country in the late nineteenth century, Latin American elites followed the Argentine and Mexican patterns. They realized that years of political in-fighting had done nothing for the country, and little for their personal wealth. Latin America offered investment opportunities for the wealth of Great Britain's expanding industry only if it could achieve political unity—foreigners were not eager to invest in countries where governments changed hands on an annual basis and the security of investments could not be guaranteed. Latin American elites cast aside their political differences in the interests of attracting foreign investment.

Positivism and Progress

Latin American elites looked longingly at the material progress being made in Great Britain, France, Germany, and the United States. Many of them had mastered French, the second language of the elite, and a few had a knowledge of English or German, which gave them direct access to information and literature from the nations whose progress impressed them. The newspapers carried full accounts of what was happening in the leading nations of the Western world, and the programs of the learned societies featured discussions of the technical advances of the industrializing nations. Many members of the elite traveled abroad and were exposed to the innovations firsthand. They returned to their quieter capitals in the New World with a nostalgia for Paris and the irrepressible desire to mimic everything they had seen there. Of course, the imports bore testimony to larger segments of the population of the manufacturing skill and ingenuity of those technically advanced societies.

The elites closely followed the intellectual trends of Europe. In fact, they could more readily discuss the novels of Émile Zola or Gustave Flaubert than those of Jorge Isaacs or Machado de Assis, and they paused to admire European painters while they ignored the canvases of their compatriots. Not surprisingly, some members of the elite became knowledgeable about the new philosophy of Positivism, formulated in Europe during the second quarter of the nineteenth century by French philosopher and sociologist Auguste Comte. They eventually imported it into Latin America, where governments warmly welcomed it.

Many of the ideas on progress that the Latin Americans extracted from the Enlightenment, Charles Darwin, Herbert Spencer, as well as from other sources, seemed to converge in Comte's Positivism. Comte maintained that societies could advance through scientific, rational processes. He defined three stages of social development: the theological, characterized by belief in the supernatural; metaphysical, a belief in ideas as reality; and the positive stage, in which phenomena are explained by observation, hypothesis, and experimentation. Outward manifestations of progress—railroads and industrialization were prime examples—assumed great importance in Positivism and emphatically so among the Latin Americans, whether they acknowledged Comte or not.

With its emphasis on material growth and well-being, Positivism ideally suited the trends of the last half of the century. It favored a capitalist mentality, regarding private wealth as sacred. Indeed, private accumulation of wealth was a sign of progress as well as an instrument for progress. Because of the weakness of domestic, private institutions, the state had to assume the role of directing progress. Deferring to the role of the state over the individual, Positivism complemented the patriarchal experience of the Latin Americans. Of course, to promote capitalism and to direct progress, the state, according to Positivist doctrine, had to maintain order and impose stability. With its special emphasis on order and progress, Positivism reached the height of its influence between 1880 and 1900. It became an official doctrine of the Díaz regime in Mexico; some of his principal ministers, who fittingly were known as *científicos,* had imbibed deeply of Comte's doctrines and tried to offer a scientific solution to the problems of organizing national life. As Mexico's Nobel-winning poet Octavio Paz would reflect, "Positivism offered the social hierarchies a new justification. Inequalities were now explained, not by race or inheritance or religion, but by science."

In Venezuela, President Antonio Guzmán Blanco governed directly or indirectly from 1870 to 1888 under the influence of Positivism. First he imposed order and then set out in pursuit of elusive progress. Order meant the consolidation of the past and admitted minimal social change, while progress signified the adoption of the outward manifestations of European civilization. Dreaming of Paris, Guzmán Blanco laid out wide boulevards for Caracas and constructed an opera house as well as a pantheon for national heroes. New railroads and expanded port facilities speeded Venezuela's exports to European markets to pay for the material progress.

Positivism also attracted many adherents in Brazil, particularly among the new graduates of the technical and military schools, members of the fledgling middle class. They favored the abolition of slavery, the establishment of a republic (albeit not a democratic one), and the separation of Church and state, changes that did occur in Brazil between 1888 and 1891. Material progress absorbed much of their concern. The flag of the Brazilian republic, created in 1889, bears to the present the Positivist motto "Order and Progress."

Where political stability and economic prosperity existed, notable material progress occurred. It is not surprising that Brazil and Chile were among the first Latin American nations to experiment with the inventions and innovations offered by Europe and the United States and correlated with progress. The steam engine made an early appearance in these two nations. In 1815, Bahia boasted its first steam-driven sugar mill. Two years later Pernambuco also possessed one. By 1834, there were 64 of them in operation, a number that rose to 144 by 1852 and then increased rapidly thereafter. At the same time, the coffee processors were beginning to acquire steam-driven machinery. In Chile, the first steam-powered flour mill went into operation in 1839. By 1863, Chile counted 132 steam engines used in sawmills, distilleries, blower furnaces, flour mills, and coal mines.

None of the innovations had more impact than the railroads. Its steel rails had the potential of linking formerly divided territories. Penetrating distant regions, the railroads tapped new sources of economic prosperity. Bulky and perishable products could be rushed over long distances to eager markets. Just as important, troops could be sent on the railroad, bringing state power to the most distant corners.

Cuba can boast of the first railroad in Latin America. The line from Havana to Güines, approximately thirty miles, began operation in 1838. Chile initiated its first railroad in 1852 and a decade later had laid 543 miles of track. A new Brazilian law in 1852 provided favorable conditions for any entrepreneur who would undertake to construct a railroad. The capitalist Viscount Mauá accepted the challenge and in 1854 inaugurated a line of ten miles. By 1874, there were approximately 800 miles of track. After 1875, construction increased rapidly: from 1875 to 1884, 2,200 miles were laid; from 1885 to 1889, 2,500 more miles. By 1889, then, trackage totaled approximately 6,000 miles. Argentina's railroad era began in 1857 with the inauguration of a seven-mile line. The government offered a variety of inducements to encourage its expansion: the duty-free entry of materials and equipment, interest guarantees, and land grants. British capital readily responded and dominated rail construction. Britain supplied technicians and engineers as well and then sold English coal to the railroad companies to run the steam engines. In 1914, Argentina boasted the most extensive railroad network in Latin America and the eighth largest in the world. In total, South America's railroad mileage grew from 2,000 miles in 1870 to 59,000 in 1900.

Mexico began its railroad construction slowly. When Díaz took power in 1876, only 400 miles had been laid. By the end of his regime, there were approximately 15,000 miles of rail. The railroads contributed to Mexican national prosperity, bringing the products of distant regions to market, making distant land valuable, and creating a national market. The railroads tapped new minerals for export. While Mexico before the railroads had sold only silver abroad, the railroads made it possible to export zinc, lead, and copper, intensifying the flow of Mexico's natural resources to the industrialized nations. It is noteworthy that Mexican exports increased eight and a half times between 1877 and 1910, coinciding with the period of intensive railroad construction. U.S. interests completed the line linking the border with Mexico City so that in May of 1880 it was possible to travel by rail from Chicago to Mexico City for the first time.

Along the newly laid rail lines, at rail junctions, and at railheads sprang up villages and towns. Older settlements took on a new life. The railroad brought the countryside and the city into closer contact, and as a result the isolated and paternalistic patterns of plantation and hacienda life were challenged as never before. The railroads opened new markets for the incipient industries of the large cities and brought into the hinterlands a greater variety of goods than those populations had hitherto seen. Railroads thus helped to promote the fledgling industries. They also provided some amusement during their early years. When the railroad finally reached Guatemala City in the 1880s, it became a custom for the capital's inhabitants of all social levels to congregate at the railroad station for the semiweekly arrivals and departures of the train. On those occasions, the National Band played in the plaza in front of the station for the further entertainment of the crowd.

While railroads perfectly illustrated Latin America's urge to progress, they exerted an ironic negative influence on development. They deepened Latin America's dependency, strengthened the neocolonial institutions, and impoverished the governments. The primary explanation for these adverse effects lay in the fact that more often than not foreigners built and owned the railroads, and put them where they would best complement the North Atlantic economies rather than Latin America's. In Argentina, as but one example, English-financed, -built, -equipped, and -administered railroads carried the resources of the rich pampas to the port of Buenos Aires for their inevitable export. As this example aptly suggests, the railroads served export markets by lowering transportation costs of bulky items, incorporating new regions into commercial agriculture, and opening up new lands and mines to exploitation. More often than not, the railroads expanded and strengthened the latifundia wherever the rails reached, since they often conferred considerable value on lands once considered marginal. Whereas previously peasants had been tolerated on that marginal land, its new value caused the landlords first to push the peasants off the land and then to incorporate them into the estate's labor force. Commercial agriculture, much of it destined for export, replaced subsistence agriculture, and the numbers and size of small landholdings declined. Indian landholdings in particular suffered incursions in those areas touched by railroads. Mexico proved perfectly the equation of railroad expansion to increased exports, growth of the latifundia, disappearance of small farms, and threats to Indian lands. The Indians, however, did not passively acquiesce as the railroad came through their lands. Historian John Coatsworth showed in a landmark study that there were 55 agrarian rebellions from 1877 to 1884; many of these rebellions were so significant that they required the deployment of federal troops to suppress them. Of those 55, 50 took place within 40 kilometers of a railroad route, and 32 of them took place within 20 kilometers.

Bolivia provided a sobering example of the contribution of railroads both to dependency on a single export and to the reduction of food production for local markets. By the end of the nineteenth century, rails connecting the highlands with Pacific ports accelerated tin-ore exports. The rail cars descended the Andes loaded with the ore. In order to fill the otherwise empty cars on their return, the trains carried agricultural products imported from Peru, Chile, and the United States. The importation of food wrought havoc on the agrarian economy of the fertile Santa Cruz region, depriving it of its national market. Production declined sharply. Bolivia became locked into a double dependency status: dependent on foreign markets for its single export and on foreign producers for a part of its food supply.

Costa Rica illustrated in a slightly different but even more disastrous way the effects of railroads on the economy of a small nation. To market larger quantities of coffee and thus earn the money to modernize, the government encouraged the construction of a railroad (1870–90) that stretched from the highlands where the coffee grew to Puerto Limón for shipment abroad. The onerous loans overburdened the treasury as the government paid outrageous interest rates to unscrupulous foreign money lenders. Further, the government bestowed on Chief Engineer Minor Keith 800,000 acres, land that fronted on the railroad and later became the center of the plantations of the United Fruit Company. Meanwhile, the railroad remained in foreign hands. British investors also controlled the ports, mines, electric lighting, major public works, and foreign commerce as well as the principal domestic marketplaces. In short, Costa Rica surrendered all its economic independence and mortgaged its future before 1890 to obtain some of the physical aspects of modernization.

Most of the other Latin American governments also contracted heavy debts to pay for their railroads. Those debts often led to foreign complications and always to some sacrifice of economic independence. One brazen example of foreign intervention triggered by railroad funding occurred in Venezuela. In 1903, German gunboats appeared off the coast to force the government to pay 1.4 million pounds sterling for loans associated with railroad building.

The telegraph furthered the communications revolution in Latin America. Both Chile and Brazil began service over short lines in 1852. The telegraph both contributed to national unity and helped to bring neighboring nations closer together. In 1866, a cable connected Buenos Aires and Montevideo; and the following year the United States opened cable communication with Cuba. The transandine telegraph united Buenos Aires and Santiago in 1872. Brazil inaugurated telegraphic contact with Montevideo in 1879 and with Buenos Aires in 1883. From the United States, the Central and South American Cable Company, formed in 1879, began stretching its cables southward into Middle America and then beyond. By 1882, its line reached as far south as Lima, and in 1890, it extended to Santiago, where it connected with the Transandine Telegraph Company. Transatlantic cables put Latin America in instantaneous communication with Europe. Pedro II dictated the first message to be cabled from Brazil to Europe in 1874. Significantly, Rio de Janeiro was linked to Europe by cable long before it could communicate by telegraph with other parts of its own empire.

The number of international steamship lines serving Latin America increased rapidly during the last half of the century. The principal ports of Europe and the United States were in direct and regular contact with those of Latin America. Sailings became increasingly frequent; ships carried more cargo; service improved. The major ports underwent renovation with the addition of new and larger warehouses, faster loading and unloading machinery, larger and sturdier wharfs, and the dredging of deeper channels.

Clearly not all of Latin America shared fully in the progress. One astonished visitor to the highlands of Ecuador and to Quito in 1885 gasped, "The country does not know the meaning of the words progress and prosperity." At that time, the only communication between Quito, the capital high in the Andes, and Guayaquil, the Pacific port, was still by mule path, a route impassable during six months of the year because of the rainy season. Under optimum conditions, it was possible to make the journey in eight or nine days over the same route in use for centuries. As a port, Guayaquil was in contact with the world and showed signs of modernization long before the isolated capital did. The public streetcar, gas lighting, and other amenities reached Guayaquil years before they could be seen in the capital. Not until the end of the first decade of the twentieth century did a railroad link Guayaquil with Quito. The 227-mile railroad climb from the port to the capital took two days. The slower growth of Ecuador was not unique; it characterized many of the nations that lagged behind the leadership of Argentina, Brazil, Chile, and Mexico.

The concern with improved transportation and communication symbolized the dedication to progress. To a great extent, material advances measured modernization. How many miles of railroads, how much horsepower generated by steam engines, how many tons handled per hour in the ports, how many miles of telegraph wires? The higher the number given in response to these questions, the greater the progress the nation could claim. In their satisfaction with these material advances, the elites seemed oblivious of another aspect of modernization: the very steamships, railroads, and ports tied them and their nations ever more tightly to a handful of industrialized nations in Western Europe and North America, which bought their raw products and provided manufactured goods in return. They failed to see the significance of the fact that many of the railroads did not link the principal cities of their nations but rather ran from the plantations or mines directly to the ports, subordinating the goal of national unification to the demands of the industrial nations for agricultural products and minerals. As the amount of loans increased to pay for the new material progress, the governments had to budget ever greater sums to pay interest rates. As foreign investment rose, the outflow of profit remittances multiplied. Increasingly the voices of foreign investors and bankers spoke with greater authority in making economic decisions for the host countries. Local economic options diminished. In short, progress as it took shape in nineteenth-century Latin America adversely affected the quality of life of the majority and contributed to deepening dependency.

Economic Prosperity

The elites' pursuit of progress had economic prosperity as the goal, and they were not disappointed. Thanks to loans, investments, and rising exports, a growing economy characterized parts of Latin America during the last half of the nineteenth century. That growth came from the consolidation of the export economy.

The demands of the industrialized nations for raw products rose impressively throughout the last half of the nineteenth century. Not only was there a rapidly increasing number of consumers in Western Europe and the United States, but also their per capita purchasing power was ever greater. The United States emerged as the principal industrialized nation of the world and as the foremost consumer of Latin America's exports. As the industrial centers bought more agricultural and mineral products from Latin America, the region's trade underwent a dramatic expansion. Plantation owners and miners produced larger amounts of grain, coffee, sugar, cotton, cacao, bananas, livestock, copper, silver, tin, lead, zinc, and nitrates for export. The natural products—such as palm oils, nuts, woods, rubber, and medicinal plants— also found a ready market abroad, and their exportation rose sharply.

Similar to well-established patterns of the colonial past, the export sector of the economy remained the most active, the dynamic focus of investment, technological improvement, official concern, and demand for labor. More often than not, foreigners, with their own agendas, dominated that sector. Dependency has become a widely used (and frequently abused) concept to describe Latin America's economy. Definitions of that concept vary. A frequently cited one holds dependency to be a situation in which the economy of one nation is conditioned by the development or growth of the economy of a second nation to which the former is subordinated. This historical survey will adopt that definition.

Foreign observers marveled at the rapid rate of increase of Latin American trade in the last half of the nineteenth century. By 1890 Latin America's foreign commerce exceeded 1 billion dollars per year and had increased roughly 43 percent between 1870 and 1884. By comparison, during the same period British trade increased by 27.2 percent. The five principal areas engaged in foreign commerce were Brazil, Argentina, Cuba, Chile, and Mexico, which together accounted for more than three-quarters of Latin America's trade. With the exception of Argentina, they exported more than they imported. Trade statistics for the individual nations were impressive. Argentine exports jumped sevenfold between 1853 and 1873 and doubled again by 1893. Mexican exports quadrupled between 1877 and 1900. The smaller nations benefited too. Exports of coffee from Costa Rica increased fourfold between 1855 and 1915, and tin shipments from Bolivia quadrupled during a four-year period, 1897–1900, and tripled again by 1913.

In Brazil, the value of foreign trade increased by six to seven times between 1833 and 1889, a record made possible by coffee, a relatively new export. At the time of independence, coffee accounted for only about a fifth of Brazil's exports, a figure that rose to two-thirds by 1889. These figures indicate an increase from 190,000 to 5,586,000 in the number of sacks of coffee

The central plaza of La Paz, Bolivia, 1863.

beans shipped to world coffee markets in a sixty-seven-year period. The value of the coffee sold during these years equaled that of all the exports during the entire colonial period. The coffee industry flourished first in the Paraíba Valley in the province of Rio de Janeiro, from which it spread into the neighboring provinces of Minas Gerais and São Paulo.

A number of inventions, among them the railroad, barbed wire, the canning process, and the refrigerator ship, facilitated the exploitation of Argentina's hitherto untamed pampas, potentially one of the world's most fertile regions. The sailing of the first primitive refrigerator ship from Buenos Aires to Europe in 1876 changed the course of Argentine economic history. The successful voyage proved that chilled and frozen beef could be sold in lucrative European markets. Measures were taken at once to improve the quality of the beef. By 1900, 278 refrigerator ships plied between Great Britain and Argentina. During the decade of the 1870s, Argentina also made its first wheat shipments to Europe, a modest 21 tons in 1876. In 1900, wheat exports reached 2,250,000 tons. During the same period, the cultivated acreage on the pampas jumped fifteen times. Exports rose fivefold from 30 million gold pesos in 1870 to 150 million by 1900. This extraordinary economic boom made Argentina the most prosperous nation in Latin America.

Chile offers an excellent but by no means exceptional example of the development of a mineral-exporting economy. Already in the first decades of independence it exported increasing amounts of silver and copper. By midcentury, Chile enjoyed a well-balanced program of exports divided between various minerals and agricultural products. That diversification ended after 1878 when the new nitrate exports grew increasingly important until, within a few years, they dominated the export sector. Dependent on the world's need for nitrates, the Chilean economy declined or prospered according to demand and price for one product. The vulnerability of the economy was obvious.

Most governmental leaders paid far more attention to the international economy than to the national, domestic economy. The export sector of the Latin American economy grew more rapidly than the domestic sector, and income from foreign trade contributed an unusually high percentage of the gross national product. Foreign trade emphatically did not mean commerce among the Latin American states. They were strangers in each other's marketplaces, frequently competitors producing the same export products. Their economies complemented the demands of the distant major capitalistic economies in Western Europe and the United States.

Mounting foreign investments also characterized the Latin American economy in the last half of the nineteenth century. Europe generously sent capital, technology, and technicians to Latin America to assure the increased agricultural and mineral production its factories and urban populations required. The more pronounced stability of Latin America engendered greater confidence and generosity among foreign investors. The politicians of Latin America discovered the advantages of foreign investment. It created new wealth, which caudillos, politicians, and elite alike enjoyed. In a pattern established throughout the hemisphere, Porfirio Díaz meticulously paid off Mexico's foreign debts and decreed laws favorable to foreign investors. Foreign investment poured into Mexico. As investments rose, profit remittances flowed out of Latin America. The foreign capitalists might have invested in part to obtain the raw products they needed, but they also expected a rich return in the form of profits, interest payments, patent fees, and commissions.

To handle the new flow of money, banks, both national and foreign, sprang up with amazing rapidity in the major Latin American cities. Only one bank existed in Brazil in 1845, but in the following twelve years, twelve new banks were founded as the Brazilians began to rapidly expand their banking system. Foreign banks made their appearance in Brazil for the first time with the inauguration of the London and Brazil Bank in Rio de Janeiro in 1862. In that same year, the Bank of London and the River Plate was established in Buenos Aires. The London Bank of Mexico and South America opened in Mexico City in 1864. Spanish, Portuguese, Italian, French, German, and North American banks followed. The banks facilitated international trade and investment.

By the eve of World War I, foreign investments totaled $8.5 billion. The English invested the most, $5 billion, or 20 percent of British overseas investment. The French were second with $1.7 billion, followed very closely by the United States with $1.6 billion. Germany was fourth with somewhat less than $1 billion. The largest share of the money went to Argentina, Brazil, and Mexico, and the most popular investments were railroads, public utilities, and mining. British investments predominated in South America; those of United States capitalists dominated in Mexico and the Caribbean area.

With sources of capital, markets, and headquarters abroad, the foreign investors and businesspeople identified neither with their host countries nor with local needs. Their ability to direct capital investment, their hostility to tariffs, and their preference for free-trade policies exerted an unfavorable influence on Latin America's economic development.

Modest Industrialization

During the last half of the century, the larger and more stable nations began to industrialize in order to meet growing internal demands for manufactured goods, to develop more balanced economies, and to protect the national economies from extremes of fluctuation in international trade. Some far-sighted statesmen believed that without such industrialization the Latin Americans would be doomed to economic dependency and backwardness. The Chilean Manuel Camilo Vial, Minister of Finance during the administration of Manuel Bulnes (1841–51), preached, "Any nation in which agriculture dominates everything, in which slavery or feudalism shows its odious face, follows the march of humanity among the stragglers. . . .That future threatens us also, if we do not promote industry with a firm hand and a constant will." The governments raised the tariffs, particularly during the final decades of the century, to encourage and protect the new industries and from time to time promulgated other legislation such as tax incentives and permission to import machinery duty-free to give further impetus to the process. Despite such disadvantages as limited capital, unskilled labor, low labor productivity, lack of coal, limited markets, and a mentality emphasizing the continued reliance on the exploitation of mineral and agricultural possibilities, industrialization grew gradually in the last decades of the nineteenth century.

The burgeoning cities provided a ready labor supply for the new industrialization. Women—and all too many children—worked in the factories. Women had always played a major role in agriculture. While traveling in Central America in the mid-nineteenth century, William V. Wells observed, "I have always found the women of the lower classes in Central America simple, kind-hearted, and hospitable, generally performing the most laborious part of the work, and never tiring under their ceaseless tasks. They are truly the hewers of wood and drawers of water." In the last half of the century, increasing numbers of females tended the new industrial machinery, working the same long hours as men but for lower wages.

In the beginning, industrialization was primarily concerned with the processing of natural products for local consumption or export. Flour mills, sugar refineries, meat-packaging plants, tanning factories, lumber mills, wineries, and breweries developed wherever the requisite resources were at hand. Then service industries appeared: gas and electric utilities, repair shops and foundries, and construction enterprises. Finally, protected industries began to manufacture other goods for home consumption, principally textiles or processed food.

In Brazil, the textile industry was by far the most important. The nine cotton mills in 1865 multiplied into 100 before the fall of the empire. The new republican government that came to power in 1889 visualized an industrial expansion for the nation. Symbolic of their ambitions, the Republicans changed the name of the Ministry of Agriculture to the Ministry of Industry. As further encouragement, they promulgated a protective tariff in 1890, raising to 60 percent the duty on 300 items, principally textiles and food products, that competed with nationally produced goods. Conversely they lowered the duty on primary goods used in national manufacturing. The tariff rose again in 1896 and still higher in 1900. Fundamental to any industrialization, the government established four new engineering schools in the 1890s.

The Argentine government began to turn its attention seriously to the encouragement of industrialization during the 1870s. In 1876, it enacted a high protective tariff. Industrialization concentrated in and around Buenos Aires, which by 1889 counted some 400 industrial establishments employing approximately 11,000 workers. During the last decade of the century, larger factories appeared and industry began to penetrate other regions, although Buenos Aires would always remain the focal point. The census of 1895 listed the number of factories and workshops as 23,000 with 170,000 employees (small workshops employing fewer than ten workers were by far the most common); the next census, 1914, raised the number of factories and workshops to 49,000 and the number of employees to 410,000. By that time, Argentina manufactured 37 percent of the processed foods its inhabitants consumed, 17 percent of the clothing they wore, and 12 percent of the metals and machinery they used.

Under Porfirio Díaz, Mexicans also used their success in export production to invest in manufacturing. By 1902, there were 5,500 manufacturing interests in Mexico. The most important industries were iron and steel, developed with a combination of foreign and domestic finance. New industries included production of cement, textiles, cigarettes, soap, bricks, furniture, flour, and beer, including José Schneider's 1890 founding of the Cerveceria Cuahtemoc, which produced Carta Blanca. Industrial production tripled during the Porfiriato, and the value of manufacturing rose by 6 percent a year. Despite these increases, manufacturing was still dwarfed by production of primary products, and industrial labor did not exceed 15 percent of the nation's workforce.

The most progress in manufacturing took place in Argentina, Brazil,

Chile, Mexico, and Peru. Among the five, domestic production of consumer goods reached 50 to 80 percent. However, the goods were largely of low quality, protected by tariffs, and no progress was made towards the creation of manufactured goods for export.

Progress on the Periphery

Few parts of Latin America were left untouched by the drive for progress of the late nineteenth century. Even areas that had been poor backwaters in the colonial period followed the same patterns as the rest of the region by orienting their economies and polities to the export market. The small Central American nation of Nicaragua is one example.

As early as 1835, the Nicaraguan government tried to promote exports by giving ten-year tax exemptions to the production of indigo, cochineal, and coffee. It soon became clear that the most likely success was coffee production on Nicaragua's fertile highlands. By 1846, the government exempted coffee planters, their family and workers from military service and exempted coffee farms from taxes. Production was encouraged in 1858 by allowing the growers to import duty-free goods equivalent to the value of the coffee they exported. The government undertook transportation and communications improvements, with an eye toward the coffee market. The first telegraph lines were established in 1876, and in 1882, underwater telegraph lines connected Nicaragua to the world's major cities; by 1890, there were 2,478 kilometers of telegraph lines, and by 1905 there were 4,330 kilometers. Construction of the railroad, Ferrocarril del Pacífico de Nicaragua, began in Corinto in 1878, and by 1886, it had reached the port of Momotombo on Lake Nicaragua. By 1893, there were 144 kilometers of railroad in the Pacific region, and by 1909, 275 kilometers. Furthermore, coffee planters were not charged for shipping their produce on the government-owned railroads. Clearly, Nicaragua's economic and political leaders were interested in developing the economy and, starting in the mid-nineteenth century, saw coffee as the way to do it. Both the Conservative governments (1862–1892) and the Liberal government of José Santos Zelaya (1893–1909) threw their support behind the new export commodity.

Nicaraguan farmers responded to the incentives provided by the government and the market: 26 million trees were in production by 1892. Exports rose from 4.5 million pounds in 1880 to 11.3 million by 1890. From 1904 to 1924, coffee exports averaged 23 million pounds a year. In 1871, coffee represented only 10 percent of the value of Nicaragua's exports, in fourth place behind indigo, rubber, and gold. By the 1880s, coffee had become the country's most important export. In 1890, coffee constituted at least 60 percent of exports.

The larger producers of cacao, indigo, and sugar quickly turned to coffee production. They sought more land to bring into cultivation, and elites in government responded with laws intended to commercialize property. A small proportion of nationally owned land was sold to large growers, and a small percentage of municipal ejidos and indigenous communal land ended up in coffee production. However, despite decrees in 1877 and 1881 that authorized the sale of communal lands, municipal governments continued to receive large tracts of land from the federal government for use as ejidos. And they gave small plots of land in the ejidos to small farmers, most of whom continued to produce subsistence crops. The donation of small plots of land continued apace, and rental plots were available at nominal fees well into the twentieth century.

By providing small plots of land, the government guaranteed a seasonal workforce for the large coffee estates that formed. Coffee requires minimal upkeep during the year, but during the harvest there are massive labor demands. The government adopted a multitude of vagrancy laws and requirements that Nicaraguans work in the harvests; most of the laws were flouted with regularity, as workers ran off to competitors. The easiest solution was to provide them with land that enabled them to grow food for subsistence, with the lure of the nearby haciendas for seasonal labor to earn the needed additional income.

While large coffee farms spread across most of the countryside, they were joined by an even greater number of small and medium-sized coffee farms. These smaller farmers produced significant amounts of coffee and became an important part of the coffee economy, lending legitimacy to the economic and political system. Men who owned even relatively small farms had the right to vote, and they participated in heated municipal and regional elections. They also made use of the legal system to protect their rights.

The various indigenous communities of Nicaragua responded differently to the new commercial incentives. In Carazo, some Indians who had produced sugar in the early national period easily switched to coffee and joined the Hispanized, or *ladino,* world. In parts of neighboring Masaya, they lost their lands and largely became a workforce for the powerful interests in the old colonial capital of Granada. In the northern province of Matagalpa, where coffee production came relatively late, many indigenous communities were more successful in keeping their land and indigenous identity.

Similar patterns appeared in Guatemala and El Salvador, where small farms were created alongside the huge plantations, and where some indigenous communities managed to hold onto their lands into the twentieth century. Some profited; others lost; but few were untouched by the spread of the export economy and the growth of government institutions that accompanied it.

The Growth of Cities

Although most of the population remained in the countryside, the export economies of the late nineteenth century fostered the growth of cities. For purposes of definition, most of the Latin American nations classify as urban those localities that have some type of local government and a population of at least 1,000 to 2,000 inhabitants.

The cities played ever more important roles in each nation. The government and administrative apparatus, commerce, and industry were located in the cities. Increasingly they served as hubs of complex transportation and communications networks. Further, they provided important recreational, cultural, and educational services. Rapid urban growth resulted from the arrival of greater numbers of foreign immigrants, a constantly increasing population (Latin America counted 60 million inhabitants in 1900), and an attraction the city exerted over many rural dwellers. Promises of better jobs and a more pleasant life lured thousands each year from the countryside to the city, a road that became increasingly more heavily trodden. On the other hand, even where that promise was lacking, the grinding poverty and modernization of the countryside pushed many desperate folk into urban areas.

But cities failed to play the role they might have in encouraging national development. The urban facade of modernization deceived. Dependency shaped the cities as well as the countryside. The high concentration of land in a few hands led to the creation of large estates. These agrarian-industrial enterprises did not require the intermediary services that support small trading, servicing, and processing towns. The export-oriented economy encouraged the prosperity of a few ports, a transportation system focusing on them, the expenditure of export wealth to beautify the capital city, and the concentration of absentee landlords in the capital to be near the center of power. The capital and the ports (in the case of Argentina, for example, the capital is also the principal port) absorbed the wealth of the export economy. The large estates, the overreliance on an export economy, and the resultant dependency help to explain why only one or two major "modern" cities dominated each Latin American nation and why urban modernity remained little more than a facade.

A correlation between class status and participation in the modernization process existed. Broadly speaking, in the upper levels of society people could more readily accept modern values. They were the ones most in contact with the world and knew what was going on. They more readily imitated the advances and changes that most struck their fancy. Indeed, they had the time and resources that permitted them the luxury of experimentation.

Individuals who subscribed to the process of modernization were willing and able to experiment, to change, to alter their environment to suit their needs. On the other hand, many of those immersed in poverty and tradition simply could not afford to experiment for fear that failure would bring the ultimate disaster. In short, institutional structures rather than personal choice kept most Latin Americans locked into a marginal existence without much possibility of experimentation with change. Although the conditions hostile to experimentation and change also existed in the cities, they permeated the countryside. But basic as agriculture was to the prosperity of the new nations, by midcentury few changes had been made in timeless production methods. The son used what his father had used, just as the father had copied his own father. An agricultural report on northern Brazil in the early 1860s characterized the local agrarian practices as "primitive" if compared to those observed on the farms of Western Europe and the United States. The hoe was the single farm implement, and the workers faithfully followed past procedures.

Urban culture with its capitalist–consumer imprint imposed a particular mentality on many city dwellers, which in turn shaped an outlook differing from that of most of the rural inhabitants. In an urban environment, traditional relationships tended to bend under necessity or examples of newer ones. In very general terms, the more intimate living conditions of the city and the greater familiarity of the city dwellers with foreign cultures exposed them to different ideas and alternative values. Many read newspapers and participated in public events. They were aware of changes the world was undergoing; they knew of the opportunities open to the trained and talented and were willing to strive for those opportunities. Consequently they laid plans for the future and, exerting every effort to realize those plans, they worked to shape their own destiny. The educational opportunities, varied careers, and job possibilities afforded by the city encouraged them to aspire toward upward mobility.

The statistics on Latin America's urban boom are impressive. Argentina's urban population doubled between 1869 and 1914, so that in the latter year the urban sector represented 53 percent of the population. In 1869, Buenos Aires had a population of a quarter of a million, a figure that increased eightfold by 1914 to encompass a quarter of the national population. Brazil witnessed similar urban growth. Between 1890 and 1914, the government created approximately 500 new municipalities. During the three decades after 1890, the population of the major cities jumped: Recife and Rio de Janeiro doubled in size, Niterói and Pôrto Alegre tripled, and São Paulo increased eightfold. São Paulo grew faster than any other major Brazilian city—in fact it was one of the fastest-growing cities in the world. It increased in population at a rate above 25 percent every five years after 1895. In 1910, the distinguished British diplomat and author James Bryce described São Paulo, a city then approaching half a million, as "the briskest and most progressive place in all Brazil. . . . The alert faces, and the air of stir and movement, as well as handsome public buildings, rising on all hands, with a large, well-planted public garden in the middle of the city, give the impression of energy and progress."

Chile well represented the urban surge in Latin America. In 1875, approximately 27 percent of the population could be classified as urban dwellers, but a quarter of a century later the figure reached 43 percent. Santiago's population shot up from 160,000 in 1880 to 400,000 in 1910, while the population of the second city and principal seaport, Valparaíso, more than doubled to 200,000 during the same period. Foreign visitors always had praise for the modernity of Chile's two major cities. They inevitably commented on the female streetcar conductors, a novel occupation for women anywhere in the Western Hemisphere. However, the Chilean women of the lower class held a variety of other jobs in the cities by the end of the nineteenth century. In addition to running the streetcars, they did most of the street cleaning and sold meats, vegetables, and fruits in the markets and on street corners. A well-known figure in Chilean society at the time was Isadora Cousiño, one of the wealthiest persons in Latin America, if not in the world. She administered her vast estates (said to number in the millions of acres), mines, and factories with a business acumen few could equal and lived amid a splendor that would have been the envy of European monarchs.

By the beginning of the twentieth century, nearly all the capitals and many of the largest cities boasted of electricity, telephones, streetcar service, covered sewers, paved streets, ornamental parks, and new buildings reflecting French architectural influence. But the cities offered more than the material trappings of modernity. Nurtured in an increasingly prosperous urban environment, intellectual activity flourished. Some of Latin America's most prestigious newspapers were founded: *El Mercurio* in Chile and the *Jornal do Commércio* in Brazil, both in 1827; *El Comercio* in Peru in 1839; and *La Prensa* in 1869 and *La Nación* in 1870 in Buenos Aires. Starting with the University of Chile in 1843, the major universities of Latin America began to publish reviews, journals, annuals, and books, an activity that further stimulated intellectual development. Romanticism, with its individuality, emotional intensity, and glorification of nature, held sway in literary circles for much of the nineteenth century. José Mármol of Argentina, Jorge Isaacs of Colombia, and José de Alencar of Brazil were masters of the romantic novel. Excesses in romanticism prompted literary experiments by 1880 in modernism and realism, already in vogue in Europe. The brilliant Nicaraguan poet Rubén Darío helped to introduce modernism into Latin America, and by the end of the century he dominated the field of poetry. Critics considered him one of the most original and influential poetic voices of his time.

Under the sway of realism, the urban writers depicted and denounced the injustices they observed in their society. Clorinda Matto de Turner wrote the first significant novel, *Aves sin Nido* (Birds Without a Nest, 1889), protesting the abysmal conditions under which the Peruvian Indians lived. She saw the Indians as victims of iniquitous institutions, not least of which in her opinion was the Church.

With two notable exceptions, Latin American culture aped European trends, particularly those set in Paris. The exceptions were Ricardo Palma, whose original *"tradiciones peruanas,"* delightful historical anecdotes of Peru, recreated with wit and imagination his country's past; and the gaucho poets, foremost of whom was the Argentine José Hernández, creator *of Martín Fierro,* a true American epic, picturing life among Argentina's rugged cowboys.

Education continued to be a privilege of the elite. Overwhelming numbers of the masses remained illiterate. In Brazil, the illiteracy rate never dropped below 85 percent in the nineteenth century. In the 1880s, with a population exceeding 13 million, the number enrolled in primary schools totaled less than a quarter of a million. Argentina dedicated much of the nation's budget to improving education. As a result, literacy in Argentina rose from 22 percent in 1869 to 65 percent in 1914, an enviable record throughout most of Latin America. In Uruguay during the 1870s, José Pedro Varela preached that education should be free, obligatory, coeducational, and secularly controlled. Under his direction, the Uruguayan educational system expanded rapidly and the illiteracy rate dropped proportionately. Chile, too, extended its schools to ever larger numbers of children. During his long administration (1873–85), President Justo Rufino Barrios of Guatemala devoted as much as 10 percent of the national budget to education. Still, at the end of his regime, Guatemala had only 934 schools enrolling 42,549 pupils, out of a population of approximately 1.25 million. In truth, despite the efforts of a number of farsighted statesmen, the illiteracy rate remained high throughout Latin America during the last half of the nineteenth century, varying from 40 to 90 percent. It was always much higher in the countryside than in the city. More males than females attended school. A marked contrast existed between the well-educated few and the ignorant many. The unschooled masses silently witnessed the events that surrounded and affected them but in which they could play only the most limited role. The children of the elite, however, seldom set foot in a public school. Their parents hired tutors or sent them to private schools for a typically classical education. Such segregation further removed the future leaders from national realities.

The modernizing elites began to worry that they could not progress as long as mothers—at least elite mothers—lacked the skills to teach their sons to be good citizens. Mexican journalist Florencio del Castillo declared in 1856, "The most effective way to better the moral condition of the land is to educate women." Just as women served as transmitters of Spanish culture during the colonial era, educated women were now to pass on the republican, progressive values so important to Latin American modernization. In Argentina, Juan Bautista Alberdi and Domingo Faustino Sarmiento included women in their vision of an educated, progressive country.

Of course, conservatives worried that education would encourage women to leave their traditional roles, and the idea of their education was not immediately accepted. It took more than just the enlightened attitudes of men like Sarmiento to win expanded education for women. Many women, particularly from the middle class, campaigned for educational opportunities. They founded journals and editorialized about the need for education. An article in the Brazilian journal *O Sexo Femenino* contended: "It is to you [men] that is owed our inadequacy; we have intelligence equal to yours, and if your pride has triumphed it is because our intelligence has been left unused. From this day we wish to improve our minds; and for better or worse we will transmit our ideas in the press, and to this end we have *O Sexo Femenino*; a journal absolutely dedicated to our sex and written only by us."

As educational opportunities improved, so did employment. Because girls and boys were usually taught in separate schools, women were trained to teach the girls. As schools later became coeducational, women were considered the most appropriate teachers of young children in primary schools. Normal schools were founded to train teachers for this role.

The bringing together of women in schools and producing journals gave impetus to an early feminist movement, concerned not just with basic education but also with the opening of higher education and the professions to women. Their actions were not taken lightly by the men at the top. Mexico's minister of state Justo Sierra made the Porfirian attitude toward female education quite clear: "The educated woman will be truly one for the home: she will be the companion and collaborator of man in the formation of the family. You [women] are called upon to form souls, to sustain the soul of your husband; for this reason, we educate you . . . to continue the perpetual creation of the nation. *Niña querida*, do not turn feminist in our midst."

Chile pioneered in offering professional education to women. A special governmental decree in 1877 permitted women to receive professional degrees, and in 1886 Eloisa Díaz became the first woman in all of Latin Amer-

Immigrants disembark in Buenos Aires, Argentina, 1907.

ica to receive a medical degree. In 1892, Matilde Throup graduated from the law school in Santiago and became the first female lawyer in Latin America. The Brazilian government opened professional schools to women in 1879.

Women also became activists in the anti-slavery movements in Cuba and Brazil. Much like women in the United States, their focus on lack of freedom for blacks led them to see the limits on their own freedom. As the slaves were freed in Brazil in 1889, one journal proclaimed, "once more we [women] ask equal rights, freedom of action, and autonomy in the home." The demands, however, remained unmet.

Continuity and Change

During the last half of the nineteenth century, new forces appeared that challenged the social, economic, and political institutions deeply rooted in the colonial past. Urbanization, industrialization, and modernization formed a trinity menacing to tradition. Once introduced, these mutually supporting forces could not be arrested. The center of political, economic, and social life, once located on the plantations and haciendas, shifted gradually but irreversibly to the cities.

By the beginning of the twentieth century, some of the Latin American states—certainly Argentina, Brazil, Chile, and Mexico—conveyed at least the outward appearance of having adopted the patterns and modes of the most progressive European states and of the United States. Their constitutions embodied the noblest principles of Western political thought. Their governmental apparatus followed the most progressive models of the day. Political stability replaced chaos. Expanding transportation and communication infrastructures permitted the governments to control a larger area of their nations than they ever had before. New industries existed. An ever larger banking network facilitated and encouraged commerce. Society was more diversified than at any previous time. In the capitals and the largest cities, the architecture of the new buildings duplicated the latest styles of Paris—in how many Latin American cities do the local citizens proudly point to the opera house and claim it to be a replica of the Paris Opera? To the extent that some of the Latin American states formally resembled the leading nations of the Western world, which they consciously accepted as their models of modernity, it is possible to conclude that those nations qualified as modern. However, many would argue that such modernity was only a veneer. It added a cosmetic touch to tenacious institutions while failing to effect the changes implied by the concept. Modernization in Latin America lacked real substance.

The superficiality of modernization guaranteed the continued domination of the past. The rural aristocracy still enjoyed power; their estates remained huge and generally inefficient; their control over their workers was complete. The latifundia actually grew rather than diminished in size during the nineteenth century, at the expense of Indian communities and their traditional landholdings, the properties confiscated from the Church, and the public domain.

By early 1888, slavery had been abolished. Still, former slaves and their descendants occupied one of the lowest rungs of the social and economic ladder. The doors to education, opportunity, and mobility remained tightly closed to them except in the rarest instances. The Indians fared no better. Debt servitude of one or another variety characterized part of the labor market. Clorinda Matto de Turner recorded in her novel *Aves sin Nido* how debt servitude worked in one shocking case. To borrow 10 pesos, the Indian had to agree to repay 120 at a specific date. Unable to repay, he saw his daughter seized by the lender and sold into servitude to make good the debt. It would have been foolish to have expected the law to intervene to restrict such abuses since the making, enforcing, and judging of the laws rested in the hands of the landowners and their sympathizers.

The wealthiest and most powerful class in Latin America in general was white or near white in complexion. Heirs of the creoles and mazombos, they enjoyed age-old economic advantages, to which, after independence, they added political power. The group that surrounded Porfirio Díaz spoke of themselves, symbolically enough, as the "New Creoles."

Rural tradition comfortably allied itself with the invigorated capitalism of nineteenth-century Latin America. Positivism even provided a handy ideological umbrella for the two. Like so much of the economic and political thought in Latin America then and since, it recognized no incompatibility in the imposition of capitalist industrialization on a traditional rural base. With its emphasis on order and hierarchy, Positivism assured the elites their venerable privileges, relative prosperity, and selective progress and held out promise of the same to the restless middle sectors. Subsumed was the inferiority of the masses who stood very little chance of "progressing" in a society in which all the institutions repressed them.

When few control the economy, few control the government. The Latin American reality at the opening of the twentieth century authenticated that equation. Without access to wealth, the majority possessed no political power. With no political power, they stood scant chance of experiencing economic development. The elites rarely thought in economic terms beyond growth. Did they ever envision an economic development that would provide for the majority? They blocked the majority and its well-being from their minds. Their vision fixed on Europe and the United States. The elite grew wealthy from serving as a complement to North Atlantic economies, and they saw their own well-being as the nation's.

But social inequality, paternalistic rule, privilege, and dependency clearly were incompatible with the new trends started during the last half of the century. The Chilean intellectual Miguel Cruchago Montt pointed out in his *Estudio sobre la organización económica y la hacienda pública de Chile* (Study of

Chile's Economic Organization and Public Finances), published in 1878, that the colonial past dominated the present and frustrated development. The past could no longer exist unchallenged once Latin Americans began to think in terms of national development.

At the opening of the twentieth century, the Colombian Rafael Uribe stated that the basic economic question concerned the quality of life of the "people": "Are they able to satisfy their basic needs?" The reality was they could not. A majority of the Latin Americans were no better off at the dawn of the twentieth century than they had been a century earlier. In fact, a persuasive argument can be made that they were worse off. The negative response to Uribe's question foretold conflict.

The Popular Challenge

The Latin American nations marched toward progress to a tune played by the elites, but not without discordant chords sounded by large numbers of the humble classes. For the majority of the Latin Americans, progress was proving to mean increased concentration of lands in the hands of ever fewer owners; falling per capita food production with corollary rising food imports; greater impoverishment; less to eat; more vulnerability to the whims of an impersonal international market; uneven growth; increased unemployment and underemployment; social, economic, and political marginalization; and greater power in the hands of the privileged few. Ironically, the more the folk cultures were forced to integrate into world commerce, the fewer the material benefits the folk reaped. But poverty through progress must be understood in more than the material terms of declining wages, purchasing power, or nutritional levels. A tragic spiritual and cultural impoverishment debased the majority, who were forced by circumstances to abandon previously satisfactory ways of life and to accept alien ones that provided them little or no psychic benefits.

The impoverished majority both bore the burden of the inequitable institutional structure and paid for the modernization enjoyed by the privileged. The deprivation, repression, and deculturalization of the majority by the minority created tensions that frequently gave rise to violence. The poor protested their increasing misfortunes as modernization increased. For their own part, the privileged were determined to modernize and to maintain the order required to do so. They freely used whatever force was necessary to accomplish both. Consequently, the imposition of progress stirred social disorder.

Indian rebellions flared up from Mexico to Chile. The Indians refused to surrender their remaining lands quietly as the large estates intensified their encroachment. The arrival of the railroads, which accelerated those encroachments, spawned greater violence. Doubtless the major Indian rebellion in terms of length, carnage, and significance in the Americas of the nineteenth century was the Caste War of Yucatán between the Mayas and the peninsula's whites and mestizos.

In the years after Mexico declared its independence, the sugar and henequen plantations had expanded to threaten the corn cultures of the Mayas by incorporating their lands into the latifundia and by impressing the Indians into service as debt peons. The Indians fought for their land and freedom. They defended their world. On the other side, the Yucatán elite professed that they fought for "the holy cause of order, humanity, and civilization." Much of the bloodiest fighting occurred during the period from 1847 to 1855, but the war lingered on until the early twentieth century. During those decades the Mayas of eastern and southern Yucatán governed themselves.

Free of white domination, the Mayan rebels took the name of Cruzob, turned their backs on the white world, and developed their own culture, a synthesis of their Mayan inheritance and Spanish influences. Four hundred years of conquest had erased the intellectual and artistic heritage from the Mayan mind, but the Cruzob retained their knowledge of agriculture and village and family organization from the pre-Columbian past. Unique to the Cruzob was the development of their own religion, based largely on their interpretation of Christianity. Unlike other syncretic regions of Latin America, it developed without dependence on the sporadic participation of Roman Catholic priests (to perform baptisms, marriages, or an occasional mass) and free from the critical eye of the white master. Incorporating the Indian folkways, it strengthened the Cruzob and provided a spiritual base for independence other Indians lacked. What was notable about the Cruzob was the emergence of a viable Indian alternative to Europeanization. Although infused with Spanish contributions, it bore a strong resemblance to the pre-Columbian Mayan society. Reviving their Indian culture by repudiating "foreign" domination and substituting their own values for "foreign" ones, the Cruzob revitalized their society. They became masters of their own land again.

Powerful forces at work in the closing decades of the nineteenth century overwhelmed the Cruzob. The poor soil of Yucatán, exhausted under corn cultivation, no longer yielded sufficient food. Disease reduced the Indian ranks faster than battle did. At the same time, Mexico, increasingly stable under Porfirio Díaz, showed less tolerance for the Cruzob and more determination to subdue them in order to exploit Yucatán. A treaty between Mexico and Great Britain closed British Honduras to the Cruzob, thus cutting off their single source of modern weapons and ammunition. Finally, the expanding wagon trails and railroads from northern Yucatán, which accompanied the spread of the prosperous henequen plantations, penetrated the Cruzob territory. A growing market for forest woods even sent the whites into the seemingly impenetrable forest redoubts of the Cruzob. Consequently, a declining Cruzob population and relentless Mexican pressures brought to an end the

Mayan independence of half a century. The long and tenacious resistance testified to the Indian preference, a rejection of the modernization preferred by the elites.

The Indians were not the only rebels. In Brazil, where slavery lingered after midcentury, the slaves vigorously protested their servitude. Sober members of the elites regarded the slave as "a volcano that constantly threatens society, a mine ready to explode," as one nineteenth-century intellectual phrased it in his study of Brazilian slavery. Foreign visitors also sensed the tensions created by slave society. Prince Adalbert of Prussia visited one large, well-run plantation, which he praised as a model. After noting the seemingly friendly relations between master and slaves, he revealed, "The loaded guns and pistols hanging up in his [the master's] bedroom, however, showed that he had not entire confidence in them [the slaves] and indeed, he had more than once been obliged to face them with his loaded guns." The decade of the 1880s, just prior to emancipation, witnessed mounting slave resistance. The slaves fled the plantations, killed the masters, and burned fields and buildings. One fiery Afro-Brazilian abolitionist leader, Luis Gonzaga de Pinto Gama, declared, "Every slave who kills his master, no matter what the circumstances might be, kills in self-defense." He also preached the "right of insurrection." Once freed, African-Americans throughout the Americas protested their poverty and the institutions that they felt perpetuated their problems. For example, Panama City seethed with racial tensions during the decades from 1850 to 1880. The African-American urban masses resented their depressed conditions and used violence—robberies, fires, rioting—as a means of protest. Many referred to the situation as a "race war," exacerbated by an economic reality in which the poor were black and the rich, white.

Rural rebellions abounded, signifying still other challenges to the elite institutions and commitment to modernization. More often than not, the ideology behind those rebellions was vague and contradictory. Somehow, the rebels hoped to save their lands, improve their standards of living, and share in the exercise of power. Two popular revolts, one in Brazil, another in Argentina, illustrate the motives, the violence, and the repression.

The Quebra-Quilo Revolt, from late 1874 to early 1875, ranked high in significance because the subsistence farmers of Brazil's interior Northeast succeeded in checking the government's new modernization drive (underway in 1871 but ineffectual by 1875). The causes of that revolt were not unique: new taxes and the threat smallholders felt from the large landowners absorbing their farms, complicated by the imposition of the metric system with the requirement of fees for official alteration and authentication of weights. A journalist covering the revolt called it "the direct consequence of the suffering and deprivation . . . of the working classes of the interior," while a participant claimed, "The fruit of the soil belongs to the people and tax ought not be paid on it." As riots multiplied in the marketplaces, the municipal and provincial authorities feared the "forces of Barbarism" were poised to sweep across the Northeast. The peasants were unusually successful. They ignored the new taxes, destroyed the new weights and measures, and burned official records and archives (thus protecting their informal title to the land by reducing to ashes the legal documentation). The subsistence farmers in most cases had taken physical possession and worked the land over the generations without title. They faced possible eviction by anyone who could show the proper paper authenticating legal ownership. By destroying the records, they removed evidence—the local notarial registers of land, for example—from use in judicial proceedings, thereby putting themselves on equal legal footing with the local landed elite. Momentarily, then, the sporadic riots that constituted the revolt achieved their goals, while temporarily frustrating the penetration of the elites into their region.

In Argentina, revolts shook the province of Santa Fe in 1893. Small farmers there protested a tax on wheat to pay for the government's innovations, including railroads, that seemed to favor the large landowners. Furthermore, they resented the fact that immigrants received land and preferential treatment denied the locals. In the meantime, social disorder rose dramatically in the Argentine province of Tucumán between 1876 and 1895. During those two decades the number of arrests, ones involving mostly illiterate workers, jumped from under 2,000 per year to over 17,000, while the total population only doubled during the same period.

Popular protest also assumed forms other than rebellion. Banditry and millenarian movements flourished in the nineteenth century. Thanks to the conceptual framework offered by E. J. Hobsbawm, it is possible with many cautions to consider banditry as a form of social protest and millenarianism as a type of popular revolution.

Religious in content, advocating a radical change in the world, millenarianism profoundly and totally rejects the present while expressing a passionate hope for a happier future. Those faithful to such ideas believe the world will come to a sudden, apocalyptic end but are vague about how this will happen and about the details of the new society that will replace the old. Although political revolutionaries also advocate a new society, they diverge from millenarianism because revolutionaries plan for and express ideas about how society will be remade. Millenarianists, on the other hand, expect the change to take place through divine intervention according to God's will and plan. Their duty is to prepare themselves for the new world. Obviously people hoping for a new and better life are expressing a form of dissatisfaction with the life they currently lead. Although they do not want confrontation, events may frequently force violence.

Brazil witnessed a remarkable array of millenarian movements. Doubtless the best known took place in the dry, impoverished backlands of the state of Bahia where the mystic Antônio the Counselor gathered the faithful between 1893 and 1897. Thousands flocked to his settlement at Canudos to listen to the Counselor preach. They stayed to establish a flourishing agrarian community. He alienated the government by advising his adherents not to pay taxes. Furthermore, his patriarchal ideas smacked of monarchism to the recently established republican government in Rio de Janeiro. The Church authorities denounced him, resenting his influence over the masses. The local landlords disliked him because he siphoned off the rural workers and stalemated the expansion of their fazendas. Those powerful enemies decided to arrest Antônio and scatter the settlers at Canudos. However, they failed to consider the strength and determination of his followers. It took four military campaigns, all the modern armaments the Brazilian army could muster, and countless lives to suppress the millenarian movement. The final campaign directed by the minister of war himself devastated the settlement at Canudos house by house. The people refused to surrender. The epic struggle inspired Euclydes da Cunha's 1902 masterpiece, *Rebellion in the Backlands.*

Messianic movements flourished among the Andean Indians after the conquest. They yearned for a return to an order, basically the traditional Incan one destroyed by the Spanish conquest, that would benefit them rather than the outsider. Exemplary of such movements in the nineteenth century was one that occurred among the Bolivian Indians of Curuyaqui in 1891–92. An individual called Tumpa, known as "the supreme being," appeared in the community announcing his mission "to liberate them from the whites." Under his prophetic new system Tumpa promised that the whites would work for the Indians. His followers took up arms as urged by the messianic leader; the whites fled to the cities, and the army arrived to brutally crush the uprising. The carnage disproved at least two of Tumpa's prophecies: first, that only water would issue forth from the soldier's guns, and second, that anyone who did die for the cause would return to life in three days.

Northwestern Mexico was the scene of the miracle cures of Teresa Urrea, referred to by hundreds of thousands of devotees as Teresita or the Saint of Cabora. In 1889, after a severe psychological shock, she lapsed into a comatose state. Considered dead, she regained life just prior to her burial. She reported having spoken to the Blessed Virgin, who conferred on her the power to cure. By 1891, pilgrims flooded Cabora seeking her help. Teresita's compassion for the poor earned her the devotion of the masses and the suspicion of the Díaz government. The Yaqui and Mayo Indians confided in her and unburdened their sufferings before her. Believing she enjoyed influence with God, they pressed her for help and advice. In 1890, the Tarahumara Indian mountain village of Tomochic adopted Teresita as their saint, placing a statue of her in their church. The village began to modify its Roman Catholicism to a more indigenous religion focused on the Saint of Cabora. The next year Tomochic rebelled against the government and requested Teresita to interpret God's will to them. The government reacted immediately and harshly, but it still took several armed expeditions to quell the rebellion. The village was destroyed, and not a man or boy over thirteen years of age survived the slaughter. In mid-May of 1892, a group of approximately two hundred Mayo

Mexico (showing the location of oilfields)

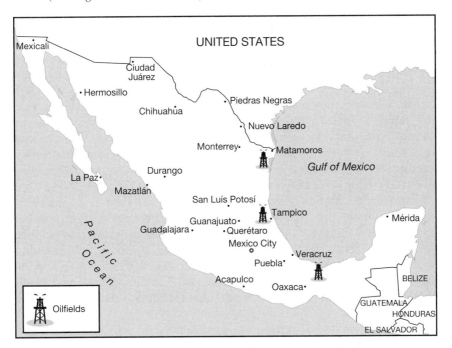

Indians attacked the town of Navojoa shouting, "Viva la Santa de Cabora!" Considering her a dangerous agitator of the masses, the Díaz government exiled Teresa Urrea to the United States. Teresita, herself opposed to violence, had served more as a figurehead, a catalyst, a remarkable charismatic personality, whose compassion gave unity of expression to the miserable masses of northwestern Mexico.

Banditry attracted the desperate, those who had lost out in the system whether they were the poor or members of the impoverished gentry. Whatever else banditry might have signified, it was as much a means of protesting injustice or righting wrongs as it was of equalizing wealth or taking political revenge. Although unsympathetic to banditry, the Brazilian jurist of the mid-nineteenth century, Tavares Bastos, realized that the bandits often were victims of the state who, no longer confiding in its laws, made their own justice.

Bandits roamed the Brazilian interior in the nineteenth century, particularly the impoverished Northeast, where many won the admiration of the poor and the respect of the wealthy, who not infrequently coopted them and utilized their services. Some scholarship correlates the rise of banditry in the late nineteenth century with the breakdown of the patriarchal order in the countryside. Brazilian popular poetry abounds with tales of the bandit hero.

A well-known poem sung at the beginning of the twentieth century related the history of Antônio Silvino, who became a bandit in 1896 to avenge an injustice: His father was slain by a police official who went unpunished by the government. Others relate the adventures of Josuíno Brilhante, also seemingly forced into banditry to avenge injustices against his family. He assaulted the rich and distributed their goods and money among the poor, boasting that he never robbed for himself.

Banditry characterized much of Spanish America as well. Mexican banditry flourished, and interestingly enough, regions that produced bandits, such as Chalco-Río Frío, eastern Morelos, and northwestern Puebla, spawned agrarian revolutionaries before the century ended, providing further evidence of the social dimension banditry could assume on occasion. Peru offers numerous examples of peasant bandits. In his study of them, Enrique López Albujar described banditry as "a protest, a rebellion, a deviation, or a simple means of subsistence." He concluded that nineteenth-century Peruvian banditry produced an array of folk heroes because those bandits corrected injustices, robbed to help the poor, and protested social and economic inequities. For their part, Chilean officials tended to lump together Indians and bandits of the rugged Andes as "criminals." They also routinely complained that local populations supported the bandits, thus facilitating their anti-establishment activities.

The motives and activities of the bandits varied widely, but at least in part they could be explained as protests against the wrongs of society, as they viewed it. Because of their strength and because they often opposed the elites and official institutions, they received the support, indeed the admiration, of large numbers of the humble classes, who often hid them, lied to the authorities to protect them, guided them through strange terrain, and fed them. To the poor, the bandits were caudillos who by default helped them to sustain their folk cultures and deflect modernization.

The folk by no means rejected change simply to preserve the past unaltered. Rather, they wished to mediate change over a longer period of time. They opposed those changes imposed by the elites which they judged harmful or potentially threatening. They perceived the threat that the export economy and the capitalist mentality promoting it posed to their remaining lands and to their control over their own labor. The elites showed little patience and less tolerance with folk preferences, caution, and concerns. They dealt severely with any protest and thus further raised the level of violence. In the last analysis the elites triumphed. After all, they controlled the police, militia, and military. Furthermore, the popular protests tended to be local and uncoordinated. Thus, despite the frequency of such protests, the elites imposed their will and their brand of progress. The triumph of that progress set the course for twentieth-century history in Latin America. It bequeathed a legacy of mass poverty and continued conflict.

The Mexican Constitution of 1857

Article 27. Private property shall not be taken without the consent of the owner, except for reasons of public utility and by prior indemnification. The law shall determine which authority shall make the appropriation and the provisions by which it shall be carried out.

No civil or ecclesiastical corporation of whatever character, designation, or object, shall have the legal capacity to acquire ownership to, or administer in its own behalf, landed property, except for buildings immediately and directly related to the services or purposes of said corporations.

In Support of Porfirio Díaz

Justo Sierra (1848–1912) was a Mexican educator and liberal reformer who served as minister of education under Porfirio Díaz. In this excerpt from *The Political Evolution of the Mexican People,* published in three volumes from 1900 to 1902, he defends the Porfirian regime.

The country's real desire, manifested everywhere, was peace. No one wanted a resumption of the war except those who thrived on anarchy, those who were misfits in any normal situation. Seldom in history has there been a people with a more unanimous, more anguished, more determined aspiration. . . .

In order to make this seemingly visionary ideal a reality, all interests, from the highest to the lowest must be involved, and the leader believed that, to accomplish this, all must have faith in him and fear him. Faith and fear, those two profoundly human emotions, have been the pillars of every religion and were to be the pillars of the new political regime. Without losing a day or wasting an opportunity, President Díaz has marched in this direction for twenty-five years: he has founded the political religion of peace. . . .

Never before had peace been so patently a matter of urgent national necessity. The industrial development of the United States, already colossal twenty-five years ago, required a concomitant development of the railroad system, for without this it ran the risk of paralysis, something American "go-ahead" could never permit. The builders of the great systems that approached our frontiers planned to complete them in Mexico, which was regarded by the communication experts as forming a single region with the southwestern United States. The financial object of the Americans in extending their railway network to Mexico was to dominate our markets to the profit of their industry. This American need could be satisfied by declaring the country to be in a state of anarchy and intervening to give the railroad builders protection, or it could be satisfied in a normal, pacific manner if they could be convinced that there was a stable and viable government in Mexico whose word in treaties and contracts could be trusted. From this moment, civil war could be considered not only as the gravest of the country's internal ills, but also as responsible for attracting the most imminent external danger. Lerdo had tried to forestall this danger by seeking the concurrence of European capital, but to no avail. European capital would come to Mexico only after long years, and then as backing for American enterprises. President Díaz had the perspicacity to understand the situation and, believing that our history and the state of our society put us in a position where we were liable to be hooked and carried off into the future by the formidable Yankee locomotive, he preferred to make that journey under the auspices and through the action of the Mexican government, as equal partners with the obligation to preserve peace and order, thereby maintaining our national integrity and achieving progress.

Many who have tried to analyze the psyche of President Díaz—who, without being either an archangel or a tyrant of melodrama, is in the true sense of the word an extraordinary man—find in his mental processes a notable inversion of logic: His decisions are quick, and deliberation follows the act of will, deliberation that is slow and laborious and modifies or even nullifies the original decision. This mental pattern, characteristic, perhaps, of the mixed family to which the majority of Mexicans belong, has given rise to imputations of political perfidy (deceiving in order to persuade, dividing in order to rule). These imputations, contradicted by the qualities that we all recognize in the private man, are mechanisms by which some individuals in Mexican society attain contact with power and identify with the powerful. This society has inherited from the idiosyncracies of the indigenous race, from colonial education, and from the perennial anarchy of the epochs of revolt an infinite distrust of rulers and all their acts; what we criticize, no doubt, is the reflection of ourselves in the other person. . . . [W]e needed a man, a conscience, a will to unify our moral forces and transmute them into national progress; this man was President Díaz. . . .

Thus, without breaking a single law, President Díaz has been invested by the will of his fellow citizens with the lifelong office of supreme arbiter. This investiture—the submission of the people in all their official manifestations, the submission of society in all its active elements, to the President's judgment—

could be given the name social dictatorship. The truth is, it has
singular features which keep it from fitting any of the classic
definitions of despotism. It is a personal government that defends
and reinforces legality, springing as it does from the national
resolution to banish anarchy once and for all. Hence, while our
government in eminently authoritarian, it can never, at the risk
of perishing, refuse to abide by the Constitution. It has been
entrusted to one man, not only for the sake of peace and economic
progress, but also in the hope of neutralizing the despotisms of
the other Powers and eradicating the caciques and disarming the
old tyrannies.

In short, the political evolution of Mexico has been
sacrificed to other phases of her social evolution. This is proved
by the plain fact that not a single political party exists in Mexico,
nor any group organized around a program rather than
a man. Every move in this direction has been blocked by the
government's distrust and the general apathy. The day that a
party succeeds in maintaining an organization, political evolution
will resume its progress, and the man, more essential in
democracies than in aristocracies, will come later: the function
will create an organ.

But if we compare Mexico's situation at the instant when
the parenthesis in her political evolution was opened with the
present moment, we must admit that the transformation has been
amazing. Only we who were witnesses of preceding events can
fully appreciate the change. A peace lasting from ten to twenty
years was an idle dream, they said. But ours has already lasted a
quarter of a century. It was mere dreaming, they said, to think of
covering the country with a railway system that would unite the
ports and the center with the hinterland and the outside world.
Only in a dream would one see a national industry in rapid
growth. But all these things have come true, and still we move
forward.

The undeniable achievement of the present administration
consists, not in having brought about this change, which an
extraneous combination of factors would probably have brought
anyway, but in having done everything possible to facilitate the
change and exploit it to the best advantage. In the course of this
task, nothing has been more beneficial to the country than the
intimate collaboration between the President's firm resolution
and his Finance Minister's application of scientific procedures to
financial problems. To this collaboration we owe the revival of our
credit, the balancing of our budget, the freedom of internal trade,
and the concomitant increase in public revenue. . . .

There exists, we repeat, such a thing as Mexican social
evolution. Our progress, made up of foreign elements, reveals,
on analysis, a reaction of our social body to those elements in
order to assimilate and make use of them in developing and

intensifying our life. Thus, our national personality has been enriched and made stronger by contact with the world. This evolution, no doubt, is just beginning. When we look back at our condition previous to the final third of the past century we see what a long way we have come, and even if we compare our progress with that made by our neighbors (and this should always be our frame of reference, without succumbing to pernicious illusions or to cowardly discouragement) it is not insignificant.

We still need to revitalize the earth by way of irrigation. We need to attract immigrants from Europe so as to obtain a cross with the indigenous race, for only European blood can keep the level of civilization that has produced our nationality from sinking, which would mean regression, not evolution. We need to bring about a complete change in the indigenous mentality through education in the school. This is our great, our urgent obligation, and we must comply with it promptly or we are lost.

To convert the native into a social asset (and it is the fault of our apathy that he is not one), to make him the principal colonist on intensively cultivated soil, to blend his spirit and ours in a unification of language, of aspirations, of loves and hates, of moral and mental criteria, to place before him the ideal of a strong and happy country belonging to all—to create, in sum, a national soul—is the goal assigned to the future, the program of our national education. Whosoever helps to attain this goal is a patriot; whosoever places obstacles in the path is an enemy.

The obstacles are familiar. There is the danger, along our frontiers, of shifting from an indigenous to a foreign tongue and rejecting the national language. There is superstition, which only the humanistic and scientific spirit, only the secular school can successfully combat. There is the civic sacrilege of the impious who, taking advantage of the Mexican's ineradicable religious feeling, persist in setting the principles that are the basis of our modern life against the ones that have been the basis of our moral life. And then, there is the skepticism of those who, doubting that we are fit for liberty, condemn us to death.

Thus, our duty is plain: to educate, which means to make strong. Liberty, the marrow of lions, has always been, among nations as among individuals, the patrimony of the strong; the weak have never been free. Mexican social evolution will have been wholly abortive and futile unless it attains the final goal: liberty.

Source: Justo Sierra, *The Political Evolution of the Mexican People,* Charles Ramsdell, tran. (Austin: University of Texas Press, 1969), 359, 361–62, 366–68. Copyright © 1969 by permission of the University of Texas Press.

A Chilean Offers a Different Vision

Few leaders arose who offered a different vision than the hegemonic liberal program for modernization via foreign investment. One of the few was José Manuel Balmaceda, president of Chile from 1886 to 1891. Balmaceda was certainly a modernizer—his administration oversaw the construction of railways, roads, and bridges, extension of telegraph and postal service, construction of fine government buildings, and increase in education. But Balmaceda also proposed a nationalist program of industrialization and increased local control of the British-dominated nitrate industry. The result: Conservatives revolted, with British support. A civil war ensued, and a defeated Balmaceda committed suicide. These excerpt from his speeches indicate Balmaceda's unusual point of view.

NATIONAL INDUSTRY

Economic developments of the last few years prove that, while maintaining a just balance between expenditures and income, we can and should undertake productive national works that will nourish, more especially, our public education and our national industry.

And since I speak of our national industry, I must add that it is weak and uncertain because of lack of confidence on the part of capital and because of our general resistance to opening up and utilizing its beneficial currents.

If, following the example of Washington and the great republic of the North, we preferred to consume our national production, even if it is not as finished and perfect as the foreign production; if the farmer, the miner, and the manufacturer constructed their tools and machines whenever possible in our country's workshops; if we broadened and made more varied the production of our raw materials, processing and transforming them into objects useful for life or personal comfort; if we ennobled industrial labor, increasing wages in proportion to the greater skill of our working class; if the state, while maintaining a balance between revenues and expenditures, devoted a portion of its resources to the protection of national industry, nourishing and supporting it during its first trials; if the state, with its resources and legislation, and all of us together, collectively and singly, applied ourselves to producing more and better and consuming what we produce, then a more vigorous sap would circulate through the industrial organism of the Republic, and increased wealth and well-being would give us the possession of that supreme good of an industrious and honorable people: the capacity to live and clothe ourselves by our unaided efforts.

FOREIGN INVESTMENT

The extraction and processing of nitrate must be left to the free competition of the industry itself. But the question of the privately owned and government-owned nitrate properties is a matter for serious meditation and study. The private properties are almost all foreign owned, and effectively concentrated in the hands of individuals of a single [British] nationality. It would be preferable that these properties belonged to Chileans as well; but if our national capital is indolent or fearful, we must not be surprised if foreign capital fills with foresight and intelligence, the void in the progress of this region [Tarapaca] left by the neglect of our compatriots. . . .

The importance of nitrate in agriculture and industry and the growing tempo of its production counsel the legislator and the statesman not to delay the solution of the problem, and to resolve it by effectively protecting the interests of our nationals. It is true that this must not be done in such a way as to effectively stifle free competition and production of nitrate in Tarapaca, but neither should we allow that vast and rich area to become a mere foreign enclave. We cannot ignore the very real and serious fact that the peculiar nature of the industry, the manner in which the nitrate properties came into being, the absorption of small properties by foreign capital, and even the temper of the races that dispute the dominion of that vast and fertile region, demand a special legislation, based on the nature of things and the special needs of our economic and industrial existence. This question has such profound consequences for the future that upon its solution will in large part depend the development of our private wealth, today removed from that fecund center of labor and general prosperity.

Source: A Chilean Offers a Different Vision from *El pensamiento de Balmaceda.* Fernando Silva Vargas, ed. Reprinted in *Latin American Civilization: History & Society. 1492 to the Present 6E* Benjamin Keen, ed. and trans. Boulder, CO; Westview Press, 1996.

6

New Actors
on
an Old Stage

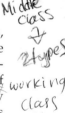

As Latin America approached its independence centennial, two trends, one of external origin and the other internal, emerged with greater clarity. The first was the emergence of the United States as a major world power. Motivated by economic interests, United States leaders adopted a philosophy of Manifest Destiny, justifying aggression by claims of concern about security and by blatantly racist attitudes toward Latin America. The second trend was the emergence of middle sectors in Latin American society. The middle sectors could be divided into two groups: the middle class, which aspired to the wealth of the elites via the path of progress shown by the United States, and the working class, which sought to improve its lot more through European examples of labor unions, introduced by the flood of immigrants to such countries as Brazil and Argentina. Together, the United States and the Latin American middle sectors helped to shape Latin American history during the twentieth century. What were their motivations and goals? How would they influence the flow of history?

The Presence of the United States

Foreign influence, and none more so than Great Britain's, shaped much of the historical course of Latin America during the nineteenth century. At first Great Britain had no serious rivals to its economic domination of the region. But as the United States grew stronger, its capitalists and politicians were determined to spread across the North American continent and to dominate the Caribbean. By the early twentieth century, the United States had succeeded in doing both and was well on its way to replacing Britain's century-long domination of Latin America. Concerns for security and desires for trade shaped U.S. attitudes and policies toward Latin America. Obviously the United States and Latin America shared the same geography, the Western Hemisphere, thus being neighbors, in a certain romantic sense, even though much of the United States was closer to Europe than it was to most of South America.

Despite the tough talk of the Monroe Doctrine in 1823, the United States was not at the time a world power, and Washington officials ignored the proclamation for decades. Meanwhile, European powers intervened in Latin America at will: The British reoccupied the Falkland Islands despite vigorous Argentine protests, the French intervened in Mexico and the Plata area, and the French and British blockaded Buenos Aires, all without the United States reminding these European interlopers of the content or intention of Monroe's statement. Only when the British and French maneuvered to thwart the union of Texas with the United States did President John Tyler invoke the principles of the doctrine in 1842 to warn the Europeans to keep out of hemispheric affairs. Indeed, as later used, the doctrine provided a handy shield for North American expansion, well underway by the mid-1840s. As President James Polk gazed westward toward California, he notified the Europeans that his country opposed any transfer of territory in the New World from one European state to another, or from a nation of the Western Hemisphere to a European nation. However, by his interpretation the Monroe Doctrine did not prohibit territorial changes among the nations of this hemisphere. Such an interpretation complemented the annexation by the United States of Texas in 1845 and of Arizona, New Mexico, and California later in the decade. Expansionist sentiment rose to a fever pitch as the Stars and Stripes fluttered across the continent toward the Pacific Ocean. An editorial in the influential *De Bow's Commercial Review* in 1848 expressed the ebullient mood of a confident nation:

> The North Americans will spread out far beyond their present bounds. They will encroach again and again upon their neighbors. New territories will be planted, declare their independence, and be annexed. We have New Mexico and California! We will have Old Mexico and Cuba!

The editorial reflected the era's dominant theme: Manifest Destiny, an expression coined in 1845 by John L. O'Sullivan, editor of the *Democratic Review*. The term meant that the United States, due to Anglo-Saxon superiority, was destined to absorb its neighbors. As O'Sullivan put it: "This continent is for white people, and not only the continent but the islands adjacent, and the Negro must be kept in slavery."

Initial U.S. expansionist efforts were deeply entwined with the issue of slavery, both in the United States and in Latin America. O'Sullivan's brother-in-law was Cristobal Madán, a Cuban planter who served as leader of the annexationist lobby in New York in 1845. Madán represented the Cuban planters who wanted to join the United States as a slave state. Slave owners in the U.S. south looked longingly at Cuba, Mexico, and Central America as potential slave states.

Great Britain served as the major check on United States expansion southward into Middle America and the Caribbean during the mid-nineteenth century. The best the United States could arrange at the time was an agreement in 1850, the Clayton-Bulwer Treaty, in which both nations promised not to occupy, fortify, colonize, or otherwise exercise domination over Central America. Specifically, neither country would seek to build an interoceanic canal. The treaty temporarily checked the territorial expansion of both nations into troubled and tempting republics that otherwise stood helpless before the two aggressive Anglo-Saxon powers. Significantly, no representatives of the targeted Latin American nations were a party to the treaty. At about the same time the attention of the United States focused inward once again, as a divided nation girded itself for internal strife.

While civil war rent the United States, several European nations pursued their own adventures in the New World. Spain reannexed the Dominican Republic and fought Peru and Chile. France intervened in Mexico. Only after it became apparent that the North was winning the Civil War and was determined to oppose European adventures in this hemisphere did Spain depart from the Dominican Republic and return the Chincha Islands to Peru. When Napoleon III hesitated to withdraw French forces from Mexico, the government in Washington dispatched a large army to the Mexican border to help the French emperor make up his mind. Once these European threats to Latin America had ended, the United States seemed content to ignore the region, at least for the moment, while the nation concentrated its energies on reconstruction, railroad building, and industrialization.

But the rapid industrial growth of the post-war years eventually prompted United States businesspeople and leaders to search for new markets, and none seemed more promising than Latin America, long the domain of European salespeople. One of the most remarkable secretaries of state, James G. Blaine, understanding the need for friendship and cooperation among the nations of the hemisphere, sought to stimulate more intimate commercial relations as a logical means to solidify the inter-American community. The United States had long appreciated the strategic importance of Latin America but had been slow to develop its trade relations with the huge area. During the last half of the nineteenth century, North American commerce with and investments in Latin America rose gradually. In the vigorous industrial age that had begun in the United States, Secretary of State Blaine envisioned a fraternal hemispheric trade in which the United States supplied the manufactured goods and Latin America the raw products. With that idea in mind, he presided over the first Inter-American Conference, held in Washington in 1889–90. Although cordiality characterized the sessions, it became increasingly obvious that the Latin Americans were less interested in placing orders for the new industrial products than they were in containing the expansion of an ambitious neighbor by obtaining a promise of respect for the sovereignty of their nations. The times augured ill for such a promise. In fact, at that very moment, a rising tide of sentiment favoring expansion once again swept the United States.

Others in the United States realized as Blaine did that Latin America contained great wealth and potential, but unlike the secretary of state they showed less subtlety in coveting it. In the eyes of many, the Latin Americans appeared too slow in fulfilling the destiny that nature had charted for the area. A growing number of United States citizens thought that Latin America needed a dose of "Protestant virtues and Yankee know-how" to turn potential into reality. The Reverend Josiah Strong summed up much of the opinion of his fellow countrymen in his influential book *Our Country*, published in 1885, when he wrote, "Having developed peculiarly aggressive traits calculated to impress its institutions upon mankind, [the United States] will spread itself over the earth. If I read not amiss, this powerful race will move down Central and South America, out upon the islands of the sea, over upon Africa and beyond. And can anyone doubt that the result of this competition of races will be the 'survival of the fittest'?" Imbued with the Spencerian and Darwinian philosophy popular at the time, the good Reverend spoke with the enthusiasm, confidence, and arrogance of his generation. Other powerful voices soon echoed his views. Senator Henry Cabot Lodge spoke of "our rightful supremacy in the Western Hemisphere." Naval officer, historian, and strategist Alfred T. Mahan lobbied for a bigger and better navy—preferably able to quickly cross the continent and protect both coasts. Senator Albert J. Beveridge put his faith in a still more potent force: "God has marked the American people as His chosen Nation to finally lead to the regeneration of the world. . . . We are trustees of the world's progress, guardians of its righteous peace." Secretary of State Richard Olney announced to the world in 1895 that the United States was supreme in the Western Hemisphere, where its will would be done.

Thus, by the end of the nineteenth century, government, religious, and business leaders alike spoke approvingly of expanding world markets and of

Wreckage of the American battleship *Maine* in the harbor of Havana after the mysterious explosion. (National Archives.)

a global foreign policy. Their talk soon led to action: American overseas expansion into the Pacific and the Caribbean. Significantly that expansion began after the conquest of the western frontier, after several decades of impressive industrial growth, and during the economic difficulties of the 1890s. The chance came in 1898, when the United States intervened in Cuba's war for independence from Spain. The Cubans were close to winning on their own when U.S. officials used the excuse of the explosion of the battleship Maine in Havana Harbor to enter the war. The United States easily defeated Spain and took possession of the Philippine Islands, Cuba, and Puerto Rico. The quick victory marked the debut of the United States as a world power embarked upon a new international course of extracontinental expansion, which one influential journalist of the day characterized admiringly as "the imperialism of liberty." Washington annexed Puerto Rico and made Cuba a protectorate, a state of dependency that officially lasted thirty-five years. Formal occupation ended only after the United States insisted in 1901 that Cuba attach the Platt amendment to its constitution. Written by U.S. Senator Orville Platt, the amendment read, "Cuba consents that the United States may exercise the right to intervene for the protection of Cuban independence, the maintenance of a government adequate for the protection of life, property, and individual liberty."

Americans doubted that Cubans could be trusted to manage their own affairs, a point of view that grew out of racism. In a speech about the status of the Philippines after the war, Sen. Beveridge articulated common views of the people both freed and conquered by the Spanish-American War:

> We will not renounce our part in the mission of our race, trustee, under God, of the civilization of the world. . . . Mr. President, this question is deeper than any question of party politics, deeper than any question of the isolated policy of our country even; deeper even than any question of constitutional power. It is elemental. It is racial. God has not been preparing the English-speaking and Teutonic peoples for a thousand years for nothing but vain and idle self-contemplation and self-admiration. No! He has made us the master organizers of the world to establish system where chaos reigns.

Next, the United States turned to the issue of constructing an interoceanic canal, spurred by military and commercial considerations. The first step toward the realization of a canal was to abrogate the old Clayton-Bulwer Treaty. Under international pressure, London agreed in the Hay-Pauncefote Treaty in 1901 to permit the United States to build, operate, and fortify a canal across the isthmus. Washington then proceeded to negotiate with Colombia for rights across Panama, but the Senate in Bogotá balked at the terms suggested. At that point, the Panamanians seceded from Colombia and declared their independence on November 3, 1903. They were helped by the presence of two U.S. gunboats, the Nashville and the Dixie, which prevented Colombian troops from countering the bloodless Panamanian insurrection. The commander of the Nashville had orders to take over the railroad, preventing the already-arrived Colombian troops from boarding the railroad to travel from Colón to Panama City. Within a week of Panama's declaration of independence, the United States also sent the Atlanta, Maine, Mayflower, and Prairie to Colón and the Boston, Marblehead, Concord, and Wyoming to Panama City.

The Panamanians found their new sovereignty heavily compromised by the treaty signed fifteen days later by U.S. Secretary of State John Hay and the Frenchman Philippe Bunau-Varilla, an international adventurer who purported to represent Panama's interests. The treaty he signed in Panama's name granted the United States "in perpetuity" control of a ten-mile strip across the Isthmus with power and jurisdiction "as if it were sovereign." It was negotiated without consulting the Panamanians. Work on the canal began in 1904 and terminated a decade later. Controversy over the canal and the treaty that made it possible raged until the canal was finally handed back to the Panamanians on December 31, 1999.

The trespassing of the North American giant on Latin American sovereignty evoked protest and aroused distrust. Many Latin American intellectuals of the period spoke out to denounce "the Yankee imperialism." Physically unable to prevent the interventions, Latin American governments sought recourse in international law. They labored long and determinedly to persuade Washington to renounce by treaty recourse to intervention.

But Theodore Roosevelt, who led his Rough Riders in Cuba before becoming U.S. president in 1904, expressed the new U.S. sentiment well in what became known as the Roosevelt Corollary to the Monroe Doctrine: "Chronic wrongdoing, or an impotence which results in a general loosening of the ties of civilized society, may in America, as elsewhere, ultimately require intervention by some civilized nation, and in the Western Hemisphere the adherence of the United States to the Monroe Doctrine may force the United States, however reluctantly, in flagrant cases of such wrongdoing or impotence, to the exercise of an international police power."

National rhetoric reflected that attitude. In his study published in 1908 of the relations between the United States and Latin America, George W. Crichfield spoke pompously of the duty to impose "civilization" on the Latin Americans: "The United States is in honor bound to maintain law and order in South America, and we may just as well take complete control of several of the countries, and establish decent governments while we are about it." More than half the nations, he huffed, had "sinned away their day of grace. They are semibarbarous centers of rapine. . . . They are a reproach to the civilization of the twentieth century."

Diplomacy dictated that such ideas be expressed more subtly, but there can be no doubt that the same sentiments governed Washington's twentieth-century behavior in Latin America in the twin pursuits of trade and security. Theoretically, the United States was ready to put aside the gunboat diplomacy of the turn of the century for the more genteel "Dollar Diplomacy." But the United States did not hesitate to send troops in to protect those dollars. President William Howard Taft (1908–12) left no doubt of where his government stood on those matters. Influenced by his experiences as the first civil governor (1901–04) of the U.S-controlled Philippine Islands and provisional governor of Cuba (1906), he announced that his foreign policy would "include active intervention to secure our merchandise and our capitalists opportunity for profitable investment." Indeed, the United States already had involved itself physically in the region that most strategically concerned it, the Caribbean and circum-Caribbean.

In the period between 1898 and 1934, the United States intervened militarily in Cuba, Mexico, Guatemala, Honduras, Nicaragua, Panama, Colombia, Haiti, and the Dominican Republic. In some nations, such as Honduras, Panama, and Cuba, the interventions occurred repeatedly. In others, like Haiti, the Dominican Republic, and Nicaragua, they lasted for years, even decades. In Haiti, the marines landed in 1915 and did not depart until 1934. Tolerating no opposition, the marines fought continuously during their interventions against outraged local patriots. For example, in Haiti, Charlemagne Peralte organized a guerrilla army in 1917 to fight the U.S. Marines. Betrayed, he died in an ambush two years later. The newspapers in the United

U.S. Military Interventions in the Caribbean Basin, 1898–1934

COUNTRY	INTERVENTION
Costa Rica	1921
Cuba	1898–02, 1906–09, 1912, 1917–22
Dominican Republic	1903, 1904, 1914, 1916–24
Guatemala	1920
Haiti	1915–34
Honduras	1903, 1907, 1911, 1912, 1919, 1924, 1925
Mexico	1916, 1914, 1916–17, 1918–19
Nicaragua	1898, 1899, 1909–10, 1912–25, 1926–33
Panama	1903–14, 1921, 1925

Source: Peter H. Smith. *Talons of the Eagle: Dynamics of U.S.–Latin American Relations* (N.Y.: Oxford University Press, 1996), p. 53.

States invariably branded those armed opponents as "bandits." Of course viewpoints conflicted. Those termed bandits by the U.S. Army were labeled "freedom fighters" or "guerillas" by others who were bearing the brunt or feeling the humiliation of the intervention.

While its interventions in Nicaragua dated back to 1849, the United States did not occupy the country until the twentieth century. Annoyed with President José Santos Zelaya (1893–1909), a fiery nationalist who talked of enlisting Japanese, British, or German help to build a canal across Nicaragua, the United States dispatched a fleet in 1909 to overthrow him. Thus began a prolonged occupation, 1909 to 1933 (with one break in 1925–26). Denouncing the seemingly endless occupation by the Yankees who "murder us in our own land," Augusto César Sandino launched a rebellion on July 16, 1927, with the announcement: "I am accepting the invitation to combat." For five and a half years, Sandino led the fight to expel the foreign occupiers.

For that challenge, the international press vilified him as a bloodthirsty bandit. His skill in harassing the marines, avoiding capture, and embarrassing the United States won the support of large numbers of Nicaraguans and the admiration of many Latin Americans. On repeated occasions, Sandino advocated changes for a "free Nicaragua": a popular, independent government, the revision of all treaties that limited Nicaragua's sovereignty, and the recovery of the nation's riches and resources for the benefit of all. He favored land reform: "I believe the state owns the land . . . . I favor a system of cooperatives to work the land." Nationalism propelled and shaped his struggle and the revolution it promised. To an occupied people, he was a patriot, a man who nourished their self-respect.

The treacherous assassination of General Sandino opened a new chapter in Nicaraguan history. After the U.S. Marines withdrew in January 1933, Sandino agreed to a cease fire and signed a protocol of peace with President

United States marines hang around on a railroad flatcar in Nicaragua.
(National Archives.)

Juan Bautista Sacasa. Sandino swore loyalty to the president, while repeatedly warning him to beware of the new Guardia Nacional (National Guard), created, equipped, and trained by the U.S. Marines. He particularly suspected the ambitions of the Guard's commander, Anastasio Somoza García. In the spring, Sandino issued a "Manifesto" declaring his moral support of President Sacasa and his intention to remain in the Segovia mountains, where he would "organize agricultural cooperatives in those beautiful regions that for centuries have been ignored by the statesmen." In February 1934, Sandino returned to Managua for more talks with the government. On that occasion, General Somoza and officers of the Guardia Nacional planned the assassination of Sandino, who was seized after leaving a dinner with Sacasa and executed. Somoza waited until 1936 to depose Sacasa and to establish a dynastic rule that lasted until 1979. But the ghost of Augusto César Sandino did not rest. Most Nicaraguans—and many Latin Americans—accorded him a position of honor as a folk hero. From his grave he would defeat the Somozas.

The rationale for U.S. interventions varied. In the cases of the Dominican Republic and Haiti, the marines landed ostensibly to forestall threatened European intervention to collect debts; in Nicaragua, the country's alleged chaotic finances partially explained the United States presence, but probably more significant was the rumor that the Nicaraguan government might sell exclusive canal rights through its territory to either Japan or Great Britain. Threats, real or imagined, against U.S. citizens or property occasioned other U.S. interventions. Nor were they limited to small republics; both Colombia and Mexico felt the weight of the "Colossus of the North."

Meanwhile, the United States eclipsed Great Britain as the dominant foreign economic influence. Investments from the United States rose rapidly. By 1897, U.S. capital in Latin America totaled $320 million, chiefly in Mexico, Cuba, and Central America. Railroads ranked as the most important investment, followed by mining and then agriculture. In the next fifteen years, investments jumped fivefold, with Chile and Peru joining the Middle American nations as the chief recipients of attention. By 1929, U.S. citizens had invested $3.5 billion, or 40 percent of all overseas investments, in Latin America.

Trade between the United States and Latin America increased with equal rapidity. The United States supplanted Europe in economic importance in Middle America. By 1914 the United States was purchasing 75 percent of Mexico's exports and supplying 50 percent of its neighbor's imports. By 1919 the United States consumed two-thirds of Central America's exports, while furnishing that area with three-quarters of its imports. Domination of the South American markets was less complete but nonetheless important and growing. New steamship lines and telegraph cables tightened the links between the United States and Latin America.

The North Americans, who had forged particularly strong economic links with Brazil, were the principal customers of Brazil's three major exports: coffee, rubber, and cocoa. Since 1865, the United States had taken the single largest share of Brazil's coffee, after 1870 buying more than half its coffee beans sold abroad. The result was that by 1912 the United States bought 36 percent of Brazil's exports, while the second most important market, Great Britain, purchased only 15 percent. Indicating the increasing importance of trade with Brazil, the National City Bank of New York in 1915 established the first two U.S. bank branches there. In the same year, an American Chamber of Commerce opened in Rio de Janeiro. Those growing commercial relations strengthened diplomatic understanding and cooperation between Brazil and the United States. In 1904, the Brazilian Foreign Office classified Washington as the "number one" diplomatic post and the following year raised its legation to the rank of embassy in the North American capital, the first South American nation to do so. The United States immediately reciprocated. The United States enjoyed a friendship with the South American giant unique in the annals of hemispheric diplomacy, a counterpoint to tensions prevailing in other regions created by U.S. concerns for security and Latin American fears of aggression.

The Middle Sectors Emerge

The rhythm of Latin America's population growth quickened. Increasing at a rate of 1.3 percent per year in the last half of the nineteenth century, the population doubled between 1850 and 1900, from 30.5 to 61 million, exceeding by two-thirds the rate of growth during the previous century. Latin

America's population grew at a much faster rate than Europe's. The rate accelerated slightly in the period from 1900 to 1930, averaging 1.7 percent per year, so that population totaled 104 million by 1930. The most rapid increase was in the southern temperate zone of South America, especially in Uruguay and Argentina.

In the cities there emerged a small middle sector, which grew in size and influence over the course of the century. Members of the liberal professions—schoolteachers and professors—as well as bureaucrats, military officers, businessmen, merchants, and those involved in the nascent industrialization composed the ranks of that group. The common denominator of the middle sectors rested on the fact that they were neither admitted to the ranks of the traditional elite nor associated with the lower and poorer ranks of society. The observant James Bryce noted during his tour of South America at the end of the first decade of the twentieth century, "In the cities there exists, between the wealthy and the workingmen, a considerable body of professional men, shopkeepers, and clerks, who are rather less of a defined middle class than they might be in European countries." They possessed a strong urge to improve their lot and tended to imitate, as far as it was possible, the elite. Still, they were not cohesive enough or sufficiently defined to compose a "class," and for that reason the purposely chosen, more nebulous term "middle sectors" is applied to them.

Initially, the heirs of the creoles and mazombos tended to predominate in the middle sectors, but increasing numbers of mulattos and mestizos entered their ranks as well. Education and military service provided two of the surest paths of upward mobility, but initially the climb was too steep for any but the exceptional or the favored. In many of the Latin American nations the mestizos or mulattos formed the largest part of the population. Mexico, Guatemala, Ecuador, Peru, Bolivia, and Paraguay, for example, had large mestizo populations, while the Dominican Republic, Venezuela, and Brazil had large mulatto populations. Representatives of the mestizos and mulattos entered the middle sectors in large numbers during the last decades of the nineteenth century and claimed their right to play a political and economic role in their nation's destiny. In some cases, the traditional social elites accommodated their ambitions; in others their frustrations mounted as they were excluded from positions of control, prestige, or wealth.

Although few in number, the dominant presence of the middle sectors in the capital city of each nation allowed them to wield influence far out of proportion to their numbers. A high percentage of the intellectuals, authors, teachers, and journalists came from their ranks, and they had a powerful voice in expressing what passed for public opinion in the late nineteenth century. By the end of the century, they had enough direction to increasingly exert influence on the course of events in some nations, particularly Argentina, Brazil, Chile, Mexico, Uruguay, and Costa Rica. Only later were they large and articulate enough to wield a similar influence in other countries.

Only an educated guess permits some approximation of the size of the middle sectors. At the end of the nineteenth century it is estimated that Mexico had an urban middle group numbering roughly three-quarters of a million, while another quarter of a million constituted a rural middle group. In contrast, there was an urban proletariat of more than one-third of a million and a huge peon class of eight million working on the haciendas. In Mexico, Chile, Brazil, Argentina, and Uruguay, the middle sectors may have included as much as 10 percent of the population by the turn of the century. In many of the other countries, it fell far short of that.

The swelling tide of foreign immigration contributed to the growth of the middle sectors. Many of the new arrivals were from the lower class, but a significant percentage represented Europe's middle class, and there was also a high incidence of upward mobility among the immigrants in the lands of their adoption. Argentina has been one of the largest recipients of immigrants in modern times. Between independence and 1914, approximately three million arrived, a majority of them Italians and Spaniards. In 1914, 30 percent of Argentines were foreign-born. These immigrants provided 60 percent of the urban proletariat and held 46 percent of the jobs associated with the middle sectors. Half of the population of Buenos Aires in 1914 was foreign-born. Alberto Gerchunoff, a Russian who arrived in Argentina in 1895, left a moving account of the problems and satisfactions of assimilation in his *The Jewish Gauchos of the Pampas* (1910).

About 100,000 Europeans migrated to Chile before World War I. They constituted at that time only 4 percent of the population. Yet the foreign-born owned 32 percent of Chile's commercial establishments and 49 percent of the industries. Brazil welcomed large numbers of Europeans, particularly Italians, Portuguese, and Spaniards. Between 1891 and 1900, approximately 112,500 immigrants arrived annually. The trend continued and reached record yearly averages just before World War I. From 1911 through 1913, half a million immigrants entered. However, the proportion of immigrants to the total population in Brazil never surpassed 6.4 percent, a figure reached in 1900. Nonetheless, because of their concentration in the south and southeast, and particularly because of their importance in the cities of these two regions, they exerted an influence far greater than their numbers might indicate. The traditional elite soon grew wary of the immigrants and blamed them for many of the ills the burgeoning urban centers began to experience.

Certain characteristics of the middle sectors increasingly became evident. The majority lived in the cities and boasted an above-average education. Their income level placed them between the wealthy few and the impoverished many. Although the heterogeneous middle sector never unified, on occasion a majority might agree on specific goals, such as improved or expanded education, further industrialization, or more rapid modernization, and on certain methods to achieve them, such as the formation of political parties or the exaltation of nationalism. They consented to the use of the government to foment change, and with minimal dissension welcomed the government's participation and even direction of the economy. Still, political preferences within their ranks varied from far right to far left.

Although the middle sectors expressed strong nationalistic sentiments, they also looked abroad for models, as did the elites. This contradiction was expressed most emphatically in their ambivalence toward the United States: on the one hand, a model of progress, and on the other a too-powerful neighbor with aggressive tendencies. Their nationalism prompted frequent outcries against "Yankee imperialism." Yet the middle sectors regarded the United States as the example of a New World nation that had "succeeded," an example of the "progress" preached but not always practiced in aristocratic Europe. True, the United States embraced impressive examples of poverty as well as wealth, but it seemed that large numbers, even a majority, lived somewhere between those extremes so characteristic of Latin American society. The aggressive strength of their counterparts in the United States inspired the Latin American middle sector.

They attributed part of the apparent success of the United States to industrialization and education, and so they prescribed industrialization as a panacea for their national ills. The high North American literacy rate seemed to provide the proper preparation for an industrial society, and the middle sectors appreciated the mobility that education afforded the citizens of that technological nation. The American educator Horace Mann became a revered figure to many Latin American leaders, and they eagerly imported not only his doctrines but also the Yankee books and schoolteachers to go with them. Domingo F. Sarmiento met Mann, imbibed his ideas, and as president of Argentina (1868–74) hired New England teachers to direct the new normal schools he established. President Justo Rufino Barrios in Guatemala (1873–85) encouraged the North American missionaries to set up Protestant schools. Finally, the comfortable lifestyle of the U.S. middle class, with its increasing arsenal of consumer goods, impressed the Latin American candidates for middle-class status.

The middle sectors favored reform over revolution. They sought entrance into the national institutions, not necessarily destruction of them. In fact, they demonstrated a preference for economic improvement and less concern with altering political structures. Although the elites at first distrusted the middle sectors, they eventually understood their potential as allies and not only incorporated them into their privileged institutions but also in due course let them administer them—a trust that the middle class did not betray.

The elites were less sure of the other significant element of the middle sectors, the working class. As urbanization and industrialization expanded, a larger, more cohesive, and militant proletariat appeared. Slowly becoming aware of their common problems and goals, these workers unionized despite relentless government opposition. The first unions appeared after 1850, evolving from mutual aid societies. They tended to be small, ephemeral, and local organizations. The typographers, stevedores, railroad employees, artisans, miners, and textile workers were the first to organize, and most of the early union activity concentrated in Buenos Aires, Montevideo, Havana, Santiago-Valparaíso, and Mexico City, as well as in the mining regions of northern Chile and central Mexico. By 1914, about half a dozen nations boasted well-organized unions, and at least some attempt had been made in the rest to institute them. At any rate, the foundation for future expansion was laid.

In the following two decades, the local unions expanded into national organizations, recruiting ever larger numbers from all urban sectors as well as from some of the rural proletariat. The economic dislocations caused by World War I and the financial collapse of 1929 induced labor unrest, mounting militancy, and strikes. A working-class consciousness took shape as labor thought in terms of changing the national institutions to suit its own needs.

In their periods of formation and expansion, the unions could and did cooperate with other urban elements, specifically the middle sectors. Both sought change, however modest, and realized they had to challenge the traditional elites to get it. The privileged oligarchy resented and opposed that alliance. Once the middle sectors achieved their more limited goals and began to participate in the national institutions, they broke their alliance and aligned with the elite.

The Middle Class in Politics

As the heterogeneous middle class emerged, its members sought to play a political role. Inexperienced, they experimented. Their first goal focused on admission to power.

In Brazil, the middle sectors were strong enough to help overthrow the monarchy in 1889 and for a short time, in conjunction with the military, to rule the nation. The composition of Brazilian society had altered considerably in the nineteenth century. At the time of independence the new empire counted barely 4 million inhabitants, of whom probably half were slaves of African birth or descent. Sixty-five years later there were 14 million Brazilians, roughly 600,000 of whom were slaves. At the other end of the social scale stood 300,000 plantation owners and their families. Most of the population fell somewhere between the two extremes. True, most of them were impoverished, illiterate rural folk who unknowingly contributed to the status quo. But there was an important, growing body of urban dwellers, many of whom qualified for the ranks of the middle sectors. The gulf between the countryside, with its many vestiges of the colonial past, and the city, with its increasingly progressive outlook, widened during the last decades of the nineteenth century. The urban dwellers were less favorably disposed to two basic institutions inherited from the past, slavery and monarchy, than was the rural population. They viewed those institutions as buttresses of the position of the elite and un-complementary to their own best interests. Indeed, they perceived the two institutions as the means by which the traditional rural elite retained most of what was colonial in Brazilian society and in the economy while still rejecting, in the stricter legal sense, colonial status. The military, hostile to slavery, ignored by the emperor, and restless, shared the view of the urban middle sectors to whom the officers were closely related both by family ties and philosophy. Together, they brought an end to both slavery and monarchy.

Not surprisingly the new republican government established by the military in 1889 reflected the goals and aspirations of Brazil's middle sector. The new chief of state, Deodoro da Fonseca, was the son of an army officer of modest means, and his cabinet consisted of two other military officers, an engineer, and four lawyers. They were sons of the city with university degrees, a contrast to the aristocratic scions who had formed previous governments. During its early years, the republic was identified with both the military and the urban middle groups much more than the monarchy had ever been. As one of their goals, they hoped to transform the nation through industrialization. The government raised the tariff on items that competed with national goods and lowered the duty on primary goods used in national manufacturing. To augment the number of technicians, four new engineering schools were opened in the 1890s. A high income from coffee exports, generous credit from the banks, and the government's issue of larger amounts of currency animated economic activity to a fever pitch. Speculation became the order of the day. Bogus companies abounded, but unfortunately for Brazil the speculation resulted in little real industrial progress. In 1893 a political crisis complicated the economic distress. The navy revolted and the southern state of Rio Grande do Sul rose in rebellion; together they threatened the existence of the republic.

The powerful coffee planters, with their wealth and control of the state governments of São Paulo, Minas Gerais, and Rio de Janeiro, held the balance of power between the government and the rebels. They promised aid to the government in return for a guarantee of an open presidential election in 1894. Both kept their sides of the bargain, and in the elections the coffee interests pushed their candidate into the presidential palace. The political victory of the coffee interests reflected the predominant role coffee had come to play in the Brazilian economy. Cheap suitable land, high profits, large numbers of immigrant workers, and a rising world demand made coffee a popular and lucrative crop. By the end of the nineteenth century it composed half of the nation's exports.

The alliance of the coffee planters and the federal government in 1894 superseded all previous political arrangements. Thereafter, the political dominance of the coffee interests characterized the First Republic (1889–1930). The new oligarchy, principally from São Paulo but secondarily from Minas Gerais and Rio de Janeiro, ruled Brazil for its own benefit for thirty-six years. The coffee interests arranged the elections of presidents friendly to their needs and dictated at will the policies of the governments. Sound finances, political stability, and decentralization were the goals pursued by the coffee presidents.

The urban middle groups, whose unreliable ally, the military, was torn by disunion and bickering, lost the power they had exercised for so brief and unsettled a period. These middle groups increasingly resented the economic and political monopoly the large planters wielded in the republic. They decried the many favors the government lavished on the planters. Occasionally they supported a presidential candidate, such as Ruy Barbosa in 1910, who understood their aims and objectives. For the elections of 1922, the urban groups and the military united in an unsuccessful effort to wrest the presidency from the coffee elite. They failed. Thereafter, violent protest erupted in Brazil.

In July of 1922, shortly after the coffee interests had once again imposed their presidential preference on the nation, a handful of junior officers revolted in Rio de Janeiro in a poorly planned effort to overthrow the moribund republic. It signaled the beginning of an eight-year period of unrest, which climaxed in 1930 with the fall of the republic. The discontented elements centered in the cities.

By 1926, the movement of the junior military officers, known in Portuguese as *tenentes* (meaning lieutenants), had acquired a somewhat more identifiable philosophy, even though it never became precise. The tenentes maintained a mystical faith that somehow the military could alter the habits of the country and provide the impetus to propel it into the modern age. Their primary concern was not democracy but reform. For the remainder of the discussion, reform denotes a gradual change or modification of established economic, political, or social structures. The tenentes wanted to retire the entrenched politicians and modernize the nation. Then, and only then, they would consent to return the nation to constitutional rule. They hoped to expand the base of the government and to eradicate regionalism. They favored a very strong, centralized government. Revealing "social democratic" tendencies, the tenentes proposed government recognition of trade unions and cooperatives, a minimum wage, maximum working hours, child-labor legislation, agrarian reform, nationalization of natural resources, and expanded educational facilities. Obviously much of the program favored the urban middle groups. However, those groups failed to understand that the various military rebellions and movements in the 1920s could have been turned to their advantage. Indicative of the weakness of the middle groups was their inability to coordinate their desires for modernization with the similar desires of the young officers. Still, by the end of the decade of the 1920s, the middle groups had some accomplishments to their credit: They had helped to abolish slavery, to bring down the monarchy, to encourage education, to promote industrialization, and to stoke the fires of nationalism, but they did not achieve the influence their counterparts did in some of the Spanish-speaking nations.

At the same time the middle sectors were maturing and tasting their first political power in gigantic Brazil, the small nation of Costa Rica felt the initial influences of its own middle group. Always remote from the activities of the Spanish empire, Costa Rica had been relatively isolated from the political turmoil of the rest of Central America. There was no privileged wealthy class from the colonial era, and this relative poverty had created a rough equality in a nation that contained only slightly more than a quarter of a million inhabitants at the close of the century. Costa Rica engaged in minimal foreign trade until the mid-nineteenth century, when it became a leading coffee producer. While there were indeed large landholdings, Costa Rica probably had a higher percentage of small and middle-range farmers than any other Latin American country at the end of the century. A society without the sharp edges of economic extremes offered good conditions for the growth of a middle class. The period from 1882 to 1917 boasted a remarkable record of constitutional government in which four-year presidential terms were honored and peacefully exchanged. Politicians and parties supported platforms substantively middle class in their goals. In the last half of the 1880s, Minister of Education Mauro Fernández laid the foundation for a system of free and compulsory public education that eventually would produce one of Latin America's most literate populations. The government also began to pay greater attention to public health. The widespread medical and health care that the government provided its citizens made them the healthiest of Central America. The relatively equitable patterns of land ownership, the positive emphasis on education, and the comparatively widespread participation of the citizenry in politics marked Costa Rica as an essentially middle-class nation.

In Chile, the middle sectors allied with the working classes in 1918 to form the Liberal Alliance, an electoral force dominant enough to win control of the Chamber of Deputies that year. The Alliance, under the banner of the popular Arturo Alessandri, went on to win the presidency in a closely contested election in 1920. Alessandri had promised many socioeconomic reforms, but once in office he found his efforts to fulfill those promises frustrated by the conservatives in congress hostile to his program. The conservatives, from their stronghold in the Senate, clearly represented the traditional values of the oligarchy as they fought off the efforts of the urban middle and working groups to implement change. A congressional election in 1924 favored Alessandri by giving him a working majority. The new congress promptly enacted his broad social-welfare program. It recognized labor unions and assured their independence. Alas, congress voted itself a handsome pay raise at an economically inopportune moment when paychecks to the military had been delayed. Contrary to its previous constitutional behavior, the army rebelled and sent Alessandri packing in September of 1924. A liberal countercoup in 1925 brought him back from exile. He served six more months in office, during which time he was able to push a new constitution through congress, a document that replaced the ninety-two-year-old constitution written by

Portales. It ended Chile's experiment with parliamentarianism and returned to the president the full measure of power he had lost in 1891. It also contained advanced labor and social welfare provisions and authorized the state to intervene in social and economic matters. The middle class has remained a dominant force in Chilean politics ever since the Alessandri presidency.

In Uruguay, the Latin American middle sector won their greatest victory in the early twentieth century. Uruguay changed dramatically under the government of the middle sectors, providing one of the best such examples of peaceful change in Latin America. Independent Uruguay emerged in 1828 as a result of the stalemate between Argentina and Brazil, which had continued the centuries-old Luso-Spanish rivalry over the left bank of the Río de la Plata. Uruguayans divided into two political camps, the conservatives (Blancos) and the liberals (Colorados). From independence until 1872 they fought each other almost incessantly for power. When the liberals got power in 1872, they managed to hang on to it, despite challenges from the conservatives and the military, until 1959. During the last decades of the nineteenth century, relative peace settled over the small republic, by then in the process of an economic metamorphosis. Prosperity helped to pacify the nation. Exports of wool, mutton, hides, and beef rose. New methods of stock breeding, fencing, the refrigerated ship, and railroad construction (the mileage jumped five times from 200 to 1,000 miles between 1875 and 1895) modernized the economy.

During the same period, Uruguay constructed the foundation of its enviable educational system. New teacher-training institutes and public schools multiplied. Uruguay was on its way to becoming South America's most literate nation. Expanded and improved education was among the foremost concerns of the middle sectors, and the attention given to education in Uruguay reflected their increasing influence.

The outstanding political representative of the middle class at that time, not only in Uruguay but in all of Latin America, was José Batlle. He first exerted influence as the articulate editor of a prominent newspaper in Montevideo that spoke for the interests of the middle sectors and, by providing them with a voice, helped to organize that always amorphous group. By the end of the nineteenth century, he led the Colorado Party. He served twice as president (1903–07, 1911–15), but his influence over the government lasted until his death in 1929. During those decades, he sought to expand education, restrict foreign control, enact a broad welfare program, and unify the republic. He succeeded brilliantly in each instance, and through his strength and foresight he transformed Uruguay into a model bourgeois nation.

At the turn of the century, the conservatives controlled some of the departments (local territorial units) to the extent that they were virtually free of the control of the central government. Batlle extended the power of his government over them by assuring the conservatives proportional representation in the central government. He managed to balance the budget, repay foreign creditors, and strengthen the national currency. National banks grew in confidence and were able to lend to Uruguayans so that they no longer had to look abroad for much of their capital. To protect national industry, congress raised the tariffs. The government began to enter business, taking over light, power, insurance, and many other formerly private enterprises, and continued to do so on an ever-increasing scale. The government entered the meat-packing business to offer competition to the foreign companies that had long been engaged in the industry, so vital to a nation dependent on stock raising. The enactment of advanced social-welfare legislation guaranteed workers their right to unionize, a minimum wage, an eight-hour day, pensions, accident insurance, and paid holidays. Batlle felt the government should play a positive role in improving the living conditions of the less-favored citizens. On one occasion he announced, "There is great injustice in the enormous gap between the rich and the poor. The gap must be narrowed—and it is the duty of the state to attempt that task." These reforms, like others taking place in Latin America at the time, affected only the urban areas and never extended into the countryside. Strong as Batlle was, he never directly challenged the landowners or the rural socioeconomic structures. In fact, he saw no reason to, as he stated in 1910: "There is no pressing agrarian problem requiring the attention of the government. The division of the landed estates will take place in response to natural forces operating in our rural industries." It was a point of view shared by the middle-sector leaders of the period. Thus they permitted the continuation of the oldest and most fundamental land and labor institutions. Obviously such a neglect restricted national reforms and circumscribed the limits of change. The neglect of rural reforms reflected the middle sectors' fear of the power of the landowners, their preoccupation with the city, their own intermarriage and connections with the landowning families, and a desire to acquire estates of their own.

The climax of the Batlle reforms came in the new constitution, written in 1917 but promulgated in 1919. It provided a model of the type of government the middle class of the period wanted, one, of course, that guaranteed them power. It authorized direct elections, reduced the powers of the president and created a National Council of Administration to share the presidential powers (with the hope of eliminating any future threat of dictatorship), established a bicameral legislature elected by means of a proportional representative system, reduced the military to a minor institution, separated the Church and state, and provided a comprehensive program of social welfare. In creating the first welfare state in the Western Hemisphere, the middle class acknowledged their political debt to the working classes and rewarded them for their support.

Uruguay prospered in the years after World War I thanks to a lively demand abroad for products from the nation's fertile pampas. The good times were auspicious for the new reforms. Batlle died in 1929, just before the Great Depression challenged his democratic welfare state. In the first three decades of the twentieth century, Batlle demonstrated to the Latin Americans how a nation once immersed in chaos, tyranny, illiteracy, social inequality, and foreign exploitation could change peacefully. Compact in size, with a small and homogeneous population, with rich land and no adverse geography, Uruguay enjoyed advantages of which few other nations could boast. These advantages doubtless smoothed the path to reform. Still, Uruguay provided an example of a nation that could peacefully alter its course. In the three decades during which Batlle exerted his greatest influence, he accomplished much of what many progressive Latin Americans of the period desired. His constitution provided the blueprint for Uruguay's development in the twentieth century. The middle class throughout Latin America venerated it.

The middle class, complaining loudly of their precarious economic position, felt confident that education, industrialization, and nationalism charted a course to enhance their positions. In theory, some of them advocated a wide variety of reforms, but in practice they proved to be essentially conservative, fearful that too much reform might harm rather than benefit them.

The Middle Sectors and Feminism

In the early twentieth century, middle-class women began to organize to demand suffrage, while their working-class sisters sought equality in the union movements and the political trends linked to them, such as the anarchist movement in Argentina. As in the United States, women in Cuba and Brazil were often drawn into the feminist movement through their roles in the struggle for abolition of slavery. But both middle-class and working women found that their middle-sector brothers, while eager to achieve their own rights, were less eager to share them with women.

The middle-class reformers who sought suffrage had no radical reforms in mind. In fact, many did not expect women to hold public office, and merely sought the right to vote for men. Their position often was a moral one: Women could bring their superior morality to bear on the political world through voting, without actually having to participate in the rough and tumble of political contests.

Dismissed by the men in power, these women sought recognition by holding international conferences, hoping that the participation of foreigners would help them gain national influence. In 1910, the Congreso Femenino Internacional was held in Buenos Aires; in 1924, the Second Pan-American Women's Conference met in Peru; in 1928, women had an important presence at the International Conference of American States in Havana, where they demanded an Equal Rights Treaty. But it was not until the 7th International Conference of American States in Montevideo that women had official presence. The Convention on the Nationality of Women, signed by twenty countries at the conference, was the first treaty in history to extend equality to women.

Women's Suffrage in Latin America

Ecuador	1929
Brazil	1932
Uruguay	1932
Cuba	1934
El Salvador	1939
Dominican Republic	1942
Panama	1945
Guatemala	1945
Costa Rica	1945
Venezuela	1947
Argentina	1947
Chile	1949
Haiti	1950
Bolivia	1952
Mexico	1953
Honduras	1955
Nicaragua	1955
Peru	1955
Colombia	1957
Paraguay	1961

Feminists also formed international organizations to fight for their rights. In 1922, the Pan-American Association for the Advancement of Women was formed, with United States feminist leader Carrie Chapman Catt as president, and Mexico's Elena Torres as vice president. Brazilian activist Bertha Lutz served as vice president of the Pan-American Association for South America.

In the early decades of the twentieth century, suffragists met with little success. Women won the vote before World War II only in four countries: Ecuador, 1929; Brazil, 1932; Uruguay, 1932; and Cuba, 1934. The circumstances differed sharply in those countries. In Ecuador, conservative politicians sought women as allies against Socialist officers, who carried out a coup in 1925. In Brazil, Cuba, and Uruguay, suffrage was gained when women who had been organizing for many years were able to take advantage of political openings. In Brazil, attorney Bertha Lutz had been one of the key organizers of the Brazilian Federation for the Advancement of Women (*Federaçao Brasileira pelo Progresso Feminino*) in 1922. In 1930, when reformers took power, Lutz and the federation lobbied the new government on women's issues, winning suffrage in 1932. Lutz was then appointed to the commission to draft a new constitution; her successful contribution to the 1934 constitution was the Thirteen Principles, which included women's suffrage, the right of married women to retain their nationality, equal pay for equal work, paid maternity leave, and the right of women to hold public positions. In Uruguay, government officials were being pressured for reforms by European immigrants, labor, and liberal politicians. Granting woman suffrage in this context was a way to unite native-born Uruguayans against perceived foreign radicals. And finally, Cuban women won suffrage in the political opening after the overthrow of the dictator Gerardo Machado.

Not all feminists agreed with the goal of suffrage. Some argued that it gave too much credence to an ineffective political system in which votes were generally meaningless anyway. Many were more concerned about material needs, and indeed, a social agenda was included by many suffragists. For example, at Cuba's Second National Women's Conference in 1925, women called for social equality between men and women, equal pay for equal work, and equality of the claims of illegitimate children. In addition to the Thirteen Principles regarding women, Lutz also supported a labor agenda for both sexes that included a minimum salary, eight-hour day, paid vacations, and compensation for illness, injury, disability, and retirement.

The labor agenda was increasingly important for women as they joined the workforce in ever greater numbers. In Colombia in 1870, some 70 percent of the artisans were women. In Mexico City in 1895, more than 275,000 women worked as domestic servants. Women led strikes in the tobacco and

This 1875 photograph by Eadweard Muybridge focuses on five major domestic tasks of Guatemalan Indian women: transporting water, grinding corn meal, spinning cotton, combing cotton, and weaving.

Receiving lower wages than men, women were widely employed in the factories as Latin America industrialized in the twentieth century. These women manufactured helmets in Santiago, Chile, circa 1929.

textile industries in Mexico as early as 1880, organized in such groups as the *Hijas de Anahuac* (Daughters of Anahuac). In Chile, working women were organizing around workplace issues long before middle-class women began to organize as feminists.

But women workers were not always welcomed as allies by men. Some anarchists urged women to stay home because they feared that by enlarging the labor pool, they depressed wages—especially since employers paid women less than men. However, women were usually relegated to the least technical and mechanized positions; in the Argentine textile industry of the turn of the century, they often still worked at home as weavers and seamstresses. As the industry slowly expanded, women's positions were limited because of social reformers who pushed for protective legislation. As late as 1914 as many women industrial workers were at work in their homes as in the factories.

Women in the cities who could not find work in industry found few options: domestic service, laundering, ironing, and prostitution. In Guatemala City starting in the 1880s, prostitution was legalized and state-run. Women over 15 years old who were found guilty of "bad conduct" could be sentenced to a house of prostitution. Both those forced into the brothels and those who went voluntarily signed contracts that amounted to debt servitude. Such bordellos existed until 1920. While Guatemala may have been alone in its sentencing of women to brothels, most Latin American countries tried to regulate the occupation, and often forced women into other kinds of employment. For example, vagrancy laws were used to force women to work in textile factories and bakeries in Mexico, where women were virtual prisoners. In Argentina, poor women were often placed into domestic service, under the theory that they would be protected by the family.

A female basketball team, Nicaragua, 1927.

Domestic service, however, has often offered the worst possible conditions of employment. Live-in servants were often given miserable lodging and food, expected to work day and night, and subjected to sexual abuse by men in the home. If they became pregnant, they were usually fired. Complaints were dismissed as signs of ungratefulness from "girls" who were supposedly regarded as members of the family.

When working women became politically active, they were more likely to join the socialist and anarchist movements than the new middle-class parties being formed. The Argentine Socialist party supported women's rights from its founding in 1896. Alfredo Palacios, the first Socialist elected to the Chamber of Deputies (1804–08, 1912–15), gave testimony before the chamber showing statistics on the deplorable conditions of women workers. He was a supporter of the Feminist Center, which demanded shorter working hours, daycare centers, and safer equipment, measures that were not enacted.

Some radicals contended that women's rights should not be separate from workers' rights and opposed what was viewed as bourgeois feminism. Perhaps the best example of this view was espoused by Magda Portál, an activist in the 1920s in Peru's *Alianza Popular Revolucionaria Americana* (American Popular Revolutionary Alliance, APRA). Founded by Víctor Raúl Haya de la Torre in 1924, APRA was opposed to foreign imperialism and dedicated to the integration of Peru's sizable indigenous population into the economic and political life of Peru. Portál was a founding member of the party, and she argued that women's issues were not separable from the larger problems of society. "The aprista woman . . . does not want to conquer her rights through

Paraguayan army officers, 1915. Throughout Latin America, the military kept a sharp eye on the middle class during its initiation into the exercise of political power.

an open fight against men, as *feministas* do, but to collaborate with him as her companion," she argued. She openly argued against giving women the vote. "What type of women should have the right to vote? The educational level of the Peruvian woman, her prejudices, her willing dependency on male influence, and often, on that of the church, would convert the feminine vote into a means of strengthening conservative rather than revolutionary ideas." Her views were shared by the Mexican revolutionaries, who also refused to grant women the vote.

José Martí: Our America

Cubans refer to José Martí (1853–1895) as the apostle of Cuban independence. He founded the Cuban Revolutionary Party in 1892 to struggle for independence from Spain. Living in exile in the United States—in the belly of the beast, as he put it—he warned Cubans in this 1891 essay not to emulate foreign solutions to their problems but to look to their own creativity. Martí was killed fighting for Cuban independence in 1895.

To govern well requires an understanding and appreciation of local realities. Anyone who would govern well in the Americas does not need to know how the Germans or the French govern themselves but rather needs to possess a basic knowledge of his own country, its resources, advantages, and problems and how to utilize them for the benefit of the nation, and needs to know local customs and institutions. The goal is to reach that happy state in which everyone can enjoy the abundance Nature has bestowed so generously on the Americas. Each must work for that enjoyment and be prepared to defend that abundance with his life. Good government arises from the conditions and needs of each nation. The very spirit infusing government must reflect local realities. Good government is nothing more and nothing less than a balance of local needs and resources.

The person who knows his own environment is far superior to anyone dependent on imported books for knowledge. Such a natural person has more to contribute to society than someone versed in artificial knowledge. The native of mixed ancestry is superior to the white person born here but attracted to foreign ideas. No struggle exists between civilization and barbarism but rather between false erudition and natural knowledge. Natural people are good; they respect and reward wisdom as long as it is not used to degrade, humiliate, or belittle them. They are ready to defend themselves and to demand respect from anyone wounding their pride or threatening their well-being. Tyrants have risen to power by conforming to these natural elements; they also have fallen by betraying them. Our republics have paid through tyranny for their inability to understand the true national reality, to derive from it the best form of government, and to govern accordingly. In a new nation, to govern is to create.

In nations inhabited by both the educated and the uneducated, the uneducated will govern because it is their nature to confront and resolve problems with their hands, while the educated dither over which formula to import, a futile means to resolve local problems. The uneducated people are lazy and timid in matters related to intelligence and seek to be governed well,

but if they perceive the government to be injurious to their
interests they will overthrow it to govern themselves. How can
our universities prepare men to govern when not one of them
teaches anything either about the art of government or the local
conditions? The young emerge from our universities indoctrin-
ated with Yankee or French ideas, aspiring to govern a people
they do not understand. Those without a rudimentary knowledge
of political reality should be barred from a public career. Prizes
should be awarded not for the best poetry but for the best essays
on national reality. Journalists, professors, and academicians
ought to be promoting the study of national reality. Who are we,
where have we been, which direction should we go? It is essential
to ask such basic questions in our search for truth. To fail to ask
the right questions or to fail to answer them truthfully dooms us.
We must know the problems in order to respond to them, and
we must know our potentials in order to realistically frame
our responses. Strong and indignant natural people resent the
imposition of foreign solutions, the insidious result of sterile
book learning, because they have little or nothing to do with local
conditions and realities. To know those realities is to possess the
potential to resolve problems. To know our countries and to
govern them in accordance with that knowledge is the only way
to liberate ourselves from tyranny. Europeanized education
here must give way to American education. The history of the
Americas, from the Incas to the present, must be taught in detail
even if we forego the courses on ancient Greece. Our own Greece
is much more preferable to the Greece which is not ours. It is more
important and meaningful to us. Statesmen with a nationalist
view must replace politicians whose heads are in Europe even
though their feet remain in the Americas. Graft the world onto our
nations if you will, but the trunk itself must be us. Silence the
pedant who thrives on foreign inspiration.

There are no lands in which a person can take a greater
pride than in our own long-suffering American republics. The
Americas began to suffer, and still suffer, from the effort of trying
to reconcile the discordant and hostile elements which they
inherited from a despotic and greedy colonizer. Imported ideas
and institutions with scant relationship to local realities have
retarded the development of logical and useful governments.
Our continent, disoriented for three centuries by governance that
denied people the right to exercise reason, began in independence
by ignoring the humble who had contributed so much in the
effort to redeem it. At least in theory, reason was to reign in all
things and for everyone, not just scholastic reason at the expense
of the simpler reason of the majority. But the problem with our
independence is that we changed political formulas without
altering our colonial spirit.

There are no lands in which a person can take a greater
The privileged made common cause with the oppressed

to terminate a system which they found opposed to their own best interests. . . . The colonies continue to survive in the guise of republics. Our America struggles to save itself from the monstrous errors of the past—its haughty capital cities, the blind triumph over the disdained masses, the excessive reliance on foreign ideas, and unjust, impolitic hatred of the native races— and relies on innate virtues and sacrifices to replace our colonial mentality with that of free peoples.

With our chest of an athlete, our hands of a gentleman, and our brain of a child, we presented quite a sight. We masqueraded in English breeches, a French vest, a Yankee jacket, and a Spanish hat. The silent Indians hovered near us but took their children into the mountains to orient them. The Afro-Americans, isolated in this continent, gave expression to thought and sorrow through song. The peasants, the real creators, viewed with indignation the haughty cities. And we the intellectuals wore our fancy caps and gowns in countries where the population dressed in headbands and sandals. Our genius will be in the ability to combine headband and cap, to amalgamate the cultures of the European, Indian, and Afro-American, and to ensure that all who fought for liberty enjoy it. Our colonial past left us with judges, generals, scholars, and bureaucrats. The idealistic young have been frustrated in efforts to bring change. The people have been unable to translate triumph into benefits. The European and Yankee books hold no answers for our problems and our future. Our problems grow. Frustrations mount. Exhausted by these problems and frustrations, by the struggles between the intellectual and the military, between reason and superstition, between the city and the countryside, and by the contentious urban politicians who abuse the natural nation, tempestuous or inert by turns, we turn now to a new compassion and understanding.

The new nations look about, acknowledging each other. They ask, "Who and what are we?" We suggest tentative answers. When a local problem arises, we are less likely to seek the answer in London or Paris. Our styles may all still originate in France but our thought is becoming more American. The new generation rolls up its sleeves, gets its hands dirty, and sweats. It is getting results. Our youth now understands that we are too prone to imitate and that our salvation lies in creativity. "Creativity" is the password of this new generation. The wine is from the plantain, and even if it is bitter it is our wine! They understand that the form a government takes in a given country must reflect the realities of that country. Fixed ideas must become relative in order for them to work. Freedom to experiment must be honest and complete. If these republics do not include all their populations and benefit all of them, then they will fail.

The new American peoples have arisen; they look about; they greet each other. A new leadership emerges which under-stands local realities. New leaders read and study in order to apply their new knowledge, to adapt it to local realities, not to imitate. Economists study problems with an historical context. Orators eschew flamboyance for sober reality. Playwrights people the stages with local characters. Academicians eschew scholastic theories to discuss pressing problems. Poets eschew marble temples and Gothic cathedrals in favor of local scenes. Prose offers ideas and solutions. In those nations with large Indian populations, the presidents are learning to speak Indian languages.

The greatest need of Our America is to unite in spirit. The scorn of our strong neighbor the United States is the greatest present danger to Our America. The United States now pays greater attention to us. It is imperative that this formidable neighbor get to know us in order to dissipate its scorn. Through ignorance, it might even invade and occupy us. Greater knowledge of us will increase our neighbor's understanding and diminish that threat.

A new generation reshapes our continent. This new generation recreates Our America. It sows the seeds of a New America from the Río Grande to the Straits of Magellan. The hopes of Our America lie in the originality of the new generation.

Source: Text adapted from "Nuestra America," *El Partido Liberal* (Mexico City), January 30, 1891, p. 4, by E. Bradford Burns, ed., *Latin America: Conflict and Creation, A Historical Reader* (Englewood Cliffs, NJ: Prentice Hall, 1993), 110–13.

Ode to Roosevelt

The Nicaraguan poet Rubén Darío (1867–1916) is best known as the father of modernism, as a cosmopolitan who lived most of his life in Europe. But when Theodore Roosevelt ordered United States intervention in Panama in 1903, he wrote this poem in protest.

To Roosevelt
The voice that would reach you, Hunter, must speak
in Biblical tones, or in the poetry of Walt Whitman.
You are primitive and modern, simple and complex;
you are one part George Washington and one part Nimrod.
You are the United States,
future invader of our naive America
with its Indian blood, an America
that still prays to Christ and still speaks Spanish.

You are a strong, proud model of your race;
you are culture and able; you oppose Tolstoy.

You are an Alexander-Nebuchadnezzar,
breaking horses and murdering tigers.
(You are a Professor of Energy,
as the current lunatics say.)
You think that life is a fire,
that progress is an irruption,
that the future is wherever
your bullet strikes.
     No.

The United States is grand and powerful.
Whenever it trembles, a profound shudder
runs down the enormous backbone of the Andes.
If it shouts, the sound is like the roar of a lion.
And Hugo said to Grant: "The stars are yours."

(The dawning sun of the Argentine barely shines;
the star of Chile is rising . . .) A wealthy country,
joining the cult of Mammon to the cult of Hercules;
while Liberty, lighting the path
to easy conquest, raises her torch in New York.

But our own America, which has had poets
since the ancient times of Nezahualcóyotl;
which preserved the footprints of the great Bacchus,
and learned the Panic alphabet once,
and consulted the stars; which also knew Atlantis
(whose name comes ringing down to us in Plato)
and has lived, since the earliest moments of its life,
in light, in fire, in fragrance, and in love—
the America of Moctezuma and Atahualpa,
the aromatic America of Columbus,
Catholic America, Spanish America,
the America where noble Cuauhtémoc said:
"I am not on a bed of roses"—our America,
trembling with hurricanes, trembling with Love:
O men with Saxon eyes and barbarous souls,
our America lives. And dreams. And loves.
And it is the daughter of the Sun. Be careful.
Long live Spanish America!
A thousand cubs of the Spanish lion are roaming free.
Roosevelt, you must become, by God's own will,
the deadly Rifleman and the dreadful Hunter
before you can clutch us in your iron claws.

And though you have everything, you are lacking one thing:
     God!

Source: *Selected Poems of Rubén Darío*, Lysander Kemp, tran. (Austin: University of Texas Press, 1965), 69–70. Copyright © 1965, renewed 1993, reprinted by permission of the University of Texas Press.

7

The Past Challenged

The export boom of the late nineteenth century produced profound changes in the social composition of Latin America. New export opportunities opened the doors of fortune, though not necessarily of political opportunity, to arriviste elites. The expanding middle sectors wanted a political voice to convince the state to address their needs—particularly to provide expanded education and opportunities for their children. And beneath the elites and middle class was the mass of urban and rural workers who longed for better economic conditions. The middle class at times joined with the urban working class to press similar demands, but continued to identify primarily with the elites, who they aspired to join. Where ruling elites allowed some change, there was reform. Where they resisted, there was revolution.

Here, Argentina provides a compelling counterpoint to Mexico. By the turn of the century, 60 percent of the Buenos Aires population consisted of manual workers, many of them foreign-born. While the United States is often viewed as the nation of immigrants, 30 percent of Argentina's population was foreign-born, compared to 13 percent in the United States. The largely Italian and Spanish immigrants brought with them ideas about socialism, anarchism, and anarcho-syndicalism. In 1895, the Socialist Party was formed, and the 1910 centennial celebration was marred by anarchist demonstrations and government repression.

The political leaders, the Generation of 1880, were members of or allied to the landowning class. They monopolized the instruments of state power—the army, the electoral system—and used fraud when necessary. They controlled the ruling Partido Autonomista Nacional (PAN), and made decisions by *acuerdo*, informal agreement. But by the beginning of the twentieth century, these elites faced challenges from newly prosperous landowners, the old aristocracy from the interior who didn't profit from the export boom, and the rising middle class. The three groups joined forces to form the Radical Party. An attempted armed revolt in 1890 ended with an acuerdo and recognition of the Radical Civil Union, formed in 1892. The 1910 demonstrations convinced the conservatives that they needed to ally with the middle classes against the masses. In 1912, President Roque Saenz Peña oversaw passage of the Saenz Peña law, giving universal male suffrage to all Argentine citizens, with compulsory voting in elections by secret ballot. The Radicals took the opportunity to seize power and retained control until the Great Depression.

In Mexico, however, the intransigence of Porfirio Díaz led to a different path.

Mexico's Violent Response to the Past

The Mexican Revolution of 1910 was the first major revolution of the twentieth century. Many considered it, at least until about 1950, as the prototype for nationalistic revolutionary change in twentieth-century Latin America. By revolution, we mean the sudden, forceful, and violent overturn of a previously relatively stable society and the substitution of other institutions for those discredited. Change by revolution thus denotes sweeping change, the destruction of old social, political, and economic patterns in favor of newer ones. Use of this definition divides genuine "revolutions" from the innumerable palace coups, military takeovers, civil wars, and the wars of independence, which were nothing more than shifts in the holding of power within the same or similar groups unaccompanied by fundamental economic, social, or political changes.

By 1910, Porfirio Díaz and the "New Creoles" had ruled for thirty-four years without popular mandate for the benefit of a privileged native elite and foreign investors. The economy still depended on foreign whims and direction, a neocolonialism clearly seen in statistics such as 75 percent of all dividend-paying mines in Mexico being owned by United States interests. Foreign capital represented 97 percent of investment in mining, 98 percent of rubber, and 90 percent of oil. Some Mexicans resented the high level of foreign investment. Others were concerned that the Porfirian prosperity was narrowly based, relying mostly on mining, utilities, commerce, and large-scale agriculture, with relatively little industry. The majority of the population did not share the wealth. Real wealth actually declined for the majority: Hacienda peons earned an average daily wage of 35 cents, which remained almost steady throughout the nineteenth century, while corn and chile prices more than doubled, and beans cost six times more than they had at the beginning of the century. Life was little better for urban workers, who worked eleven- to twelve-hour days, seven days a week, and lived in squalid housing with one bathhouse per 15,000 residents.

Land, a principal source of wealth, remained in the hands of a few. Foreigners owned between 14 and 20 percent of it. Ninety-five percent of the rural population owned none. Not even 10 percent of the Indian communities held land. Fewer than 1,000 families owned most of Mexico. In fact, fewer than 200 families owned one-quarter of the land. Private estates reached princely proportions. The De la Garza hacienda in the state of Coahuila totaled 11,115,000 acres; the Huller estate in Baja, California, sprawled over 13,325,650 acres. Productivity was low; absentee landlords were common. The fact that a majority of the Mexicans lived in the country and worked in agriculture made the inequity of the land distribution all the more unjust.

At the same time, the growing mestizo urban classes were dissatisfied with the inequitable institutions inherited from the past. The mestizos had grown rapidly in number over the centuries. By the end of the nineteenth century they surpassed the Indians in number and totally overshadowed the tiny "creole" class. It was obvious from their size, skill, and ambitions that the mestizos held the key to Mexico's future. The mestizo working and middle sectors of the cities voiced discontent with their inferior and static position in Porfirian Mexico. The inflexibility of Mexico's neocolonial institutions retarded their mobility and inhibited their progress.

The theoretical justification for the Porfiriato was "Order & Progress"— but order had become rigidity, and progress had slowed. Others wanted political power, and they questioned the dictatorship. The voices for change

Land Distribution in the Mexican Revolution

	ejidos	*0.1–1,000 hectares*	*1,000+ hectares*
1910	1.6%	26.6	71.8
1923	2.6	19.6	77.9
1940	22.5	15.9	61.6

Source: Adolfo Gilly, *The Mexican Revolution* (London: Verso, 1983).

came not from the most oppressed groups but from disaffected elements of the elite and the rising middle class. When Díaz announced in a 1908 interview in Pearson's Magazine that he would not seek reelection, his opponents immediately began to express their views. In 1909, Francisco I. Madero published *The Presidential Succession of 1910,* calling for political change. Díaz chose to run again in 1910, and Madero, the scion of a wealthy ranching family from Coahuila, was chosen as the candidate of the anti-Re-electionist Party. He called for political reform, free and open elections. When asked about economic issues, however, Madero replied that the Mexican people wanted liberty, not bread.

To the surprise of no one, Díaz declared his victory at the polls and took office for the eighth time. Madero, by then, had seen the popular response that his political opposition to the old dictator had aroused. In November of 1910, he crossed the frontier from the United States into Mexico with the intention of overthrowing the government. His Plan of San Luis Potosí announced the simple motivation of his movement: the forced resignation of Díaz and electoral reforms. Repeatedly his followers voiced the slogan "Effective suffrage and no reelection," a clue to the exclusively political, urban, and middle-sector origin of the Revolution. Díaz resigned in May of 1911, and fled to a European exile. (He died in Paris in 1915.)

Madero took office quite unprepared for the task he faced. His political platform contained some vague planks on political reform and almost nothing solid on social or economic change. He represented the traditional liberalism of the nineteenth century, which at last many realized had not benefited Mexico. At any rate, it did not harmonize with the newer demands being made. Madero's importance derived first from his significance as a symbol of the revolt against the Porfirian past and second from the political freedom he permitted for open discussion in which the needs and aspirations of the nation were thoroughly aired.

While Madero demonstrated his incompetence, the demand for agrarian reform mounted, encouraged by a small farmer from Morelos named Emiliano Zapata in his Plan of Ayala in 1911. Crying "Land and Liberty," he and his determined rural followers, based in the region where sugar plantations had been squeezing out smallholders, demanded land. In many cases, they seized haciendas for themselves. A new force had been unleashed and it represented what distinguished the Mexican Revolution from previous movements in Latin America: the stirring of the masses. It became clear that a social revolution had begun.

To enact change or to redirect the course of the Revolution required power, and many were the leaders vying for it. In February 1913, General Victoriano Huerta, a representative of the *porfiristas,* overthrew the ineffectual Madero and then permitted his assassination. Uniting to oppose the reactionary general, Venustiano Carranza, Alvaro Obregón, Plutarco Elías Calles, Francisco Villa, and Emiliano Zapata, all marched against Huerta's armies.

They all agreed that Huerta was a reactionary who represented a return to the Porfirian past. But after Huerta fell in March of 1914, the victors began to struggle among themselves, as they could not agree on what kind of government and society should replace him.

The revolutionary leaders represented different sectors of the Mexican population. Carranza, the governor of Coahuila, came from an old colonial family. He represented the new northern ranching and entrepreneurial interests that looked toward the United States and resented the way Díaz had refused to allow them a political voice commensurate with their economic power. As a northerner, he was able to take on Madero's mantle, and he enlisted the support of such effective generals as Alvaro Obregón of Sonora, who had worked as a farmer and factory worker before joining the military, where he worked his way up to become one of Madero's generals. Obregón, then, represented the rising middle sectors. By mid-1915, Carranza and his allies emerged to direct the Revolution.

But the Carrancista forces were challenged by Zapata in the South and Villa in the North. Zapata represented the small farmers, whose lands had been encroached upon by the expanding sugar producers in Morelos. Many of his followers still spoke Nahuatl, and they sought a return to the village life of the past. Villa, on the other hand, represented the peon and cowboy of the north. He was born on a hacienda and became head of his family when he was 16 and his father died. One version of his life story contends that he fled the hacienda after shooting and wounding the hacendado, who had raped his sister. Legend has it that he lived as a bandit until meeting the revolutionary Abraham Gonzalez, who convinced him that while banditry attacked a few of the wealthy, only revolution could really redistribute the wealth.

Unfortunately, neither Zapata nor Villa was able to articulate a message that went beyond their regional and social bases. In 1919, Zapata was tricked into an ambush and killed. In 1920, Villa agreed to put down his arms in exchange for a modest ranch. The greater wealth of the elite and middle sectors, and the support offered them by U.S. forces that fought against Villa, helped the Carrancista forces to win. In 1920, the violent phase of the revolution ended with the election of Obregón to the presidency.

During the early years of the Revolution, as the winds of change blew with gale force across Mexico, the absence of a plan, a philosophy, intellectual leadership, or a directing party became painfully obvious. The Revolution assumed its general characteristics slowly. In time, it became apparent that many of the institutions closely identified with the Spanish past—foremost of which, and most fundamental, was the land-tenure system—would be destroyed or altered beyond recognition. To solve national problems, the Mexicans looked deeply into themselves for an answer. As a result, the Revolution became increasingly native and conversely more antiforeign.

The Revolution swept all before it. The destruction was as total as the

Revolutionary leader Pancho Villa on horseback among his troops on a dusty trail in 1916 during raids in the United States and northern Mexico. (Library of Congress.)

chaos. It cost more than a million lives. It ruined much of the agrarian, ranching, and mining economy. No major bank or newspaper that predated the Revolution survived. Exceptions to the economic dislocation were the henequen and oil industries, whose output rose. By 1921, Mexico ranked third among the world's oil producers, furnishing one-quarter of the world's total. From the disorder and destruction that lasted throughout most of the period of 1910 to 1920, a new Mexico arose.

The constitution promulgated in 1917 contained the blueprint for the future, the first general statement of the aims of the Revolution. Carranza called a constituent assembly, expecting it to approve a document similar to the liberal constitution of 1857, but it quickly became apparent that he exercised little control over the proceedings. Ideological differences split the delegates. The radicals, supported by Obregón, gained control and imposed their views. The constitution that emerged after two months of bitter debate at Querétaro contained many of the traditional enlightened ideas characteristic of the former constitution. In the customary Latin American fashion, the constitution conferred strong authority on the president. However, it went on to alter significantly some fundamental and traditional concepts, to eliminate some hoary institutions, and to point the way to new solutions for old problems.

Mexican revolutionary Emiliano Zapata, shown here in a patriotic sash, dual bandoleers, a sombrero. He stands tall in front of a brick staircase while holding a Winchester single action rifle and a sheathed saber. (Library of Congress.)

The new constitution exalted the state and society above the individual and conferred on the government the authority to reshape society. The key articles dealt with land, labor, and religion. Article 27 laid the basis for land reform and for restrictions on foreign economic control. It declared government ownership of mineral and water resources, subordinated private property to public welfare, gave the government the right to expropriate land, annulled all alienations of ejidos since 1857, and recognized communal ownership of land. Article 123 protected the Mexican workers from exploitation by authorizing the passage of a labor code to set minimum salaries and maximum hours, provide accident insurance, pensions, and social benefits, and guarantee the right to unionize and to strike. Because foreign investment in Mexican industrialization was heavy, this article potentially could be used as one means of bridling the operations of the foreign capitalist. Finally, Article 130 placed restrictions on the Church and clergy; churches were denied juridical personalities, they could not own property, states could limit the number of clerics by law, no foreigner could be a minister or priest, nor could priests vote, hold office, or criticize the government, and the Church could not participate in primary education.

Carranza dutifully promulgated the constitution, but he showed little intention of carrying out most of its provisions, many of which were not put into effect for years. For example, fourteen years passed before the enactment of a labor code to give meaning to Article 123. Nonetheless, the constitution stands as the single most important event in the history of the Revolution, marking off Mexico's neocolonial past from the modernized nation that was rising from the fury of revolution. It provided the point of departure for the creation of a new national state based on local experience. The history of Mexico since its promulgation has been the story of the struggle to carry out the provisions of the document and thereby to put into effect the social, economic, and political changes it envisaged.

With the inauguration of Obregón in 1920, the first efforts were made to implement the socioeconomic changes authorized by the Constitution. After years of slogans, the land-reform program got underway. Obregón distributed 3 million acres to the peasants. To combat illiteracy, the president appointed the energetic José Vasconcelos as Minister of Education. Accelerated school construction and teacher-training programs received an impetus from him. With the encouragement of the Revolution, educational opportunities continued to expand, and illiteracy slowly declined from a high of 80 percent in the early 1920s. Vasconcelos was a fiery cultural nationalist, in the vanguard of a movement enveloping Latin America. Negating the pessimistic racism and European cultural imperialism of the past, he preached the triumph of the new mestizo "race," *la Raza Cósmica* (the Cosmic Race). He made available space and funds to encourage such artists as Diego Rivera, José Clemente Orozco, and David Alfaro Siqueiros to paint monumental murals glorifying Mexico's Indian past. With his encouragement, Carlos Chávez composed music in a Mexican idiom. Desirous of an authentically Mexican culture, Vasconcelos declared the nation's spiritual and cultural independence of Europe: "Tired, disgusted of all this copied civilization . . . we interpret the vision of Cuauhtémoc as an anticipation of the . . . birth of the Latin American soul. . . . We wish to cease being [Europe's] spiritual colonies." Mexico's intellectuals rallied to the cry. A new sense of nationality and pride—brilliantly evident in art, architecture, music, dance, and literature—engulfed Mexico.

Plutarco Elias Calles, who became president in 1924, carried forward the trends begun during his predecessor's administration, but he soon found himself embroiled with the Roman Catholic Church. The Constitution horrified the Catholic hierarchy, who saw in several of its articles the power to debilitate the Church. The Church-state issue exploded in 1926, when Archbishop José Moray del Rio publicly announced that the clergy and all Catholics were to combat the articles of the constitution that secularized society. The government reacted by enforcing those articles more rigidly than ever before. In response, the Church went on strike. The priests refused to perform their functions, although the government kept the churches open for the faithful. Conservative Catholics revolted against the government, and blood flowed anew in Mexico. Not until the late 1930s did the Church and state show more tolerance toward each other, and relations gradually improved.

The bullet of a religious fanatic felled Obregón before he could return to the presidency to which he was reelected in 1928. Calles continued to dominate politics, and in 1929 he founded the National Revolutionary Party (PNR) to help fill the political vacuum. The PNR assumed responsibility for selecting and electing presidents as well as ensuring that the transfer of power took place and took place peacefully. It thus helped to solve basic political problems that had nagged Mexico, indeed most of Latin America, since the declarations of independence. In 1938, the party reorganized as the "official party" under the name of Mexican Revolutionary Party (PRM) and broadened its base of support. In 1946, the party once again changed its name, this time to Party of the Institutionalized Revolution (PRI). With each change, the party strengthened its role as an institution that would dominate Mexican politics, replacing the old domination by individuals. It gave Mexico a political stability in sharp contrast to the nation's own past and unusual in Latin America.

As stability increased, the role of the military diminished. The Constitution assigned the military the conventional tasks of maintaining order and defending the nation from outside attack, and the officers accepted their more restricted position. After 1929, the budget provided increasingly less funds for them. In that year, one-third of federal expenditures went to the military; by 1950, the figure had dropped to one-fourteenth; by 1964, to one-thirtieth.

Basic to the Revolution was land reform. If carried out successfully, it threatened to destroy the hacienda, perhaps the most debilitating and influential institution from the past, and substitute for it communal and small private holdings. Obregón modestly initiated the redistribution of the land, and his successors continued the policy. The titles the president handed out conferred on the small farmers a new dignity. The reform put into use formerly idle or inefficiently cultivated lands. It also strengthened the powers and prestige of the government, which could grant land or withhold it for political considerations. Lázaro Cárdenas, president from 1934 to 1940, accelerated the redistribution of land by handing out titles to 45 million acres, a staggering amount when one considers that between 1910 and 1945 the grand total of land redistributed was 76 million acres. By 1984, the government had distributed 253 million acres to 2.3 million small farmers. Despite that trend, 4 million landless rural workers clamored for land that year.

After 1940, following a period of decline, agricultural productivity began to rise. It increased 46 percent during the following two decades, far above the world's average increase of 12 percent and contrary to the general decline in Latin America's agricultural output. One prominent Mexican economist, Edmundo Flores, affirms that the rapid industrialization of his nation has been achieved only because of the reformed agrarian structures that made possible political stability, high rates of capital formation, and increased agricultural production and productivity.

In many respects, the six-year term of Cárdenas marked the apogee of the Revolution. Cárdenas based his energetic use of the presidency on the support of the peasants and the urban laborers, who in turn benefited the most from his reaffirmation of revolutionary principles. He was the first Latin American president in the twentieth century to shift the power base to the popular masses. He also well understood the potential force of economic nationalism. Cárdenas boldly declared Mexico's economic independence by nationalizing the railroads in 1937 and the oil companies in 1938. The foreign oil companies, accustomed to a privileged status in Mexico, had refused to accept a decision of the Mexican Supreme Court ruling as legal the pay raise requested by the workers. In response to the companies' defiance of the court, Cárdenas expropriated the oil firms and thus became a national hero. All Mexicans, of every level and background, enthusiastically supported the government. Even the Church nodded its approval, the first gesture of cooperation between the two in several decades. What was more, Mexico proved to itself, to the former oil monopolies, and to the world that it could produce its own oil, and contrary to predictions, it proceeded to do so more efficiently than the foreigners had done. Oil production climbed. By 1950, it doubled the output reached during the low point of 1932; by 1963 it doubled again. Mexico was in the process of redeeming itself, of limiting foreign control over its land and its industry.

The major governments of Western Europe and the United States endorsed none of these changes. The endangered investments of their citizens prompted them to complain bitterly to the Mexican government about the new laws, to apply pressure to thwart them, to threaten reprisals, and to speak

Mexican national hero President Lázaro Cárdenas. (Library of Congress.)

of intervention. Also, the Roman Catholic Church maintained strong pressures on other governments to force the Mexican officials to accommodate
themselves to the interests of the Church. No nation intervened in Mexican
affairs more vigorously than the United States, whose officials, with the exception of Ambassador Dwight W. Morrow and President Franklin D. Roosevelt, lacked even the haziest notion of the significance of the Mexican Revolution. Ambassador Henry Lane Wilson unabashedly supported General

Huerta, although the brutal assassination of Madero shocked President Woodrow Wilson into refusing to recognize the Porfirian general. The U.S. Navy blockaded the Gulf coast in 1914, then shelled and occupied the port of Veracruz. After Villa raided Columbus, New Mexico, and killed seventeen Americans, President Wilson ordered General John Pershing and an army into northern Mexico in a quixotic search of nearly a year for the evasive Villa. The Constitution of 1917 caused further concern in Washington over U.S. investments in Mexico as talk of confiscation circulated. The United States did not want Article 27 to be applied retroactively. Because of the violent death of Carranza, the Department of State refused to recognize Obregón when he became president in 1920. It used the issue of recognition as a lever to pry from the Mexicans an agreement to pay compensation for any land expropriated. Relations between the two neighbors improved in 1927 when Dwight W. Morrow arrived as ambassador to Mexico. Astute and able, he understood the significance of the Mexican Revolution and attempted to deal fairly with the Mexicans in their drive for rapid change. Later, President Roosevelt possessed a similar perceptiveness and withstood heavy pressures from the Roman Catholic Church and the oil companies for intervention. Mexico's agreement to compensate the oil companies and the improvement of Church–state relations within Mexico in the late 1930s lifted at least part of the pressures on him, and improved relations between Mexico and the United States were the result.

Cárdenas was the last strong man to dominate Mexico. After 1940, Mexican presidents derived their power from the office they held, not from their own personal strength, prestige, or following. In short, the institution possessed greater strength than the individual, a new development in Mexico and Latin America. At the same time, public opinion grew in influence to the point where it exerted considerable pressure on the government. The Revolution created a novel social flexibility, and as one consequence the middle class grew both in size and importance.

Impressive as the material results of the Revolution were, the psychological changes in the Mexicans surpassed them. As Octavio Paz would write: "The Revolution was a sudden immersion of Mexico in her own being, from which she brought back up, almost blindly, the essentials of a new kind of state. In addition, it was a return to the past, a reuniting of the ties broken by the Reform and the Díaz dictatorship, a search for our own selves, and a return to the maternal womb. . . . Like our popular fiestas, the Revolution was an excess and a squandering, a going to extremes, an explosion of joy and hopelessness, a shout of orphanhood and jubilation, of suicide and life, all of them mingled together."

Unfortunately, that explosion of joy became muted. After 1940, the Revolution entered a conservative phase. Institutions took on a greater rigidity. Indeed, the Revolution itself had become institutionalized. Peruvian novelist Mario Vargas Llosa dubbed Mexico the perfect dictatorship as he watched

PRI win every election for 70 years. (It was not until 2000 that a non-PRI candidate, Vicente Fox of the Partido de Acción Nacional, won the presidency.) A new privileged elite emerged to absorb most of the national income, with the sharp division between wealth and poverty all too evident. Foreign capital reentered to play a dominant role, and growth began to outstrip development. The low point was reached in 1968, when hundreds of students protesting against the government were slaughtered. Finally, in 1992, President Carlos Salinas did the unthinkable—he abandoned the ejido system, the most sacred icon of the Revolution.

Clearly the Revolution did not change all the institutions, and its failure to make a total transformation permitted the resurgence of old neofeudal and capitalist practices that apparently have thwarted many of the original revolutionary goals of those who wanted to alter Mexican society. The weaknesses of the Revolution obviously were great, but nonetheless it will stand as a major landmark in Latin American history: the first effort of the twentieth century to divide the past from the present and future.

Nationalism as a Force for Change

The new Mexico was characterized by a profound nationalism, and nationalism, perhaps more than any other single force, impelled change in twentieth-century Latin America. Difficult to define precisely, nationalism in this text means a group consciousness that attributes great value to the nation-state, to which total loyalty is pledged. Members of the group agree to maintain the unity, independence, and sovereignty of the nation-state as well as to pursue certain broad and mutually acceptable goals. Two of these goals in the twentieth century have been modernization and economic independence. The nationalists have been in the vanguard of those encouraging the development of Latin America, and thus they have served as eager agents propelling change. Nationalism can trigger a powerful emotional response. Much of the nationalistic sentiment intertwines with feeling, loyalty, and group spirit.

Nationalism is not a novelty introduced by the twentieth century. It can trace its roots far back into the Latin American past. It evolved slowly over the centuries. Latin American historians affirm that the spiritual and emotional maturity of their countries predates political independence. The nation in the historical sense preceded the nation in the political sense.

The declarations and wars of independence gave a much sharper focus to nationalism. The rhetoric, symbols (flags, anthems, heroes), and battles infused enthusiasm and determination into many ranks of the Americans, particularly into the elite, the intellectuals, and the urban dwellers. Wars, boundary disputes, and foreign threats helped to maintain or intensify that political nationalism throughout the nineteenth century. Juan Manuel de Rosas ably manipulated the Argentine distrust of foreigners to weld diverse and distrusting regions into a national union. In Brazil, the throne of the emperor provided a convenient focal point that rallied the loyalty of all regions and classes of the enormous and sprawling empire. During the course of the nineteenth century, internal trends buttressed the sporadic demonstrations of defensive nationalism. The fast rate of racial mixing obscured ethnic origins to create a mestizo or mulatto citizenry distinctive to the New World, and some of the racial combinations were unique to specific countries. As the nations became more conscious of their peculiar personalities, they developed a stronger sense of national identity. Railroads, telegraph lines, and steamships further unified each nation. Together they successfully combated the major threat to national unity: regionalism.

As the twentieth century opened, a wave of cultural nationalism swept the hemisphere. The intellectuals, long slavish imitators of European styles, turned their backs on their former mentors to seek the indigenous roots of national culture. They probed national psychology, questioned national motives, and reexamined the past. Intellectuals offered novel introspective theories to explain national development (or the lack of it) that relegated the usual emphasis on Europe to a secondary plane. In reinterpreting the past, historians paid greater attention to the influence of the interior, the hinterlands, and the frontier. Nowhere was that trend more evident than in Brazil. In a brilliant essay presented in 1889, Capistrano de Abreu was the first to point out the influence of the interior on the formation of Brazil.

According to him, the interior was the true Brazil; the more heavily populated coast was just an extension of Europe. Only when the coastal inhabitants turned their backs to the sea and penetrated the interior did they shed their European ways and become Brazilianized. Euclydes da Cunha confirmed that thesis in *Rebellion in the Backlands* (1902). From his perceptive study of the interior, he concluded that on the frontier, in the hinterland, he beheld the real Brazil and the true Brazilian. He spoke of the backwoodsmen as "the very core of our nationality, the bedrock of our race," and of their society as "the vigorous core of our national life." Ricardo Rojas came to similar conclusions about the Argentine interior. Essays, poems, and novels on the gaucho, now perfectly romanticized as the frontier "type," were the vogue throughout the Platine region.

As the battle lines hardened between nationalism and foreign influences, Ricardo Rojas cried for the salvation of Argentine youth "from the foreign clergy, from foreign gold, and from foreign books." At the same time in Brazil, Ronald de Carvalho, one of the major exponents of the new cultural nationalism, exhorted his followers, "Let us forget the marble of the Acropolis and the towers of the Gothic cathedrals. We are the sons of the hills and the forests. Stop thinking of Europe. Think of America!" A Latin American renaissance in art, literature, music, and dance resulted from these proddings. It originated in Mexico, then appeared in Brazil, and spread to the rest of the republics.

The Aula Magna of the University of Caracas, Venezuela (1954). The architect was
Carlos Raul Villanueva: the sculptor, Antoine Pevsner; the muralist, Matteo Manaure.

Architecture, too, bore the impress of nationalism. The architects turned
their attention away from Europe to contemplate the environment in which
they built. Slowly, they suggested a new architectural idiom, notable for its
integration with the arts (murals, sculptures, tiles) and nature (gardens and
decorative plantings). In some regions, bold splashes of color enhanced the
buildings. In Brazil, Lúcio Costa led a vigorous movement to adapt architecture to the tropical environment. One of the first and finest examples of the
distinctively Brazilian architecture was the Ministry of Education and Health
(1937–43) in Rio de Janeiro, a project that combined the genius of Costa, Oscar Niemeyer, and others. In Venezuela, Carlos Raúl Villanueva led a movement to create distinguished modern architecture.

The invention of the motion picture camera coincided with a rising tide
of nationalism in Latin America, and the Latin Americans at once seized on
film as an appropriate means to encourage the nationalism. It offered an obvious advantage in those countries where a majority of the citizenry was illiterate.

The fledgling Mexican film industry actively promoted fictional documentaries to glorify the past. As part of the centennial celebrations in 1910,
Felipe de Jesús Haro produced *El Grito de Dolores* (*The Cry of Dolores*), a patriotic hymn to Miguel Hidalgo, the hero of Mexican independence. The
appearance of *Cuahtémoc* in 1918 reflected the revived interest in Mexico's

Indian past, so notable in music, literature, dance, and art as well. At about the same time the Ministry of War expressed an interest in filmic interpretations of the Revolution and financed such films as *Juan Soldado* (*John Soldier*), *El Precio de la Gloria* (*The Price of Glory*), and *Honor Militár* (*Military Honor*). The Revolution provided filmmakers with a seemingly endless inspiration.

Lacking the intense nationalistic impetus that the Revolution gave Mexicans, the early Brazilian filmmakers paid only partial attention to historical themes. In 1911, Salvatore Lazzaro made the first filmic version of *O Guarany* (*The Guaraní Indian*), that quintessence of Brazilian nationalism. In its romantic plot, an Indian chief and the daughter of a Portuguese noble fall in love, the symbolic intertwining of the New World and the Old to create Brazil. First as a novel, then as an opera, and, after 1911, as a movie, *O Guarany* appealed mightily to the national spirit. In fact, the overture to the opera (always played along with the film) is considered on a par with the national anthem as a major hymn to Brazilian patriotism.

Beginning in 1915, filmmakers paid greater attention to historical themes. Doubtless the approach of Brazil's first centenary celebration of independence encouraged the new film industry to turn to historical epics. In 1918, Brazilians could watch *Tiradentes*, episodes from the life of a martyr to independence, and *O Grito do Ipiranga* (*The Cry of Ipiranga*), an account of events surrounding the declaration of independence. As in Mexico, the Ministry of War favored such enterprises with its cooperation and encouragement.

The Argentines shared a fascination with historical films with other Latin American filmmakers of the early twentieth century. Likewise, part of the impetus to explore the past through film came from the elaborate preparations underway to commemorate the first centenary of Argentine independence in 1910. In fact, the first story-film made in Argentina concerned the independence period; called *El Fusilamiento de Dorrego* (*The Execution of Dorrego before the Firing Squad*), it was filmed in 1908 by Mario Gallo. In 1910, the public viewed an entire series of patriotic films based on history.

In their concern with national identity and reality, early Argentine films, like those of Mexico and Brazil, dealt with the Indians, the prime symbol of the uniqueness of America and of nationality. Starkly contrasting with the romanticism of the Mexican and Brazilian treatment of the subject, one of the early Argentine masterpieces of the screen depicted the Indian with a realism unusual for the time. The remarkable *El Ultimo Malón* (*The Last Indian Uprising*), filmed in 1917 by Alcides Greca, focused on an uprising of the Mocovi Indians in Santa Fe in April 1904. The first part was purely documentary, showing the conditions of the Mocovi in 1917 and commenting on their poverty and exploitation by the local landowners. The second part recreated, using the Indians themselves, the actual uprising. The film identified the Indians with the land as the worthy progenitors of Argentine nationality.

Also, as might be expected, the filmmakers focused on the gaucho, a mixture both culturally and ethnically of the Indian and European, who offered an obvious symbol for national identity. The gaucho already had left his stamp on Argentine literature and José Hernández published his epic *Martín Fierro* in 1872 and 1879; the highly successful gaucho novel, *Juan Moreira,* by Eduardo Gutiérrez appeared in 1879–80. The novel was dramatized to much acclaim in 1886. By then a group of Argentine artists, among whom Prilidiano Pueyrredón and Juan Carlos Morel would be outstanding representatives, had painted vivid scenes of gaucho life. Therefore, it seemed only natural for the new medium, the film, to take up that highly national theme, and the filmmakers did, producing in 1915 one of the great hits of the Argentine screen, *La Nobleza Gaucha (Gaucho Nobility).* Many of the explanatory titles for this silent film came directly from *Martín Fierro.* The plot concerned a beautiful country girl, sweetheart of a hardworking gaucho, who was kidnapped by a city villain and, of course, eventually rescued by the brave gaucho so they could live happily ever after in the simplicity and wholesomeness of the countryside. A simple plot, indeed a melodramatic one, it gave another perspective to an intensified search for national identity, at least part of which became increasingly associated with the broad pampas and its distinctive gaucho inhabitants. *La Nobleza Gaucha* also contained social commentary in its implied denunciation of the precarious situation of the gaucho. Within a few years, the theme of the gaucho emerged in yet another form: music. Felipe Boero's *El Matrero,* which premiered in 1929, projected a romanticized vision of the gaucho, in some respects akin to the tragic *Martín Fierro,* and has been sanctified as the national opera.

Argentina's first professional film director, José Augustín Ferreira (1889–1943), one of the most prominent of the nation's twentieth-century Afro-Argentines, freely drew inspiration from the growing exaltation of the gaucho and made four early popular films on the gaucho theme. However, in the final analysis, he was a devoted son of Buenos Aires, a city he knew intimately and always loved. His best films, in fact, testify to that devotion. He used his camera to explore and dissect the city, and he found beauty in the most commonplace incidents and localities. Almost invariably his films showed the lifestyles of the ordinary people, and many of them were shot in the suburbs, rather than using the more sophisticated locales in the center of the capital. These films provide a subtle study of changing Buenos Aires, 1915–40, a city multiplying in size and illustrative of the dominant role cities assumed in the twentieth century, not only in Argentina but throughout Latin America. The film *Calles de Buenos Aires (Streets of Buenos Aires,* 1933) typified the director's style, concerns, and themes. The simple plot focused on the lives of two young ladies of humble origin—many of his films depicted and moralized on the contemporary roles of women. One sought to escape her poverty and fell victim to the easy promises of a seducer and the ruin that followed. In contrast, the other, steadfastly maintaining her honesty and faith in the face of adversity, found true love and fulfillment in the arms of an impoverished singer.

Like so many of his plots, that of *Calles de Buenos Aires* recalled tango lyrics. Indeed, it should. Ferreira loved tangos; he composed lyrics for them. Many of his films included the singing of that distinctive music of Buenos Aires. In one of his earliest films, *El Tango de la Huerta* (*The Tango of Death*, 1917), he made clear his association of the tango with the film. To the female lead in this film, the tango simultaneously symbolized her condemnation to misery and her final liberation. More often than not, Ferreira's films were visual recreations of the sentiments pervading the tango. Appearing first in Buenos Aires in the 1880s, the tango offered a partial insight into the spirit and feelings of all Argentines. Ferreira succeeded in combining the city (particularly the poorer districts), the common people, and the tango into films that both depicted a broad segment of the nation and expressed popular sentiments. No other Argentine filmmaker has succeeded so brilliantly in making that combination.

Film reached huge audiences, proved to be the most effective medium to address the populace at large, and often discussed national themes. Still, its importance should not be exaggerated, since most of the screens in Latin America showed foreign movies that had nothing to do with local realities. In fact, they contained antinational messages and served more as social soporifics than stimulants.

Changing Racial Attitudes

The nationalists in the twentieth century came to appreciate a long-neglected or avoided fact: the rich and varied racial heritage of Latin America accounted for the region's uniqueness and vitality. Unfortunately, although the Indian, African, and European contributed jointly to the formation of Latin American civilization, the three groups by no means enjoyed equality. The Europeans and their New World descendants occupied the highest level of society, with the mestizos, mulattos, Indians, and blacks relegated to lower rungs of the social ladder. Without the benevolent protection of the Iberian monarchs, the position of the Indians and blacks, if anything, deteriorated in the nineteenth century. Some intellectuals contributed to their misery. In their eagerness to mouth European ideas, they circulated the specious racist doctrines so in vogue among Europeans in that century.

The wealth of biological thought in the nineteenth century, the popularity of Darwinism and Spencerianism, and the complex ethnic composition of Latin America aroused a lively interest in race and racial theories. Latin America's cultural mentor, France, offered a poisonous array of pseudoscientific books attesting to the superiority of the Northern European. Widely read by the end of the century was the social psychologist Gustave Le Bon, who methodically classified all humankind into superior and inferior races, with the Europeans indisputably at the top. Among other things, he asserted that miscegenation produced an offspring inferior to either parent. Another champion of the Aryan, the anthropologist Georges Vacher de Lapouge, minced no words in his chief work, *L'Aryen, son Role Social,* to support the theory of racial significance in cultural development. In line with his thesis, he characterized Brazil as "an enormous Negro state on its way back to barbarism." Bombarded by such influence, and inheritors of a sociopolitical system in which the Europeans and their offspring ruled while the Indian, the African, and their offspring obeyed, most Latin Americans equated whiteness with beauty, intelligence, and ability. Conversely, the darker the people the less likelihood they could possess those desired characteristics. Intellectuals throughout the hemisphere blamed miscegenation for the backwardness and anarchy of Latin America.

The rising tide of nationalism caused some Latin Americans to question those racial concepts. To accept the European doctrines, they finally realized, would condemn Latin America perpetually to a secondary position. The nationalists concluded that the doctrines were simply another means devised by the Europeans to humiliate and subjugate Latin America. In due course, many Latin Americans rejected foreign racist doctrines, and in so doing they took a major step toward freeing themselves from European cultural domination.

In the early twentieth century, the Latin Americans began to take a new interest in the Indians, who had been cheated, robbed, overworked, suppressed, and massacred throughout the nineteenth century. Disturbed by the rapid decline of the Indian population as well as by the terrible tales of brutal exploitation of the natives by the rubber barons of the Amazon, the Brazilian government created the Indian Protection Service in 1910 to defend them and to incorporate their diminishing numbers into the national family. The *Aprista* movement appeared in Peru by the end of the second decade of the twentieth century and spread thereafter to other countries. Advocating an Indian renaissance, it strove to uplift the Indian and glorified America's indigenous past. In 1919, President Augusto Leguía of Peru declared the Indian community once again to be a legal corporation.

As in so many other ways, the Mexican Revolution set a new model for depiction and treatment of the Indians. Lázaro Cárdenas, more than any other Mexican president, served the Indians; in order to institutionalize his concern, he created the Department of Indian Affairs in 1936. Unjust biases against America's Indian past were finally challenged, and Indian themes became respectable for art, literature, music, and dance. Latin Americans at last pointed with justifiable pride to their Indian past. Mexico City's famed Museum of Anthropology extolled the virtues of the Indian past. However, the reality of the Indian present lagged far behind the symbolic role of the glorified past.

At the same time attitudes toward the Latin Americans of African descent also underwent change. As the first step, it was necessary to end slavery. The Spanish-speaking republics abolished it between 1821 and 1854. The institution lingered in Spain's Caribbean islands and in Brazil. Tremendous international pressures bore down on Spain and Brazil to free their slaves. After midcentury internal pressures welled up. Spain feared that to liberate the slaves would drive the insular landowners to declare their independence. Cautiously the Spanish government abolished slavery in Puerto Rico in 1873, freeing approximately 31,000 slaves. The process in Cuba was slower. The Moret Law, passed in 1870 but only published in Cuba in 1872, liberated children born of slaves after September 18, 1868, although subjecting the freeborn black to a system of tutelage until eighteen years of age. In 1880, the government ended slavery but with the proviso that former slaves had to continue to work for eight years for their former masters. Finally, in 1886, the crown abolished the tutelage system, freeing all blacks from compulsory labor.

The abolition movement in Brazil was even more protracted. No one in authority seriously advocated an immediate end to slavery. The economy could not absorb the shock of so radical a move. The abolitionists therefore favored a gradual emancipation, to take place over a lengthy period of time. The emperor, too, counseled the gradual approach in order to avoid disturbing the economy and committed his prestige to such a course. The conservative government headed by the Visconde do Rio-Branco enacted the Law of the Free Womb in 1871, which declared all children born to slave mothers to be free. At the time there were approximately 1.5 million slaves and a free population of 8.6 million. The law slowly doomed slavery in Brazil. Africa as a source of slaves had been closed since 1850; after 1871, the only other source, the womb, could bring forth no more slaves. However, patience with the slow results of the Rio-Branco Law wore thin. Before the end of the 1870s, the slavery question once again confronted the public. The concern for the welfare of the remaining slaves called forth some forceful spokesmen and prompted the formation of some active abolitionist societies.

Several highly articulate African-Brazilians contributed to the leadership of the abolitionist campaign: José Carlos do Patrocínio, a persuasive journalist, wrote ceaselessly for the cause and became a symbol of the campaign; André Rebouças, one of the empire's most prominent engineers, organized abolitionist clubs and spoke and wrote profusely in support of abolition; and Luís Gonzaga de Pinto Gama spent his youth as a slave and later became a distinguished lawyer who specialized in defending slaves in court. He claimed credit for freeing 500 slaves through the courts. A fiery advocate of immediate abolition, he declared, "Every slave who kills his master, no matter what the circumstances may be, kills in self-defense." He also preached "the right of insurrection." Given to poetry, he began one of his better-known verses, "My loves are beautiful, the color of night."

The slavery issue forced itself to the forefront of politics as one group after another favored the abolitionist cause until only the slave owners themselves were left as apologists of a discredited institution. Finally, on May 13, 1888, to cries of approval from those in attendance, the parliament passed the Golden Law, liberating the remaining three-quarters of a million slaves. When

Princess-Regent Isabel put her signature to the law, slavery finally disappeared from the Western Hemisphere.

If the slaves expected the Golden Law to transport them to a promised land, however, they became disillusioned quickly enough. Life continued to be hard for them. The battle for their freedom had ended, but they faced a second struggle against the deep-seated racial biases that had divided Brazil for all of its history.

During the early twentieth century, interest in the African-Latin American's new struggle as well as in their contributions to the New World grew. The new interest was most evident in those areas where the populations of African descent were largest, the Caribbean and Brazil. In Cuba, the prolific intellectual Fernando Ortíz began publishing his studies of the African-American as early as 1906. Together with the Afro-Cuban Nicolás Guillen, the originator of the *negrismo* school of poetry, he founded the Society for Afro-Cuban Studies in 1926 and thereafter devoted himself with increasing fervor to the study of the African-Americans and their cultures.

The intellectual search for black identity did not preclude violence generated by frustration and injustice. In Cuba in 1912, the Afro-Cuban leader Evaristo Estenoz, disillusioned by the failure of the island's independence to institute equality of all peoples, organized the Independent Party of Color to support African-Cuban rights. Regarding the new party as subversive, the government sent troops to disband it, and a race war erupted that claimed the lives of 3,000 blacks and engendered lasting hostilities.

Meanwhile the concept of "Negritude" swept the Caribbean. In Haiti in the 1920s, Jean Price-Mars took up his pen to urge fellow Haitians to accept their African heritage and to use it as a cultural resource. Aimé Césaire, an outstanding intellectual from Martinique, a Caribbean island under French rule, whose contributions include the widely read *Return to My Native Land*, defined Negritude as follows:

> I have always thought that the black was searching for identity. And it has seemed to me that if what we want is to establish this identity, then we must have a concrete consciousness of what we are—that is, of the first fact of our lives: that we are black; that we were black and have a history, a history that contains certain cultural elements of great value; and that the Negroes are not . . . born yesterday, because there have been beautiful and important black civilizations. . . . Therefore we affirmed that we were Negroes and that we were proud of it, and that we thought that Africa was not some sort of blank page in the history of humanity; in sum, we asserted that our Negro heritage was worthy of respect, and that this heritage was not relegated to the past, that its values were values that could still make an important contribution to the world.

Generations of Caribbean intellectuals have pursued the goals of Negritude. At the same time, the Brazilians looked with clearer vision on their

African past. Afonso Celso refused to accept the negative predictions about Brazil's innate inferiority. In his blatantly nationalistic *Porque Me Ufano do Meu Pais* (*Why I Am Proud of My Country*), Celso proudly affirmed, "Today it is a generally accepted truth that three elements contributed to the formation of the Brazilian people: the American Indian, the African Negro, and the Portuguese. . . . Any one of those elements, or any combination of them, possesses qualities of which we should be proud." His book contained a chapter praising the heroic resistance of the blacks to slavery.

The pioneer of anthropological studies of the African in Brazil, Dr. Raimundo Nina Rodrigues, worked in Bahia from 1890 to 1905. Although not free of the prejudices of his day, he felt a great sympathy toward the African-Brazilians and manifested a lively interest in their condition. He studied the African cultures in order to identify their survivals in Brazil, and in that manner was able to indicate more correctly than previously the contributions of various African civilizations to the formation of Brazil. For example, he disproved the long-accepted idea that the Bantu predominated among Brazilian blacks by pointing out the strong cultural presence of the Sudanese groups, particularly the Yoruba, in Bahia. A few years later, another scholar, Manuel Raimundo Querino, emerged in Bahia to write about the African-Brazilians, their religions, and their contribution to Brazilian history. Querino is of special interest and significance because he was Brazil's first black historian, and he has provided a unique and extremely valuable perspective on Brazilian history. His major historical essay, "The African Contribution to Brazilian Civilization," first reached print in 1918. It was fitting that the intellectuals of Bahia—an area where the African always predominated—first discovered the Brazilian blacks and began to emphasize the heroic role they had played in Brazil's development.

Writers also turned their attention to the same subject. Several novelists of the late nineteenth century, Aluísio Azevedo in his *O Cortiço* (*The Tenement*), and Adolfo Caminha in his *O Bom Crioulo* (*The Good Negro*), described at length the Afro-Brazilian as a member of the urban proletariat. In some of his best novels, Afonso Henriques Lima Barreto raised his voice to protest the discrimination against the black that manifested itself in Rio de Janeiro, described it in some of its ugliest aspects, and called for justice. Menotti del Picchia characterized the Brazilian as a mulatto in his lengthy poem "Juca Mulatto"; it was the first time in Brazilian poetry that a mulatto appeared as the hero.

Gilberto Freyre helped to break the last chains binding the intellectuals to their racial uncertainties when he published *Casa Grande e Senzala* (*The Masters and the Slaves*) in 1933. The national and international acclaim that greeted his study freed the intellectuals from any remaining cultural complexes. Freyre's cogent discussion of the creation of a unique, multiracial civilization in Brazil opened vast new areas for research and study. In 1934 the first Afro-Brazilian Congress met in Recife, and three years later a second one convened in Salvador. The papers read during those sessions and the discussions that followed emphasized the revised opinion about the blacks and their newly assigned place within the Brazilian family.

The more realistic appraisal of the African presence improved the black's position in Brazilian society, but it would be wrong to conclude, as is so often done, that Brazil knows no racial prejudice. The facts prove otherwise. Newspapers regularly ran help-wanted advertisements seeking whites only. Until well after the mid-twentieth century, both the diplomatic corps and the naval officer corps remained lily-white. After World War II, it was necessary to promulgate a law to punish overt discrimination.

The change in representation of the African and Indian in Latin America was more symbolic than real, and it was related to the new sense of nationalism that dawned with the early twentieth century. This nationalism would focus more strongly, however, on the need for economic development and independence.

The Plan of Ayala

Emiliano Zapata (1880–1919) was the most popular of the leaders of the Mexican revolution. In contrast to Francisco I. Madero, who launched the revolution, Zapata stood for economic and social, not just political, reforms. When Madero refused to entertain his request for land reform, Zapata issued a call to arms, The Plan of Ayala, on November 28, 1911. His slogan: *Tierra y libertad!* (*Land and Liberty!*)

The revolutionary junta of the State of Morelos will not sanction any transactions or compromises until it secures the downfall of the dictatorial elements of Porfirio Díaz and Francisco I. Madero, because the nation is tired of traitors and false liberators who make promises and forget them when they rise to power . . . as tyrants.

As an additional part of the plan that we proclaim, be it known: that the lands, woods, and water usurped by the hacendados, científicos, or caciques, under the cover of tyranny and venal justice, henceforth belong to the towns or citizens in possession of the deeds concerning these properties of which they were despoiled through the devious action of our oppressors. The possession of said properties shall be kept at all costs, arms in hand. The usurpers who think they have a right to said goods may state their claims before special tribunals to be established upon the triumph of the Revolution.

. . . [T]he immense majority of Mexico's villages and citizens own only the ground on which they stand. They suffer the horrors of poverty without being able to better their social status in any respect, or without being able to dedicate themselves to industry or agriculture due to the fact that the lands, woods, and water are monopolized by a few. For this reason, through prior compensation, one-third of such monopolies will be expropriated from their powerful owners in order that the villages and citizens of Mexico may obtain *ejidos,* colonies, town sites and rural properties for sowing or tilling, and in order that the welfare and prosperity of the Mexican people will be promoted in every way.

The property of those hacendados, científicos, or caciques who directly or indirectly oppose the present plan shall be nationalized, and two-thirds of their remaining property shall be designated for war indemnities—pensions for the widows and orphans of the victims that succumb in the struggle for this plan.

Source: *Revolution in Mexico: Years of Upheaval, 1910–1940,* James R. Wilkie and Albert L. Michaels, eds. (NY: Knopf, 1969) 45–46.

Carlos Fuentes on the Revolution

Carlos Fuentes (1928–), is one of Mexico's foremost novelists, essayists, and diplomats. Along with Colombia's Gabriel García Marquez and Peru's Mario Vargas Llosa, he was part of "the boom" in Latin American fiction in the 1960s. Fuentes has written eloquently of the paradoxes of Mexico and the mixed blessings of the Revolution. In *The Death of Artemio Cruz* (1962) he writes of a common soldier who gains success and betrays the ideals of the Revolution. In *Where the Air Is Clear* (1958), he analyzes where the Revolution has left Mexican society in the 1950s.

THE DEATH OF ARTEMIO CRUZ

you will inherit the land
you will never again see those places and faces you knew in Sonora and Chihuahua, the faces of soldiers that you saw sleeping and enduring today and tomorrow enraged, thrown into battle with neither reason nor palliative, into the embrace of the killers, the set-apart, the next day thrown into the cry of here I am and I exist with you and with you too, with all our outlawed hands and outcast faces: love, a strange common love that will die away of itself: you will tell yourself about it, because you lived it and while you lived it did not understand it: but dying you will accept that love and will admit openly that even without understanding, you feared it all the days of your power: you will be afraid that those love-filled meetings between men of hatred will explode again; and now you will die and no longer fear: but you will tell others that they had better be afraid: distrust the false tranquillity you bequeath them, the fiction of concord, the magic formula, the sanctioned greed: let them fear this injustice so pervasive it does not even know its limits: so habitually unjust it no longer knows itself as unjust at all:
they will accept your legacy: the decency that you acquired for them: they will offer up thanks to bare-foot Artemio Cruz because he made them people of position: they will give thanks to him because he was not content to live and die in a Negro hut; they will thank him because he ventured away and gambled his life: they will justify you because they will not have your justification: they will not be able to speak of their battles and captains, as you can, and shield themselves behind glory to justify rapine in the name of the Revolution, self-aggrandizement in the name of working for the good of the Revolution: you will think about them and will wonder: what justification will they find? what wall will they oppose? But they will not think about it, they will merely enjoy, while they can, what you leave them: they will

live happy, show themselves, in public, and you ask no more, to
be mourning and grateful, while you wait with three feet of earth
above your head, wait until you feel the tramp of feet over your
dead face, and then you will say

"They have returned. They didn't give up."
and you will smile, mocking them, mocking yourself, which is
your privilege: nostalgia will tempt you to make the past more
beautiful but you will refrain:

you will bequeath the futile dead names, the names of so
many who fell that your name might stand: men despoiled of
their names that you might possess yours: names forgotten that
yours might be remembered:

you will bequeath this country: your newspaper, the hints
and the adulation, the conscience drugged by lying articles
written by men of no ability; you will bequeath the mortgages,
a class stripped of natural human affection, power without
greatness, a consecrated stultification, dwarf ambition, a fool's
compromise, rotted rhetoric, institutionalized cowardice, coarse
egoism:

You will bequeath them their crooked labor leaders and
captive unions, their new landlords, their American investments,
their jailed workers, their monopolies and their great press, their
wet-backs, hoods, secret agents, their foreign deposits, their
bullied agitators, servile deputies, fawning ministers, elegant tract
homes, their anniversaries and commemorations, their fleas and
wormy tortillas, their illiterate Indians, unemployed laborers,
rapacious pawnshops, fat men armed with aqualungs and stock
portfolios, thin men armed with their fingernails: they have their
Mexico, they have their inheritance.

Source: Carlos Fuentes. *The Death of Artemio Cruz,* Sam Hileman, tran. (N.Y.:
Farrar, Straus, Giroux, 1986), 268–69. Copyright © 1964, renewed 1992 by Carlos
Fuentes.

WHERE THE AIR IS CLEAR

Look outside. There are still millions of illiterates, barefoot
Indians, poor people starving to death, farmers who don't have
even one miserable acre of their own, factories with no machinery,
nor parts, unemployed workers who have to flee to the United
States. But there are also millions who can go to schools that we
of the Revolution built, millions for whom company stores and
hacienda stores are gone forever, and there are some factories in
the cities. Millions who, if this were nineteen hundred ten, would

be peons are now skilled workers, girls who would be cooks and maids are now typists, there are millions who in only thirty years have moved into the middle class, who own cars and use toothpaste and spend five days a year at Tecalutla or Acapulco. Our plants have given those workers jobs, our commerce has given them time-payment plans and savings accounts. For the first time in Mexican history a stable middle class exists, the surest protection against tyranny and unrest. Men and women who do not want to lose their jobs, their installment plan furniture, their little cars, for anything in the world. Those people are the one concrete result of the Revolution, . . . and we made them. We laid the foundation for Mexican capitalism. . . . What if we did get our percentage from every highway contract? What if the collective farm directors do steal half the appropriations they are given? Would you prefer that in order to avoid these evils, we had done nothing at all? You want us to have the honesty of angels? I repeat, because of what we went through, we are entitled to everything. Because we were born in dirt-floor shacks, we have the right now to live in mansions with high ceilings and stone walls, with a Rolls-Royce at the door. Only we know what a revolution is. A revolution is fought by flesh and blood men, not by saints, and every revolution ends with the creation of a new privileged class. I assure you that if I had not been a man able to take advantage of his breaks, I would still be scratching corn rows in Michoacan, and just as my father was, I would be satisfied. But the fact is that I got my breaks and I am here, and I am more useful to Mexico as a businessman than as a farmer. And if I hadn't, someone else would have seized what I have seized, stand where I stand now, do what I do. We, too, were of the common people, and our homes and gardens and automobiles are, in a way, the people's triumph.

Source: Carlos Fuentes, *Where the Air Is Clear* (N.Y.: Noonday Press, 1960), 87–88. Copyright © 1960, renewed 1988 by Carols Fuentes.

From World Wars to Cold War

By the early twentieth century, the export economy was well entrenched throughout Latin America, making the region extremely dependent on the well-being of foreign economies. Latin American food sales depended on working-class buying power in Europe and the United States. The expansion of tin, henequen, and other raw material production depended on technological advances abroad. National governments became dependent on export revenues to balance their budgets, keep the armed forces paid and equipped, and meet domestic demands for services.

Then three international crises disrupted Latin American foreign trade in fairly rapid succession: World War I, the Great Depression, and World War II. Economic downturns led to political instability, and throughout the region dictators came to power. These strongmen increased government's role in the economy, and new institutions were created to help stem the crisis. Import substitution industrialization and agriculture made the Latin American region less dependent on the international economy and more interdependent.

In the aftermath of World War II, the United States replaced Europe as the model for Latin Americans. They looked north and considered two issues: democracy and development. The U.S. rhetoric of the war years in the fight against fascism made Latin Americans see their dictators in a new light. And the unprecedented wealth of the United States in the post-war years made Latin Americans reconsider how to modernize their economies. By the 1950s, however, Latin Americans would discover that their own attempts at democracy and development would become entangled with United States economic expansion and the new Cold War realities.

Old questions surfaced again: Why had Latin America not developed? How could development be achieved? Can democracy and development occur simultaneously?

Economic Crises

From 1914 to 1945, Latin America was buffeted by international affairs, paying a price for its extensive openness to the world economy. As Europe became immersed in World War I, investment in Latin America plummeted. Public loans to Brazil fell from $19.1 million in 1913 to $4.2 million in 1914, to zero in 1915. Commodity exports suffered from both shortages of shipping and a decline in European demand for goods. Because most Latin American governments relied on import tariffs, there was a precipitous decline in government revenue. Chile, for example, saw government revenues drop by two-thirds from 1911 to 1915.

World War I did provide opportunities for a few Latin American countries. Venezuela began exporting oil, and Mexican oil imports increased. Peruvian copper, Bolivian tin, and Chilean nitrates were in demand. Despite the success of these products, economies suffered as import prices rose along with trade surpluses and budget deficits, fueling inflation. Inflation eroded urban real wages, leading to political upheavals.

The curtailment of trade with Europe benefited the United States, which became the main supplier not just of Mexico and Central America, but of the entire region. The United States proved to be a limited market, however, for any products competing with American products, such as grain and beef. At the end of the war, Great Britain's slow recovery led the United States to consolidate its new prominence in Latin America by becoming the dominant lender. U.S. capital, however, was usually tied to foreign policy concerns. This was the era of dollar diplomacy, and the United States gave substantial loans —then took over customs houses to guarantee their repayment.

Europe's recovery in the 1920s did little to help Latin America. A drop in the birth rate in Europe led to a slowdown in the demand for Latin American primary products. European investors turned their attention to their own continent. And new synthetic substitutes dried up the market for Latin American cotton, rubber, forest dyes, timber, and nitrates. The instability of commodity prices led Latin Americans to increase production, which in turn led to a decline in prices. Furthermore, the increase in worldwide production of strategic war products, such as oil, copper, and tin, led to market gluts and a drop in prices.

To rebuild their economies, Latin Americans sought loans. The United States responded with so much money—$1 billion from 1926 to 1928—that it became known as the dance of the millions. Some of the money went into the still-small industrial sector, which by 1914 was well-established in Argentina, Brazil, Chile, Mexico, Peru, and Uruguay. However, most expansion of industrial production involved a more intensive use of existing facilities. By the end of the 1920s, almost all export earnings were still earned from production of primary products, and as few as three products accounted for at least half of all foreign exchange earnings. Seventy percent of foreign trade was conducted with the United States, Great Britain, France, and Germany. By the end of the 1930s, Argentina was the only country in Latin America where industry's share of gross domestic product exceeded 20 percent. Most of the region continued to rely on exports.

When the Great Depression hit in 1929, Latin American governments saw the markets for their products shrivel. As industries contracted in the industrialized countries, they stopped importing minerals from the developing world. Demand and prices for primary products fell, with the unit value of exports dropping more than 50 percent from 1928 to 1932. In Argentina, export values dropped from $1,537 million in 1929 to $561 million in 1932. But while prices and volume of exports fell, the interest on the sizable foreign debts of the 1920s did not. Governments began to default on their loans, and new credits were not forthcoming.

The economic turmoil caused Latin American attention to shift to yet another form of nationalism: economic. The difficult years once again emphasized the dependency and vulnerability of the Latin American economies. Their monocultural export economies collapsed. Cuba's economy broke down: Foreign trade in the early 1930s was 10 percent of the 1929 figure. Uruguay's exports dropped 80 percent in the early 1930s. Brazil's exports plummeted from $445.9 million in 1929 to $180.6 million in 1932. In short, by 1932, Latin America exported 65 percent less than it had in 1929, proving once again that foreign trade contributed mightily to the cyclical fluctuations of the Latin American economy. The nationalists demanded that steps be taken to increase the viability of the national economies and conversely to reduce their dependency on the gyrations of the international market caused by the buying whims of a few highly industrialized nations. Plans were made to increase economic diversification and to promote industrialization. Industrialization appealed to both common sense and pride. For one thing, it promised to diversify the economy; for another, it kept foreign exchange from being spent to import what could be manufactured at home. At the same time, an acute shortage of foreign currencies meant that either the nations manufactured their own goods or they did without.

The economic crisis motivated the governments to play an increasingly active role in the national economies. They introduced long-range economic planning, exerted new controls, and offered incentives. Devalued currency, import controls, and higher tariffs stimulated national industry, and all these measures received the support of the nationalists. The wider participation of the governments in the economies and the mounting demands for faster development shifted the leadership of the nationalist movement from the intellectuals, who had long enjoyed a near monopoly, to the governments themselves, which began to understand the potential power of nationalist thought. At the same time the base of support for nationalism expanded to sometimes include the urban working classes.

Latin America responded to the Great Depression with domestic production of formerly imported goods, both manufactured and agricultural products. Land that had been devoted to export crops was turned to the production of food. The two strategies—import-substituting industrialization (ISI) and import-substituting agriculture (ISA)—coupled with export promotion, helped foster domestic demand for goods. Some countries made fast recoveries as a result: Brazil, Mexico, Chile, Cuba, Peru, Venezuela, even Costa Rica and Guatemala. Recovery came much more slowly for the rest of the region, and particularly lagged in Honduras, Nicaragua, Uruguay, Paraguay, and Panama. Some of the recovery can be attributed to new trade partners. From 1932 to 1938, Germany, Italy, and Japan became important importers of Latin American goods. The European market was purchasing 55 percent of exports and supplying 45 percent of imports by 1938.

Those new markets, of course, were cut off with the outbreak of World War II. But the Second World War also presented new opportunities for Latin America, which became the only raw material producer in the world that was not a site of hostilities. Trade increased between Latin America and the United States, particularly for tin and oil, and trade increased among Latin American countries, with the larger, industrializing regions exporting to the rest. Argentina, Chile, Brazil, and Mexico even developed a limited capital goods industry. Brazil's President Getulio Várgas (1930–45, 1951–54) played Germany off against the United States, convincing the United States to replace Krupp's planned investment in a steel industry. As a result, the United States funded construction of the Volta Redonda steel mill.

Nationalism remained an amorphous sentiment, but passions could be brought to a boil over certain issues and none was more inflammable than oil. It symbolized economic nationalism and represented the longing many Latin Americans felt to control their own natural resources. Nationalists argued that the discovery and exploitation of their own petroleum was not only economically desirable but also the guarantee of real national independence and, in the case of several of the larger countries, of world-power status. "Whoever hands over petroleum to foreigners threatens our own independence," one Latin American nationalist leader warned. No acts in recent memory received more popular acclaim than the nationalization of foreign oil industries in Bolivia in 1937 and in Mexico in 1938. On the other hand, the alienation of a nation's petroleum through concessions to foreign companies has contributed to the fall of several Latin American governments, as President Arturo Frondizi (1958–62) learned in Argentina and President Fernando Belaúnde Terry (1963–68) in Peru.

When the oil question is handled adroitly, it can serve as a strong prop buttressing a nationalist government. Brazil's Várgas ably used the oil issue to his advantage. Sensing the growing importance of oil, emotionally and economically, he created the National Petroleum Council in the 1930s to coordinate and intensify the search for oil. In 1939, the first successful well was drilled. The excited nationalists at once called for the creation of a national oil industry. In a bid for wider popular support, Várgas urged the creation of a state oil monopoly to oversee exploration and to promote the development of petroleum resources. Its creation in 1953 followed a passionate national campaign and marked a major victory for the nationalists. They had triumphed over those who argued that it would be more economical for experienced foreign companies to drill for oil and pay Brazil a royalty on whatever was pumped out. The nationalists denounced that argument. After all, the issue was an emotional, not an economic, one. They wanted Brazil to retain control over one of its most precious and important resources. Their arguments convinced the masses that a national oil industry represented sovereignty, power, independence, and well-being. The masses responded with enthusiastic support, a demonstration of the power economic nationalism can muster.

Dictators and Populists

As the prosperity of the 1920s gave way to the depression of the 1930s, unrest rippled through Latin America, and governments fell in rapid succession. In 1930, the armed forces overthrew the governments in the Dominican Republic, Bolivia, Peru, Argentina, Brazil, and Guatemala. In 1931, the pattern continued in Panama, Chile, Ecuador, and El Salvador.

The men who came to power in the 1930s tended to be personalist dictators who put their own stamps on government. They were all known for their brutality and corruption, and they amassed fortunes during their years of absolute control. Some came to power through the institutions founded during the years of United States occupation: Rafael Léonidas Trujillo, who dominated the Dominican Republic 1930–61, was the commander of the Army that formed out of the constabulary that the United States established before withdrawing its occupation forces in 1924. Anastasio Somoza García came to power as head of the National Guard that the United States created in Nicaragua to guarantee order when U.S. troops withdrew in 1934. Somoza took power in 1936 and ruled until his assassination in 1956. His elder son, Luís, inherited the mantle until his own death in 1967, when he was succeeded by his younger brother, Anastasio. Both Trujillo and Somoza censored the press, suppressed or coopted labor movements, and used the police force to punish enemies and dissenters.

Their brutality paled, however, next to Maximiliano Hernandez Martínez, who took power in El Salvador in 1932 after overthrowing the constitutionally elected president Alberto Araujo. Araujo had adopted as his campaign the ideas of Salvadoran intellectual Alberto Masferrer, who called for redistribution of wealth, providing the "vital minimum." Araujo named Martínez as his vice president, and he watched the fledgling Communist Party under Faribundo Martí conduct hunger strikes and protests, while the countryside grew restive as the coffee economy collapsed. (The average price of coffee dropped from $15.75 per hundredweight in 1928 to $5.97 in 1932.) An easily defeated uprising in the province of Sonsonate led the Martínez government to respond with that has become known as *la matanza* (the massacre), a brutal attack on the rural, mostly indigenous, population, leaving an estimated 30,000 dead. After the *matanza*, Martínez became known as El Brujo, the warlock, because of his devotion to the occult. He held seances in the presidential palace, encouraged children to go barefoot so they could "better receive the beneficial effluvia of the planet, the vibrations of the earth," and hung colored lights across the streets in San Salvador to stem a smallpox epidemic.

In Cuba, the path to dictatorship was a bit different: A democratically elected president became a dictator. Gerardo Machado was elected in 1924 on the "Platform of Regeneration." His reform program included diversification of exports, encouragement of new industry, and tariff reform, and his efforts won him reelection in 1928. But his reforms depended on prosperity, which came to an end with the Great Depression. Sugar had sold for 22.5 cents per pound at the height of 1920s prosperity, but by 1930 it dropped to 2.5 cents. Sugar production dropped by 60 percent, sending shock waves through the economy. Machado greeted the inevitable social and political unrest with repression. By 1931 there was open warfare as moderate leaders were jailed. His brutal attempts to hold power, however, led the army to overthrow him in 1933 rather than face the possibility of U.S. intervention.

A longer-lasting rule was demonstrated in Brazil by Getúlio Várgas, a defeated presidential candidate who took power in a military coup in 1930. Várgas suspended congress, the state legislatures, and local governments and ruled by decrees. In 1934 he staged elections and instituted a new constitution, which nationalized banking and insurance. He also emphasized industrialization and oversaw the formation of the national oil industry, Petrobras, and the founding of the steel mill Volta Redonda. The resulting increase in the working class led to worker mobilizations and fears of social revolution. Várgas responded in 1937 with the Estado Nôvo, or New State, an idea he took from Mussolini's Italy. His government became increasingly authoritarian, and he relied on press censorship and secret police to prevent dissent.

Várgas discovered, however, that he could win the masses to his side via a new political tool: populism. Populism was the political movement that characterized much of Latin America from roughly 1930 to 1965. It was labeled as a people's movement, since it was based on mass electoral participation and pledged to address popular concerns. But populism was also hierarchical and was directed from above by a charismatic leader. These urban movements relied largely on a coalition of the working class, labor unions, middle classes, and industrial elites. In the process, they coopted the more radical ideas of the masses and redirected them in a nonrevolutionary direction. Growing poverty, first because of the Depression, next because of the nature of industrial development and urban growth, led to fears of revolution. Populism was the answer, and it seemed to please most sectors of the increasingly diverse Latin American society—all except the oligarchic elites and their revolutionary opposition.

Those charismatic leaders spoke the nationalist vocabulary. Rhetorically convincing, ideologically weak, they offered immediate benefits—better salaries, health services, the nationalization of resources—rather than institutional reforms. With the notable exception of Mexico's Lázaro Cárdenas, they focused their attention on the cities.

Várgas clearly understood the importance of the growing proletariat in Brazil. Almost at once after taking power in 1930, he created the Ministry of Labor to serve as the means by which the government dealt with the workers. By careful maneuvering, he used the urban workers to help check the formerly overwhelming power of the traditional elite. The workers pledged their support to him in return for the benefits he granted them. With a highly paternalistic—and some say demagogic—flourish, Várgas conceded to the workers more benefits than they had previously obtained through their own organizations and strikes. A decree ordered the Ministry of Labor to organize the workers into new unions under governmental supervision. By 1944, there were about 800 unions, with membership exceeding half a million. The government prohibited strikes but established special courts and codes to protect the workers and to provide redress for their grievances. Under the government's watchful eye, the unions could and did bargain with management. Further, Várgas promulgated a wide variety of social legislation favoring the workers. He decreed retirement and pension plans, a minimum wage, a work week limited to forty-eight hours, paid annual vacations, maternal benefits and child care, educational opportunities and literacy campaigns, safety and health standards for work, and job security. In short, Várgas offered labor, in less than a decade, the advances and benefits that the proletariat of the industrialized nations had agitated for during the previous century. Little wonder, then, that the urban working class (for the benefits did not extend into the rural areas) rallied to support the president. In 1945, Várgas created the Brazilian Labor Party, which frankly and aggressively appealed to the urban worker. Small at its inception, the party grew in size and strength during the following two decades, while the other two major parties declined in strength.

Simultaneously Cárdenas wooed Mexico's urban laborers in an attempt to counteract the growing influence of conservatives in the government. To strengthen labor, he advised the workers to organize into one monolithic confederation and in 1936–37 oversaw the establishment of the Confederación de Trabajadores de México (Confederation of Mexican Workers, CTM), which included most of the nation's unionized labor. At the same time, he restructured the official governmental party so that it rested on four sectors of support, one of which was labor. Organized labor, thus encouraged and directed by the government, achieved an unprecedented importance in Mexico. Both sides benefited. The standard of living of the workers rose and so did their sense of dignity as active participants in the national government. The government intervened to settle most labor–management disputes in favor of labor. Further, the workers assumed management of the National Railways Company and cooperated in the management of the petroleum industry. With the encouragement of Cárdenas, the labor movement reached its highest degree of organization, greatest prestige, and strongest influence. Cárdenas profited from the vigorous and loyal labor organization. Partially as a result of the strength labor lent him, he triumphed over party and political rivals, promulgated the revolutionary reforms he favored, and improved his position in bargaining with foreign economic interests and local industrialists.

One of the icons of Latin American populism was Juan Domingo Perón, who came to power in Argentina as part of the string of military governments that took power beginning with a coup in 1930. Previous Argentine governments had done little to favor the workers, despite the industrial surge and expansion of labor's ranks. Perón perceived the potential of the working class and utilized it after the military coup d'etat of 1943 to project himself into power. As secretary of labor in the new government he lavished attention in the form of wage increases and social legislation on the hitherto neglected workers, who responded with enthusiastic endorsement of their patron. During the two years Perón held the labor portfolio, the trade unions nearly quadrupled in size. Perón adroitly manipulated the labor movement so that only leaders and unions beholden to him were officially recognized. When military leaders, suspicious and resentful of Perón's growing power, imprisoned him in October of 1945, workers from around the country angrily descended on the center of Buenos Aires and paralyzed the capital. The military, devoid of any visible popular support, immediately backed down and freed Perón. With the full backing of labor, he easily won the presidential elections of 1946 with 56 percent of the vote, and his followers dominated the new congress.

Argentine President Juan Domingo Perón. (Library of Congress.)

During his decade of government, Perón relied heavily on the approval and support of organized labor. Urban workers, many of whom were inadequately integrated into city life, constituted the basis for Perón's highly successful mass movement.

Eva Duarte de Perón (1919–52) had played a fundamental role in organizing and coordinating the popular support of the working class that first brought her husband to power and then helped to maintain him there. Probably more radical than he, she exhibited a greater sensitivity to the needs and aspirations of the masses. She partially contributed to their well-being through the huge Social Aid Foundation she administered. She devoted much time to strengthening the Peronist Women's Party and was instrumental in achieving the enfranchisement of Argentine women in 1947. In the 1951 elections, more than 2 million women voted for the first time, and six women senators and twenty-four deputies, all Peronistas, were sent to Congress. "Evita," as the Argentine masses affectionately called her, helped handle government relations with the workers, welding them into an effective force complementary to the government's goals.

It would be too simplistic to lament the demise of labor's freedom under the Peróns. In truth, it never had enjoyed much liberty—at best it was

Emphatic Argentine first lady Eva Perón (1919–1952) gestures while delivering a speech. (Hulton Getty / Liaison Agency, Inc.)

tolerated—under previous governments, and certainly prior to Perón the unions had gained few victories for their rank and file. They did compromise their liberty but they did so in return for undisputed advantages and for a greater feeling of participation in government than they had ever felt under the elitist leaders who had governed Argentina, with the possible exception of the middle-class government of Irigoyen. Perón's nationalist rhetoric cheered the workers, who identified more closely with his programs than with those of any previous government. They rallied behind him to taunt the foreign and native capitalists who they believed had exploited them. Perón, like the other populist leaders of the time, exuded a charismatic charm. He never lost the support of the working class. His fall from power in 1955 resulted from economic problems, loss of Church approval, the firm and increasingly effective opposition of the traditional oligarchy, and—most importantly—the withdrawal by the military of its previous support. The middle class and the elite rejoiced in his fall; the event stunned great multitudes of the masses who had given their leader enthusiastic support in return for more benefits and dignity than they received from all the previous governments combined.

Obviously such populist governments as the one Perón so well represented found little favor among Latin America's elite, both the traditional elite and those who, thanks to greater social fluidity in the twentieth century, had recently achieved that exalted status. They resented any erosion of their power from below. Increasingly, the middle class seemed frightened by the prospects of populist government and consequently they tended to align with the elite. Certainly the previous accords between urban labor and the middle class, noticeable in some instances during the first decades of the twentieth century, disintegrated as the middle class became apprehensive of a threat, real or imagined, to their status and ambitions from labor. By the mid-twentieth century, identifying more with the elite against whom they had once struggled but whose lifestyle they incessantly aped, the middle class when forced to select between the masses and change and the elite and the status quo tended to opt for the latter.

Latin America Turns Inward

As World War II ended, Latin America faced a new world order, dominated by the United States and dedicated to free trade. The new order was established by the allied powers meeting at Bretton Woods, where they determined how to rebuild the post-war economy. The United States guaranteed a more international economy by providing a market, through open borders and unilaterally reduced tariffs; a stable currency, by pegging the dollar to gold at $35 an ounce; and capital, by investing in the rest of the world. Institutionally, the new order rested on three pillars: The International Monetary Fund, which would stabilize monetary relations by lending money to governments; the International Bank for Reconstruction and Development (IBRD, or World Bank), which was to lend money at long-term rates to developing countries to build the infrastructure that would attract private investment; and the International Treaty Organization, which led to formation of the General Agreement on Trade and Tariffs (GATT), designed to negotiate tariff reductions and free world trade.

At the Eighth Inter-American Conference held in Chapúltepec, Mexico, in 1945, U.S. representatives announced their commitment to free trade, ending the wartime agreements that had provided guarantees to Latin America. The United States then turned its attention to rebuilding the destroyed European economies via the Marshall Plan. Now that the United States could once again access Asian raw material supplies that had been cut off by the war, Latin America became a low priority.

Latin America tried to turn back to its former European markets, but Europe was struggling to rebuild and could buy little of Latin America's products. Export volume grew slowly, but export prices increased dramatically. Foreign exchange reserves grew, but they were quickly depleted by repayment of debts and the high demand for imports that once again flooded the region. Pessimistic about exports and buoyed by economic nationalism, Latin American leaders chose to look inward.

The Plaza of the Three Cultures, Mexico City, perfectly illustrates the past and the present. In the foreground is an excavated Aztec, temple foundation, upon which the Spaniards constructed a church, while in the background stand modern apartment buildings.

Their view was bolstered by the theories of the United Nations Economic Commission for Latin America, founded in 1948 and headed by Argentine economist Raúl Prebisch. ECLA and Prebisch contended that over time the terms of trade went against Latin America because it exchanged low-priced primary products for higher valued manufactured goods. Furthermore, international markets were dangerously unreliable and commodity prices were subject to boom-and-bust cycles. Their recommendation was to take the unofficial import-substitution industrializing policy of the war and depression years and make it a conscious policy decision. The policy of ISI gained a number of adherents: nationalists who believed it was important to have local industries to meet national needs; urban industrialists and workers, who wanted to see an expansion in industry; the middle class, who anticipated the growth of the service sector associated with industrialization.

Argentina, Brazil, Chile and Uruguay enthusiastically adopted the ISI model, erecting tariff barriers to limit imports that would compete with fledgling industries. They subsidized inputs needed for industrial production, provided low-rate credit to create and expand an industrial base, and passed legislation requiring particular levels of domestic content for goods on the market. Brazil amply illustrated the growing importance of industry within the economy. Whereas in 1939, the industrial sector provided 17.9 percent of the national income, it furnished 35.3 percent by 1963.

All nations of Latin America did not participate equally in the industrial surge. Industrialization concentrated in a few favored geographic areas. At the end of the 1960s, three nations, Argentina, Brazil, and Mexico, accounted for 80 percent of Latin America's industrial production. In fact, more than 30 percent of the total factory production was squeezed into the metropolitan areas of Buenos Aires, Mexico City, and São Paulo. Five other nations—Chile, Colombia, Peru, Uruguay, and Venezuela—produced 17 percent of Latin America's industrial goods, leaving the remaining 3 percent of the manufacturing to the twelve other republics. Industrialization sowed the seeds of new problems for Latin America. For one thing, it was creating a new type of dependency in which Latin America relied ever more heavily on foreign investment, technology, technicians, and markets. For another, it funneled wealth increasingly into the hands of a few industrial elites.

Furthermore, the ties between industrialists and large landowners were closer than most people realized or cared to admit. While at times there were separate landowning and industrialist classes, in many instances the two groups overlapped. Thus, one could observe a growing industrial concentration in the hands of a few alongside a great concentration of land ownership, and very often the same persons played the dual role of landowner and industrialist. Such an interrelationship of interests complicated reform efforts.

One significant consequence of industrialization has been the growth of a better-defined urban proletariat class conscious of its goals and powers. As the labor movement expanded in the decades between 1914 and 1933, its leadership spoke increasingly in terms of major social changes. The ideological content of the labor programs, the increasingly efficient organization of the unions, and the new power that labor wielded worried the elites and the middle class. Governments yielded to some basic labor demands to limit working hours, set minimum wages, provide vacations, ensure sick and maternal leave, and legislate other social-welfare laws. But at the same time they moved to dominate, control, and finally coopt the labor movement.

One of the things that labor demanded, especially when it could not secure higher wages, was cheap food. Yet, while agriculture still formed the basis for the area's economy, few nations tried to reform the centuries-old agrarian structure. Mexico was the sole exception until the 1950s. The landowning system in most of Latin America remained flagrantly unjust, based, at least in part, on the accumulation of huge tracts of land often by means of force, deceit, and dubious measures approved by the passage of time and the connivance of bureaucrats.

In no other area of comparable size in the world did there exist a higher concentration of land in the hands of a few than in Latin America. As of 1950, 2 percent of the Argentine estates accounted for 60 percent of the land; in Brazil, 1.6 percent of the fazendas covered 50 percent of the land; in El Salvador, 1 percent of the haciendas included 50 percent of the land; in Paraguay, 11 haciendas controlled 35 percent of the land. The figures were comparable in most of the rest of the countries. And the general tendency in this century has been for the large properties to increase in both number and size. (By the late 1960s, 17 percent of the landowners controlled 90 percent of the land.)

On the opposite end of the scale lay another problem: the minifundium, a property so small that often it failed to sustain its owner, much less to contribute to the regional or national economies. That problem, too, was widespread. As of 1950, 42 percent of the farms in Argentina claimed only 1 percent of the land; in Brazil, 22 percent of the rural properties possessed only 0.5 percent of the land; in El Salvador, 80 percent of the farms had fewer than 12 acres each; in Paraguay, 44 percent of the farms had fewer than 12 acres each. Statistics for the early 1960s showed that 63 percent, or 18 million adult farmers, owned no land; another 5.5 million owned insufficient amounts of land; 1.9 million possessed sufficient land; and 100,000 owned too much land for the social and economic good of the area.

In very general terms and with notable exceptions, a lack of efficiency characterized the large estates. They included much land their owners either did not cultivate or undercultivated. Experts estimated that Latin Americans in the mid-twentieth century farmed only about 10 percent of their agricultural holdings. In Brazil, Venezuela, and Colombia, approximately 80 percent of the farmland was unused or unproductively used for cattle raising at the end of the 1950s. A 1960 study of Colombia revealed that the largest farmers, in control of 70 percent of the agricultural lands, cultivated only 6 percent of it. Farmers of fewer than thirteen acres, on the other hand, cultivated 66 percent of it. Another study illustrating the underuse of farmland showed that only 14 percent of Ecuador's tillable land was cultivated in the early 1960s. The landowners continued to hold their property, not to farm, but for purposes of prestige, investment, and speculation. As in the past, control of the land ensured control of the workforce as well because the resulting landlessness forced people to work on the great estates. With such great supplies of cheap labor, estate owners saw no need to modernize their farming techniques. The slash-and-burn method remained the most popular means of clearing the land. The farmers rarely spread fertilizer or did so sparingly. Consequently, the land eroded, became easily exhausted, and depleted quickly. Productivity, always low, fell. The farmer used the hoe, unmodified for centuries. The plow was rare, the tractor even rarer.

Increasingly, Latin America needed to import food. Chile, for example, shifted in the 1940s from being a net agricultural exporter to becoming a net importer. By the mid-1950s, agricultural products accounted for 25 percent of Chile's total imports. In short, that nation was spending about 18 percent of its hard-earned foreign currency on food that Chile could grow itself, a tragedy by no means unique to Chile. By 1965, foodstuffs constituted 20 percent of Latin America's purchases abroad. Even with imports supplementing careless local production, the food available to feed the population properly was insufficient. Starvation was not unknown and malnutrition was common in wide regions of Latin America.

Agriculture in the twentieth century lost none of the speculative, reflexive nature so characteristic of the mercantilist past. For its prosperity, agriculture continued to rely heavily on a few export commodities, which were always very vulnerable on the international market. Prices depended on the demands of a few industrialized nations. Further, new producers and substitutes appeared to challenge and undersell them, thus increasing Latin America's economic vulnerability. Africa, in particular, emerged as a formidable competitor for international markets. After World War II, the prices of agricultural products gradually declined to the dismay of the Latin Americans (while at the same time the prices of imported capital goods spiraled upward). Still, the latifundia by and large followed their usual practice of offering one crop for sale. At the end of the 1950s, the well-being of an alarming number of Latin Americans depended, for example, on a fair price for coffee. Coffee composed 67 percent of Colombia's exports, 42 percent of El Salvador's, 41 percent of Brazil's, 38 percent of Haiti's, 34 percent of Guatemala's, and 31 percent of Costa Rica's. Other Latin American economies depended on the export of sugar, bananas, cacao, wheat, beef, wool, and mutton.

Furthermore, despite the ISI emphasis on building national industry, the strategy actually resulted in an influx of foreign investment. Foreign producers who wanted access to Latin American markets but were discouraged by high tariff barriers simply established subsidiaries in Latin America. Governments welcomed this direct foreign investment: It brought in needed capital for investment, along with technology, marketing and management expertise, and guaranteed access to foreign sources of supply and markets. Most foreign investment concentrated in petroleum, manufacturing, mining, and public utilities. United States investment, by far the most predominant, reached $9 billion by the mid-1960s. Foreign capital controlled a disproportionate share of the industries in each nation. For example, the extent of foreign investment in Brazilian industry in 1970 was approximately 22 percent of the capital of all industrial firms, or 32 percent of medium and large firms. Of the fifty-five largest companies operating in Brazil during the l960s, thirty-one were foreign-owned. Argentine industry likewise felt the influence of foreign capitalists. Of the ten principal industrial firms operating in Argentina in 1971, foreigners owned eight and the government the remaining two. Foreigners also owned more than half of the private banks in Argentina. In Mexico, too, foreign economic influences remained considerable. Well over $1 billion of U.S. direct investment concentrated in Mexico, over two-thirds of that in manufacturing. In the early 1960s, foreign interests, predominantly those of the United States, controlled 28 percent of the 2,000 largest companies in Mexico, and their influence was clearly evident in another 14 percent. Despite impressive industrial growth and diversification in Latin America, the area still relied heavily on foreign interests and capital.

The foreign investors were attracted by high profits. Indeed, investors received more return than they could expect from similar investments in the United States, Canada, or Western Europe. Between 1950 and 1965, U.S. citizens invested $3,800 million in Latin America and earned $11,300 million, a mind-boggling profit of $7,500 million.

A Flirtation with Democracy

The economy was not the only aspect of Latin America to change in the post-war years. The rhetoric that accompanied the United States as it marched into World War II was heard throughout the hemisphere. The Allies' victory marked democracy's triumph over dictatorship, and the consequences shook Latin America. Questioning why they should support the struggle for democracy in Europe and yet suffer the constraints of dictatorship at home, many Latin Americans rallied to democratize their own political structures. A group of prominent middle-class Brazilians opposed to the continuation of the Várgas dictatorship mused publicly, "If we fight against fascism at the side of the United Nations so that liberty and democracy may be restored to all people, certainly we are not asking too much in demanding for ourselves such rights and guarantees."

In the surge toward democratic goals, the ideals of the nineteenth-century liberals revived. The times favored the democratic concepts professed by the middle class. Governments out of step with them toppled. A wave of freedom of speech, press, and assembly engulfed much of Latin America and bathed the middle class with satisfaction. New political parties emerged to represent broader segments of the population. Democracy, always a fragile plant anywhere, seemed ready to blossom throughout Latin America.

Nowhere was this change more amply illustrated than in Guatemala, where Jorge Ubico ruled as dictator from 1931 until 1944. Ubico, a former minister of war, carried out unprecedented centralization of the state and repression of his opponents. Although he technically ended debt peonage, the 1934 vagrancy law required the carrying of identification cards and improved the landlords' position in disputes with workers. The landlords, in turn, supported his regime, since he prohibited independent labor organizing. He massacred Indians who rebelled, killed labor leaders and intellectuals, and enriched his friends.

In May and June of 1944 there were a series of anti-Ubico protests, led primarily by schoolteachers, shopkeepers, skilled workers, and students. They were influenced by Franklin Delano Roosevelt's four freedoms: freedom of speech and religion, freedom from want and fear. They were also influenced by the Mexican example of Lázaro Cárdenas, who had nationalized the oil industry and carried out agrarian reform.

Ubico could not count on the United States for support against his opponents. U.S. officials viewed him as unreliable. He was openly pro-Nazi until the United States pressured him to support the Allies, and he was so untrustworthy that FBI agents were sent to oversee his confiscation of German property. The establishment of a U.S. air base near Guatemala City was as much to keep an eye on Ubico as to watch over the Panama Canal.

The series of nonviolent protests that led to Ubico's overthrow began when teachers refused to march in the annual teachers' day parade. During one of their protests, the Guatemalan cavalry was ordered to charge, killing and injuring some 200 people. Ubico then declared a state of siege. As the crisis mounted, a group of prominent teachers, lawyers, doctors, and businessmen, who supported the protesters, drew up the Petition of the 311, calling on Ubico to step down. The petition was presented to Ubico by several prominent citizens who he considered to be friends. Defeated, he resigned on July 1, 1944, and turned power over to Gen. Federico Ponce. Ponce stood for election that fall, and the opposition recruited as their candidate Dr. Juan José Arévalo, a prominent educator, author of several textbooks on history, geography and civics, who was in exile in Argentina.

Arévalo considered himself a "spiritual socialist," an inspiration he credited to FDR. In his inaugural address, Arévalo said of the U.S. president: "He taught us that there is no need to cancel the concept of freedom in the democratic system in order to breathe into it a socialist spirit." Arévalo dissolved the secret police, removed all generals from their positions, dissolved the National Assembly, and repealed the constitution. An elected constitutional assembly wrote a new constitution and elected a new national assembly. The four priorities of the new government were to carry out agrarian reform, protect labor, improve education, and consolidate political democracy.

The challenge was formidable: An experienced bank clerk in Guatemala earned about $90 a month. A farmworker earned about five to twenty cents a day. Only 2 percent of all landowners owned 72 percent of the land. Ninety percent of landowners held only 15 percent of productive acreage. Indians were still held by debt labor for 150 days of the year. Illiteracy was 75 percent in the general population, and 95 percent among the indigenous, who constituted more than half of the population. Life expectancy for ladinos was 50 years; for Indians only 40. Coffee production was dominated by Guatemalan elites, and banana production was dominated by the U.S. giant, the United Fruit Company (UFCO). Arévalo addressed these problems by adopting a labor code, setting a minimum wage, and creating a National Production Institute to distribute credit, expertise, and supplies to small farmers. He distributed the confiscated German landholdings, made sure smallholder titles were registered, and passed the Law of Forced Rental to guarantee that land would be rented to anyone with less than one hectare (2.5 acres). He also established a national bank and national planning office.

In 1950, after historic free elections, Jacobo Arbenz took office, having won 65 percent of the vote in an election that all observers agreed was fair and honest. While democracy had been consolidated by Arévalo, it fell to Arbenz to work for economic change. In 1950, the annual per capita income of agricultural workers was $87. Of 4 million acres in plantations, less than 25 percent of the land was cultivated. In his inaugural address, Arbenz pledged to convert the country from a dependent nation to economic independence, to convert from a "feudal" to a modern, capitalist economy, and to raise the standard of living for the masses.

His blueprint was a report issued in 1950 by the International Bank for Reconstruction and Development. The report recommended government regulation of the energy companies and autonomous National Power Authority; setting wages to take prices into account; regulation of foreign business; industrialization to decrease reliance on foreign trade; and institution of a capital gains tax. The report criticized Guatemalan elites for raking in exorbitant profits and then investing them abroad.

Arbenz knew that the place to begin was the countryside, which he claimed was feudal and needed to be restructured for successful capitalism. The tool was to be the Agrarian Reform Law of 1952. The law declared that the uncultivated land on estates over 220 acres where less than two-thirds of the estate was under cultivation was subject to expropriation and redistribution. It left untouched farms smaller than 220 acres, and any size farm was allowed as long as it was fully cultivated. Confiscated land was to be paid in 25-year bonds at 3 percent interest, based on the value of the property as declared by the owners for tax purposes as of May 1952. Land was redistributed in maximum parcels of 42.5 acres, and 1.5 million acres of land were distributed among 1000,000 people. Among the property confiscated was 1,700 acres taken from Arbenz himself. Arbenz had a firm legal base for the reform he intended. The Constitution of 1945 declared large estates to be illegal and conferred on the government the power to expropriate and redistribute land. Nonetheless, the landowning elite immediately and vociferously charged that the reform was communistic.

The charge of communism was guaranteed to get the attention of U.S. officials. The United States had never been friendly to socialism and communism and had been wary since the beginning of the Soviet Union, with whom they were reluctant allies in World War II. But after the "hot" war of fighting the Axis powers was over, the United States became immersed in a new war: the Cold War. This time there would be no fighting—at least not directly between the United States and the USSR. But the United States was determined to stop the spread of communism—or anything perceived as communism—around the world. Communism is based on a planned rather than a market economy; the United States, on the other hand, was committed to markets, now more than ever.

Guatemala's agrarian reform was far less severe than the one carried out in neighboring Mexico. But it came at the wrong time, and in the wrong place. In another decade, the United States would encourage programs such as these. But in the 1950s, the attack on the UFCO was seen as an attack on U.S. capital. And in the zero-sum game of the Cold War, anything that limited capitalist development must be socialist. And socialism equaled the supposedly monolithic communism of the Soviet Union.

In Washington, the State Department watched apprehensively but said nothing until in 1953 the Guatemalan government seized 233,973 acres of unused land claimed by the United Fruit Company, a figure later raised to 413,573 acres. The company exercised formidable economic powers. Not only was it the largest single agricultural enterprise in the country but it also owned and controlled the principal railroad and the facilities in the major port, Puerto Barrios. It was extremely unpopular among the nationalists and vulnerable because it was foreign and exercised too powerful an influence over an economy being challenged as semifeudal and exploitative. As a matter of record, the company paid the Guatemalan government in duties and taxes about 10 percent of its annual profits, a sum regarded by indignant nationalists as far too low.

The State Department rushed to support the claims of the United Fruit Company against the Guatemalan government on the basis that the compensation offered was insufficient. Yet, the sum offered equaled the value of the lands declared by the company for tax purposes. At that point, the State Department began to charge that the Guatemalan government was infiltrated with, if not controlled by, communists. Some critics of U.S. foreign policy wondered at the motivations of the U.S. government. They pointed out the close connections between Central Intelligence Agency Director Allen Dulles, his brother, Secretary of State John Foster Dulles, and the United Fruit Company, a relationship that suggested some conflict of interests. The law office of John Foster Dulles had written the drafts of the United Fruit Company's 1930 and 1936 agreements with the Guatemalan government. For that matter, the family of John Moors Cabot, then assistant secretary of state for inter-American affairs, owned stock in the banana company; Cabot's brother, Thomas, had been president of the company. As the verbal attacks of the State Department on Guatemala mounted, it became difficult, indeed, nearly impossible, to distinguish its charges from those of the United Fruit Company, and both of them sounded remarkably similar to the statements of the native oligarchy. All three were preoccupied with the communist "menace," but none of them seemed concerned with the abysmal misery on which communism might well feed in Guatemala and other underdeveloped nations in the hemisphere.

Despite the mounting pressure, Arbenz pushed ahead with his program to decrease Guatemala's dependency. He announced the government's intention to build a highway from Guatemala City to the Atlantic coast and thereby end the transportation monopoly of the International Railways of Central America, owned and operated by the UFCO. Further, he decided to construct a national hydroelectric plant. Until that time, foreigners produced Guatemala's electrical power, and the rates charged were among the highest in Latin America.

By late 1953, the Arbenz government feared intervention. Arbenz repeatedly requested arms since he felt his more conservative neighbors, Honduras and El Salvador, were encouraging exiles to prepare an attack on his country. The State Department responded with an embargo on arms sales to Guatemala. Unable to equip the army with materiel from the United States, the president turned to another source. On May 17, 1954, a shipment of arms arrived from Poland. To the State Department, its arrival served as final proof that Guatemala had fallen under communist control. The U.S. Air Force at once ferried military supplies to Tegucigalpa in order to equip a small army under the command of a Guatemalan army exile, Colonel Carlos Castillo Armas. On June 18, 1954, Castillo, Armas and approximately 150 men crossed the border into Guatemala. They penetrated about twenty-five miles but engaged in no significant action. They did not need to. The Arbenz government fell because the army refused to act and the workers were not armed. A series of air attacks on the unarmed capital terrorized the population and broke the morale of the people. The attacks caused more psychological than physical damage. The planes were furnished by the CIA and flown by U.S. pilots, as former President Dwight D. Eisenhower revealed in a publicly recorded interview. U.S. Ambassador John Peurifoy handled the changing of the government, and with the enthusiastic endorsement of Washington, installed Castillo Armas in the presidency. In violation of United Nations and Organization of American States treaties and international law, the metropolis blatantly intervened in the small country. In a radio address on June 30, 1954, John Foster Dulles informed the American people of the changes in the

Guatemalan government, which prompted him to declare, "The events of recent months and days add a new and glorious chapter to the already great tradition of the American States."

A year after the United States placed Castillo Armas in power, Vice-President Richard Nixon wrote, "President Castillo Armas' objective, 'to do more for the people in two years than the Communists were able to do in ten years,' is important. This is the first instance in history where a communist government has been replaced by a free one. The whole world is watching to see which does the better job."

In a yes-or-no plebiscite echoing the Ubico practice of the 1931–44 period, Castillo Armas confirmed himself in power. Deriving his major support from the local elites, the United Fruit Company, and the U.S. State Department, he ruled for three years without ever offering to hold elections, free or otherwise. Nonetheless, he took the precaution of abolishing all political parties that did not please him and disenfranchising all illiterates, thus canceling the voting rights of more than half the adult population. The police jailed, tortured, exiled, and executed political opponents, excusing their crimes with the accusation that the victims were communists. Castillo Armas eradicated whatever traces of communism might be found or fabricated, but in the process also eliminated democracy and reform.

Guatemala after 1954 offered the first Latin American example of the reversal of a land reform. Castillo Armas returned to the United Fruit Company the lands his predecessor had nationalized. What is more, he signed a new contract that facilitated the company's exploitation of Guatemala until 1981, limiting its taxes to a maximum of 30 percent of the profits. (That figure contrasted with the 69 percent oil companies had to pay Venezuela.) Approximately 1.5 million acres, which under the 1952 Agrarian Reform Law had been confiscated as idle and distributed to 100,000 landless rural families, reverted back to the original owners. The newly created peasant class suffered severely. Much of the land returned to the original owners lay fallow, while Guatemala imported food that the country was perfectly capable of growing.

Castillo Armas was assassinated by one of his own presidential guards in 1957, but that did not put an end to the country's political repression. A series of military governments during the last half of the twentieth century, always under the banner of anti-communism, ignited the fires of a holocaust for the Indian population. Reflecting on the brutality and arrogance of military rule in Guatemala, the *Los Angeles Times* (July 5, 1984) termed the CIA intervention in 1954 and its dismal aftermath "one of the most shortsighted 'successes' in the history of U.S.–Latin American relations."

Evita: A Different Feminism?

Eva Duarte de Perón (1919–52) was more than the first lady of
Argentina as the wife of populist leader Juan Perón. Evita, as she
was affectionately known, was the poor girl from the country
who grew up to be a beautiful actress, the wife of a powerful
man, and the champion of the poor. While it may be argued that
structural reforms would have done more to help the poor, her
Eva Duarte de Perón Foundation distributed a great deal of aid
to the lower classes, making her a symbol of beneficence. As a
woman in the spotlight, Evita presented a contradictory image.
A childless public activist who urged the adoption of women's
suffrage, she also believed that women belonged at home.
Within the home, however, she advocated for a radical set of
women's rights and guarantees. The following excerpts are from
her autobiography, *My Mission in Life*.

WOMEN AND MY MISSION
My work in the woman's movement began and grew, just like my
work of social service and my trade-union activities, little by little,
and more by force of circumstances than through any decisions of
mine. . . .

All I brought by way of preparation to the scene of these
struggles were those same *feelings* which had made me think of
the problem of the rich and the poor.

But nothing more.

I never imagined it would fall to my lot someday to lead a
woman's movement in my country, and still less a political
movement.

Circumstances showed the way.

Ah! But I did not remain in my comfortable position of Eva
Perón. The path which opened up before my eyes was the path I
took if by it I could help Perón's cause a little—the cause of the
people.

I imagine many other women have seen the paths I pursue
long before I did.

The only difference between them and me is that they
stayed behind and I started. Actually, I should confess that if I
girded myself for a struggle it was not for myself but for him . . .
for Perón!

He encouraged me to rise.

He took me out of the "flock of sparrows."

He taught me my first steps in all my undertakings.

Afterward I never lacked the powerful and extraordinary
stimulus of his love.

I realize, above all, that I began my work in a woman's movement because Perón's cause demanded it.

It all began little by little.

Before I realized it I was already heading a woman's political movement . . . and, with it, had to accept the spiritual leadership of the women of my country.

This caused me to meditate on women's problems. And, more than that, to feel them, and to feel them in the light of the doctrine with which Perón was beginning to build a New Argentina.

I remember with what extraordinary fondness, as friend and master, General Perón explained to me innumerable women's problems in my country and in the world.

In these conversations I again became aware of the kindliness of his nature.

Millions of men have faced, as he has faced, the ever more acute problem of woman's role in humanity in this afflicted century; but I think very few of them have stopped, like Perón, to penetrate it to its depth.

In this, as in everything, he showed me the way.

The world's feminists will say that to start a woman's movement in this way is hardly feministic . . . to start by recognizing to a certain extent the superiority of a man!

However, I am not interested in criticisms.

Also, recognizing Perón's superiority is a different matter.

Besides . . . it is my intention to write the truth.

FROM THE SUBLIME TO THE RIDICULOUS

I confess I was a little afraid the day I found myself facing the possibility of starting on the "feminist" path.

What could I, a humble woman of the people, do where other women, more prepared than I, had categorically failed?

Be ridiculous? Join the nucleus of women with a grudge against woman and against man, as has happened to innumerable feminist leaders?

I was not an old maid, nor even ugly enough for such a post . . . which, from the time of the English suffragettes down to today, generally belongs, almost exclusively, to women of this type . . . women whose first impulse undoubtedly had been to be like men.

And that is how they guided the movements they led!

They seemed to be dominated by indignation at not having been born men, more than by the pride of being women.

They thought, too, that it was a misfortune to be a woman. They were resentful of women who did not want to stop being women. They were resentful of men because they would not let them be like them; the "feminists," the immense majority of feminists in the world, as far as I could see, continued to be a strange species of woman . . . which never seemed to me to be entirely womanly!

And I did not feel very much inclined to be like them.

One day the General gave me the explanation I needed.

"Don't you see that they have missed the way? They want to be men. It is as though to save the workers I had tried to make oligarchs of them. I would have remained without workers. And I do not think I should have managed to improve the oligarchy at all. Don't you see that this class of 'feminists' detests womanhood? Some of them do not even use makeup . . . because that, according to them, is womanly. Don't you see they want to be men? And if what the world requires is a woman's political and social movement . . . how little will the world gain if the women want to save it by imitating men! We have done too many strange things and made such a mess of everything that I do not know if the world can be arranged anew. Perhaps woman can save us, on condition that she does not imitate us."

I well remember that lesson of the General's.

His ideas never seemed to me so clear and bright.

That is how I felt.

I felt that the woman's movement in my country and all over the world had to fulfill a sublime mission. . . and everything I knew about feminism seemed to me ridiculous. For, not led by women but by those who aspired to be men, it ceased to be womanly and was nothing! Feminism had taken the step from the sublime to the ridiculous.

And that is the step I always try to avoid taking!

HOME OR THE FACTORY

Every day thousands of women forsake the feminine camp and begin to live like men.

They work like them. They prefer, like them, the street to the home. They are not resigned to being either mothers or wives.

They substitute for men everywhere.

Is this "feminism"? I think, rather, that it must be the "masculinization" of our sex.

And I wonder if all this has solved our problem

But no. All the old ills continue rampant, and new ones, too, appear. The number of young women who look down upon the occupation of homemaking increases every day.

And yet that is what we are born for.

We feel that we are born for the home, and the home is too great a burden for our shoulders.

Then we give up the home. . . go out to find a solution . . . feel that the answer lies in obtaining economic independence and working somewhere. But that work makes us equal to the men and—no! We are not like them! They can live alone; we cannot. We feel the need of company, of complete company. We feel the need of giving more than receiving. Can't we work for anything else than earning wages like men?

And, on the other hand, if we give up the work which makes us independent so as to form a home . . . we burn our boats once and for all.

No profession in the world has less of a chance of a comeback than our profession as women.

Even if we are chosen by a good man, our home will not always be what we dreamed of when we were single.

The entire nation ends at the door of our home, and other laws and other rights begin . . . the law and the rights of man—who very often is only a master, and also, at times, a dictator.

And nobody can interfere there.

The mother of a family is left out of all security measures. She is the only worker in the world without a salary, or a guarantee, or limited working hours, or free Sundays, or holidays, or any rest, or indemnity for dismissal, or strikes of any kind. All that, we learned as girls, belongs to the sphere of love . . . but the trouble is that after marriage, love often flies out of the window, and then everything becomes "forced labor" . . . obligations without any rights! Free service in exchange for pain and sacrifice!

I do not say it is always like this. I should have no right to say anything, since *my* home is happy . . . if I did not see the suffering every day of so many women who live like that . . . with no outlook, no rights, with no hope.

That is why every day there are fewer women to make homes.

Real homes, united and happy! And the world needs more homes every day, and for them more women willing properly to fulfill their destiny and their mission. That is why the first objective of a feminine movement which wishes to improve things for women—which does not aim at changing them into men—should be the home.

We were born to make homes. Not for the street. Common sense shows us the answer. We must have in the home that which we go out to seek: our small economic independence—which would save us from becoming women with no outlook, with no rights and no hope!

AN IDEA

. . . I think one should commence by fixing a small monthly allowance for every woman who gets married, from the day of her marriage.

A salary paid to the mothers by all the nation and which comes out of all the earnings of all the workers in the country, including the women.

Nobody will say that it is not just for us to pay the work

which, even if it is not seen, demands the efforts of millions and millions of women whose time, whose lives, are spent on the monotonous but heavy task of cleaning the house, looking after clothes, laying the table, bringing up children, etc.

That allowance could be, for a start, half the average national salary, and thus the woman, housekeeper, mistress of the home, would have an income of their own apart from what the man wishes to give her.

Later increases for each child could be added to this basic salary, an increase in case of widowhood, lost if she joins the ranks of the workers—in a word, in all the ways likely to be of most help so that the original purpose shall not be lost sight of. . . .

I offer this solution so that the woman who starts a home shall not feel herself below the woman who earns her living in a factory or in an office. . . .

I know my solution is more a remedy than a solution. I know it is only a beginning, a gesture. I think a great deal more will still have to be done.

Because it is not a matter of trying to return to the home a prestige it is losing, but of giving it an entirely new one. . . .

THE GREAT ABSENCE

I think the feminist movement organized as a vital force in each country and in all the world should and would do a great good to all humanity.

I do not know where I once read that in this world of ours the great need is for love.

I would modify this a bit and say that rather does the world today suffer from a great absence: that of woman.

Everything, absolutely everything in this contemporary world, has been made according to man's measure.

We are absent from governments.

We are absent from parliaments.

From international organizations.

We are in neither the Vatican nor the Kremlin.

Nor in the high commands of the imperialists.

Nor in the commissions of atomic energy.

Nor in the great business combines.

Nor in Freemasonry, nor in other secret societies.

We are absent from all the great centers constituting a power in the world.

And yet we have always been present in the time of suffering, and in all humanity's bitter hours.

It would seem as though our calling were not substantially that of creating, but rather that of sacrifice.

Our symbol should be the Mother of Christ at the foot of the Cross.

And yet our highest mission is nothing but to create.

I cannot understand, then, why we are not in those places where an attempt is being made to create man's happiness.

Haven't we, by any chance, a common destiny with man? Shouldn't we perhaps share in creating the happiness of the family?

Perhaps man has failed in his attempts thus far to make mankind happy, precisely *because* he has not invited us to join his great social organizations.

Source: Eva Perón, *My Mission in Life*, Ethel Cherry, tran. (New York: Vantage Press, 1953), 181–186, 189–180, 192–196.

Raúl Prebisch: The Periphery v. the Center

Raúl Prebisch (1901–86) was an Argentine economist who served as the first director of the United Nation's Economic Commission for Latin America (ECLA, often known by its Spanish acronym CEPAL) from 1948 to 1963. Prebisch's thoughts about the problems that late-developing Latin America faced because of its position on the periphery, subjected to the needs of the developed countries at the center, was a trail-blazing approach that led the way for the development of Latin American dependency theory, which dominated economic debate through the 1980s.

In Latin America, reality is undermining the out-dated schema of the international division of labor, which achieved great importance in the nineteenth century and, as a theoretical concept, continued to exert considerable influence until very recently.

Under the schema, the specific task that fell to Latin America, as part of the periphery of the world economic system, was that of producing food and raw materials for the great industrial centers.

There was no place within it for the industrialization of the new countries. It is nevertheless being forced upon them by events. Two world wars in a single generation and a great economic crisis between them have shown the Latin American countries their opportunities, clearly pointing the way to industrial activity.

The academic discussion, however, is far from ended. In economics, ideologies usually tend either to lag behind events or to outlive them. It is true that the reasoning on the economic advantages of the international division of labor is theoretically sound, but it is usually forgotten that it is based upon an assumption which has been conclusively proved false by facts. According to this assumption, the benefits of technical progress tend to be distributed alike over the whole community, either by the lowering of prices or by the corresponding raising of incomes. The countries producing raw material obtain their share of these benefits through international exchange, and therefore have no need to industrialize. If they were to do so, their lesser efficiency would result in their losing the conventional advantages of such exchange.

The flaw in this assumption is that of generalizing from the particular. If by "the community" only the great industrial countries are meant, it is indeed true that the benefits of technical progress are gradually distributed among all social groups and classes. If, however, the concept of the community is extended to include the periphery of the world economy, a serious error is implicit in the generalization. The enormous benefits that derive from increased productivity have not reached the periphery in a measure comparable to that obtained by the peoples of the great industrial countries. Hence, the outstanding differences between the standards of living of the masses of the former and the latter and the manifest discrepancies between their respective abilities to accumulate capital, since the margin of savings depends primarily on increased productivity.

Thus there exists an obvious disequilibrium, a fact which, whatever its explanation or justification, destroys the basic premise underlying the schema of the international division of labor.

Hence, the fundamental significance of the industrialization of the new countries. Industrialization is not an end in itself, but the principal means at the disposal of those countries of obtaining a share of the benefits of technical progress and of progressively raising the standard of living of the masses. . . .

Admittedly much remains to be done in the Latin-American countries, both in learning the facts and in their proper theoretical interpretation. Though many of the problems of these countries are similar, no common effort has ever been made even to examine and elucidate them. It is not surprising, therefore, that the studies published on the economy of Latin-American countries often reflect the points of view or the experience of the great centers of world economy. Those studies cannot be expected to solve problems of direct concern to Latin America. The case of the Latin American countries must therefore be presented clearly, so that their interests, aspirations and opportunities, bearing in mind, of course, the individual differences and characteristics, may be adequately integrated within the federal framework of international economic cooperation. . . .

The industrialization of Latin America is not incompatible with the efficient development of primary production. On the contrary, the availability of the best capital equipment and the prompt adoption of new techniques are essential if the development of industry is to fulfill the social objective of raising the standard of living. The same is true of the mechanization of agriculture. Primary products must be exported to allow for the importation of the considerable amount of capital goods needed.

The more active Latin America's foreign trade, the greater the possibility of increasing productivity by means of intensive capital formation. The solution does not lie in growth at the expense of foreign trade, but in knowing how to extract, from continually growing foreign trade, the elements that will promote economic development.

Source: Raúl Prebisch, *The Economic Development of Latin America and its Principal Problems*, 27 April 1950. United Nations, New York. Reprinted by permission.

9

The Revolutionary Option

By the late 1950s, much of the promise of development and democracy seemed hollow. In most nations and for major segments of the populations, reforms came too slowly and too ineffectively, if, indeed, they came at all. On five occasions in the twentieth century, Latin Americans despairing of evolutionary change and reform opted for revolution as a quicker and surer path to change. The Mexican Revolution marked the first half of the twentieth century. Four more countries would erupt in revolution during the second half of the century: Bolivia, Cuba, Chile, and Nicaragua.

All four revolutions had some common patterns: They were led mainly by young men and women who were the children of the middle class and sometimes even the elites, but who had opted to reject their class privileges and work for social change. The leaders created a coalition of middle-class, urban working-class, and poor rural groups, joined by disaffected sectors of the elites. They wanted revolution—a sweeping change of economic, political, social and cultural structures—not just reform. And they wanted to create programs that would benefit the poor masses. But the specific circumstances of each country, and the international circumstances at the time of each revolution, led to differences in the paths taken and in the outcomes.

People choose the extreme option of revolution—sudden, forceful, and usually violent overturn of a previously stable society and the substitution of other institutions for those discredited—when legal and peaceful paths to change fail. Revolutions make sweeping and fundamental change, not just in political organization but in social and economic structures and the predominant ideology. These are not just personnel changes, like the numerous coups d'etat (or golpes de estado) that changed the individual in the presidential palace but none of the social structures.

Bolshevik leader Leon Trotsky famously opined that if all one needed to make revolution was poverty and oppression, then there would be revolutions every day all around the world. The causes of revolution do not develop overnight but are the result of long-term problems. Foreign control of the economy or political processes can cause local resentments. The public's perception of economic conditions—rising expectations because of economic growth and development programs, or the social dislocations caused by rapid changes in the economy, as well as the hardship of economic crises—can be a cause of revolution.

Political disputes can also lead to revolution, particularly when new economic leaders want political power. Political openings can create rising expectations for democratization, and a violent reaction when increased freedoms are not granted. A government's inability to meet the needs or desires of various constituencies can weaken its bases of support. When the government becomes the target of protest, threatened officials often respond with brutality, which turns more people against the government.

For revolutions to occur, there must be both leaders and followers. Eloquent leaders focus the discontent of the masses and plan acts, frequently violent ones, to ignite the revolution. But they also need the support of the masses, or their exhortations to action will fall on deaf ears. No leaders can make a revolution on their own. Importantly, the leadership offers guidance and justification for revolution, shattering old myths and creating new ones. They articulate the goals of the revolution, which frequently focus on nationalism and some form of socialism or redistribution of wealth.

Although Bolivia led the new wave of revolutions, it would turn out to be the least influential of the four. The Bolivian revolution fell apart because of internal problems. Furthermore, it was atypical because it was not actively opposed by the United States.

Like Guatemala, Bolivia is a mostly indigenous country, and in the 1950s its population was characterized by illiteracy, undernourishment, sickness, low per capita income, and short life expectancy. Bolivia depended primarily on exports of tin, and the mines were owned by three Bolivian families: Patiño, Hochschild, and Aramayo. Patiño's annual income exceeded the national government's, and the annual allowance of one of his sons was greater than the government's education budget.

In 1941, urban intellectuals under the leadership of Victor Paz Estenssoro organized the National Revolutionary Movement (*Movimiento Nacional*

Revolucionario, or MNR). Its two primary goals were to nationalize the tin mines and to combat international imperialism. In the presidential election of 1951, as was customary, the government controlled the electoral machinery and suffrage was restricted to literate males, about 7 percent of the population. Despite these handicaps, the MNR won a resounding victory. The government and army refused to let Paz Estenssoro take office, leading to a bloody struggle in April 1952, in which the MNR seized power by force. The revolution represented a broad-based alliance of the progressive elements of the middle class, intellectuals and students, organized labor, and the rural landless. The urban and rural workers' militias provided the backbone of armed strength and emerged as a key power group.

President Paz Estenssoro nationalized the tin mines without compensating the owners, a move nearly the entire population supported. More controversial was the unexpected rural agitation that forced the urban movement to undertake agrarian reform. Indians rose up and took land, and Paz responded to the reality: He formalized the Indian reforms in a decree-law of August 2, 1953.

After serving his four-year term, Paz Estenssoro turned over the presidency to MNR stalwart Hernán Siles, who won the 1956 elections. A term out of office permitted Paz Estenssoro to run again for the presidency in 1960, and the voters enthusiastically endorsed his new bid for office. But when Paz tampered with the constitution in 1964 to allow himself another term, the army took the reins of power. Revolutionary activity declined, then disappeared.

The United States had few investments in Bolivia and did not consider the isolated country to be strategically important. Instead of aggressive opposition, Washington lavished funds, technical aid, and support on the MNR governments of Bolivia as a way to support the moderate, middle-class leaders of the revolution, Paz Estenssoro and Siles, against the radical, working-class factions. George Jackson Eder, who the Bolivian government was required to accept in 1956–57 as the director of its stabilization program, reminisced in his book *Inflation and Development in Latin America* (1968) that he helped to break the power of the radical labor unions over the government. His stabilization program "meant the repudiation, at least tacitly, of virtually everything that the Revolutionary Government had done over the previous four years."

For the rest of Latin America, Bolivia was an example of a revolution that had imploded. It was coopted by the middle classes and destroyed by its leadership's greater concern for power than for the goals of the revolution. As a result, its impact was minimal. It did little to inspire other revolutionary movements. In fact, by 1967, Bolivia's situation was so dismal that Cuban revolutionary hero Ernesto "Che" Guevara tried to start a new revolutionary movement there, ending in his death. The Cuban, Chilean, and Nicaraguan revolutions would have a much greater impact on the region, and the role of the United States would become crucial in all three.

As historians, we need to ask three main questions. What did these revolutionaries want to achieve and why? How did they go about it? And why has the United States so vigorously opposed them?

Cuba

Perhaps no other event in Latin American history has had the impact of the Cuban Revolution of 1959. It became the model for revolutionary change throughout Latin America and beyond. It also became a model for United States Cold War policy. The Cuban Revolution particularly rankled Washington leaders, partly because of the historically close relationship between the two countries and partly because it occurred a mere 90 miles from U.S. shores.

At first glance, Cuba seemed an unlikely place for revolution. By Latin American standards, Cubans enjoyed a high literacy rate and high per capita income. It was an urbanized nation with a relatively large middle class. However, aggregate statistics can be misleading. Much of the population lived in the countryside, and the story there was quite different: 43 percent of adults were illiterate, 60 percent lived in homes with dirt floors and palm roofs, 66 percent had no toilets or latrines, and only one in fourteen families had electricity. The largest group in Cuba was the rural wage workers, 600,000 strong. They were mostly sugarcane cutters, and they were fully employed only during the harvest. Agricultural wage workers averaged only 123 days of work a year. Cuba was dependent on one crop, sugar, which brought in 75 to 85 percent of all export earnings. And it was further dependent primarily on one market, the United States.

The United States has loomed overly large in Cuba's history ever since stepping in just as Cubans were about to win their independence from Spain in 1898. Afterward, U.S. military occupation deprived Cubans of the opportunity to reorganize their economy. In the process, the United States consolidated its hold on the Cuban economy: As early as 1890–95, U.S.-owned mills produced 10 percent of Cuba's sugar. In 1953, U.S. owners produced 40 percent of the sugar and owned 50 percent of the railways and 90 percent of the utilities. In 1958, U.S. investment totaled more than $1 billion. The large scale and attendant capital requirements of sugar production kept Cubans from expanding their share of ownership, and the development of secondary industries occurred in the United States rather than Cuba.

The United States was Cuba's most important market, and the amount of sugar Cuba could sell depended on quotas set by the U.S. Congress, with an eye toward the needs of American sugar growers and refiners. This dependence on Congressional action goes well beyond the disadvantageous position in which most agricultural-exporting peripheral countries find

Cuba

themselves in a world market controlled by the industrialized countries. In addition, in exchange for the quota, Cuba gave preference to more than 400 U.S. products, in essence trading away the island's industrialization opportunities.

All that was left to the Cubans was the government, and it became synonymous with theft and corruption, which was clearly demonstrated by the dictator Gerardo Machado. Machado was overthrown in 1933 in an army coup led by Sgt. Fulgencio Batista and replaced by Ramón Grau San Martín, a doctor and professor who proclaimed a socialist revolution. Washington officials immediately became worried and urged Batista to step in again. This time, Batista took power himself, and he dominated Cuba for the next 25 years. From 1934 to 1940, puppets held the presidency while Batista held the real power. He ruled directly 1940–44, then retired to Miami an estimated $20 million richer. He returned in 1948 and served in the Cuban Senate during the presidency of Carlos Prio Socorrás, which reached new lows of political corruption. Batista responded with a coup in 1952, and ruled with dictatorial powers until the 1959 revolution. Many Cubans felt there had been no change from 1924, when Machado took power, until 1959, when Batista was toppled. The system was corrupt, elections were fraudulent, and the island was dominated by the United States.

Batista was toppled in a popular revolution led by Fidel Castro, a brash young representative of middle-class students and intellectuals. Castro, the illegitimate son of a Spanish-born landowner and his maid, was an attorney who represented the poor. He was an Orthodox Party candidate for Congress, but elections were aborted by Batista's coup. Fidel used the creative approach of filing a lawsuit charging Batista with violating the 1940 constitution, but, of course, Batista's courts would not hear the suit. At that point Fidel followed

Cuba's long historical tradition of armed uprising. In 1953, he and a ragtag band of 162 men set out to attack the Moncada Barracks, failing miserably. After Fidel's release from prison, he escaped to Mexico, where he organized an invasion force.

Among the trainees in Mexico was the young Argentine medical doctor Che Guevara. Guevara had traveled the length of Latin America and come to the conclusion that many of the medical problems he had hoped to solve were related to poverty. He arrived in Guatemala in 1954 and was impressed by Arbenz's attempts to change society, only to see the government toppled by the U.S. coup. He gladly joined Fidel's invasion force in 1956. Most of the men were lost at sea or killed in the landing. But twelve survived, and they drew support from the poor farmers of the Sierra Maestra, as well as from urban forces. Eventually, Batista fell, and the triumphant revolutionary forces marched into Havana in January 1959.

Castro visualized a reformed Cuba. He said his struggle was to end the latifundia, limit foreign ownership, establish cooperatives, nationalize public services, enact social legislation, spread education, and industrialize the nation. Those programs appealed to broad segments of the Cuban population and stirred the island's nationalism. They echoed the basis upon which Grau San Martín had founded his middle-class party in 1935: "nationalism, socialism, anti-imperialism."

The changes that Castro advocated rested on a strong historical precedent, dating back to Cuba's struggle against Spain. The hated Platt amendment, repeated U.S. intervention and support for Batista, and dominance of Cuba's economy left a bitter legacy. Cubans resented Washington's hegemony, and succeeding generations of patriots challenged it. Castro also looked to Cuba's 1940 constitution, which banned latifundia, discouraged foreign ownership of the land, and permitted the expropriation of property "for reason of public utility or social interest." The constitution authorized the state to provide full employment, claimed the subsoil for the nation, empowered the government to "direct the course of the national economy for the benefit of the people," and conferred on the state control of the sugar industry. The succeeding middle-class governments turned their backs on the new constitution and governed as though it never existed. But in the writings of Martí, in the rhetoric of the forces that overthrew Machado, and in the Constitution of 1940, Fidel found much of the inspiration for the changes he proposed.

Despite Castro's intense nationalism, he tried to initiate good relations with the United States. In April 1959 he was invited to Washington by the National Press Club. In meetings with Vice President Richard Nixon and Secretary of State Christian Herter, Fidel sought an increase in Cuba's sugar quota, but the officials refused. Fidel assured them that Cuba would remain a member of the Organization of American States, that it would not abrogate the treaty giving the United States rights to its base at Guantánamo, and that the

Cuban leader Fidel Castro reviews Cuban troops with his brother Raúl, the commander of the Cuban armed forces. Looming behind them is a statue of Jose Martí. (National Archives.)

island would continue to welcome U.S. investment and protect U.S. strategic interests. Nonetheless, the officials offered no United States or World Bank aid, although there had been a great deal of financial support for Batista.

His attempts to reform the economy, however, brought him into conflict with Cuban elites and the United States. One of the revolution's first acts was to cut the exorbitant utility rates charged by U.S. companies, providing compensation via state bonds. The next step was the agrarian reform law. Sugar companies owned 70 to 75 percent of the arable land, and 3 percent of the sugar producers controlled more than 50 percent of production. At the same time, while most of the arable land stood uncultivated, 70,000 Cubans had no jobs and the country imported fully 50 percent of the food its people ate. In June of 1959, the Castro government issued the Agrarian Reform Law. The confiscated estates were worked as cooperatives under the management of the National Institute of Agrarian Reform. (As late as the early 1970s, approximately 34 percent of Cuba's tillable soil still remained in private hands, divided into family-sized farms of no more than 165 acres each.) In September 1959, Eisenhower recalled the U.S. ambassador, citing the utility cuts and agricultural expropriation, even though no property had been nationalized without compensation.

In February 1960, Cuba negotiated an agreement with the Soviet Union for $200 million in trade over four years, which was less than Soviet trade had been with the Batista government. The United States, however, chose to interpret the agreement as a sign of the Cuban government's allegiance. In June, tension between the United States and Cuba intensified when Texaco, Royal Dutch Shell, and Standard Oil demanded payment for imports, rather than extending credit. Fidel canceled the exclusive contract held by the three and established the Cuban Petroleum Institute to find other supplies. When no one in the West would sell to him, Fidel turned to the Soviets, who traded crude oil for sugar. The next day, Eisenhower cut Cuba's sugar quota. In retaliation, on October 12, 1960, Cuba expropriated the oil companies. On October 14, the United States announced a trade embargo on all goods except medicine. On January 4, 1961, Washington broke diplomatic relations.

By then the United States had labeled the Cuban revolution a Communist one and saw Cuba as a tool of the Soviet Union. This judgment ignored the rights of sovereign countries to shape their own economy and polity unmolested and showed a profound misunderstanding of the domestic roots of the Cuban revolution. Further, the United States helped create Cuba's relationship with the Soviet Union by spurning Fidel's offers for friendly relations. In the end, however, the break in relations was probably inevitable given the genuine desire of the Cuban masses for egalitarian programs, which forced confrontations with international capital. Cuban social welfare and U.S. investment as constituted were not compatible.

Ironically, Fidel at that point did not consider himself or the revolution to be socialist or communist. He distrusted the Cuban Socialist Party, which had allied itself to Batista in exchange for privileges. The Communists, in turn, had believed that a socialist revolution could not be made until the country had gone through the stages predicted by Karl Marx; therefore, no revolution could happen in Cuba until it became fully capitalist and industrialized. They dismissed Fidel as a bourgeois adventurer.

Fidel turned to the communist party because he needed administrative help. First the Batista property fell into state hands; then expropriated property became the state's. The new state enterprises had to be managed, and much of the bourgeoisie with administrative skills had fled the island. Furthermore, the well-organized masses pushed the revolution, calling for more and more social programs to meet their needs, and the Communists provided organizing know-how. When the United States refused aid, and pressured its allies to isolate Cuba, the Soviets became the only alternative for aid. In part to facilitate relations with the Soviets, the Cubans formed the Partido Comunista de Cuba (PCC, Communist Party of Cuba), though no party congress met till 1975.

Castro did not declare Cuba's revolution to be socialist until the U.S. invasion in 1961. Not content to break ties with the revolution, Washington's Cold War mentality demanded the revolution had to be defeated and rolled back. The United States launched an invasion at the Bay of Pigs, using anti-Castro exiles trained by the Central Intelligence Agency. To prepare for the landing, CIA operatives strafed several airfields, killing seven. At the funeral the next day, Castro declared for the first time that the Cuban revolution was a socialist one—"This is the Socialist and Democratic Revolution of the humble, with the humble, for the humble"—a cry for help to the Soviet Union, which had promised to aid socialist revolution anywhere in the world. While Soviet help would be crucial in the future, however, it was Cubans who defeated the Bay of Pigs forces. Fidel himself was at Playa Gijón, the beach at the Bay of Pigs, to lead the forces. His popularity soared.

Fidel became a heroic symbol of anti-imperialism throughout the Third World. But his domestic popularity also came from the programs that the new government carried out. He regarded education as one key to the new future. Teacher-training institutes sprang up; in a decade the number of teachers tripled; the number of schools quintupled; young, eager volunteers fanned out into the remotest corners of the island to teach reading and writing. Within a few years illiteracy virtually disappeared. By 1971, nearly one-quarter of the country's 8 million inhabitants were in school. Education was free from nursery school through the university. Reading became a national pastime. In 1958, Cuba published 100 different titles and a total of 900,000 books. In 1973, it published 800 titles and a total of 28 million books. Cuba has the highest per capita book production in Latin America, and the highest literacy rate in the hemisphere.

Health care also became a revolutionary priority. Hospitals were built in remote cities and doctors became available in the countryside for the first time. All medical services were free. By 1965, Cuba spent $19.15 per person per year for medical care, a figure that contrasted sharply with the $1.98 Mexico spent or the $.63 Ecuador spent. As a consequence the health of the nation improved dramatically and life expectancy lengthened. Cuban medical care became the envy of the hemisphere, and Latin Americans from throughout the region traveled to the island to seek medical help.

Public housing received attention from the government, and the living conditions of the masses were better than ever before. The real estate market had been one of the prime areas of investment, speculation, and corruption. New laws provided everyone with their own housing, and no family needed to pay more than 10 percent of its income for rent.

The government encouraged the arts, and painting, literature, and music flourished. The National Ballet of Cuba emerged as one of the principal dance companies of the world and frequently toured to critical and popular acclaim. The *nuevo canción* movement, led by such singer/songwriters as Silvio Rodriguez, brought revolutionary themes to 1960s music, combining rock and Latin sounds, leading a musical movement that swept Latin America.

It was probably in film, however, that the Cuban Revolution reached its maximum cultural achievement. The first law of the revolutionary government in the field of culture created the Cuban Film Institute (*Instituto Cubano del Arte e Industria Cinematográficos*) in March 1959. It has produced documentaries, newsreels, and feature-length films in addition to publishing the most serious Latin American journal on film, *Cine Cubano*. Cuban film retrospectives have been organized in New York, San Francisco, and Los Angeles, and Cuban films have become regular features of film festivals, where they consistently win international awards.

Much of the Cuban filmmakers' attention focused on reinterpreting their country's past. In his alternatingly lyric and realistic *Lucia*, Humberto Solas studied the woman's role in three Cuban struggles that have shaped the history of modern Cuba: the war for independence in 1895, the fight to overthrow the Machado regime in 1933, and the literacy campaign of the 1960s. The final segment's focus on continuing *machismo* in Cuban society shows a fascinating element of Cuban cinema—its capacity for criticism of the revolution. Double standards penalizing women were again criticized in *Portrait of Teresa*, the story of a woman trying to balance a job, union activism, cultural work, and a family. Her husband, widely recognized as a good worker and staunch revolutionary, does nothing to help in the home and indulges in extramarital affairs. It was a theme that struck a chord with Cuban women.

Che talked about the selfless virtues of the Cuban "new man" that the revolution was creating. But women found that all too often the new man was much like the old man, despite some of the efforts made by the new government. Fidel targeted women as a group from the beginnings of the revolution, encouraging the formation of the *Federación de Mujeres Cubanas* (FMC, Federation of Cuban Women) just three months after the triumph of the revolution.

Their first goal was to mobilize women to support the revolution through work, participation in the literacy campaign, and in neighborhood projects. The government responded to women's increased activity outside the home by providing day care centers. Their health needs were particularly targeted through perinatal care and the legalization and availability of abortions. Female participation in education soared, and women entered professions in record numbers. To balance work and home, legislation guaranteed women eighteen weeks of paid maternity leave

But in the home, the double standard prevailed. The revolution responded with the 1975 Family Code, which required a revolutionary couple to be equal partners. Article 26 required both parents to participate in child rearing and housework. Of course, there were no revolutionary police knocking on doors to make sure that men did their part, but at least the moral weight of the revolution was behind the idea of equality.

The change in women's roles was just one of the many social changes that discomfited the old oligarchy, most of whom fled within the first two years of the revolution. As changes were instituted, the traditional power of the old oligarchy, military, and Church vanished; the state and new mass organizations, like the FMC, filled the vacuum. Eschewing the sterile forms of the democratic farce that had previously characterized Cuban government, Castro claimed his government to be one of the people. To prove his confidence in popular support, he distributed arms to the peasants and workers to defend their new government. He frequently convoked the people to mass meetings where he spoke extemporaneously for hours, to the delight of the masses who had never felt so close to the source of power. New systems of power were formalized starting in 1976 with the formation of *Poder Popular,* or people's power. Neighborhoods elect representatives to municipal assemblies, which in turn elect provincial assemblies, deputies to the National Assembly, and judges for municipal courts. The National Assembly elects the council of state, and Fidel serves as president of both the council and the Council of Ministers, his cabinet.

By the early 1970s the testimony of the overall success of the Cuban experiment became irrefutable and much of it emanated from surprising sources. Pat M. Holt, chief of staff of the Senate Foreign Relations Committee, made a brief visit to Cuba and then wrote *A Staff Report Prepared for the Use of the Committee on Foreign Relations, United States Senate* in which he concluded that all Cubans enjoyed the necessities of life and indeed as a group had an impressive standard of living. The *Los Angeles Times* carried an article by Frank Mankiewiez on September 22, 1974, that concluded:

> I traveled throughout Cuba for nearly four weeks in July, and during that time did not see one shoeless child or one child with the classic signs of malnutrition. Cuba now has the lowest infant mortality rate of all Latin American nations, illiteracy is practically nonexistent, and by a shrewd

concentration of resources in the countryside—where the great majority of development has taken place—Castro has avoided the terrible problem of almost every developing country, namely the flight of hundreds of thousands to the capital city. As a result, Havana is the only Latin capital I have seen which does not have the typical ring of shantytown misery surrounding it. . . .What it does have is a government free of corruption, with the support of the people who live there, whose economy appears to be stable and indeed is growing without our assistance.

Cuba was able to make these changes in part because the Soviet bloc paid above-market prices for sugar, on the theory that the market price did not reflect adequate compensation for Cuban labor and profit. At first Cuba vilified sugar and strove to diversify the economy and to industrialize, including food processing, and manufacture of fertilizers, sugarcane derivatives, agricultural supplies, pharmaceuticals, textiles, apparel, machinery, steel, and construction materials. By 1961, there was a renewed emphasis on sugar production to pay for the industrialization; nonetheless, sugar dropped from 90 percent of exports in 1975 to 65 percent in 1985. Domestically, the government allowed private peasant markets to function until 1986, when fears of exploitation by middle men led to their closure. Other private businesses were discouraged, however, and in 1968 they were confiscated, sending a second wave of Cuban exiles to Miami.

Cuba's growth rate has generally been better than Latin America as a whole, averaging 6 percent in the 1970s and 5 percent in the 1980s. But the world economic crises eventually were felt on the island as well, leading to shortages. As growth rates fell, the Revolution alienated that part of the labor force in a precarious or marginal position, people who had sacrificed all they were able to for the Revolution and who could accept no more discipline in the name of socialism. They, too, wanted out. Castro opened the doors (the safety valve?) in mid-1980, and over 100,000 Cubans migrated to the United States from the port of Mariel.

The 1990s presented Cuba with new challenges. With the fall of the Soviet Union, Cuba began the "special period," a time of both austerity and market incentives. Private businesses were allowed to open, and Fidel agreed to allow foreign investment, particularly in tourism. "Not only do [foreign companies] have an opportunity to do business with Cuba, but they will find in Cuba the only market in the world where they don't have to compete with United States companies," noted Carlos Lage, vice president of Cuba's Council of State. The government refuses to let the market, however, determine the distribution of housing, health care, education, and basic necessities. After an initial downturn, the economy began to revive, albeit along with some of the problems that come with greater openness; for example, the new tide of tourism has also brought a resurgence of prostitution.

Cuba also faced criticism, even from supporters, over two key issues: handling of the AIDS crisis, and ongoing censorship. While Cuba has provided extensive health care services for people with AIDS, bias against homosexuals has also stigmatized the population. The price of health care was quarantine, albeit in facilities that were the envy of AIDS activists in other parts of the world. U.S. gay rights groups were instrumental in the Cuban government's decision to end the quarantine in 1994. Internal criticism of the system was muted, however, by the continuing censorship. Writers who disagreed with the government found they could not get their work published, and they were denied jobs and travel opportunities. The government, however, continued to see the revolution as embattled, in no small part due to the United States.

Beginning with the Bay of Pigs, U.S. hostility has been unremitting. Successive U.S. governments employed the CIA to finance and influence myriad Cuban exile organizations in support of U.S. policies toward the Castro government. The machinations of the CIA included commando raids on the island, false news reports, assassination attempts, the overthrow of Latin American governments that refused to break relations with Cuba (the government of President J. M. Velasco Ibarra of Ecuador in 1961, for example), and the cynical manipulation of the patriotic sentiments of many sincere Cuban exiles.

While the U.S. government continues to wait for Fidel Castro to die—he has outlasted nine U.S. presidents—Cubans have their own plans for the future. These plans will likely include a mixture of social programs and greater political freedoms. They are unlikely to include a return of confiscated property and a full rollback of the revolution to the old days for which so many exiles long. For Latin Americans, Fidel has become a Latin American elder statesman, welcome at international conferences, and still preaching the gospel of equality and independence.

Cuba's Impact

The Cuban revolution forced the United States to acknowledge that there were, indeed, many deep-rooted causes for revolution in Latin America. Coupled with the fear of communism, the United States reacted in two ways. First was the ill-fated attempt to overthrow the revolution by a rerun of the coup in Guatemala. But the failed intervention showed instead the strength of Fidel's government. If the United States could not overthrow the Cuban revolution, perhaps it could prevent similar revolutions throughout the region. As President Kennedy declared, "Those who make peaceful revolution impossible make violent revolution inevitable."

In 1961, President Kennedy launched the Alliance for Progress, a small-scale Marshall plan for Latin America designed to encourage economic development, which presumably would promote the growth of democracy. The alliance charter, drawn up at the 1961 Inter-American Conference at Punta del Este, Uruguay, called for an annual increase of 2.5 percent in per capita income, the establishment of democratic governments, more equitable income distribution, land reform, and economic and social planning. Latin American countries (with the exception, of course, of Cuba) were to see investment of $80 billion during the next ten years. The United States pledged $20 billion.

The alliance struggled along for ten years. The goals were often contradictory, such as to raise agricultural productivity while redistributing land in the countryside. Large landowners were loathe to reduce their landholdings so that property could be redistributed. In fact, the aim of increased productivity was often achieved through further concentration of landholdings, with greater mechanization, leading to more rural unemployment and unrest. Alliance funds too often ended up paying for infrastructure that benefited large landowners and did nothing for the rural poor.

The Alliance failed because the traditional oligarchy had no intention of freely volunteering to give away or sell its lands, to tax itself more heavily, or to share power with a broader base of the population. A decade after the Alliance's creation, there were more military dictatorships and less evidence of democracy than at any time in recent memory. In a ten-year span, military rule replaced thirteen constitutional governments, with the United States supporting the Latin American military lavishly. In truth, over two-thirds of Alliance for Progress funds went to military dictators or to military-controlled civilian governments, despite the intention that funds would be used to buttress democracy. Economically, the area's condition was certainly more precarious in 1971 than it was in 1961. The rate of economic growth per capita over the decade averaged a pitiful 1.8 percent, lower than it was in the years before the Alliance for Progress and far from the minimal goal of 2.5 percent set by the Alliance. In November of 1968, President Richard Nixon concluded that the alliance had "done nothing to reduce the ominous difference which exists between North and South America."

Disappointment, almost disbelief, in the meager results of the Alliance, after funneling nearly $10 billion into Latin America, was widespread both there and in the United States. Senator Frank Church, chairman of the Senate's Subcommittee on Western Hemisphere Affairs, voiced that dismay when he mused, "We thought we were seeding the resurgence of democratic governments; instead, we have seen a relentless slide toward militarism. We thought we could remodel Latin societies, but the reforms we prescribed have largely eluded us."

The fears of U.S officials were realized as revolutionary movements proliferated throughout Latin America, with the United States cynically blaming revolutionary movements on Soviet and Cuban provocateurs. But Latin Americans did not need foreign agents to foment revolution—they were well aware of their own problems of poverty and oppression. What Cuba provided was an example and an inspiration.

Starting in the 1960s, guerrilla movements developed throughout Latin America. By the 1980s, armed groups had appeared in seventeen of the nine-

Latin American Guerrilla Groups

COUNTRY	GROUP	YEARS
Argentina	Tiger-Men *Uturuncos*	1959–60
	Guerrilla Army of the People	
	Ejército Guerrillero del Pueblo (EGP)	1963–64
	Peronist Armed Forces	1967–74
	Fuerzas Armadas Peronistas (FAP)	
	Revolutionary Armed Forces	1967–73
	Fuerzas Armadas Revolucionarias (FAR)	
	Montonero Peronist Movement	1969–77
	Movimiento Peronista Montonero (Montoneros)	
	Armed Forces of Liberation	1969–74
	Fuerzas Armadas de Liberación (FAL)	
	People's Revolutionary Army	1970–77
	Ejército Revolucionario del Pueblo (ERP)	
Bolivia	Army of National Liberation	1966–70
	Ejército de Liberación National (EBN)	
	EBN/Commando Nestor Paz Zamora	1989–90
	EBN/Nestor Paz Zamora Commando	
Brazil	October 8th Revolutionary Movement	1960s–70s
	Movimiento Revolucionario de Outubre 8 (MR-8)	
	National Liberating Action	1968–71
	Acao Libertadora Nacional (ALN)	
	Popular Revolutionary Vanguard	1968–70s
	Vanguardia Popular Revolucionaria (VPR)	
Chile	Movement of the Revolutionary Left	1965–
	Movimiento de Izquierda Revolucionaria (MIR)	
	Manuel Rodríguez Patriotic Front /	1980–
	Communist Party of Chile	
	Frente Patriótico Manuel Rodriguez /	
	Partido Comunista de Chile (FPMR/PCC)	
Colombia	Movement of Workers, Students and Peasants	1959–61
	Movimiento de Obreros, Estudiantes y Campesinos (MOEC)	
	Army of National Liberation	1964–
	Ejército de Liberación National (EBN)	
	Revolutionary Armed Forces of Colombia	1966–
	Fuerzas Armadas Revolucionarias de Colombia (FARC)	
	Popular Army of Liberation	1967–84
	Ejército Popular de Liberación (ECL)	
	April 19th Movement	1974–90
	Movimiento 19 de Abril (M-19)	
Costa Rica	The Family *La Familia*	1981–83
	Santamaria Patriotic Organization/Army of Democracy and Sovereignty	1985–88
	Organización Patriótica Santamaria/Ejercito de la *Democracía y la Soberanía* (OPS)	

continued

Latin American Guerrilla Groups—*Continued*

COUNTRY	GROUP	YEARS
Cuba	July 26th Movement *Movimiento 26 de Julio* (M-26)	1953–59
Dominican Republic	June 14th Movement *Movimiento 14 de Junio* (M-14)	1963, 1970
Ecuador	Alfaro Lives, Damn It! *¡Alfaro Vive, Carajo!* (AVC)	1981–92
El Salvador	People's Revolutionary Army *Ejército Revolucionario del Pueblo* (ERP)	1970–92
	Popular Forces of Liberation-Farabundo Martí (FPL) *Fuerzas Populares de Liberación-Farabundo Martí*	1970–92
	Armed Forces of National Resistance *Fuerzas Armadas de Resistencia National* (FARN)	1975–92
	Revolutionary Armed Party of the Workers of Central America /Armed Revolutionary Forces of Popular Liberation *Partido Revolucionario de Trabajadores de Centroamerica/* *Fuerzas Armadas Revolucionarias de Liberación Popular* (PRTC / FALP)	1976–92
	Armed Forces of Liberation *Fuerzas Armadas de Liberación National* (FAL)	1977–92
	Farabundo Martí National Liberation Front *Frente Farabundo Martí de Liberación National* (FMLN) (Union of FPL, ERP, FARN, PRTC, FAL)	1980–
Guatemala	Rebel Armed Forces *Fuerzas Armadas Rebeldes* (FAR)	1960–96
	Revolutionary Organization of the People in Arms (ORPA) *Organización Revolucionaria del Pueblo en Armas*	1971–96
	Guerrilla Army of the Poor *Ejército Guerrillero de los Pobres* (EGP)	1972–96
	Guatemalan Labor Party/Revolutionary Armed Forces *Partido Guatemalteco del Trabajo/Fuerzas Armadas* *Revolucionarias* (PGT-FAR)	1968–96
	Guatemalan National Revolutionary Unity *Unidad Revolucionaria Nacional Guatemalteca* (URNG) (Union of EGP, FAR, ORPA, PGT / FAR)	1982–
Honduras	Morazanist Front of Honduran National Liberation (FMLNH) *Frente Morazanista de Liberación National Hondureña*	1967–91
	Revolutionary Party of Central American Workers- Honduras *Partido Revolucionario de Trabajadores Centroamericanos-* *Honduras* (PRTCH)	1977
	Popular Revolutionary Forces Lorenzo Zelaya (FPR-LZ) *Fuerzas Populares Revolucionarias Lorenzo Zelaya*	1981–91
	Popular Movement of Liberation "Chinchoneros" *Movimiento Popular de Liberación "Chinchoneros"* (MPL-Chinchoneros)	1980–90

continued

Latin American Guerrilla Groups—*Continued*

COUNTRY	GROUP	YEARS
Mexico	Revolutionary Party of Workers and Peasants / Party of the Poor *Partido Revolucionario de Obreros y Campesinos/Partido de los Pobres*	1969–74
	Communist League September 23rd *Liga Comunista 23 de Septiembre* (L-23)	1973–76
	Zapatista Army of National Liberation *Ejército Zapatista de Liberación Nacional* (EZLN)	1994–
Nicaragua	Sandinista National Liberation Front *Frente Sandinista de Liberación Nacional* (FSLN)	1961–
	ParaguayUnited Front of National Liberation *Frente Unido de Liberación Nacional*	1960
Peru	Revolutionary Leftist Front *Frente Izquierdista Revolucionario* (FIR)	1961–63
	Army of National Liberation *Ejército de Liberación Nacional* (EBN)	1962–65
	Movement of the Revolutionary Left *Movimiento de Izquierda Revolucionaria* (MIR)	1962–65
	Tupac Amaru Revolutionary Movement *Movimiento Revolucionario Tupac Amaru* (MRTA)	1975–93
	Communist Party of Peru Through the Shining Path of the Thought of José Carlos Mariátegui *Partido Comunista del Peru por el Sendero Luminoso del Pensamiento de José Carlos Mariátegui* (Sendero Luminoso)	1980–
Uruguay	Movement of National Liberation—Tupamaros *Movimiento de Liberación National Tupamaros*	1962–72
Venezuela	Movement of the Revolutionary Left / Armed Forces of National Liberation (MIR-FALN) *Movimiento de Izquierda Revolucionaria/Fuerzas Armadas de Liberación National*	1960s
	Communist Party of Venezuela /Armed Forces of National Liberation *Partido Comunista de Venezuela/Fuerzas Armadas de Liberación Nacional* (PCV-FALN)	1961–68

Source: Liza Gross, *Handbook of Leftist Guerrilla Groups in Latin America and the Caribbean.* (Boulder, Co: Westview Press, 1995).

teen countries in Latin America. Some of the groups were ephemeral, disappearing a year or less after their formation. Others continued struggling for a decade or more, sometimes going underground only to appear again when conditions seemed more propitious. While there had been only three armed uprisings in the region in the 1950s, including the Cuban revolution, there were 25 armed groups founded in the 1960s. They were generally met by the arm of the Alliance for Progress that the Kennedy administration did not publicize—government counterinsurgency forces armed and trained by the United States.

But in 1970, one country offered an alternative—a peaceful revolution.

Chile

Chile has always been a little different from its neighbors. From its earliest independence days, the country enjoyed greater stability than the rest of the region. It also enjoyed a long democratic tradition: From 1833 to 1973, Chile only had two constitutions. They provided for a strong presidency but also a strong voice from Congress. Chile's constitution gave political parties proportional representation, fostering an active political process.

Chile first became a regional power after the War of the Pacific (1879–83), in which it fought Bolivia and Peru over the nitrate-rich region of the Atacama Desert. At the end of the nineteenth century, Chile was positioned as a serious aspirant to world power. It had a stronger navy than the United States and tremendous wealth from the export of nitrates, which were used for fertilizer and for making explosives. During World War I, Germany developed synthetic nitrates, and Chile lost its position in the market. During World War II, Chile accelerated development of its copper industry to take the place of nitrates. But by the twentieth century, Chilean entrepreneurs had exhausted the easily accessible copper deposits and needed foreign capital and technology to access the rest. Two U.S. companies came to dominate the industry: Anaconda and Kennecott.

By 1960, some 30–35 percent of the Chilean population had reached the upper or middle class. This sector was even larger in Santiago and Valparaíso, where almost half of Chile's population lived. Seventy percent of the country's population was urban, and 90 percent of them were literate. Nationwide, literacy was 84 percent. Yet the image of Chile as urbane, educated, and well-to-do hid gross inequality: While the per capita income of the top 5 percent was $2,300, the lower 50 percent only earned $140. Copper earnings paid for limited industrialization, while the countryside was little changed from the nineteenth century. Change was clearly needed.

Chile in the 1960s became a showcase for the Alliance for Progress, which invested heavily in the government of President Eduardo Frei (1964–70). Frei represented a new political trend of the era, the Christian Democrats, who stressed the moral responsibility of government to mitigate societal ills, but stopped short of advocating revolutionary change. The Frei government promised "a revolution in liberty," and it did make some substantial changes. By 1970, the state had acquired ownership of most of Chile's copper mines. An agrarian reform gave land to 30,000 families. Farm laborers were unionized and given a minimum wage. Much of the change was funded by U.S. aid and high prices for copper fueled by the Vietnam War.

Frei's reforms had two political results: Some felt that he did not go far enough, and ended up joining the left; others felt he had gone too far, and joined the right. The center lost its strength, and in 1970 the presidency was won by Salvador Allende, a medical doctor and committed Marxist who had been one of the founders of the Socialist Party in 1931. He was the candidate of six parties that had joined in *Unidad Popular* (Popular Unity). Allende was a dedicated democrat: He had served as president of the Chilean Senate, was in Congress for 30 years, and ran for president four times. He had won a plurality of the vote, but not a majority, which was typical in Chilean elections because of the large number of parties participating.

Allende's election redefined revolution. Chileans in 1970 believed they had shown the world that a socialist revolution could be made without resorting to violence and force of arms. Chile had acted within its 140-year democratic tradition. But the experiment was doomed to failure. Three years later, the presidential palace was in flames, Allende was dead, the military controlled the streets, and Gen. Augusto Pinochet established a brutal dictatorship that would rule Chile until 1989. Allende's defeat came at the hands of a familiar alliance: Chilean right-wing forces and the United States.

Allende's program was a radical one, calling for the abolition "of the power of foreign and national monopoly capital and of large units of agricultural property, in order to initiate the construction of socialism." His economic advisors were influenced by Marxist theory but also by the structuralist theories popular in Latin America after World War II and propounded by Raúl Prebisch and ECLA, which was based in Santiago. The structuralist analysis contended that the economy could not grow because the market was limited by lack of buying power. The answer was to redistribute income, thereby increasing consumer demand. Income was to be redistributed by increasing wages while holding prices down, and by expropriating large businesses, especially those that were foreign owned, so that the government could rechannel profits into social spending. Finally, a more widespread agrarian reform would make agriculture more efficient, producing enough low-cost food to feed the workforce without expensive imports. The government increased wages, gave low-interest housing loans to the poor, and created new social programs, including day care centers, health and welfare programs, and school lunches.

For the first year, Allende's policies were effective, fueled by a foreign-reserve surplus from the high prices of copper. The government also simply printed more money, and borrowed money to pay for imports of food and consumer goods. But in 1971, the economy took a sharp decline. First, copper prices dropped precipitously, then world food prices rose, and Chile had hit the limits of industrial expansion possible without increased investment. Then the United States stepped in.

The United States was wary of Allende from the start. Secretary of State Henry Kissinger commented tartly, "I don't see why we must sit with our arms folded when a country is slipping toward communism because of the irresponsibility of its own people." President Richard Nixon gave orders to "make the economy scream." Some $8 million of CIA funds were used to support the opposition, including support for a truckers' strike that paralyzed the country and infiltration of the newspaper, *El Mercurio*, which kept up a drumbeat of denunciations, blaming the Allende government for limits imposed by the world market and the United States. The United States cut off loans and influenced other western sources to do so as well.

By 1973, middle-class housewives were marching in the streets, banging pots and pans, while radical workers were taking over factories and urging Allende to take even more drastic action. The right wing, elites, and the middle class clamored for a change. The military became restive, and when it was clear that his officers did not support him, Gen. Carlos Prats, chief of the army, resigned. The next in command was Gen. Augusto Pinochet. Under his direction, coordinating with the navy, Valparaíso, Concepción, and Santiago were occupied. On September 11, the presidential palace, La Moneda, was bombed, and Allende was dead, apparently having committed suicide.

Chileans were shocked. Theirs was a peaceful, democratic country. Now, it was a country of brutal military rule. Santiago's two stadiums were filled with prisoners, many of whom were brutally murdered. Between 3,000 and 10,000 people were killed during and after the coup. Left-wing political parties were outlawed, and Pinochet systematically eliminated rivals in the military and removed both the left wing and moderates in unions, universities, and other institutions. Chile descended into a state of siege.

For the rest of Latin America, the lesson was clear. Revolutions were not won at the ballot box. As Augusto César Sandino said, "Liberty is not won with flowers but with gunshots."

Nicaragua

The dominant reality of twentieth-century Nicaraguan history has been the lack of opportunity the Nicaraguan people have had to govern themselves. The United States intervened in 1909 to overthrow President José Santos Zelaya and occupied the country, with some brief interruptions, until early 1933, a period characterized by the disintegration of both the state and the economy. During its final years of occupation, the United States created the Guardia Nacional and appointed as its commander Anastasio Somoza García. The maintenance of order and stability were the primary duties of the Guardia, and it received the training, financing, and equipment to fulfill them. The Somoza dynasty, the father and two sons, ruled from the mid-1930s until 1979. One political scientist termed the Somoza rule as "government by kleptocracy." The family robbed everything it could put its hands on. By 1979, the Somozas owned 20 percent of the arable land (the best lands with good soil and ready access to roads, railroads, and ports); the national airline; the

After the revolution, Nicaragua's two medical schools vastly increased enrollments. More than half the students were female. This second-year class is studying microbiology in the Faculty of Medicine, the National University, Managua, 1984.

national maritime fleet; and a lion's share of the nation's businesses and industries. The Somoza hand never left the national coffers; the family built up accounts in foreign banks that in time ranked it among the world's wealthiest.

The Somozas were loyal only to the Guardia, a small coterie of relatives and members of the old elite who supported the regime, and the United States. Nicaragua's voting record in both the Organization of the American States and the United Nations, for example, conformed 100 percent with that of the United States. The Bay of Pigs invasion was launched from Nicaragua's Atlantic Coast; indeed, Luís Somoza was on hand to send them off and asked that they bring him back a hair from Fidel's beard.

During the long Somoza decades, the Nicaraguan people exercised neither political power nor influence, and the Guardia dealt swiftly and brutally with anyone courageous or foolish enough to try. The voice of the Nicaraguans remained muted from 1909 to 1979.

An opposition group emerged in 1961 to challenge the Somozas. Its youthful leadership drew inspiration from the struggle of Augusto César Sandino against the U.S. Marines. His example and ideas guided them in the creation of the *Frente Sandinista de Liberación Nacional* (FSLN, Sandinista Front for National Liberation). The Sandinistas were also inspired by the success of the Cuban revolution. The Sandinista program advocated entrusting political and economic power to the people; agrarian reform; national unity; emancipation of women; the establishment of social justice; and an independent foreign policy. The struggle of the Sandinistas against the well-armed and trained Guardia Nacional proved to be long and bloody. Determination sustained them; the greed, corruption, and brutality of the Somozas were their effective allies. By the late 1970s, even the small but potent middle class and members of the tiny elite joined the opposition to the third dynastic dictator, Anastasio Somoza Debayle, whose military arsenal could no longer repel popular wrath. The Guardia, and thus the government, collapsed, and the victorious rebels led by the FSLN entered Managua triumphantly on July 19, 1979.

The challenge of reconstruction surpassed even the task of overthrowing the Somozas. The victors inherited an economy in shambles. Somoza had bombed the cities and industries. War damages amounted to approximately $2 billion; 40,000 were dead (1.5 percent of the population); 100,000 wounded, 40,000 children orphaned; 200,000 families without homes. The national treasury was empty; the foreign debt exceeded $1.6 billion. Add to these woes the reality of an underdeveloped country: 52 percent of the population was illiterate; life expectancy was slightly more than 53 years; infant mortality was 123 per 1,000 live births; and malnourishment plagued 75 percent of the children.

During the early months after the victory, a wide variety of political groups supported and participated in the revolution. However, as the realization dawned on some of the representatives of the middle and upper classes that the revolution had been made by the peasants and workers and was to benefit them, they withdrew their cooperation and became critical, some even hostile. Such behavior followed the classic model of revolutions. United to overthrow a common enemy, a heterogeneous group brings about the final victory. Later, the temporary alliance disintegrates as some realize that their own interests will not be served by revolutionary change. As a last resort, the disaffected try to stop the revolution by force, more often than not by allying themselves with some sympathetic foreign power in order to enhance their strength. Events in Nicaragua followed that predictable pattern.

The Roman Catholic Church split in its support of the revolution. The Nicaraguan Church had taken a stand against Somoza and, finally, in favor of armed resistance to him. Thus, the religious hierarchy gave its blessings to the revolution, an extremely unusual position for the Church in Latin America. Many priests participated in the revolution, and a few later held high office, including cabinet posts, in the Sandinista government. Liberation theology played an active role in the overthrow of the Somoza dynasty and contributed to Sandinista ideology. The revolution, according to those theologians, embraced three Christian-related principles: satisfaction of basic needs through a new economic development model; broad popular participation; and the emergence of a new consciousness, a new dimension of human awareness and justice. But as the hierarchy of the Church became uncomfortable with the revolutionary process, perhaps fearful of losing some of its own power and authority (in particular to the so-called "popular Church" based on liberation theology), the archbishop and bishops sought to distance themselves from it. Yet, many priests and religious through the Christian base communities and the popular Church maintained close ties with the revolution. A papal visit to Managua in 1983 widened rather than bridged the growing split in the Church.

The government embarked on an ambitious program to improve the quality of life of the majority. A literacy campaign in 1980 reduced illiteracy from 52 to 12 percent. Following up that campaign, the government doubled the number of schools in four years, quintupled the number of public libraries, and made education free from preschool through graduate studies. In 1988, more than a million Nicaraguans (40 percent of the population) were studying. Attention focused on expanded health care. Nicaragua eliminated measles, diphtheria, and polio, diseases that once took a heavy toll among children. Clinics and hospitals sprang up in the countryside and in small towns. The number of health centers multiplied from twenty-six to ninety-nine. Cuban physicians and nurses volunteered to staff them. Infant mortality fell 50 percent. Despite the shortage of medicine, medical equipment, and physicians, health-care delivery was so impressive that the World Health Organization cited Nicaragua in 1983 as a model nation. A proper diet further explained the improving health of Nicaraguans. Caloric intake rose because more basic foods were now available to larger numbers of people.

One of the three founders of the FSLN, Carlos Fonseca, had vowed, "In Nicaragua, no peasant will be without land, nor land without people to work it." A far-reaching agrarian reform law based on Sandino's hopes, Fonseca's promise, and global experiences with rural restructuring was promulgated in 1981. It provided land for anyone who wanted it and would work it. As the largest nation in Central America, Nicaragua (54,864 square miles) had more than enough land for its relatively small population (3.2 million). The principal goal of the reform was to put the land into use so that Nicaragua could both feed itself and export crops for needed foreign exchange. For six years, the government distributed only land that once belonged to the Somozas or their closest allies, abandoned lands, and unused lands. On January 11, 1986, after successfully distributing nearly 5 million acres of land to 83,000 families, the government made significant changes in the Agrarian Reform Law, permitting the expropriation of any unused land without compensation and, indeed, of any land needed for the goal of assuring anyone who wanted to farm access to land. For the first time the government began to distribute lands already in production in areas where rural workers demanded land. At the same time, the government continued to guarantee the right to private property, and the majority of the land remained in private hands.

In the redistribution of land, the government gave preference to those willing to organize themselves into cooperatives. Cooperative organization facilitated governmental services—clinics, schools, child-care centers, credit, machinery, and technical aid. Further, cooperatives enjoyed a reputation for efficiency. Nonetheless, the government also conferred individual land titles as well. Title holders received the land gratis but could not sell or alienate it, a safeguard to prevent future land concentration. While land titles could be inherited, the land could not be divided among heirs, thus averting the problems of minifundia.

Within this revolution, Nicaraguans looked into themselves to rediscover their own roots and expressed them in music, dance, a resurgence of folk arts, painting, and poetry. Nicaragua is a land of poets, where Rubén Dario, the father of modernist poetry, is a national hero. Popular Poetry Workshops sprang up in barracks, factories, cooperatives, and neighborhoods.

Women played an important role in the Sandinista revolution, starting from the days of armed conflict, when they made up 30 percent of the people bearing arms. The revolution targeted women as a group to mobilize, opened day care centers, and broadened employment opportunities. While no women served on the Sandinista directorate until the 1990s, there were several women in high positions, including Dora Maria Telles, the secretary of health, who had been the second in command in the daring takeover of the National Palace in 1978 and headed the column that took León in 1979. However, many women chafed against the continuing double standard and the tendency to prioritize the armed conflict over all domestic needs. For example, the Sandinistas refused to legalize abortion to avoid further conflict with the Church; but the leading cause of death among women of child-bearing age was self-induced abortions. Despite these conflicts, many women felt that the Sandinista revolution provided more opportunities for them and benefits for society than any previous system.

Nationalism, socialism, and Christianity converged in Nicaragua to offer on a modest scale one model of change for the Third World. The model attracted international attention because it addressed the major concerns of most of the world's population. It challenged dependency, pursued economic development, embraced human dignity, and sought social justice. After all, the access to land, the availability of health care, and the education that the revolution provided the Nicaraguan people are the very benefits that most of the people of the Third World crave.

Thus, in the final half of the twentieth century, Nicaragua enacted the drama of the Third World. One Nicaraguan revolutionary, Bayardo Arce, captured that reality when he asked:

> Isn't the true threat of what is happening in Nicaragua and Central America that the small, poor, underdeveloped countries are offering a new term of reference to all of the Third World? How are the new social changes made that are needed by two-thirds of humanity so as to reach a minimum level of life and survival, while at the same time retrieving the dignity, respect, and self-determination that as independent nations our peoples are demanding now

at the end of the twentieth century? These questions are not rhetorical. They attempt to raise a whole problematic: what we have called a challenge for the peoples of Europe, for the international community and its institutions, and very particularly for the North American people.

In the eyes of the majority of the planet's population comprising the Third World, Nicaragua represented the dynamic of change.

In the eyes of Washington, however, it represented the dynamic of challenge. The revolution, the rhetoric of the Sandinista government, and a nonaligned foreign policy infuriated Washington. The U.S. government expressed deep suspicions of the socialist inclinations of the Sandinistas, fearful that Managua might become a focal point for the "destabilization" of the rest of Central America, too friendly with Havana and Moscow, a security threat to the Panama Canal and to the United States itself.

Washington allied itself with the remnants of the discredited National Guard, the dispossessed elite, and members of the frightened middle class to terminate the revolution and drive the Sandinistas from power. That profound changes alienated many Nicaraguans at all social levels was not an uncommon trend in any revolutionary history. That the challenge angered the metropolis was no less uncommon.

The CIA financed, trained, and armed counterrevolutionaries, known as the *contras*, short for the Spanish term *contrarevolucionario*. They invaded Nicaragua as early as November 1979 from Honduras and later from Costa Rica. The war, intensified after 1984, brought destruction and death to Nicaragua. In 1984, the CIA mined the harbors of Nicaragua in violation of international law, drawing the outrage and condemnation of the international community. In 1985, President Ronald Reagan, an implacable foe of the revolution, imposed a trade embargo on Nicaragua. With an annual budget of less than $2 billion dollars, Managua tried to meet the goals of the revolution while fighting a war against the surrogates of the most powerful nation in the world. The war plunged Nicaragua into multiple crises. It deflected funds and people from development projects, although it has also strengthened the unity, determination, and resolve of the Nicaraguan people.

On July 19, 1989, the Nicaraguans celebrated the tenth anniversary of the triumph of their revolution. They made, taking into consideration their limited resources, the hostility of the United States, and the disastrous contra war, impressive strides toward development. The quality of life for the workers and peasants improved; the new social statistics for Nicaragua stood in marked contrast to the dismally declining ones for Guatemala, El Salvador, Honduras, and even, sadly enough, Costa Rica. Nicaraguans clearly manifested a new pride in themselves and professed great hopes for the future. Undeniably, the opposition from the United States greatly complicated the efforts of the Nicaraguans to carry out the goals of their revolution.

In early 1990, the revolution celebrated its second presidential election;

and, like the first one six years before, it was open, free, and democratic. However, much had occurred during the intervening years. In 1984, Nicaraguans were buoyant, hopeful, and proud of the achievements of the revolution; by 1990, they were anxious about the prolonged war and its destruction. The powerful pressure of Washington weighed ever more heavily on the small and impoverished nation. The FSLN lost the 1990 presidential elections to a heterogeneous political coalition, the National Opposition Union (UNO), financed, advised, and otherwise encouraged by Washington. It took twenty-one parties united in UNO and backed by the United States to defeat the Sandinistas, who still garnered 41 percent of the vote. The new president, Violeta Chamorro, had promised that her close ties to the United States would benefit Nicaragua by bringing in aid and investment. But now that the United States had achieved the goal of unseating the Sandinistas, Nicaragua receded from the U.S. agenda.

The revolutions in Cuba, Chile, and Nicaragua were landmark events in Latin American history. Cuba showed what was possible, but also showed the limits of being a small country torn between superpowers. Chile tried to show that a peaceful path was possible, but as the revolution died in flames, Latin American revolutionaries contended that it could have survived had Allende dismantled the armed forces and armed the workers and farmers. Nicaragua tried to show a new way via political pluralism and a mixed economy, but it met the usual intransigence from Washington, unwilling to let Latin Americans decide their own fate. By 1990, many wondered whether the era of revolutions had indeed come to an end.

Leonel Rugama: A Nicaraguan Revolutionary Poet

Leonel Rugama (1950–70) was a native of Estelí, Nicaragua, who joined the Frente Sandinista de Liberación National (FSLN) in 1967 and was killed in a shootout with the National Guard in 1970. Like many Nicaraguans, Rugama was a poet. He insisted that the role of everyone in a repressive society, but particularly of the student, the intellectual, and the poet, was to make revolution, in word and in deed.

THE EARTH IS A SATELLITE OF THE MOON

Apollo 2 cost more than Apollo 1
Apollo 1 cost plenty.

Apollo 3 cost more than Apollo 2
Apollo 2 cost more than Apollo 1
Apollo 1 cost plenty.

Apollo 4 cost more than Apollo 3
Apollo 3 cost more than Apollo 2
Apollo 2 cost more than Apollo 1
Apollo 1 cost plenty.

Apollo 8 cost a fortune, but no one minded
because the astronauts were Protestant
they read the Bible from the moon
astounding and delighting every Christian
and on their return Pope Paul VI gave them his blessing.

Apollo 9 cost more than all these put together
including Apollo 1 which cost plenty.

The great-grandparents of the people of Acahualinca were less
        hungry than the grandparents.
The great-grandparents died of hunger.
The grandparents of the people of Acahualinca were less
        hungry than the parents.
The grandparents died of hunger.
The parents of the people of Acahualinca were less
        hungry than the children of the people there.
The parents died of hunger.
The people of Acahualinca are less hungry than the children
        of the people there.
The children of the people of Acahualinca, because of hunger,
        are not born
they hunger to be born, only to die of hunger.
Blessed are the poor for they shall inherit the moon.

Source: Leonel Rugama, *The Earth Is a Satellite of the Moon*, Sara Miles, Richard Schaaf, and Nancy Weisberg, tran. (Willimantic, CT: Curbstone Press, 1984), 11, 13. Reprinted with permission of Curbstone Press. Distributed by Consortium.

NICOLÁS GUILLÉN: CUBA'S POET LAUREATE

Nicolás Guillén (1902–89) first made his mark in the world of poetry in 1930. He had been recognized as one of Latin America's most important poets long before the triumph of the revolution in 1959. Guillén embraced the revolution, particularly its commitment to improving the conditions of Afro-Cubans.

I HAVE

When I look at and touch myself,
I, John-only-yesterday-with-Nothing
and John-with-Everything-today,
with everything today,
I glance around, I look and see
and touch myself and wonder
how it could have happened.

I have, let's see:
I have the pleasure of walking my country,
the owner of all there is in it,
examining at very close range what
I could not and did not have before.
I can say cane,
I can say mountain,
I can say city,
I can say army,
army say,
now mine forever and yours, ours,
and the vast splendor of
the sunbeam, the star, the flower.

I have, let's see:
I have the pleasure of going,
me, a peasant, a worker, a simple man,
I have the pleasure of going
(just an example)
to a bank and speaking to the manager,
not in English,
not in "Sir,"
but in *compañero* as we say in Spanish.

I have, let's see:
that being Black
I can be stopped by no one at
the door of a dancing hall or bar.
Or even at the desk of a hotel

have someone yell at me there are no rooms,
a small room and not one that's immense,
a tiny room where I might rest.

I have, let's see:
that there are no rural police
to seize me and lock me in a precinct jail,
or tear me from my land and cast me
in the middle of the highway.

I have that having the land I have the sea,
no country clubs,
no high life,
no tennis and no yachts,
but, from beach to beach and wave on wave,
gigantic blue open democratic:
in short, the sea.

I have, let's see:
that I have learned to read,
to count,
I have that I have learned to write,
and to think
and to laugh.
I have that now I have
a place to work
and earn
what I have to eat.
I have, let's see:
I have what was coming to me.

Source: *Latin American Revolutionary Poetry/Poesía Revolucionaria Latinoamericana: A Bilingual Anthology*, Robert Márquez, ed. (N.Y.: Monthly Review Press, 1974), 165, 167. Copyright © 1974 by Monthly Review Press. Reprinted by permission of Monthly Review Foundation.

Liberation Theology: A Voice for the Poor

In the 1960s, the Roman Catholic Church raised an influential voice in favor of democracy and reform. The Vatican's Council II (1962–65) expressed concern for a more democratic Church and for greater social and economic justice. Pope Paul VI visited Bogotá in 1968, where he identified with Latin America's poor and tried to stir the social conscience of the elite. Thus encouraged, a small but dedicated part of the clergy abandoned the neighborhoods of the wealthy and middle class to enter the slums, where they set up schools and clinics. A new "theology of liberation" eclipsed traditional dogma in those areas. It held that the poor must understand the causes of their poverty as well as the Church's desire to support them in their quest for justice. This commitment was expressed at the Second General Conference of Latin American Bishops meeting in Medellín, Colombia, in 1968 and reiterated at the Third General Conference of Latin American Bishops in Puebla, Mexico, in 1979. The movement came under attack by Pope John Paul II in the 1980s, who equated all movements for social change with the communism he experienced in his native Poland. The Pope hounded liberation theologians, threatening them with excommunication. Only a handful of bishops remained devoted to liberation theology by the end of the century. The following is an excerpt from the Medellín Document on Peace.

PASTORAL CONCLUSIONS

20. In the face of the tensions which conspire against peace, and even present the temptation of violence; in the face of the Christian concept of peace which has been described, we believe that the Latin American Episcopate cannot avoid assuming very concrete responsibilities, because to create a just social order, without which peace is illusory, is an eminently Christian task.

To us, the pastors of the church, belongs the duty to educate the Christian conscience, to inspire, stimulate, and help orient all of the initiatives that contribute to the formation of man. It is also up to us to denounce everything which, opposing justice, destroys peace.

In this spirit we feel it opportune to bring up the following pastoral points;

21. To awaken in individuals and communities, principally through mass media, a living awareness of justice, infusing in them a dynamic sense of responsibility and solidarity.

22. To defend the rights of the poor and oppressed according to the gospel commandment, urging our governments

and upper classes to eliminate anything which might destroy social peace: injustice, inertia, venality, insensibility.

23. To favor integration, energetically denouncing the abuses and unjust consequences of the excessive inequalities between rich and poor, weak and powerful.

24. To be certain that our preaching, liturgy, and catechesis take into account the social and community dimensions of Christianity, forming men committed to world peace.

25. To achieve in our schools, seminaries, and universities a healthy critical sense of the social situation and foster the vocation of service. We also consider very efficacious the diocesan and national campaigns that mobilize the faithful and social organizations, leading them to a similar reflection.

26. To invite various Christian and non-Christian communities to collaborate in this fundamental task of our times.

27. To encourage and favor the efforts of the people to create and develop their own grass-roots organizations for the redress and consolidation of their rights and the search for true justice.

28. To request the perfecting of the administration of justice, whose deficiencies often cause serious ills.

29. To urge a halt and revision in many of our countries of the arms race that at times constitutes a burden excessively disproportionate to the legitimate demands of the common good, to the detriment of desperate social necessities. The struggle against misery is the true war that our nations should face.

30. To invite the bishops, the leaders of different churches, and all men of good will of the developed nations to promote in their respective spheres of influence, especially among the political and financial leaders, a consciousness of greater solidarity facing our underdeveloped nations, obtaining, among other things, just prices for our raw materials.

31. On the occasion of the twentieth anniversary of the solemn declaration of Human Rights, to interest universities in Latin America to undertake investigations to verify the degree of its implementation in our countries.

32. To denounce the unjust action of world powers that works against self-determination of weaker nations who must suffer the bloody consequences of war and invasion, and to ask competent international organizations for effective and decisive procedures.

33. To encourage and praise the initiatives and works of all those who in the diverse areas of action contribute to the creation of a new order which will assure peace in our midst.

Source: Excerpt from the Medellin Document on Peace. (Bogotá: General Secretariat of CELAM, 1970), 71–82.

10

Modern Problems

The central dynamic of Latin American history in the late twentieth century was the tension between equity and efficiency, democracy and dictatorship. Leaders searched for ways to make their economies grow, and sometimes for ways to redistribute some of the wealth. Reformers tried to appease the masses to forestall revolution, but all too often their failures led to reaction and repression. Throughout the 1970s and 1980s, Latin American economies careened from boom to bust, democratic openings alternated with brutal military regimes, and the specter of revolution continued to haunt and inspire.

The 1970s saw the rise of a new economic strategy. Import-substitution industrialization seemed to have reached its limits by the late 1960s: The spurt of growth fueled by foreign investment in protected markets was limited by the small market comprising a limited elite and middle class. The decline in exports that accompanied ISI meant lower export earnings, and therefore less money to invest in further expansion. Latin America turned outward once again, seeking foreign loans to finance expansion. But worldwide recession limited the market for Latin America's exports, and by the 1980s, Latin America could not pay back the debt. The 1980s became the lost decade, when growth declined and Latin America's social indicators slipped back to where they had been a decade earlier.

Politically, the limits on growth and development of the 1960s led to unrest that, coupled with the example of Cuba and the rise of internal dissent, led to right-wing reaction in the 1970s. Military dictatorships took the helms of most Latin American countries, claiming that democracy fostered dissent, which discouraged foreign investment and economic growth. Initially, dazzling growth rates made military models appealing. But when the debt crisis destroyed Latin America's economies in the 1980s, the dictatorships came tumbling down.

Latin Americans continued to wrestle with the questions of the century: What happens to civil life and democracy when military leaders take charge? Does an efficient economy require inequity? Is democracy incompatible with economic development?

New Economic Patterns

As early as 1965, some countries in Latin America were experiencing the limits of the strategy of import-substitution industrialization (ISI) that had dominated the region either by default or as a conscious policy for much of

This astonishing poster from Patzcuaro, Mexico, shows a curious blend of modern commercial influence with established religious practice in the mid-1960s. The poster reads, "September 8. A pilgrimage of the entire town of Patzcuaro to the Basilica. The Most Holy Virgin of Health awaits all the inhabitants of Patzcuaro, her favorite children. At 6:30 in the afternoon everyone should meet in the Guadalupe Sanctuary before proceeding to the Basilica where we will arrive at 7:00. Everything tastes better with Pepsi."

the twentieth century. Import substitution was blamed for chronic inflation because tariffs and overvalued exchange rates artificially raised prices of foreign goods, while local producers had no incentive to produce more efficiently. While many countries produced more consumer goods, they still needed to import the capital goods, the sophisticated machinery needed in manufacturing. Capital-intensive industry, which relied more on machines than people, did little to increase urban employment. But increased mechanization and production of export crops drove more people to the cities. Policies to foster industrialization tended to concentrate income among the upper sectors, who created a limited market for the new consumer goods.

One theory held that Latin America needed more money to invest in improved infrastructure and to expand industrialization for export. The multilateral and official lending organizations, such as the World Bank, did not offer the large amounts needed or carried too many restrictions on the use of the funds. Latin American leaders looked elsewhere and found that their interest in borrowing large sums of money coincided with an increase in international banking and investment.

In the 1970s, the money poured in. The lending was fueled in part by the oil crisis of 1973, when the Organization of Petroleum Exporting Countries (OPEC) raised prices after the Arab-Israeli War in 1973. The enormous sums of money the oil producers earned were deposited in banks that eagerly sought investment opportunities. Latin America seemed to be an ideal place for investment, and the investment of "petrodollars" deposited in "Eurobanks" led to a new dance of the millions, echoing the boom of the 1920s. As long as the money yielded productive investments, then debts could be paid. World trade was growing, and Latin America was prospering.

The problem came with the second oil crisis of 1979, which followed the fall of the Shah of Iran. In the lending countries, interest rates rose sharply, but not just on new debts. The loans that had been made to Latin America had floating, not fixed, interest rates. Suddenly, the Latin American governments found their interest rates soaring from 9 percent to 19 percent. The new increase in oil prices was felt not just in the price of oil itself but in the price of imported goods, which had been produced with higher energy costs. Then came the final blow: Due to the worldwide recession, buyers in other countries stopped or drastically reduced their purchases of Latin American goods. Without sales, there were no earnings to repay the spiraling debt.

Even oil-rich Mexico, which discovered more oil reserves in the 1970s, dipped into the international lending pool. The oil crisis of the decade made Mexico rich, but the wealth was squandered and by 1982, when the international recession hit, Mexico defaulted on the massive loans it had contracted. Mexico's default sent shock waves through the international lending system. Negotiations led to refinancing, rather than forgiveness. Mexico's foreign debt jumped from $14.5 billion in 1975 to $85 billion in early 1984, surpassing $110 billion by 1989.

The price was paid by the masses. In 1983, President Miguel de la Madrid, following the recommendations of officials of the International Monetary Fund (IMF), cut government spending in half, eliminating subsidies for some basic foods. While inflation continued in the 75 to 100 percent range, the president held wage increases between 15 and 25 percent. From 1981 to 1987, consumer prices increased 13.8 times. Unemployment and underemployment rose to approximately 45 percent; the austerity program created no jobs, even though Mexico needed 700,000 new jobs a year to absorb the new entrants into the workforce. In the 1980s, Mexico experienced neither development nor growth. While President de la Madrid's austerity program might have rehabilitated Mexico's international credit rating, it further impoverished average Mexicans. They reacted in the presidential elections of July 1988. The PRI candidate collected barely 50 percent of the votes from the heavy turnout at the polls. The Mexican political commentator Adrian Lajous observed, "The [one-party] system is dead, but it doesn't know it yet."

By the end of the decade, the debt crisis had driven Latin America back to 1970s levels of growth, production, and well-being, making the 1980s the "lost decade." By the 1990s, the region's foreign debt exceeded a staggering $420 billion, several times Latin America's annual income. Payment of interest alone came to absorb more than 40 percent of all export earnings. Mexico was not alone in following the IMF austerity prescription: abolish social subsidies, freeze wages, end public works projects, emphasize exports. The measures frequently led to public protests. In the Dominican Republic in 1984, for example, the reduction or elimination of subsidies on basic food items led people to riot for three days; sixty died before the army restored order. The masses were not the only ones who had doubts about the IMF approach. The economist Thomas Scheetz observed, "The IMF's model makes for neither good theory nor good policy.... Because the disease is inadequately perceived, the cure can, at best, be a stopgap measure, and, at worst, lead to disaster."

The leadership that adopted the disastrous economic strategies of the 1970s and 1980s were mostly military regimes. Their initial success—along with a willingness to use brutality as needed—kept them in power. The failure of the economic policies led to their downfall.

Military Models for Change

The shadow of the military has loomed large over Latin America. First it was the caudillos of the early independence era who ruled by force. Professionalization of the armed forces in the late nineteenth century seemed to successfully subordinate the institution to its proper role as defender of national interests, led by civilian governments. The unrest of the depression era brought a new military figure, a caudillo-like dictator who rose from the professional armed forces. Yet another military model emerged in the 1960s–80s—a bureaucratized military, which believed it could rule better than civilians. It could restore order and bring development. It tended to rule as an institution, rather than under the leadership of a caudillo-like personalistic dictator, with the notable exception of Chile's Augusto Pinochet. It was a military that distrusted civilians, and it was fully willing to use force to enforce its will.

The traditional concern of armed forces is to defend the country against foreign attack. While some Latin American countries resorted to arms to set-

Brazil

tle border disputes, in general the region did not face any foreign attacks in the late twentieth century. But the military believed that it faced an internal threat from the forces of the political left. They were encouraged in this view by the United States, which poured money into the coffers of Latin American armed forces. The Cold War between the Soviet Union and the United States that began in the years after World War II came to be fought not in their own countries but in developing nations that were seen as vulnerable to Communist propaganda. The Cuban Revolution became the proof that there was a clear and present danger.

Brazil was the first country in the region to fall under the rule of the new military model, but the military coup was not a response to a guerrilla threat. In fact, guerrilla groups did not appear in Brazil until after the military took power. Brazil's generals were unhappy with the legitimate, elected civilian government's faltering attempts to foster economic growth.

Brazil's President Juscelino Kubitschek (1955–60) was the very model of the post-war modernizer. Kubitschek tried to achieve "fifty years of progress in five." He made concessions to foreign businesses, while simultaneously promoting import-substituting industrialization. For example, he encouraged foreign car manufacturers to locate in Brazil, but he made sure that Brazil was not just an assembly point for imported parts by requiring that a significant portion of the vehicle parts be made in Brazil, preferably by Brazilian companies. His masterpiece was to be the new capital, Brasilia, built on a grand scale and signifying the opening of the interior and all of Brazil's resources to the future of the country, which had long been centered on a narrow strip of coast. But Kubitschek's economic progress also had problems: Inflation ran rampant. The quality of the goods produced in the new industries was inferior. And corruption in government and business was endemic.

Kubitschek was succeeded in office by his former vice president, Janio Quadros. Quadros had campaigned with the symbol of a broom with which he would sweep away corruption and economic problems. The inexperienced and eccentric leader quit in 1961, a mere ten months after taking office. He was succeeded by his vice president, João Goulart. Goulart had served as minister of labor and had been a protégé of Getúlio Vargas. The elites feared that Goulart was far more radical than the populist Vargas, and the military tried to prevent him from taking office. In the context of the times, the reforms that Goulart proposed seemed to bear out his radical label. He announced a modest land reform program, restrictions on the repatriation of profits by foreign investors, legalization of the Communist Party, and extension of voting rights to illiterates.

To the landed elites, any land reform was anathema. Foreign investors, and Brazilians in partnership with them, would brook no limits on their profits. And the political measures, along with recognition of Castro's government, smacked of communism to both Brazilian elites and the United States. Soon Goulart found the economy further crippled as foreigners stopped investing and Brazilians sent their money out of the country. Inflation soared, coupled with shortages of consumer goods. Goulart responded with fiery rhetoric designed to rally support but that instead roused opposition. The middle class, many of them women, took to the streets in protest. Front-page editorials in middle-class newspapers called for Goulart's ouster. In 1964, the military complied. They seized power and put Gen. Humberto Castelo Branco in the presidency. The coup received the full backing of the United States, which secretly sent a carrier task force to Brazil in case the military needed assistance.

The new regime was different than any the region had seen before. It was not led by one charismatic or all-powerful military caudillo; there was no Perón, no Somoza, not even a Vargas. The new model, labelled bureaucratic authoritarianism by Argentine political scientist Guillermo O'Donnell, marked the emergence of the military as an institution devoted to economic administration. In Brazil, they were determined to build the country's *grandeza*. This nationalistic urge to greatness would require strong measures of control, particularly over labor. A strong economy was essential to Brazil's national security, and that meant that anyone who disagreed with this agenda was not just a political opponent but a threat to the nation's security. Economically, growth was to be achieved by government investment in infrastructure and industry aimed at exports. But instead of the traditional "dessert" exports of coffee, sugar, and bananas, Brazil would export manufactured goods. Industrialization would be the goal, but the days of import-substituting industrialization, protected from the international market and aimed at the domestic market, were over. The emphasis now would be on export promotion.

The Brazilian government sought foreign loans to finance huge developments in infrastructure: highways, dams, hydroelectric plants. They encouraged foreign and domestic investment in the economy, changing its structure. And the economy was indeed transformed. While in 1960, industrial goods constituted a mere 3 percent of the country's exports, the industrial share of exports jumped to 30 percent by 1974. Brazil's factories turned out steel, automobiles, military equipment—including tanks and submarines—and computers. The results, measured in terms of gross national product, were stunning: growth rates of 10 percent a year. *The Economist* dubbed the impressive growth the "Brazilian miracle."

The so-called miracle was achieved by shifting income from lower to upper sectors, concentrating wealth at the top to create investors and a market, and by contracting large foreign loans to make up for the lack of investment by elites, who largely chose to pocket their newfound wealth. The loans were also necessary because Brazil's low rate of taxation limited government funds available for investment.

The generals and their apologists spoke glowingly of an economic "miracle," but the sober might ask what is miraculous about the rich getting richer. As the *Los Angeles Times* pointed out in an editorial on July 21, 1974, "Despite

Brazil's impressive growth rate, the gap between the rich and the poor is wider than ever." Grim statistics support that conclusion. Of the total gain in Brazilian income during the 1964–74 period, the richest 10 percent of the population absorbed 75 percent, while the poorest 50 percent got less than 10 percent. Compounding that inequity was a regressive tax system that put the heaviest burden on the working class.

Five generals then ruled successively until 1985. They highly concentrated all power, while at the same time depoliticizing the people and repressing every form of freedom and liberty. Economically they concentrated on controlling inflation and accelerating the growth rate. Politically, they instituted a brutal dictatorship, notable for its efficiency. However, the phenomenal economic growth of Brazil during the years 1969–74 attracted considerable admiration and much envy throughout the rest of Latin America. For that reason, Brazil seemed to offer a worthy model to many, especially in the southern cone, where dictators came to rule in Uruguay, Chile, and Argentina.

As in Brazil, military leaders in Argentina came to believe that civilian control was irresponsible and left the country in chaos. At first, the military would step in to restore order, then turn the government back to civilians. In 1955, the armed forces ousted Juan Domingo Perón, who fled to exile in Paraguay. The Peronist party was outlawed as the military ruled from 1955 to 1958. The military then allowed elections, won by Radical Civic Union candidate Arturo Frondizi, who concentrated during his 1958–62 term in office on building the steel and oil industries. Following the common pattern, economic restructuring led to economic difficulties, which in turn led to unrest and the intervention of the military. A new election in 1962 brought Radical Arturo Illia to power, but in 1966 he was ousted. This time the military kept power until 1973, when Juan Perón returned from exile to reclaim his mantle as leader of the workers. His vice president was his new wife, Isabel, an inexperienced young woman who had been his secretary while in exile. In July 1974 Perón died, and Isabel found herself trying to solve problems that would have challenged an experienced politician. Economic chaos reigned, armed guerrillas challenged the government, and finally the 1973 oil crisis crippled the economy.

This time the military stepped in with a vengeance. From 1976 to 1983, a series of generals ruled the country. Like the Brazilian generals, they worried about national security. And like the middle classes of Brazil who had urged the 1964 coup against Goulart, the Argentine business sector turned to the military. The business community was concerned about guerrilla kidnapping of foreign businessmen (170 kidnappings in 1973), violence at factories, and inflation rising to 30 percent despite price controls. The result was a meeting in September 1975 between the leading business organization, the Argentine Industrial Union, and Army Chief-of-Staff General Jorge Rafael Videla, in which the two groups agreed on a coup, which took place six months later. "The 1976 coup was either silently accepted or overtly supported, since virtually no political party tried to mobilize society in defense of the democratic system," according to Luis Moreno Ocampo, who later prosecuted the generals. "The coup was not simply a case of the military imposing its will upon a reluctant civil society but the result of a civic-military alliance, which found support in the international community."

The generals disbanded Congress and the Supreme Court and launched a campaign of murder and torture that killed perhaps 30,000 people. However, the generals were concerned about their international image, especially since the brutal regime of Gen. Augusto Pinochet across the Andes in Chile was drawing international outrage. The Argentine generals wanted to keep their targeting of dissidents clandestine. In Argentina, supposed subversives were kidnapped and tortured in some 340 secret detention centers. The bodies of more than 10,000 who were killed were dropped from planes or buried in mass graves. Because civilian government had been destroyed, and all means of communication were censored, the government was simply able to deny that anything had happened. A new noun entered the Argentine vocabulary—*desaparacido* (disappeared).

The obvious limits on dissent enabled the business sector cooperating with the government to carry out economic liberalism, which consisted largely of dropping the tariff barriers established under ISI and forcing local industry to compete with lower-priced imports. Government would do its part by cutting back on the public sector, which had become bloated through years of populism and ISI. The government sold public enterprises, cut wages, and increased taxes. Some domestic manufacturers collapsed in the face of competition, and their laid-off workers swelled the ranks of the unemployed, allowing the surviving firms to pay lower wages. New investments were funded by massive foreign borrowing.

Finally, the generals were brought down in 1983 by their failure in the one legitimate role they could claim—defenders of the nation. In an attempt to divert domestic attention from the crumbling economy and increasing repression, the generals launched a war to reclaim the Malvinas Islands from the British, who had de facto control of the islands since the 1830s. The Falklands, as the British called them, were populated by a tiny number of English-speaking residents and thousands of sheep. The generals assumed that Great Britain would not fight over the distant possession, and successfully rallied the population around the flag. But British Prime Minister Margaret Thatcher had her own problems, and she chose to meet the Argentine challenge as a way of rousing British patriotism and deflecting attention from Britain's economic crisis. The much stronger British forces easily defeated the Argentines, killing thousands of young, ill-trained troops. It was the last straw for the Argentine military government.

Economic failure characterized military governments throughout the hemisphere, and everywhere they brutally suppressed freedom as they reinforced outmoded and unjust institutions. Chile provided a particularly sad example of the military's political repression and economic failure. Pinochet ended Chile's long history of rule by democratic institutions, and thousands were killed in the aftermath of the coup that replaced the democratically elected Allende government in 1973. In addition to that open brutality, however, was the long-term toll taken by Pinochet's economic policies.

The Pinochet government subscribed to monetarist economic policies. Popularized by the conserative economists of the University of Chicago, monetarism advocated minimizing governmental control over the economy, extensive budget cuts, reduction of tariffs, and incentives for foreign investments. The Chilean dictatorship sought to limit governmental participation in the economy; during the 1970s it divested the state of more than 550 businesses. It virtually dismantled social security and pension plans. Between 1977 and 1980, it balanced the budget, reduced inflation, and witnessed substantial economic growth. In 1982, Milton Friedman, Chicago's theoretician of monetarism, wrote, "Chile is an economic miracle." Friedman conveniently confused growth with development. Chilean economic growth certainly did not improve the living standards of the majority.

Chile's indisputable economic growth depended largely on a substantial inflow of foreign credit spent to finance acquisitions rather than for productive investments—that is, to import luxury items rather than to construct industries capable of manufacturing basic needs. It also depended on high prices for copper, which alone accounted for 95 percent of export earnings. But after 1975, the world price of copper plummeted, from $1.70 per pound to $.52 in 1982.

To many the miracle was a myth. A rising foreign debt accompanied by falling export earnings revealed the fragility of Chile's economic growth. In 1982, the gross national product fell 14 percent; in 1983, it dropped another 3 percent. (Chile holds a record for the steepest drop in GNP in Latin America.) By the mid-1980s, the economy lay in ruins. A foreign debt, by 1988 in excess of $20 billion, gave Chile the dubious distinction of having one of the highest per-capita debts in the world. Servicing that debt consumed fully 80 percent of the nation's export earnings. Bankruptcies multiplied. Unemployment soared. The *Los Angeles Times* (February 22, 1983) reported, "Businesses are going bankrupt at a record pace, the banking industry has all but collapsed, and the country is dangerously near default on its foreign debt." The poor and the middle class felt the brunt of the economic deterioration. Chile's Cardinal Raul Silva Enriquez observed, "I could be wrong, but never in my life have I seen such a disastrous economic situation." One Chilean wryly observed, "The free-market policies of the Chicago Boys destroyed more private enterprises in the past year than the most radical sectors of Allende's coalition dreamed of nationalizing in three years; they have turned more middle-class people into proletarians or unemployed than any Marxist textbook ever described." British economist Philip O'Brien labeled the Chilean economy in 1984 as a "spectacular example of private greed masquerading as a model of economic development."

The military dictatorship's economic experiments left 7 million out of 12 million Chileans impoverished. Observers estimated a sevenfold increase in the number of people living in substandard conditions. They concluded that 10 percent of the population benefited from the "miracle" at the expense of the other 90 percent. Although the economic experiments under the Chilean military bore the fancy name of "monetarist," they were in reality a return to older types of policies that had amply proven their inability to encourage development.

War in Central America

While the countries of the Southern Cone experimented with open economies and hidden "dirty wars," in Central America the conflicts were more open and more basic. The countries of Central America had remained poor, with limited industrialization and continued dependence on agricultural exports. Small groups of elites and military dictators ruled throughout the region, with the notable exception of Costa Rica.

In fundamental ways, Central America serves as both an exaggerated and instructive example of the crises of underdevelopment besetting late twentieth-century Latin America. The region can be described by the classic dependent growth model, an emphasis on exports rather than internal production, on profits rather than on wages. The economies grew but could not develop. Growth depended on highly cyclical external demand for their primary products: coffee, bananas, cotton, sugar, and beef. Any benefits from periodic growth accrued to a small portion of the population; the majority remained marginalized and voiceless in a society that was run neither by nor for them. Conservative estimates place 60 percent of the population in the impoverished category. No amount of economic growth could help—or had helped—that majority achieve a satisfactory standard of living. In late 1986, in a homily during Mass at the cathedral in San Salvador, Archbishop Arturo Rivera y Damas stated, "The real cause of underdevelopment is the ideological, economic, and political dependence of our countries."

Most of Central America afforded its citizens few democratic rights. Occasionally the elite and, much later, the middle class, exercised the formalities of democracy for their own enhancement, but the military always kept a sharp eye on such rare experiences and readily intervened if the ballot box suggested even a hint of social, economic, or political change in the offing. The electoral farces in Guatemala, El Salvador, Honduras, and Nicaragua in the 1960s and 1970s confirmed the traditional forces in power or served as excuses for further military intervention. To those who wanted to challenge underdevelopment, poverty, dependency, authoritarian rule, and a long catalog of social iniquities, the ballot box offered no opportunity, a realization that gave form to the guerrilla movements in Guatemala and the formation of the Sandinistas in Nicaragua in the 1960s.

Central America

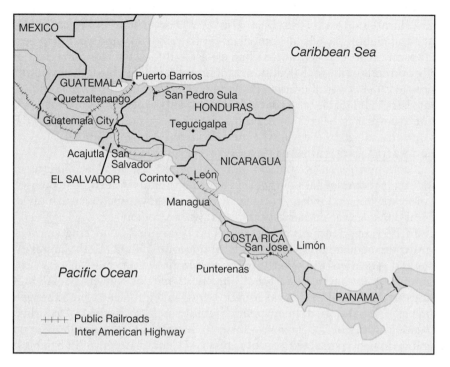

The economic collapse of the region in the mid-1970s detonated a social explosion. Since the end of the nineteenth century, the local economies remained intimately linked with those of the North Atlantic marketplaces. Economic recessions in the metropolises destroyed the fragile export-oriented economies of Central America. The most severe examples occurred in the 1930s and again after 1975. Prices for primary exports declined, while the need for ever more expensive imports rose. The governments borrowed abroad to bridge the gap. The economic disaster further threatened an already unstable industrialization.

The creation of a Central American Common Market in 1960 had opened a regional market able to sustain some import-substitution industries that no single Central American nation could support. But the Market had problems and weaknesses from the start. Industrialization proved to be capital intensive, therefore creating few jobs. Heavy expenditures for machinery and technology drained hard currencies. Many of the plants assembled rather than manufactured—importing component parts, putting them together, and then exporting the finished product. Such assembly plants did little for the local economy except employ a few workers at modest salaries. Foreign capital predominated. About 62 percent of all industries were in the hands of non-nationals. Unequal industrial growth characterized the Market, igniting local rivalries and jealousies. Guatemala and El Salvador boasted of the lion's share of the industrialization, to the annoyance and economic disadvantage of Honduras, Nicaragua, and Costa Rica. The 1969 "Soccer War" between El Salvador and Honduras, whose immediate cause was rivalry and riot on the soccer field but whose more fundamental causes included the Honduran fear of rising numbers of illegal Salvadoran immigrants and El Salvador's economic supremacy, destroyed the Common Market. Defeated in the "One-Hundred Hours War," Honduras refused to allow shipments of goods to or from El Salvador to cross its territory. The Common Market had not recovered from the disruptions caused by the war when the world recession of the mid-1970s sent the prices for Central America's exports into a tailspin.

Economic reverses sparked political unrest. A nervous alliance of landowners, commercial bourgeoisie, and the military forcefully repressed the protest when and where it occurred. To do so, they turned increasingly to the United States for military support to thwart rebellion.

In 1979, the Sandinista revolution had triumphed in Nicaragua, guerrilla warfare accelerated in Guatemala, and a coup d'etat brought liberal officers and reformers to power in El Salvador. In the official eyes of Washington, Central America had burst into the flames of subversion. Always suspicious of change in Central America, the United States viewed the new trends as a threat to both hemispheric stability and U.S. security. Disturbed by Iran's holding of U.S. hostages in 1980, the U.S. government showed no tolerance for any perceived security threat in Central America. El Salvador felt the full brunt of U.S. suspicions.

That small Central American nation represented one of the few examples in Latin America of true overpopulation. More than 6.5 million people inhabited 8,260 square miles. Thus, El Salvador had twice the population of Nicaragua packed into less than one-sixth the area. A few families traditionally owned most of the best land (roughly 2 percent of the population owned 60 percent of the 4 million acres of arable land). That minority dominated the nation's coffee and cotton economy and maintained an intimate alliance with the army. In 1932, after one of Latin America's most dramatic peasant uprisings under the intellectual inspiration of Farabundo Martí, the military dominated the Salvadoran government. Like their counterparts elsewhere, the military ruled in the name of the elites. When years of frustration came to a head over the military's rigging of the 1977 presidential elections, the nation disintegrated into civil war. A military coup staged by junior officers on October 15, 1979, turned the government over to a civilian-military junta.

In early 1980, the junta, even though it had become more conservative in its composition, made some serious efforts to institute reforms. It nationalized the banking system and the sale of coffee. Most significantly, on March 8, 1980, the junta promulgated Decree 153, a land reform. In the first phase of the reform, the government nationalized estates exceeding 1,250 acres and turned them into cooperatives run by the workers themselves. The government promised payment in bonds to former owners. Those estates grew mainly cotton and sugarcane, although some produced coffee and raised cattle. A second phase was to have nationalized estates exceeding 375 acres, later raised to 612 acres. A third phase was intended to benefit the peasants directly. The "Land to the Tiller" phase was to have transformed renters of small plots into owners. Over 80 percent of such plots measured fewer than five acres each. The land reform sounded good on paper, and efforts were made to implement it, but unfortunately they did not succeed. Jorge Villacorta, a former undersecretary of the Ministry of Agriculture, observed, "In reality, from the first moment that the implementation of the agrarian reform began, what we saw was a sharp increase in official violence against the very peasants who were the supposed 'beneficiaries' of the process." No one has better described that brutal violence than the Salvadoran novelist Manlío Argueta in his riveting novel *One Day of Life*.

Later in 1980, after the junta of reformers had been pushed aside by more traditional figures, the advocates of change formed a political alliance, the FDR (*Frente Democratico Revolucionario*, the Revolutionary Democratic Front), and a united military front, the FMLN (*Frente Farabundo Martí para la Liberación Nacional*, the Farabundo Martí Front for National Liberation). Together, they created a viable infrastructure for revolution. The FDR issued a broad program of its objectives. It called for (1) national independence, priority to Salvadoran needs, and subservience to no foreign country; (2) profound political, economic, and social reforms to guarantee human dignity, welfare, liberty, and progress; (3) nonalignment in international affairs; (4) democratic government; (5) a new national army; (6) support for private enterprise; and (7) religious freedom. Obviously the implementation of this program would revolutionize El Salvador. In the process it would eliminate the army and reduce the influence of the agrarian-industrial elite. The lines were clearly drawn between the beneficiaries of the traditional society and the advocates of change. A smoldering struggle between the army and the guerrillas erupted into a full-scale civil war as the rebel ranks expanded.

Until 1979, the military and the elite had been capable of dealing effectively with any challenge to their authority. The events of 1979–80 demonstrated they could no longer frighten their opponents, regardless of how violent their death squads became. For the first time, they had to reach out to the United States for direct support. Their tactic was a simple one that had already proven effective in many parts of the hemisphere. The Latin American elites identified any longing for change, no matter how modest, with communism. They fully appreciated the Pavlovian response of U.S. officials to any charge that communism was afoot in the Western Hemisphere. Once the alert to a "communist threat" in El Salvador had been sounded, military aid from Washington cascaded over the nation.

U.S. intervention exacerbated the civil war that intensified during the decade. By 1989, the FMLN forces, estimated to number 10,000, fought in all parts of the nation. They collected their own taxes along the national highways and their attacks and sabotage nearly destroyed the national economy. Successful in penetrating the largest cities, they were attacking military and other targets in San Salvador by early 1989. Pentagon officials concluded that the demoralized army could not fight without U.S. support. With more than 60,000 people killed in eight years—many of them civilian victims of right-wing death squads—El Salvador suffered one of the bloodiest civil wars in Latin American history. The tragic history of modern El Salvador illustrates the lengths to which those who hold power will go to keep it and to prevent change.

While the revolutionaries proved themselves capable of dispatching the Salvadoran army, they could not defeat the United States. In response to lengthening, bloody stalemate, the FMLN signed peace accords with the U.S.-sponsored government on January 16, 1992. On paper; the accords announced a compromise. The government would reduce the size of the armed forces and open the political process to the FMLN. The revolutionaries, for their part, would disband their forces and operate within the preestablished constitutional framework. Thus, both foregoing force and access to force, those revolutionaries agreed to pursue their program of change under a constitution devised by the oligarchy, including the military, and within the capitalist neo-democratic, elitist institutions that spawned underdevelopment, dependency, privileges for the few, and misery for the many.

Reactions to the civil war in El Salvador and the revolution in Nicaragua shaped the contemporary histories of Guatemala, Costa Rica, and Honduras. All three experienced the economic problems of underdevelopment: high and rising trade deficits, crippling debts, stagnant or declining prices for exports, increasing land concentration accompanied by peasant protests, and mounting unemployment.

Costa Rica, for its part, wanted to be isolated from the turmoil. The presence of Nicaraguan exiles, particularly the counterrevolutionary forces that operated until 1986 from the uninhabited Costa Rican side of the border with Nicaragua, involved Costa Ricans in Nicaragua's revolution more than they wanted. The United States exerted considerable pressure on Costa Rica both to support the counterrevolutionaries and to oppose the Sandinistas. Confronting a faltering economy, which could not be addressed let alone solved in a war-ravaged Central America, President Oscar Arias seized the diplomatic initiative after his inauguration in 1986, calling for a broad, peaceful settlement by Central Americans of their region's political problems. He won the Nobel Peace prize in 1987 for his imagination and energy. Carrying out his broad proposals for peace challenged him and the Central Americans, partially because the United States gave only lip service to the plans.

Guatemala suffered its own brutal war in the years following the CIA overthrow of Jacobo Arbenz in 1954. Some 200,000 Guatemalans were killed in the struggles following the fall of Arbenz, most of them by death squads, while another 250,000, mainly Indians, fled across the border into Mexico to escape the holocaust. The wars began with a 1960 revolt by Guatemalan military officers, angered that the government allowed the CIA to use national territory to train Cuban exiles for the unsuccessful invasion of Cuba at the Bay of Pigs. The civilian-led government of Julio César Mendez Montenegro (1966–74) responded with brutal counterinsurgency techniques, while a paramilitary death squad called the Mano Blanco targeted anyone who dissented against the government, including labor organizers, students, and professors. Several guerrilla armies fought throughout the 1970s and united in 1982 as the Unidad Revolucionaria Nacional Guatemalteca (URNG, Guatemalan National Revolutionary Unity). In response, the military pursued a scorched earth policy, burning the villages of suspected guerrilla sympathizers, torturing and killing thousands. In 1986, the Central American peace talks aimed at ending the contra war in Nicaragua created an opportunity for change. Guatemalans elected a civilian president, Vinicio Cerezo, but neither he nor his successor could control the armed forces. Finally, Guatemalan peace talks began in 1990, and accords were signed in 1996. The limits to peace, however, were clearly shown two years later, when Auxiliary Bishop Juan Gerardi Conedera was beaten to death two days after presenting a scathing report on human rights violations that blamed the Guatemalan army and civilian paramilitary groups for nearly 80 percent of rights abuses in the civil war.

More than Guatemala and Costa Rica, Honduras became completely involved in the crises. It has the uncomfortable geographic distinction of being bordered by three nations in the throes of change or challenge: simmering guerrilla warfare in Guatemala, a civil war in El Salvador; and a revolutionary government in Nicaragua. At the same time, monumental economic problems challenged Honduras, the poorest of the Central American states and the second most impoverished nation of Latin America, after Haiti. Its population of 5.1 million grew at an annual rate of 3.5 percent, one of the highest in the world. All of its economic statistics indicated widespread social injustice. Approximately 53 percent of the population was illiterate; infant mortality was 118 per 1,000 live births. Nearly 90 percent of the rural population and 66 percent of the urban population lived below the poverty level. The economy rode a roller coaster of rising fiscal deficits and foreign debts and falling export income and foreign reserves.

Honduras exemplified the classic enclave economy. In the first half of the twentieth century, three companies—United Fruit, Standard Fruit, and Rosario Mining—dominated the economy. The first two grew and exported bananas, and the third extracted gold and silver. Foreigners owned those companies; they shipped their products abroad from specific locales, leaving only an insignificant residue of the wealth in Honduras, making them classic enclave economies. Those companies owned and operated the railroads as well as several of the principal ports. The banana companies controlled the oil, beer, and tobacco industries. In 1950, the three companies earned sums equal to the entire Honduran budget. Occasionally Hondurans made efforts to regulate the companies. A major strike against the banana companies in 1954 strengthened the unions and increased salaries and benefits for the workers. The victory instilled a better sense of nationalism among the Hondurans and made the unions a new social and economic force. President Ramón Villeda Morales (1958–64) tried to further curb the fruit companies as well as to institute a modest land reform and social security program.

The victorious strike and the reforms of Villeda Morales unnerved the landowners and military. The generals overthrew him during his final days in office and, with a brief exception in 1971–72, ruled Honduras directly until 1982. Corruption and ever greater conservatism characterized the military governments. When the military turned the government over to an elected civilian in early 1982, the economy was in a shambles from which it has failed to recover.

At that moment, the administration of President Ronald Reagan discovered the strategic location of Honduras and resolved to use it in order to destabilize Nicaragua and contain the Salvadoran rebels. Consequently, U.S. military aid to Honduras jumped impressively. The United States held joint military exercises with Honduras throughout the 1980s. Honduras provided ample opportunity for the United States to construct air bases and strips, a seaport, radar sites, military encampments, and tank traps. After 1983, Honduras was for all intents and purposes an occupied country.

Much was being done to militarize Honduras under the rationale that the military would guarantee democracy. Yet, no example exists in Honduran history (or in Central American history for that matter) in which the military contributed to the strengthening of democracy. To the contrary, examples abound of the military's consistent hostility to democracy. While the Honduran government poured money into joint military maneuvers with the United States, it halted desperately needed public-works projects for lack of funds. While the economy disintegrated, Honduras boasted of the most modern air force in Central America.

In a close working alliance with the United States during the 1980s, Honduras actively supported the government of El Salvador against the FDR/FMLN. It permitted the Nicaraguan counterrevolutionaries to train on its territory and to launch repeated attacks into Nicaragua. It willfully meddled in the affairs of its neighbors; some say it fulfilled an historic role, since Honduras contributed to the CIA invasions of Guatemala (1954) and Cuba (1961) and to the U.S. intervention in the Dominican Republic (1965). In every way possible, the Honduran governments sabotaged peace efforts in Central America, including those of President Arias. As the surrogate of Washington, Honduras intensified the Central American crises and probably in the long run its own internal conflicts as well. Accelerated militarism in an impoverished nation undermined democracy and delayed development. The international dimension of that militarism made Honduras the center of the Central American crises of the 1980s.

Do Elections Make Democracies?

One by one, from the mid-1980s to 1990, the countries of Latin America returned to electing civilians to run their governments. Officials in Washington applauded the new but fragile "democracy" in the region. But the mere existence of electoral politics is not all that is required for a country to be democratic. A true democracy requires a change in the power balance among the various groups in society, with institutions that are responsive to the majority. For Latin America, true democracy has been elusive.

In Brazil, the transition to civilian government was ushered in during the government of Ernesto Geisel (1974–79), when opposition to the military in power mounted. The Roman Catholic Church raised its voice against social injustice and demanded economic opportunities for the masses and freedom for all. Labor showed a renewed independence. In May of 1978, a strike in São Paulo involving some 50,000 workers was the first in a decade. The students, too, became vocal again. In 1977 they organized a number of important demonstrations. More surprising, the business community began to voice criticism. In November of that year, some 2,000 businesspeople gathered in Rio de Janeiro and called for democratic liberties, and in July of 1978 a document signed by eight wealthy industrialists advocated a more just socioeconomic system. Finally, within the ranks of the military, reform sentiment was growing, and it became increasingly difficult for the governing generals to disguise the cracks in the facade of unity they wanted to project.

Unlike his military predecessors, Geisel did not consult his colleagues in selecting a consensus candidate to replace himself in the presidency. Arbitrarily he picked General João Baptista Figueiredo, a relatively unknown figure who formerly had directed the National Intelligence Service. Assuming a six-year presidency on March 15, 1979, Figueiredo expressed his hope to preside over the political transition from dictatorship to democracy. In 1985, the government enfranchised illiterates (perhaps as much as 40 percent of the adult population), and an electoral college selected a civilian president, Tancredo Neves, who died shortly after his election and was succeeded by José Sarney. In 1989, the first direct presidential election was held since the election of Goulart. But the transition to electoral politics was not an easy one: the winner, Fernando Collor de Mello, was impeached after a scandal in 1992.

In Argentina, the generals allowed elections in 1983, and the winner was Radical Party candidate Raúl Alfonsín. In an historic decision, Alfonsín vowed to prosecute the generals who carried out the Dirty War. In 1985, after detailed testimony about disappearances and torture, five men were convicted: Gen. Jorge Rafael Videla and Admiral Emilio Eduardo Massera were sentenced to life imprisonment. Gen. Roberto Viola was sentenced to seventeen years in prison, while Brigadier Ramón Agosti was sentenced to only four and half years. Brigadier Omar Graffigna, air force commander of the second junta, was acquitted, along with three members of the third junta, Gen. Leopoldo Galtieri, Admiral Jorge Anaya, and Brigadier Basilio Lami Dozo. But Argentina remained a deeply divided country. During the first term of Peronist Carlos Saúl Meném (elected in 1989 and 1995), he responded to a military uprising by pardoning Videla, Viola, Massera, and top commanders of the Buenos Aires police force who had been convicted.

In Chile in 1988, Pinochet agreed to a plebiscite to determine whether he should leave office. He agreed to step down, although he retained his military rank and a position as a senator for life. In 1989, Christian Democrat Patricio Aylwin was elected, and he was succeeded in 1994 by Eduardo Frei, son of the former president. In 1999, Spanish magistrate Baltasar Garzón tried to have Pinochet arrested while in England and extradited to Spain to face charges for atrocities committed by his regime. Although Garzón failed and Pinochet returned to Chile, the Chilean Supreme Court stripped Pinochet of his immunity, and Pinochet was indicted on charges in Chile. Demonstrations both for and against Pinochet showed that there, too, society remained deeply divided, despite the fact that in 2000 Chileans elected as president Ricardo Lagos, a socialist who had served in the Allende government.

The civilian regimes have simultaneously increased and narrowed the spaces for political participation and the development of an involved, politicized civilian society. Clearly, there is more freedom of speech and freedom to organize groups to work for social change. But there is little support from the new governments for the kinds of social movements that appeared in the 1970s and '80s, the "new social movements" that were hailed as having the potential to transform civil society in Latin America.

These movements developed under oppressive rule, when official opposition parties and labor unions—the traditional organizers—were harassed, repressed, and sometimes outlawed. They tended to organize around specific issues: the need for water in a community; the establishment of neighborhood kitchens to feed the hungry during the worst years of the recession; the struggle to protect environments endangered by reckless economic policy. Most importantly, they organized around the issue of human rights. Frequently, they were led by women, who were seen as nonthreatening by the military dictatorships and were not immediately repressed as men would have been.

The most famous of the groups to emerge among the new social movements was Argentina's *Madres de la Plaza de Mayo* (Mothers of May Plaza), who marched in front of the Casa Rosada on the Plaza de Mayo once a week for many years to demand the return of their disappeared loved ones. At first dismissed as crazy, the mothers skillfully built foreign contacts and became internationally famous. The mothers were mostly traditional housewives, who had never considered entering politics. It was that very maternal role that led them into the streets to search for missing loved ones, to keep their families intact. But the mothers have not weathered the transition to electoral government well. First the group split on the issue of whether to support Alfonsín: Some were satisfied with the return of electoral politics and the trials for the Dirty War. Others still demanded a full accounting of what had happened, that their children be brought back alive or their deaths fully explained. Some childless women resented the group's emphasis on motherhood, although the Madres represent a radicalized and socialized maternity, a maternity that defines the entire population of the nation as the children who all must be fed, housed, educated, and protected. In this way, they struggle to make maternal values society's dominant paradigm, in place of the traditional patriarchal values that have exalted economic competition and authoritarianism.

But the new governments saw such groups as the Madres as necessary only during the struggle against dictatorship. The civilian leaders presented themselves as the logical successors of the aspirations of the new social movements. Demands for economic and social democratization fell on deaf ears, especially since the new governments represent the same economic interests as the old. This was seen most clearly in Chile during the Aylwin government. Six months before the election, Aylwin and Alejandro Foxley met with Eduardo Matte, president of Cape Horn Methanol, one of the largest transnational corporations in Chile. Matte later told an interviewer, "[T]hey gave us all sorts of guarantees that economic policy would continue to be the same as what we had known before: an open market, favorable investment terms, in sum, all the good things that we inherited from the military government. And a year later, there is no doubt in my mind that the warranty that this country has, in fact, is precisely Alejandro Foxley as Minister of Finance." Another businessman observed that Foxley, a Christian Democrat, and economics minister Carlos Ominami, a member of the Socialist Party, "could perfectly well have been members of Pinochet's cabinet."

While the new governments represent an interest in electoral politics, they also share the same economic interests as their predecessors. They, too, are elites. Their interest in pushing social change from the top is minimal, and the pressures for change from the bottom come from a weakened, disorganized mass whose political parties and representative groups were destroyed during the dictatorships. The social movements that arose in their place, since they tended to be specific to issues of the dictatorship, frequently are not in a position to take up the struggle.

Meanwhile, the institutions of governance—and even many of the individuals within them—remain unchanged. Military officers, supreme court justices, bureaucratic appointees, are freqently holdovers from the dictatorships. In most of the transitions to elected government, guarantees were given to the outgoing governments about just such continuity. The strength of such institutions was made clear with the military uprising in Argentina that prompted Meném's pardons. Clearly, the military still has a key role to play.

Furthermore, history has shown that human rights violations are not restricted to military regimes. Thousands of Latin Americans have been killed by death squads during the rule of civilian regimes in the Dominican Republic, Guatemala, El Salvador, Peru, Brazil, and Mexico.

Much of the open violence to which people were subjected during the dictatorships has disappeared. But the violence of everyday life that comes from unequal economic structures, that causes malnutrition and high infant mortality, has not changed. In Brazil under the Sarney and Collor governments, agrarian reform proposals were blocked; a program to provide low-income housing was first re-targeted to the middle class and then dropped; and emergency distribution of food to the poor became an opportunity for corruption and political patronage.

Even with regular elections, there is always the possibility of fraud. Nicaragua had its first free elections in the twentieth century under the Sandinistas in 1984, which foreign observers found to be remarkably clean and fair. The Sandinistas won that election with 67 percent of the vote. In 1990, the Bush administration poured money into the electoral campaign of Violeta Chamorro, at per capita amounts exceeding what the president spent on his own reelection campaign. Bush also told Nicaraguans that if the Sandinistas won, the United States would assume that there had been voter fraud and would continue to fund the contra war. Unsurprisingly, voters turned the Sandinistas out of office, although incumbent president Daniel Ortega still received 41 percent of the vote.

In 1996, however, there was an outcry over the election of Arnoldo Alemán. A Costa Rican observer said that if such irregularities had occurred in his country, the election would have been voided and new elections scheduled. Reports of fraud were widespread, as Nicaraguans told of problems at the polls as well as finding boxes of ballots floating in rivers. Still, the Sandinistas polled 40 percent of the vote. Since then, Ortega has negotiated agreements with Alemán's Liberal Party, and many Sandinistas lament that Ortega's continued leadership amounts to a new caudillismo.

In El Salvador, the former guerrillas seem to be faring better as an electoral force. The FMLN participated in four elections from 1992, when peace accords were signed, to 2001. Although the party's candidates for president did not do well, the FMLN succeeded in many congressional races, culminating in 2000 with winning more seats than the ruling Nationalist Republican Alliance (ARENA). The FMLN was still outvoted in Congress, since the conservative Partido de Conciliación Nacional (PCN, National Conciliation Party) voted with ARENA to constitute a majority. But the FMLN also won 77 of 262 mayoral races, an increase of 60 percent over the 1997 elections, while the number of ARENA victories in mayoral races dropped by 34 percent. Most importantly, the FMLN's candidate for mayor of San Salvador, Hector Silva, has won two consecutive terms in office.

The FMLN gains much of its support by allying with the social movements that formed during the 1980s. Such an alliance can also been seen in

Brazil in the links between the Partido dos Trabalhadores (Workers' Party) and the Movimento dos Trabalhadores Rurais Sem Terra (MST, Landless Workers Movement). The MST is the largest social movement in Latin America, representing hundreds of thousands of landless workers. According to the MST, 60 percent of Brazil's agricultural land is idle, while 25 million people lack year-round agricultural work and access to land. Since the MST organized in 1985, with the help of the Catholic Church, more than 250,000 families have occupied 15 million acres of idle land under MST auspices and won land titles from the government. These victories were hard fought. Land occupations have been greeted with violence, both from landowners and the police. From 1989 to 1999, more than 1,000 people were killed in land conflicts, but as of August 1999, only 53 suspects had been brought to trial.

The MST has adopted the kinds of strategies carried out by revolutionary governments—creation of food cooperatives, small agricultural industries, and a literacy program—and their efforts have been supported by such international organizations as UNESCO. Within Brazil, the group also enjoys widespread support. A 1997 public opinion poll showed that 77 percent approved of the MST and 85 percent supported their nonviolent occupation of idle farmland.

The MST has joined forces with the Workers' Party, whose leaders include landless workers as well as representatives of the industrial proletariat. And both groups have linked to new international movements to fight globalization and its effects on local economies. In January 2001, the Workers' Party sponsored the World Social Forum, which attracted an estimated 5,000 scholars, politicians, labor union leaders, and representatives of grassroots organizations from around the world to challenge the business elite who were meeting at the same time at the World Economic Forum in Switzerland. "It is the first time I see people of many different countries facing the same problems and intending to resolve them together," said Luiz Inacio da Silva, popularly known as Lula, the founder of the Workers' Party. Lula has failed in his bids for the presidency, but the party has won the leadership of the city of Porto Alegre, where the forum met, and has experimented with participatory democracy, involving the public in decisions about how public funds are spent. A highlight of the gathering came when 1,300 members of the MST, joined by forum participants, invaded the grounds of the U.S. biotechnology firm Monsanto. The protesters were led by Joao Pedro Stedile, head of the MST, and French trade unionist Jose Bove, a French sheep farmer who became famous when his Farmers Confederation stormed a McDonald's restaurant in rural France to draw attention to the risks of genetically modified crops to farmers, consumers and the environment.

The forum showed the possibilities of linking social movements with progressive political parties to work for change. The social movements and progressive political parties are winning more visibility and support by making international alliances, a move that has become more possible thanks to the internet, and more necessary in the age of the World Trade Organization.

Manuel José Arce: Reasons for War

Manuel José Arce (1935–85) was a well-respected Guatemalan intellectual who, like so many of the region's writers, took up his pen to write of the ills of his society that inevitably led to revolutionary movements in the late twentieth century. Although Arce went into exile in France, his poems spoke of Guatemala.

ARMS
You have a gun
And I am hungry.

You have a gun
because
I am hungry.

You have a gun
Therefore
I am hungry.

You can have a gun
you can have a thousand bullets and even another
        thousand
you can waste them all on my poor body,
you can kill me one, two, three, two thousand,
        seven thousand times
but in the long run
I will always be better armed than you
if you have a gun
and I
only hunger.

Source: "Arms" by Manuel José Arce. English translation by Susanne Jonas. Reprinted by permission.

Never Again: Reports on Torturers in Argentina, Brazil, and Guatemala

Throughout Latin America in the 1980s, governments formed commissions to investigate the reports of kidnaping and torture. The results shocked people within these countries and around the world. The reports revealed that the armed forces of these Latin American countries were trained to torture people, and they carried out this torture systematically. Here are excerpts from three such reports from Argentina, Brazil, and Guatemala.

ARGENTINA

Many of the events described in this report will be hard to believe. This is because the men and women of our nation have only heard of such horror in reports from distant places. The enormity of what took place in Argentina, involving the transgression of the most fundamental human rights, is sure, still, to produce that disbelief which some used at the time to defend themselves from pain and horror. In so doing, they also avoided the responsibility born of knowledge and awareness, because the question necessarily follows: how can we prevent it happening again? And the frightening realization that both the victims and their tormentors were our contemporaries, that the tragedy took place on our soil, and that those who insulted the history of our country in this way have yet to show by word or deed that they feel any remorse for what they have done. . . .

Carlos Alberto Campero (file No. 1806) relates the following unforgettable episode:

> My mother was taken to the shop and, threatening her life, they beat her in a way that should not even be used on wild animals. In the shop we had a ventilator fan. They cut the cable, plugged it in and used it to give her electric shocks. So that it would have more effect, they poured mineral water over my mother, whom they had tied to a chair. While they were committing this savagery, another one of them was beating her with a belt until her body was bleeding and her face disfigured. After some considerable time they decided to take us all with them, except for the six-month-old Viviana, who was left behind with Griselda, my thirteen-year-old sister.

Dr. Norberto Liwsky (file No. 7397) . . .
> . . . For days they applied electric shocks to my gums, nipples, genitals, abdomen and ears. . . . They then began to beat me systematically and rhythmically with wooden

sticks on my back, the backs of my thighs, my calves and the soles of my feet. At first the pain was dreadful. Then it became unbearable. Eventually I lost all feeling in the part of my body being beaten. The agonizing pain returned a short while after they finished hitting me. It was made still worse when they tore off my shirt, which had stuck to the wounds. . . .In between torture sessions they left me hanging by my arms from hooks fixed in the wall of the cell where they had thrown me.

BRAZIL

Dulce Chaves Pandolfi, student, 24, was . . . obliged to serve as a guinea pig in the barracks on Barão de Mesquita Street, in Rio, according to a statement attached to military court records dated 1970:

> At the Military Police, the defendant was stripped naked and subjected to beatings and electric shocks and other torments such as the "parrot's perch." After being taken to her cell, the defendant was assisted by a doctor and, after a while, was again tortured with exquisite cruelty in a demonstration of how torture should be carried out. . . .

The torturers not only bragged about their sophisticated technology of pain, but boasted that they were in a position to export it to repressive systems in other countries. This was stated in a letter from Haroldo Borges Rodrigues Lima, engineer, 37, dated 12 April 1977 and appended to military court records:

> Tortures continued systematically. They were accompanied by threats to subject me to new and harsher torments, which were described to me in detail. They said, with great pride, that in this matter they owed nothing to any foreign organization. On the contrary, they told me, they were already exporting know-how on the subject. . . .

The "parrot's perch"
> The parrot's perch consists of an iron bar wedged behind the victim's knees and to which his wrists are tied; the bar is then placed between two tables, causing the victim's body to hang some 20 to 30 centimeters from the ground. This method is hardly ever used by itself: its normal "complements" are electric shocks, the pamatória [a length of thick rubber attached to a wooden paddle], and drowning . . . [Augusto César Salles Galvão, student, 21, Belo Horizonte, 1970] . . .

Insects and Animals
>   There was also, in his cubicle, to keep him company, a boa
>   constrictor called "Miriam" . . .
>   [Leonardo Valentini]. . . .

>   The defendant also wants to state that, during the first
>   phase of her interrogation, cockroaches were placed over
>   her body, and one of them into her anus.
>   [Lúcia Maria Murat Vasconcelos, 23, student, Rio and
>   Salvador, 1972.] . . .

When José Leão Carvalho, advertising agent, was detained
in São Paulo, on 24 June 1964, his children were not spared:

>   . . . making threats to his younger children, which resulted
>   in the boy Sérgio having to have medical-psychiatric
>   treatment. He was three years old at that time. . . .

In 1973, in Rio, the military court heard the testimony of
Maria da Conceição Chaves Fernandes, proofreader, 19:

>   that she was subjected to sexual violence in the presence
>   and in the absence of her husband. . . .

GUATEMALA
The strategy of terror in Guatemala degenerated into the most
extreme displays of disregard for human life with public torture
sessions, public display of corpses, and the appearance of
mutilated bodies bearing signs of torture.

>   *They had cut out his tongue. His eyes were blindfolded with a
>   wide bandage or wide tape and there were punctures everywhere
>   on his rib cage, and it seemed that one of his arms was broken.
>   They left him unrecognizable. And I could tell it was him only
>   because I had lived with him for many years and I knew about
>   certain scars. . . .* Case 30310 . . . Cuilapa, Santa Rosa, 1981 . . .

>   *The soldiers had begun to kill, without a word. They weren't
>   asking whether anyone had done anything wrong or not; they
>   were killing that day.* Case 6629, Alta Verapaz, 1981.

>   *It was necessary to leave the ancestors behind, the dead were far
>   away, the sacred sites too.* Case 569, Cobán, Alta Verapaz,
>   1981.

>   *Well, they told my sister—since among the soldiers there was one
>   who spoke our language—and he told my sister that they had*

> *to finish off all the men and all the male children in order to
> eliminate the guerrillas. "And why?" she asked, "and why are
> you killing the children?" "Because those wretches are going to
> come some day and screw us over." That was their intention when
> they killed the little ones too.* Case 1944 . . . , Chiché, Quiché,
> 1983.

Source: *Nunca Más: The Report of the Argentine National Commission on the
Disappeared.* (NY: Farrar Straus Giroux, 1986), 9, 18, 20, 22. *Torture in Brazil: A
Shocking Report on the Pervasive Use of Torture by Brazilian Military Governments,
1964–1979,* Secretly prepared by the Archdiocese of São Paulo. Jaime Wright,
tran. (Austin: University of Texas Press, 1985), 14–15, 16, 21–22, 27, 30. *Guatemala:
Never Again! The Official Report of the Human Rights Office, Archdiocese of Guatemala*
(Maryknoll, NY: Orbis Books, 1999), 7, 9, 14, 31. Reprinted by permission of
Farrar, Straus and Giroux, LLC. Copyright © 1986 by Writers and Scholars
International Ltd.

11

The Enigma Remains

In December 2000, the volcano Popocatépetl erupted in Mexico. It was the worst eruption in 500 years. "In Mexican culture, Popo's activity represents a premonition of historic events," said poet Homero Aridjis. "It is full of omens."

At the close of the twentieth century, there was an eerie return to old patterns throughout Latin America: Neoliberalism and its love affair with the world market reprised the free-trade liberalism of the late nineteenth century. A new revolutionary movement arose in Mexico, resurrecting an historic name and claim—Zapata and the land. Some old patterns were glossed with new issues: The United States continued to intervene in Latin America, but this time the rationale was the drug war instead of the Cold War.

The political landscape looked different in the 1990s, as former revolutionaries refashioned themselves as politicians: the FSLN in Nicaragua, the FMLN in El Salvador. But at the same time, new social movements challenged political parties as the locus for change. Groups that organized around such issues as women's rights and the environment attracted activists who had not been reached by labor unions and traditional political parties.

But beneath the new veneer, old problems remained. Widespread poverty, inequality, and lack of democracy still plagued the region. And the pressures to keep peace, at any cost, have not decreased. One hundred years ago, leaders like Porfirio Díaz championed "Order and Progress"—an enforced order designed to create the stability that attracts foreign investment, the supposed guarantor of progress. With international investment and trade at dizzying new heights in the new millennium, the pressure for stability is just as great. And the inequalities that simmer below the surface remain a threat to elite plans for progress.

What do the omens portend? A new future? Or a future that echoes the past?

Neoliberalism: The Return of an Old Model

The original liberals were Adam Smith and David Ricardo, who touted free markets and comparative advantage as the routes to prosperity. Neoliberalism is a return to that unfettered capitalism, and in Latin America, its achievement means undoing years of state involvement in the economy. The tenets of neoliberalism in Latin America are privatization of public activity, deregulation of private activity, cuts in social spending, encouragement of market solutions to social problems, and, of course, free trade.

Neoliberalism is backed by the United States, in what is known in development circles as the "Washington consensus," and the basic ideas are embedded in the development strategy advocated by the International Monetary Fund, the World Bank, and the Inter-American Development Bank (IADB). This development strategy advocates export-oriented manufacturing linked to multinational corporations. The approach often includes the devaluing of currencies in order to lower costs for foreign investors, which results in higher costs for imports. The increased production of exports often coincides with a decrease in production of domestic consumer goods, which translates to a higher cost of living, as these goods must now be imported.

The IADB strategy also prefers private-sector development, encouraged through privatization of state-owned companies and deregulation of industries. State companies tend to end up in few hands, so there is greater concentration of wealth. In Mexico, 25 holding companies produce 47 percent of the gross national product. The reduction of the size of government is not carried solely through the sale of state companies. It is also managed through cutbacks in public spending, which means that many of the rights that were won through years of struggle—such as labor rights, public maintenance of water and sewage, education—are now being eroded or abandoned.

Nonetheless, international agencies are simultaneously concerned that social inequity leads to unrest, and unrest is bad for international business. But there are no suggestions of how Latin America countries are to avoid social unrest while further opening their economies and cutting government spending and services. Much of the expanded trade taking place is between branches of international firms—by the 1980s, 40 percent of global trade was within the largest 350 transnational corporations and their affiliates—which means that it doesn't penetrate into the Latin American economy. Further, these companies are attracted by low-cost labor, and low wages means little buying power and a low standard of living.

Low wages traditionally have been justified by invoking classic economic theories regarding productivity, which assert that wages are low because the output per hour of these workers is low. However, Latin American workers producing for export are now working with advanced machinery, and their productivity is increasing, while wages are not. Plants owned by U.S. companies in Mexico are 85 percent as productive as those in the U.S., but Mexican workers only get 6 percent of United States wages.

Advocates of neoliberal policies frequently point to Chile under Pinochet and the "Chicago boys," monetarists who studied at the University of Chicago, as an example of a success story because of the high growth rates produced. But there is another side to the story. Banks were deregulated and labor unions were repressed so that wages could be lowered. As a result, while the economy grew, so did the percentage of people living in poverty, rising from 20 to 40 percent of the population. The richest 20 percent of the population increased their consumption from 45 percent of income in 1969 to 60 percent in 1989. In 1989, wages were 8 percent lower than they had been in 1970. By the end of the century, wages were just returning to the levels achieved twenty-five years earlier. Forty percent of the workforce had been shifted into the informal economy. Meanwhile, thousands of small businesses went bankrupt. But Pinochet government officials, such as Admiral José Toribio Merino, had no problem with such economic Darwinism: "Let fall those who must fall. Such is the jungle of . . . economic life. A jungle of savage beasts, where he who can kill the one next to him kills him. That is reality."

Mexico was a model of nationalism until the 1980s, when it embraced neoliberal policies with a vengeance. There were 1,050 state companies in 1983, but only 285 were left in 1990. The buyers were wealthy, and their new acquisitions added to their wealth. While Mexico had only one billionaire in 1988, there were twenty-four in 1994. Meanwhile, unemployment was 20 percent, and underemployment was 40 percent. The expansion of the maquiladora zone hurt Mexico's domestic industry in Mexico City, Monterrey, and Guadalajara. Mexican industries that had employed 2.5 million workers were replaced by international corporations that employed only 500,000.

If Mexico is a bellwether for Latin America, then we should look closely: The country's 1982 default on foreign debt signaled the end of 1970s prosperity. Mexico was the first to acknowledge the debt crisis, and the first to employ neoliberal adjustment and reform. It was the first Latin American country to form a free trade zone with the United States, signing the North America Free Trade Agreement (NAFTA), joining with the United States and Canada in 1994. And the results have been discouraging. While the volume of trade has skyrocketed, the competition has not been healthy for all involved. Not only have many Mexican businesses collapsed in the onslaught of U.S.-produced goods, but small farmers who grow corn cannot compete with the imports grown by U.S. agribusiness.

NAFTA differs in significant ways from free trade zones of the past. When the European Common Market was formed, it allowed goods, capital, and labor to freely cross borders. Workers from low-wage zones rushed to those offering higher pay, forcing their home countries to raise wages in order to keep workers. The result was an equalization of wages across the region. However, NAFTA only permits the free movement of goods and capital, not labor. The result has been a worsening of conditions for Mexican workers. The Mexican government reports that the number of Mexican workers earning less than the legal minimum or $3.40 a day rose 20 percent from 1993 to 1997, for a total of 7.7 million workers. By 1997, salaries slumped to 60 percent of their 1994 value. Meanwhile, workers in the maquilas, foreign-owned assembly plants with special privileges along the border, earned barely enough to cover basic necessities. A basic market basket (food, utilities, housing, transportation) cost $54 a week in 1998, and the average net pay for a maquila worker was $55.77, leaving a meager $1.77 a week for education, clothing, health care, and other essentials. Further, Mexican salaries declined in relation to U.S. salaries: In 1980, Mexican workers earned 22 percent of the wages earned by U.S. workers; in 1998, they earned only 9.6 percent.

While Mexican elites pushed for NAFTA as their salvation, others viewed it as a "death sentence." On the day that NAFTA took effect, a new revolutionary movement was launched as well in the jungle of Chiapas.

A New Kind of Revolution

In the nineteenth century, Chiapas was a timber and coffee region where Indians lived as virtual debt slaves. The region was split between the relatively prosperous west, which was fertile and characterized by commercial development, and the poor, subsistence-oriented east. The struggle between ranchers, landowners, and subsistence farmers was intensified at the turn of the century by competition with Guatemala.

Many say that Mexico's 1910 revolution never reached Chiapas. Large estates remained intact, leaving most of the population to compete for the remaining land. As the Mexican economy industrialized in the 1950s, state economists advocated the production of cheap food for urban workers. Low food prices meant low prices for small farmers, low wages on large farms. To earn more, commercial farmers in western Chiapas expanded, encroaching on subsistence farming in the east. Desperate indigenous farmers colonized the Lacandón jungle.

In the 1970s, the government built two hydroelectric plants in Chiapas on the Grijalva River, and in the 1980s large landowners converted the land they had once rented to small farmers into cattle grazing. More land was lost to subsistence production as areas were marked off by the government for bioreserves.

Meanwhile, Chiapas could be characterized overall as the poorest and most indigenous state in Mexico. Only 11 percent of the population earned a moderate income, compared to 24 percent nationwide. Less than 50 percent had running water, compared to 67 percent nationwide. While Chiapas has only 3 percent of Mexico's population, it produces 13 percent of the nation's corn, 54 percent of its hydroelectric power, 13 percent of its gas, and 4 percent of its oil—yet nearly half of Chiapas is without electricity.

In 1983, the *Ejército Zapatista de Liberación Nacional* (EZLN, or Zapatistas) began organizing. On January 1, 1994, the day that NAFTA took effect, the Zapatistas rose up and occupied government buildings in the town of San Cristobal. They stated, "This is our response to the implementation of the North American Free Trade Agreement, because this represents a death sentence for all of the indigenous ethnicities in Mexico."

The Zapatistas are different from other revolutionary groups in Latin American history. They reject vanguardism, the idea that only a tiny revolutionary elite knows the way to effect change. Although the media have focused on their charismatic leader, Subcomandante Marcos, the organization runs on communal decision making. And while the majority are indigenous, it is not just an ethnically based movement. The Zapatistas have urged Mexicans of all walks of life to join them, not by also taking up arms but by calling on the Mexican government to create true democracy, to develop the country rather than just growing the economy, and to give the regions such as Chiapas their autonomy.

The Mexican government responded by keeping some 40,000 troops, one-quarter of the armed forces, stationed in Chiapas. Although negotiations resulted in accords signed in February 1996, no legislation was sent to Mexico's congress, leading the Zapatistas to again take up arms. In a March 1999 referendum, three million Mexicans went to 15,000 Zapatista polling places and voted that the 1996 accords should be implemented, but the matter was not resolved.

Fearful of international publicity, especially because of NAFTA, Mexico's National Migration Institute has kept close tabs on foreigners traveling to Chiapas, and hundreds of observers have been deported. In 1998, Interior Minister Francisco Labastida claimed there was an "international movement to intervene in the internal affairs of our country." Labastida was later tapped as PRI's presidential candidate in the historic 2000 elections, in which PRI allowed an opposing candidate to win the elections for the first time since the party took power 71 years earlier. New president Vicente Fox prioritized a resolution of the Chiapas crisis, and began withdrawing troops from the region.

318 The Enigma Remains

But foreigners don't have to travel to Chiapas to find out about the Zapatistas. They can visit the EZLN's website, a phenomenon that has led some to call the Zapatistas the first post-modern revolutionaries. It is certainly the first post-Cold War rebellion, and it confronts all the contradictions of the post-Cold War dynamic.

The Post-Cold War United States

In some ways, the main interest of the United States in Latin America has not changed since the nineteenth century—government and business want the maintenance of free markets for U.S. investment. Threats to the U.S. economy traditionally are seen as threats to national security. The Cold War threat to national security was supposedly instability that could lead to revolution and communism, which would close markets. The communist threat also became the justification for huge military budgets and the expansion of U.S. military industries. Without the Cold War threat, how do military leaders and weapons manufacturers justify the still-rising annual military budget, which reached $280 billion dollars a year in 2000? The threat now has been defined as the drug war and immigration, with both issues framed as the 21st-century mission for our military. "It's their new meal ticket now that the commies are not their big threat," a congressional staffer told *Newsweek* in 1990.

Gen. Barry R. McCaffrey, commander of the U.S. Southern Command (Southcom), told Congress in 1995: "On our southern flank, there is no regional aggressor seeking military hegemony, no specter of a regional arms race, nor the grave danger of the development and proliferation of weapons of mass destruction. Our neighbors are allies who, in general, share similar values. Nevertheless, there are real problems in the Americas. Widespread social and economic inequalities are exploited by insurgents, narco-traffickers, and highly armed bands of criminals. Latin America also has the world's most skewed income distribution. The benefits of the recent economic turnaround infrequently trickle down to the poor. These problems can be catalysts for significant migration, both internal and international."

Without the bogeyman of international communism, leaders in Washington now speak more openly about what the United States is really trying to protect—trade and oil supplies. According to Richard Feinberg, director of inter-American affairs at the National Security Council, "Exports have become a major engine of our economic growth, and Latin America is one of our most dynamic markets. U.S. exports to Latin America have more than doubled in seven years to nearly $80 billion in 1993." Rear Adm. James B. Perkins of the U.S. Navy, acting commander in chief of Southcom, told the Senate Armed Services Committee in 1996: "In the 1990s U.S. exports to the region grew by $36 billion while over the same period, U.S. exports to the European

Union, Japan, and China increased by just $12 billion. Latin America purchases over 40 percent of its imports from the United States. For instance, Costa Rica with a population of just 3 million buys more U.S. goods than does all of Eastern Europe with some 100 million people. In 1994, the United State sold more to Chile's 14 million people than to India's 920 million people. Today, the United States trades more with Venezuela than with Russia, and more with Brazil than with China."

A significant component of our trade with Venezuela is oil. Gen. Charles E. Wilhelm, Marine Corps commander of Southcom, told the Senate in 1998: "No one questions the strategic importance of the Middle East, but Venezuela alone provides the same amount of oil to the U.S. as do all the Persian Gulf states combined. The discovery of major oil reserves in Colombia, and existing oil supplies in Trinidad-Tobago and Ecuador, further increase the strategic importance of this region's energy resources." The next year, Wilhelm made the oil-trade-defense link even clearer: "Our growing dependence on oil from the region, which includes Venezuela as our single largest source of imported fuel—8 percent annually—combined with the region's growing dependence on U.S. imports, fully justifies a consistent and balanced engagement strategy in the region. Latin Americans currently spend 44 cents of every dollar on imports from the U.S. By 2000 Latin America is expected to buy more U.S. goods than Europe, and by 2010 more U.S. goods than Europe and Japan combined. These figures are expected to increase as initiatives of the Free Trade Area of the Americas take root."

So what threatens oil and trade? "A threat which knows no borders," according to Wilhelm. That threat is drugs. "Narcotraffickers don't think in terms of borders. Indeed they take advantage of this mind set. They violate sovereignty. So the only way to deal with the narcotrafficking problem is to treat it as a regional problem," said William Perry, President Bill Clinton's Secretary of Defense.

In the past, United States officials discredited guerrilla groups in Latin America by calling them communists. Today they are vilified in a new way. According to U.S. Navy Rear Adm. James B. Perkins, acting commander in chief of Southcom, in testimony to the Senate Armed Services Committee in 1996: "The guerrilla forces that plagued Colombia for 30 years are today motivated by economic gain, not ideology. They render protection to narcotraffickers and extort money from legitimate businessmen."

More importantly, the military leaders contended, the drug problem comes home to the United States: 10,000 deaths a year and a social cost of $66 billion a year. However, critics have noted, use of tobacco kills an estimated 400,000 Americans and costs some $88 billion a year, but the U.S. government subsidizes tobacco production and its export rather than trying to eradicate it. Of course, tobacco is grown in the United States, and coca is not.

In addition to the drug threat, officials also fear increased immigration. Rear Adm. Perkins testified that some 900,000 illegal migrants from Latin

America were arrested in the United States in 1995 alone. Perkins also expressed concerns about immigration within Latin America, with the most dramatic examples including the 600,000 Nicaraguans illegally in Costa Rica and three million to five million Colombians in Venezuela.

To fight these problems, U.S. armed forces have sought increased funds for themselves and their counterparts in Latin America. Some argue that Latin American militaries will modernize their weaponry one way or another—either by buying from the United States, or buying leftover Soviet weapons on the international market. In 2001, Congress responded with Plan Colombia: $1.3 billion in aid, much of it military, to help with eradication of cocaine. Amnesty International, which has long been monitoring human rights abuses, opposed the military aid program for Colombia, saying the organization "believes that it will escalate the armed conflict and the human rights crisis. The organization has documented overwhelming evidence of the responsibility of illegal paramilitary organizations for widespread, systematic and gross human rights violations. There is also conclusive evidence that paramilitary groups continue to operate with the tacit or active support of the Colombian armed forces. Evidence has also emerged that Colombian army personnel trained by U.S. special forces have been implicated by action or omission in serious human rights violations, including the massacre of civilians. Military equipment provided by the U.S. to the Colombian armed forces has reportedly been used in the commission of human rights violations against civilians."

In addition to direct aid to Latin American countries, the United States has focused on beefing up the U.S. Southern Command [Southcom], which states its mission clearly on its website: "The mission of U.S. Southern Command is to shape the environment within our area of responsibility by conducting military to military engagement and counterdrug activities throughout the theater to promote democracy, stability, and collective approaches to threats to regional security. The command will, when required, respond unilaterally or multilaterally to crises that threaten regional stability or national interests, and prepare to meet future hemispheric challenges."

Southcom can trace its beginnings to the arrivals of Marines in Panama in 1903, just days after the province declared its independence from Colombia. Army troops arrived in 1911, three years before the Panama Canal opened. U.S. military presence in Panama peaked at 67,000 individuals during World War II. Southcom went on to became one of seven regional combat commands created on December 14, 1946, when President Harry S Truman signed Outline Command Plan, and eventually the United States maintained twelve military bases in the zone, including Ft. Amador and Ft. Gulick. It was at Ft. Amador that the U.S. Army School of the Americas was created in 1946 to train Latin American officers and foster anti-communism. The school was later moved to Ft. Gulick, where it became known as the "School of Coups" and "School of Assassins" because of its training of right-wing officers throughout Latin America. In 1984 the school was ordered out of Panama and moved to Fort Benning, Georgia. On January 17, 2001, the School of the Americas was replaced by the Western Hemisphere Institute for Security Cooperation, but critics feared that only the name and not its mission had changed.

Historically, the bases in Panama were seen as a backwater of U.S. international operations. But in 1983, as wars raged in Central America, 9,000 Army, Navy, and Air Force personnel were based in the zone, which came to be seen as, in the words of the *Washington Post*, "the nerve center of a . . . continent-wide war against Soviet–Cuban expansion." As the Central American wars began to wind down toward the end of the 1980s, U.S. attention shifted to the drug war. In 1988 Congress designated the Department of Defense as the lead agency to stop drug smuggling, and in 1990 the DOD planned to spend $450 million in the drug war.

The plan was for the United States to provide training, logistics, materiel, and leadership. At the time, officials told *Newsweek* that there would be no joint drug raids: "Lawmakers in Congress would be loath to see the United States repeat the mistake of Vietnam and be drawn into direct combat in the Andean highlands." And indeed, Massachusetts Senator John Kerry, a Vietnam veteran, commented, "We want to examine this policy before body bags come back to this country."

By 1991, the department was spending $1.2 million on the fight against drugs, and in 1992 the number of military personnel based at Southcom reached 10,250. Those numbers were a fraction, however, of the visiting military personnel that rotated through the region on maneuvers. In 1994, more than 60,000 airmen, sailors, marines, and soldiers were operating in the region; 20,000 of them were reservists, primarily from Army National Guard, Army Reserve, Air Guard. By 1995, the zone was home to 7,500 men and women from all branches of the armed services, along with representatives of the Department of State, the Central Intelligence Agency, Drug Enforcement Agency, Defense Intelligence Agency, National Security Agency, Coast Guard, Customs. They had shifted from the traditional bilateral combat scenarios to multilateral peacekeeping efforts, humanitarian assistance, and operations against narco-traffickers. Rear Admiral Walker F. Doran, acting commander-in-chief of Southcom, told Congress in 1997 that, while federal statutes prohibited actual involvement in operations to interdict drugs, U.S. forces provided "robust support" in intelligence, detection (radars), logistics support (airlift), training, and communications.

In fulfillment of the Panama Canal treaty, on December 31, 1999, the United States withdrew all personnel from U.S. bases and turned the facilities over to the government of Panama. Southcom moved its headquarters to Miami and shifted many personnel out of Howard Air Force Base to existing bases in Aruba and Ecuador. The military came up with a new plan of action, focusing on Miami and Puerto Rico. Gen. Charles E. Wilhelm, Southcom's Marine Corps commander, told the Senate: "There, our active component planners and programmers can join forces with nearly 15,000 aggressive, hard-charging, bilingual Guardsmen and reservists. The result will be a unique total force team, focused on the region and sensitive to its cultures. With the Southcom Headquarters at the strategic hub in Miami, . . . [U.S. Army Southern Command] in Puerto Rico, Joint Task Force Bravo minding the store in Central America from Soto Cano [Honduras], and with . . . [the Department of Defenses's Joint Interagency Task Force] South as the United States element of a Multinational Counterdrug Center, in Panama or elsewhere, we will be well-postured to execute our theater strategy and prosecute the war on drugs as we enter the third millennium."

The U.S. military commanders and political leaders never address the reasons for the spread of coca growth and cocaine production in Latin America. Aside from the abundant demand in the United States, which consumes the lion's share of the drug crop, it is useful to remember the weak condition of Latin America's economies. With few other alternatives to earn a living, cocaine becomes just another cash crop. The fact that the drug is illegal makes it possible to charge enormous profits and leads to the web of corruption and violence to which the drug trade has led, particularly in Colombia.

The Environmental Cost

One of the casualties of the drug war is the Latin American environment. Colombia uses aerial fumigation, spraying toxic herbicides on regions where drugs are produced. The spraying contaminates everything—schools, houses, water, pastures, farms, and the workers who toil in those fields. Residues are left in the ground and water, and many areas are defoliated.

In reaction, subsistence farmers move farther up steep hillsides or into the Amazon rain forest. The rain forest is a fragile, integrated region of relatively weak soils that are enriched by the dense canopy of the trees. Once the trees are cut down, soils are washed away and the region is destroyed. In Brazil, the attack on the rain forest began with the steady push into the interior after the inauguration in 1960 of Brasilia. Relentlessly since then, machete, ax, fire, and bulldozer have felled the forest. By 1992, approximately 160,000 square miles of rain forest had disappeared, an area equal in size to the nation of Paraguay or to the five Central American nations. In 1998, according to the World Bank, "six million hectares of tropical rain forest were cleared or went up in smoke, 1,244 vertebrates were in danger of extinction, and three hundred million hectares of agricultural land had lost productivity due to soil erosion."

Violence against the forest triggered other forms of destruction. As the ecologist Susanna Hecht pointed out, "In the Amazon, when trees fall, people die." Indians fought against encroaching ranchers, loggers, and miners. The poor immigrants clashed with large landowners. Land conflicts during the 1980s claimed the lives of more than 1,000 rural workers, a figure that excluded the number of Indians killed. Westward expansion decimated the Indians. Divided into 180 tribes, they numbered between 200,000 and 225,000 by the final decade of the century. The advancing frontier incorporated some of the Indians into miserable, marginal existences, the inevitable victims of "progress." The government gathered others into reservations, frequently relocated, always reduced in size. Manoel Gomes da Silva, a Caxinaua Indian, explained the indigenous plight to Pope John Paul II during his visit to the Brazilian West in 1991:

> In the name of modernity, technology and progress they criminally invade our territories, kill our leaders, poison our rivers, destroy our environment and treat us as sub-races, turning us into foreigners within our own country. . . . If they exterminate the Indian nations, they are exterminating the forests and the environment and life on the planet will become unsustainable.

Environmental degradation is occurring just as rapidly in Latin America's burgeoning cities. In the decades after World War II, the cities in Latin America grew at a faster rate than those in any other part of the world. From 1945 to 1955, the urban populations of seven countries—Brazil, Mexico, Bolivia, Peru, El Salvador, Panama, and the Dominican Republic—increased approximately 55 percent, while those in another four countries—Cuba, Chile, Venezuela, and Uruguay—went up nearly 45 percent. In 1950, only 39 percent of Latin Americans lived in urban centers (that is, more than 2,000 inhabitants). But as export agriculture expanded in the countryside, pushing small farmers off the land, and factories beckoned in the cities, internal migration rose.

By 1960, more than half of Latin America's population was urban. In 1975, 61 percent lived in areas of 2,000 or more people, and 41 percent lived in locales with 20,000 or more. And by the end of the century, 75 percent of the population was urban. Increasingly, much of the urban population is concentrated in the capitals, which with few exceptions are disproportionately large. By the 1990s, the population of São Paulo reached 18 million and Mexico City reached 20 million. In Brazil, hundreds of thousands live in shantytowns that began as temporary housing in the 1950s migrations and have since evolved into permanent slums. In Mexico City, the inability of the government to adequately house and provide services to its millions was spotlighted when a 1985 earthquake destroyed flimsy housing and left many homeless. Only Cuba has been able to manage urbanization by placing controls on population movement, developing the countryside, and developing urban centers other than Havana.

Urban population growth can be attributed in part to the high birthrate. Between 1920 and 1960, Latin America witnessed a phenomenal demographic rise, an average of 2.9 percent per year, which amounted to a 126 percent increase. The figure becomes even more impressive when compared to

Europe's population growth of only 23 percent for the same period. In recent years, Latin American population growth has slowed, now rising by about 1.5 percent a year, comparable to the world average of 1.4 percent.. The United Nations Population Fund reports that population growth rates have fallen by more than one-third from 1970 to 2000, and on average women in the region bear three children.

Most urban workers, however, have not found jobs in the industrial sector that attracted them. Industry is capital-intensive and offers little employment. If lucky, the urban masses find jobs in the low-paid but regulated formal service sector of shops, restaurants, and offices. If they are unlucky, they scrape by in the informal sector, doing everything from shining shoes and selling cheap goods at traffic lights to picking through garbage in the sprawling dumps. The two economies are linked, though, as salaried workers hire domestics and handymen from the informal sector, and workers move between the two sectors depending on fate and opportunity.

The massive cities are centers of environmental contamination as urban-based industry pollutes with few, if any, controls, and motor vehicles create such high carbon monoxide levels that respiratory illness has become rampant, especially among children. Because of the neoliberal emphasis on deregulation, environmental controls are frowned upon. This is especially true in Mexico, where U.S. companies have relocated to avoid costly environmental requirements at home. The World Bank reports, "On the human health side, only 2 percent of wastewater is treated in cities such as Santiago and San Salvador, and the air-sheds of many of the major cities in the region fail to meet WHO [United Nations World Health Organization] standards, thus imposing substantial and long-lasting effects on the health of urban dwellers."

The Enigma Remains

As Latin America moves into the twenty-first century, there have been tremendous changes but also remarkable continuities. Unfortunately, what seems to continue is the maldistribution of wealth, leaving many Latin Americans impoverished. Hunger, disease, malnutrition, and illiteracy still plague the region. "Latin America has made minimal progress in reducing poverty and improving wealth distribution," Nora Lustig, chief of the Interamerican Development Bank's poverty and inequality advisory unit, noted in 1999. She estimated that one in three Latin Americans earned less than $60 a month, the bank's definition of extreme impoverishment.

Conditions actually worsened from 1980 to 1990, as the percentage of people in poverty in the region rose from 35 to 39 percent, and those who were indigent increased from 15 to 18 percent. Statistics from the CIA's *The World Factbook 2000* show that the bottom 10 percent of Latin America's population receives 1.3 percent of all income, while the top 10 percent on average receives 40 percent. The CIA puts the percentage of people below the poverty line as high as 70 percent in Bolivia and 67 percent in oil-rich Venezuela.

The effects of poverty are manifested in a variety of indicators of quality of life. The Pan American Health Organization reported that for the period 1995–2000, the infant mortality rate was 35.7 percent, compared to 7 percent in the United States. United Nations figures for the Food and Agricultural Organization (FAO) at the end of the 1990s showed that 13 million Latin American children had retarded growth, 6.7 million had insufficient weight, and 1.5 million under the age of five suffered from loss of weight due to disease, while UNICEF reported that 800,000 children die in Latin America and the Caribbean due to preventable diseases.

Latin America showed improvements in some areas—annual cases of cholera dropped from 357,483 in 1980 to 17,686 in 1997. But at the same time, the number of cases of tuberculosis rose from 195,748 in 1980 to 231,437 in 1997. Malaria cases skyrocketed from 526,777 to 1,007,903. Undoubtedly the health problems of the population can be attributed to living conditions. Twenty-seven percent of the region's population does not have access to drinking water, and 30 percent do not have access to sewage facilities. Meanwhile, regional expenditures on health care as a percentage of gross national product increased only slightly, from 10.5 percent in 1984 to 13.9 percent in 1995.

Latin America did seem to improve on one social indicator—literacy— but a closer look shows the improvement to be illusory. In 1980, 21 percent of Latin Americans were illiterate, ranging from under 10 percent in Chile, Costa Rica, Argentina, and Uruguay, to 51 percent in Guatemala. In 1995, the overall rate of illiteracy had dropped to 14.3 percent, with Colombia, Venezuela, and Paraguay succeeding in dropping rates below 10 percent, and all other countries in the region dropping below 30 percent except for Guatemala (44 percent) and Nicaragua (34 percent). However, the definition of literacy may not include much schooling. The regional average is a mere five years, with a high of 7.2 years for Argentina. For eight Latin American countries, literacy means an average of less than five years of schooling.

That such deplorable conditions can still exist in the midst of plenty, of growth, of structural changes in the economy, indicates the continued limitations of the development models used in the region. Subcomandante Marcos described the current program as the "destruction of Mexico as a nation and its transformation into a department store, something like a mega 'little shop' which sells human beings and natural resources at prices dictated by the world market."

Some Latin American intellectuals wonder whether the core of the problem is not just Latin America's position in the international economy but the idea of development itself and the way development programs have been carried out since the end of World War II. At that time, officials in the United

States were concerned about conditions in what became known as the Third World—everyone outside of the industrialized First World and the Soviet bloc's Second World. United States officials and businessmen had multiple concerns: Poor people make poor markets, and U.S. post-war strategy for rebuilding the world economy depended on trade. Furthermore, poor people are likely to rise up to protest their conditions, and that instability is bad for business. Unrest might also result in a successful revolution. At its worst, the revolution could result in the elimination of a market and source of cheap labor and primary goods—which is the essence of the communist threat. At best, it might result in a government trying to mitigate the ills of the marketplace by insisting on higher prices for products, higher wages for labor, and the freedom to choose from multiple trade partners instead of being locked into exclusive relationships.

There were also many sincere people in the industrialized world who wanted to improve the standard of living for the masses in Latin America. Many of these people, with the best of intentions, went to work for the Agency for International Development and the Alliance for Progress in the United States, or for the many new development-oriented committees and agencies of the United Nations: World Health Organization, International Labor Organization, Food and Agriculture Organization.

Meanwhile, in Latin America, there was also a concern about development. Some elites, in an echo of nineteenth-century patterns, wanted to modernize their countries to be like the United States in the classic combination of wanting to make money and wanting to appear "modern"—no one said "civilized" anymore. At the same time, there were many Latin Americans who sincerely wanted to improve the lives of the majority. The question was how to do it.

The practical implementation of aid and investment programs designed to "modernize" Latin America was underpinned by a theoretical discussion that began with the ideas laid out by U.S. economic historian W.W. Rostow in his *The Stages of Growth: A Noncommunist Manifesto*, published in 1960. Rostow argued that modernization followed a set of stages from traditional to advanced societies, and that all of the world could develop by simply following the lead of their predecessors. The problem, in his argument, was that traditional societies needed to become more capitalist. His book launched entire schools of thought about modernization and served as the basis for many modernization programs.

The reaction in Latin America, however, was a bit different. Starting from the analyses by Raúl Prebisch and ECLA, Latin Americans concluded that the problem was not a lack of capitalism but the way that capitalism unfolded in Latin America. Because the United States and Europe already had highly industrialized economies, Latin America could not compete; limited, then, to production of primary products, the region was trapped into low growth, low wages, and declining terms of trade.

Out of this analysis came the dependency school, which turned modernization on its head. The problem was not too little capitalism but too much and in too unequal a form. *Dependentistas* described Latin America as the periphery, trapped by the desires of the metropolis, usually the United States. Instead of prescribing more capitalism, the theorists frequently advocated either disconnecting from the international market or turning toward some form of socialism.

Dependency challenged traditional paradigms that the so-called Third World could, through proper programs and economic policies, become like the First World. And the theories took the focus off the countries at the center, and turned the spotlight on the periphery. The theory was articulated by Latin Americans themselves: Fernando Henrique Cardoso, Enzo Faletto, Theotonio Dos Santos (joined by U.S. and European scholars, most notably Andre Gunder Frank.)

From the 1950s to the 1990s, people concerned about Latin America focused on the issue of development. For some, it was just another word for progress or modernization. As we have pointed out in this text, development was often used to describe mere growth in gross national product. Others defined it as structural change in the economy, especially via industrialization. We have focused on development as providing the most good for the most people.

But half a century after the focus on development began, some argue, Latin America is in worse shape than it was before. Development programs frequently displaced people and disrupted traditional subsistence cultures that met people's basic needs and provided them with cultural well-being. Before 1960, when the majority of people still lived in the countryside, there were indeed subsistence cultures that provided a lifestyle that to North Americans might look impoverished, but that might really be a more simple way of life that amply met community needs. These communities were frequently displaced by the spread of agro-industry and the so-called green revolution, using many chemical inputs to increase yield and bring underutilized land into production. To the extent that development aid was aimed at modernizing Latin America, it facilitated the further expansion of commercial activity on the theory that subsistence equaled poverty. The end result was often the production of a greater absolute poverty, both rural and urban, as well as the poverty that comes from destruction of community.

If, as Burns has argued elsewhere, the modernization of the nineteenth century brought with it the "poverty of progress," then the modernization of the twentieth century might be seen as the "devastation of development." How else can one view a situation where the cure has often been worse than the supposed disease? For example, many countries that were not only self-sufficient in food but were actually food exporters ended up as food importers after the implementation of development programs that focused on exports, resulting in the creation and spread of hunger rather than its prevention.

Once again, Latin American scholars are challenging the dominant paradigm. In *Encountering Development: The Making and Unmaking of the Third World*, Arturo Escobar shows how development programs created a discourse of problematic categories: peasants who needed to be modernized, mothers whose fertility needed to be controlled. The process of development created the problems, then failed to solve them. Yet, the discourse has not changed:

> The rural development discourse repeats the same relations that has defined development discourse since its emergence: the fact that development is about growth, about capital, about technology, about becoming modern. Nothing else. "Traditional peasants need to be modernized; they need to be given access to capital, technology and adequate assistance. Only in this way can production and productivity be increased." These statements were uttered pretty much in the same way in 1949 . . . as in 1960 . . . and in 1973 . . . and today they are still repeated ad nauseam in many quarters. Such a poverty of imagination, one may think.

Escobar encourages us to a richer imagination, asking us to imagine a post-development era, in a postmodern world. The debates about modernity and postmodernity are long and complex. To oversimplify, the modern was the project of the enlightenment and industrialization, the optimistic belief in progress and universal truths. Postmodernity is the twentieth-century condition of having seen the modern project fail so profoundly in so many ways— wars, pollution, oppression, destruction. In postmodernity, there is no one truth, but many truths, many ways of interacting with and viewing the world. It is a decentered, fragmented world.

Some argue that postmodernity is irrelevant for Latin America, a region that is still not modern—or at least not modern*ized*—in so many ways. Others quip that Latin America is the original land of the postmodern, since it has always been fragmented, always been a mixture of past, present and future. Néstor García Canclini offers the view of *hybridity*—not the syncretism usually connected with religion, nor the mestizaje usually connected to race, but elements of the traditional and the modern, creating new forms, with a new hybrid emerging. This hybridity is the product of Latin America's distinctive interaction with the modern.

What does that hybrid, postmodern, post-development world look like? Perhaps it is exemplified by the Kayapo Indians of Brazil, who use video-cameras in their fight to preserve a traditional way of life. Or by the Zapatistas, who evoke the figure of Emiliano Zapata from the Revolution of 1910 to preserve elements of an older indigenous culture—albeit modified by colonialism and neocolonialism—in a new project of sustainable economics that seeks autonomy within rather than conquest and control of the nation-state.

There appear to be new enigmas in Latin America's reality. But whether the analysts are modernists or postmodernists, they seem to agree that still the central enigma remains: Poor people inhabit rich lands.

Zapatistas: A New Voice from the Lacandón Jungle

In 1983, the *Ejército Zapatista de Liberación Nacional* (EZLN, Zapatista Army of National Liberation, or Zapatistas) began organizing in the Mexican state of Chiapas. On January 1, 1994, the day that NAFTA took effect, the Zapatistas rose up and occupied government buildings in the town of San Cristobal. They stated, "This is our response to the implementation of the North American Free Trade Agreement, because this represents a death sentence for all of the indigenous ethnicities in Mexico." Their chief spokesman has been the charismatic Subcomandante Marcos, but the following communiques are attributed to the Comité Clandestino Revolucionario Indígena, Comandancia General (CCRI-CG, Revolutionary Indigenous Clandestine Committee—General Command).

Communiqué from the CCRI-CG of the EZLN
January 20, 1994
"The land that gives life and struggle belongs to all of us."
To our indigenous brothers and sisters in other organizations
To the people of Mexico
To the people and governments of the world
We address you, indigenous brothers and sisters of other independent and honest organizations of Chiapas and all of Mexico. We, the indigenous people of the CCRI-CG of the EZLN, speak to you in order to say the following:
First. We, the Zapatistas, have always respected and will continue to respect different honest and independent organizations. We have not obligated anyone to enter our struggle. All who have entered have done so of their own free will.
Second. We respect your form of struggle; we salute your independence and honesty, as long as they are authentic. We have taken up arms because they left us no other choice. You have our support if you continue on your own road, because we are struggling for the same thing, and the land that gives life and struggle belongs to all of us.
Third. Our form of armed struggle is just and true. If we had not lifted our rifles, the government would never have worried about the indigenous people of our lands and we would now continue to be not only poor, but forgotten. Now the government is very worried about the problems of indigenous people and campesinos, and that is good. But it was necessary for Zapatista rifles to speak so that Mexico could hear the voice of the poor people of Chiapas.

Fourth. We will continue respecting you and your forms of struggle. We invite you, your organizations, and your own independent forms of struggle to join in our heartfelt hope for freedom, democracy and justice.

All organizations united in the same struggle!

From the mountains of the Mexican Southeast
CCRI-CG of the EZLN
Mexico, January 1994
Subcomandante Marcos

Communiqué from the CCRI-CG of the EZLN, Mexico
January 20, 1994
"We want all those who walk with truth, to walk together."
To the people of Mexico
To all honest and independent people, civil organizations, and democratic politicians of Mexico
To the peoples and governments of the world
Brothers and sisters,

The worthy struggle of the soldiers of the EZLN has received the sympathy of different people, organizations, and sectors of Mexican and international civil society. These progressive forces, through their honorable actions, have opened the possibility of a just political solution to the conflict that darkens our skies. Neither the political will of the federal executive nor the glorious military actions of our soldiers have been decisive in this turn of events. What have been crucial are the public demonstrations in the streets, mountains, and the media by many organizations, and by the honest independent people who are part of what is called Mexican civil society.

We, Mexico's last citizens and first patriots, have understood since the beginning that our problems, and those of the entire nation, can only be resolved through a national revolutionary movement with three principal demands: freedom, democracy, and justice.

Our form of struggle is not the only one; for many it may not even be an acceptable one. Other forms of struggle exist and have great value. Our organization is not the only one, for many it may not even be a desirable one. Other honest, progressive, and independent organizations exist and have great value. The Zapatista Army of National Liberation has never claimed that its form of struggle is the only legitimate one. It's just the only one we were left. The EZLN salutes the honest and necessary development of all forms of struggle that will lead us to freedom, democracy, and justice. The EZLN has never claimed its organization to be the only truthful, honest, and revolutionary one in Mexico, or even in Chiapas.

In fact, we organized ourselves this way because we were not left any other way. The EZLN salutes the honest and necessary development of all independent and progressive organizations that fight for freedom, democracy, and justice for the entire nation. There are, and will be, other revolutionary organizations. There are, and will be, other popular armies. We do not claim to be the one and only true historical vanguard. We do not claim that all honest Mexicans can fit under our Zapatista banner. We offer our flag. But there is a bigger and more powerful flag that can shelter us all. The flag of the national revolutionary movement can cover the most diverse tendencies, opinions, and different types of struggle, as long as they are united in a common desire and goal: freedom, democracy, and justice.

The EZLN calls on all Mexicans to unfurl this flag: not the flag of the EZLN, not the flag of the armed struggle, but the flag of all thinking beings, the flag of freedom, democracy, and justice. Under this great flag our Zapatista flag will wave, under this great flag our rifles will be raised.

The struggle for freedom, democracy, and justice is not only the task of the EZLN, it is the task of all Mexicans and all honest, independent, and progressive organizations—each one with its own ground, each one with its own form of struggle, each one with its own organization and ideas.

All who walk in truth should walk together on a single path: the one that leads to freedom, democracy, and justice.

Our struggle did not end, nor was our cry silenced, after we said, "Enough," on January 1, 1994. There is still more to go, the paths are different but the desire is one: Freedom! Democracy! Justice!

We will continue to struggle until we win the freedom that is our right, the democracy that is our reason, and the justice that is our life.

From the mountains of the Mexican Southeast
CCRI-CG
Mexico, January 1994

Source: *Shadows of Tender Fury: The Letters and Communiqués of Subcomandante Marcos and the Zapatista Army of National Liberation*, Frank Bardacke, Leslie López and the Watsonville, California Human Rights Committee, tran. (NY: Monthly Review Press, 1995), 90–91, 92–93. Copyright © 1995 by Monthly Review Press. Reprinted by permission of Monthly Review Foundation.

A Poet for the Millennium

José Emilio Pacheco (1939–) has been described as "the most important Mexican poet of the generation following Octavio Paz." His work has been hailed as the first of Latin America's post-modern writing. Pacheco demands an active reader who participates in the process as he tries to find meaning in the fractured, de-centered world of the late twentieth and early twenty-first centuries.

THE TWENTIETH-CENTURIANS

I

Because someone in the sixth century counted up
and called the inconceivable year when Christ
was born
Year One,
now the terror of the millennium,
the torments of the *fin-de-siecle* are ours.

Pity those who know
they are walking straight toward the abyss.
No doubt there is hope
for humanity.
For us, on the other hand,
there is only the certainty that tomorrow
we shall be condemned:
—the stupid twentieth century,
its primitive, savage inhabitants—

with the same fervor we used to banish
the *nineteenth-centurians,* authors,
with their ideas, their acts and inventions,
from the twentieth century, which only exists
in the imagination of those who watch
night gathering on this field of blood,
this planet of barbed wire fences, this
endless slaughterhouse that is dying
beneath the weight of all its victories.

II

A net full of holes is our legacy to you,
passengers of the twenty-first century. The ship
is sinking for lack of air,
there are no more forests, the desert
shimmers in an ocean of greed.

We filled up the earth with trash,
poisoned the air, made
poverty triumphant on the planet.

Above all we killed.
Our century was
the century of death.
So much death,
so many dead in every country.

So much blood
spilled on this earth.
And everyone
said they were killing for the sake of tomorrow:
the quicksilver future, the hope
sifting like sand through our fingers.

In the name
of Good
Evil was imposed.

Doubtless there were other things.
It is up to you
to recognize them.
For now
the twentieth century has ended.

It encloses us
like prehistoric amber traps the fly,
says Milosz.
Let us plead, along with Neruda,
for *pity for this century.*

Because after all
this present created the future that is crashing
into the past.

The century lasted an instant
and ended in a second.

We say good-bye
and go to sleep in the amber prison.

Source: José Emilio Pacheco, *City of Memory and Other Poems.* Cynthia Steele and David Lauer, tran. (San Francisco: City Lights Books, 1997), 31, 33, 35. Reprinted by permission of City Lights Books.

A Chronology
of Significant Dates
in Latin American
History

1492	Columbus reaches the New World.
1494	The Treaty of Tordesillas divides the world between Spain and Portugal.
1500	Cabral discovers Brazil.
1503	Spain legalizes the encomienda in the New World; Casa de Contratación created.
1512	The Laws of Burgos regulate the treatment of the Indians.
1513	Balboa discovers the Pacific Ocean.
1521	Hernándo Cortés completes the conquest of the Aztec empire.
1524	Creation of the Council of the Indies.
1532	First permanent settlements in Brazil.
1535	Francisco Pizzaro completes the conquest of the Incan empire; the first viceroy arrives in Mexico.
1542	The New Laws call for an end of the encomiendas.
1543	The first viceroy arrives in Peru.
1545	The Spaniards discover silver at Potosí.
1630–54	The Dutch control as much as one-third of Brazil.

1695	The Luso-Brazilians discover gold in the Brazilian interior.
1763	The capital of the Viceroyalty of Brazil is moved to Rio de Janeiro.
1776	Creation of the Viceroyalty of La Plata.
1804	Haiti declares its independence.
1808	The royal family of Portugal arrives in Brazil.
1810	Padre Miguel Hidalgo initiates Mexico's struggle for independence.
1811	Paraguay and Venezuela declare their independence.
1816	Argentina declares its independence.
1818–43	Jean-Pierre Boyer, a populist caudillo, rules Haiti.
1819	Brazil puts a steamship into service, the first in South America.
1821	Mexico, Peru, and Central America declare their independence.
1822–23	Emperor Agustín I rules the Mexican empire.
1822	Prince Pedro declares Brazil's independence and receives the title of emperor.
1823	President James Monroe promulgates the Monroe Doctrine.
1824	The Battle of Ayacucho marks the final defeat of the Spaniards in South America.
1824–38	The United Provinces of Central America in existence.
1825	Bolivia declares its independence.
1825–28	The Cisplatine War between Brazil and Argentina to possess Uruguay results in a stalemate and Uruguayan independence.
1829–52	The populist caudillo Juan Manuel de Rosas rules Argentina.
1830	The political union of Gran Colombia dissolves, leaving Colombia, Venezuela, and Ecuador to go their independent ways.
1838	The first railroad in Latin America is inaugurated in Cuba.
1839–65	The populist caudillo Rafael Carrera governs Guatemala.
1846–48	War of North American Invasion (Mexican-American War). The United States gains California, New Mexico, and Arizona from its victory.
1847–1903	The Cruzob rebellion in Yucatan and Mayan self-government.
1848–55	The popular caudillo Manuel Belzú governs Bolivia.
1850	The United States and Great Britain sign the Clayton-Bulwer Treaty to check the expansion of each in Central America. Unionization of workers slowly begins in the largest Latin American nations.
1852	Chile inaugurates the first railroad in South America. Chile and Brazil initiate telegraphic systems.

1864–67	Archduke Maximilian of Austria rules Mexico under French protection.
1865–70	In the War of the Triple Alliance, Argentina, Brazil, and Uruguay fight and eventually defeat Paraguay.
1876	The first refrigerator ship carries beef from Buenos Aires to Europe.
1876–1911	Porfirio Díaz governs Mexico.
1879–84	The War of the Pacific pits Chile against Peru and Bolivia.
1886	The University of Chile awards the first medical degree to a woman in Latin America.
1888	Brazil abolishes slavery.
1889	The military dethrones Emperor Pedro II of Brazil; Brazil becomes a republic.
1889–90	The first Inter-American Conference meets in Washington, D.C.
1898	As a result of the Spanish-American War, Cuba gains its independence from Spain and the United States takes possession of Puerto Rico.
1901	In the Hay-Pauncefote Treaty, Great Britain acknowledges U.S. supremacy in Central America.
1903	Panama gains its independence and signs a treaty with the United States for the construction of an interoceanic canal.
1903–29	José Batlle dominates Uruguayan politics, bringing stability and economic growth as well as the middle class to power.
1909–33	U.S. intervention and occupation of Nicaragua.
1910–40	The Mexican Revolution.
1911	Emiliano Zapata advocates agrarian reform in his Plan of Ayala.
1912	Argentina adopts the Saenz Peña law, giving all male citizens the right to vote, without property or literacy requirements.
1914	The Panama Canal opens.
1915–34	The United States occupies Haiti.
1916–22	Hipólito Irigoyen governs Argentina as its first middle-class president.
1916–24	The United States occupies the Dominican Republic.
1917	Promulgation of the Mexican constitution, the blueprint for the Revolution.
1919	Promulgation of the Uruguayan constitution, the blueprint for middle-class democracy.
1920–24	Arturo Alessandri, a representative of middle-class interests, governs Chile.

1927–33 Augusto César Sandino leads the guerrilla struggle in Nicaragua to expel the U.S. Marines.

1929 The world financial collapse reduces Latin American exports but encourages import-substitution industrialization. Ecuador grants the vote to women, the first in Latin America.

1932–35 Bolivia and Paraguay fight the Chaco War.

1934–40 The Mexican Revolution reaches its apogee under President Lázaro Cárdenas.

1937 Bolivia cancels foreign oil contracts and takes control of oil industry.

1938 Mexico nationalizes foreign oil companies.

1940 Promulgation of the Cuban constitution, a middle-class and nationalist blueprint for change.

1944–54 The era of Guatemalan democracy.

1945 Gabriela Mistral, Chilean poet, is the first Latin American to receive the Nobel Prize in literature.

1952 Guatemala promulgates its land reform.

1952–64 The Bolivian revolution.

1953 Bolivia puts into effect its land reform.

1954 The CIA overthrows President Jacobo Arbenz of Guatemala.

1959 Triumph of the Cuban revolution and the advent of Fidel Castro to power. Cuba issues its Agrarian Reform Law.

1960 For the first time, urban Latin Americans equal in number their rural counterparts.

1961 Washington breaks diplomatic relations with Cuba. The CIA sponsors the Bay of Pigs invasion in an attempt to overthrow Castro. President John F. Kennedy announces the Alliance for Progress.

1964 The Brazilian military deposes President João Goulart and establishes a dictatorship.

1965 The United States invades and occupies the Dominican Republic.

1967 Che Guevara is killed in Bolivia while attempting to spark a revolutionary uprising.

1968 The Mexican government squelches a significant student movement by firing on peaceful protestors at the Plaza of Tlatelolco in Mexico City. Hundreds are killed.

1970–73 President Salvador Allende sets in motion profound reforms to peacefully and democratically change Chile.

1973 The Chilean military overthrows President Allende, who dies in the attack on the presidential palace. The Uruguayan military terminates their nation's twentieth-century experiment with democracy.

1974–76 Isabel Perón serves as president of Argentina, the first female chief of state in the Western Hemisphere.

1976–83 Thousands are "disappeared" in the Dirty War in Argentina.

1977 Panama and the United States sign a treaty returning the Canal Zone to Panamanian control and putting the canal under Panamanian direction by 1999.

1979 Triumph of the Nicaraguan revolution. Young military reformers stage a coup d'etat in El Salvador.

1980 Sendero Luminoso initiates its armed struggle in Peru.

1981 Nicaragua promulgates its agrarian reform law. Latin America enters a severe economic crisis. President Ronald Reagan begins the contra war against Nicaragua.

1982 Argentina invades the Falkland Islands and is defeated by Great Britain.

1983 The United States invades Grenada and overthrows government. Economic reverses highlight Latin America's increasing difficulty in making international debt payments.

1984 Latin America's foreign debt reaches an unmanageable $350 billion.

1985 Brazil returns to democracy and civilian rule. Latin American population surpasses the 400 million mark.

1987 President Oscar Arias of Costa Rica wins the Nobel Peace prize.

1988 PRI (Partido Revolucionario Institucional) candidate Carlos Salinas de Gortari's defeat of Cuauhtemoc Cárdenas is decried as open fraud.

1989–90 United States invades and occupies Panama.

1990 Sandinistas lose presidential election to Violeta Chamorro, widow of the late newspaper editor Pedro Joaquin Chamorro, effectively ending the Sandinista Revolution.

1992 Quincentennial of European–American encounter. Sendero Luminoso controls much of rural Peru. Mexico's Carlos Salinas de Gortari amends the constitution to allow ejidos to be sold, rented, and mortgaged. Privatization of state firms begins.

1994 The North American Free Trade Agreement (NAFTA) links the markets of the United States, Mexico, and Canada. The day it takes effect, a rebellion breaks out in Chiapas, Mexico, led by the Zapatista Army of National Liberation.

1996   A peace agreement is signed in Guatemala.

1998   Former Chilean dictator Augusto Pinochet is arrested in England, on a Spanish warrant, on charges of human rights violations.

1999   The Panama Canal zone is returned to Panamanian control.

2000   For the first time in 71 years, PRI allows a free election in Mexico, and the voters elect Vicente Fox of the National Action Party (Partido de Acción Nacional). Augusto Pinochet is indicted in Chile.

STATISTICS ON THE NATIONS OF LATIN AMERICA

COUNTRY	POPULATION (Millions)	POPULATION GROWTH RATE (percent)	INFANT MORTALITY PER 1,000 LIVE BIRTHS	FERTILITY RATE	LIFE EXPECTANCY	LITERACY (Percent)	GDP PER CAPITA PURCHASING POWER PARITY	POPULATION BELOW POVERTY LINE (Percent)
Argentina	36.9	1.16	18.31	2.47	75	96.2	$10,000	36
Bolivia	8.1	1.83	60.44	3.66	64	83.1	3,000	70
Brazil	172.8	0.94	38.04	2.13	63	83.3	6,150	17.4
Chile	15.1	1.17	9.6	2.2	76	95.2	12,400	22.0
Colombia	39.6	1.68	24.7	2.69	70	91.3	6,200	17.7
Cuba	11.1	0.39	7.5	1.6	76	95.7	1,700	NA
Dominican Republic	8.4	1.64	35.93	3.0	73	82.1	5,400	25
Ecuador	12.9	2.04	35.13	3.18	71	90.1	4,300	50
El Salvador	6.1	1.87	29.22	3.38	70	71.5	3,100	48
Guatemala	12.6	2.63	47.0	4.66	66	55.6	3,900	75
Honduras	6.2	2.52	31.29	4.26	70	72.7	2,050	50
Mexico	100.3	1.53	26.19	2.67	72	89.6	8,500	27
Nicaragua	4.8	2.2	34.79	3.27	69	65.7	2,650	50
Panama	2.8	1.34	20.8	2.32	75	90.8	7,600	NA
Paraguay	5.6	2.64	30.8	4.16	74	92.1	3,650	32
Peru	27.0	1.75	40.6	3.04	70	88.8	4,400	54
Uruguay	3.3	0.77	15.14	2.37	75	97.3	8,500	NA
Venezuela	23.5	1.60	26.17	2.51	73	91.1	8,000	67
United States	275.5	0.91	6.82	2.06	77	97.0	33,900	12.7

Source: *The World Factbook 2000*, Washington, D.C.: Central Intelligence Agency, 2000.

COUNTRY	AGRICULTURE (percent)	GDP BY SECTOR INDUSTRY (percent)	SERVICES (percent)	GDP REAL GROWTH	UNEMPLOYMENT RATE	EXPORTS (In billions)	IMPORTS	EXTERNAL DEBT (billions)
Argentina	7.0	29.0	64.0	-3.0	14.0	23.0	25.0	149.0
Bolivia	16.6	35.5	47.9	2.0	11.4	1.1	1.6	5.7
Brazil	14.0	36.0	50.0	0.8	7.5	46.9	48.7	200.0
Chile	6.0	33.0	61.0	1.1	9.0	15.6	13.9	39.0
Colombia	19.0	26.0	55.0	-5.0	20.0	11.5	10.0	35.0
Cuba	7.4	36.5	56.1	6.2	6.0	1.4	3.2	11.2
Dominican Republic	13.6	30.8	55.6	8.3	13.8	5.1	8.2	3.7
Ecuador	14.0	36.0	50.0	-8.0	12.0	4.1	2.8	15.3
El Salvador	12.0	22.0	66.0	2.2	7.7	2.5	4.15	3.3
Guatemala	23.0	20.0	57.0	3.5	7.5	2.4	4.5	4.4
Honduras	20.0	25.0	55.0	-3.0	12.0	1.6	2.7	4.4
Mexico	5.0	29.0	66.0	3.7	2.5	136.8	142.1	155.8
Nicaragua	34.0	22.0	44.0	6.3	10.5	0.57	1.5	5.7
Panama	8.0	25.0	67.0	4.4	13.1	4.7	6.4	7.0
Paraguay	28.0	21.0	51.0	-1.0	12.0	3.1	3.2	2.7
Peru	13.0	42.0	45.0	2.4	7.7	5.9	8.4	31.0
Uruguay	10.0	28.0	62.0	-2.5	12.0	2.1	3.4	8.0
Venezuela	4.0	63.0	33.0	-7.2	18.0	20.9	11.8	32.0
United States	2.0	18.0	80.0	4.1	4.2	663.0	912.0	862.0

COUNTRY	HOUSEHOLD INCOME		TELEPHONES		TELEVISIONS	RADIOS
	TOP 10	BOTTOM 10	MAIN LINES	CELLULAR		
Argentina	NA	NA	7,500,000	1,800,000	7,950,000	24,003,000
Bolivia	31.7	2.3	368,874	7,229	900,000	5,025,000
Brazil	47.9	0.8	19,000,000	4,000,000	36,500,000	71,000,000
Chile	41.3	1.2	2,603,000	197,300	3,150,000	5,180,000
Colombia	46.9	1	5,433,565	1,800,229	4,590,000	21,000,000
Cuba	NA	NA	353,000	1,939	2,640,000	3,900,000
Dominican Rep.	39.6	1.6	569,000	33,000	770,000	1,440,000
Ecuador	37.6	2.3	748,000	49,776	1,550,000	4,150,000
El Salvador	38.3	1.2	380,000	13,475	600,000	2,750,000
Guatemala	46.6	0.6	342,000	29,999	640,000	835,000
Honduras	42.1	1.2	190,200	0	570,000	2,450,000
Mexico	36.6	1.8	9,600,000	2,020,000	25,600,000	31,000,000
Nicaragua	39.8	1.6	140,000	4,400	320,000	1,024,000
Panama	42.5	0.5	325,300	0	510,000	815,000
Paraguay	46.6	0.7	167,000	15,807	515,000	925,000
Peru	34.3	1.9	1,509,000	504,995	3,060,000	6,650,000
Uruguay	NA	NA	622,000	40,000 782,000	1,097,000	
Venezuela	35.6	1.5	2,600,000	2,000,000	4,100,000	10,700,000
United States	28.5	1.5	178,000,000	55,312,000	219,000,000	575,000,000

A Glossary of Spanish and Portuguese Terms

Adelantado An individual in colonial Spanish America authorized by the crown to explore, conquer, and hold new territory. He pushed back the frontier and extended Spanish claims and control of the New World.

Alcaldes mayores In colonial Spanish America, appointed officials who held administrative and judicial responsibility on local or district level.

Aldeia An Indian village or settlement in Portuguese America administered by the religious orders until the mid-eighteenth century and then by secular officials thereafter.

Audiencia The highest royal court and consultative council in colonial Spanish America.

Ayllu A communal unit in the Incan empire that worked the land in common, part for themselves and part for the Incan ruler and priestly elite.

Bandeirante Particularly active during the 1650–1750 period, these individuals penetrated the interior of Brazil to explore, to capture Indian slaves, or to search for gold.

Cabildo The municipal government in Spanish America.

Cabildo abierto The municipal council in Spanish America, which expanded under special circumstances to include most of the principal citizens of the municipality.

Campesino   A farmer or peasant.

Capitão-mor (plural, *capitães-mor*)   A military rank given to commanders of the local militia in colonial Portuguese America.

Capitulación   A contract between monarch and *adelantado* stating the duties and rewards of the latter.

Casa da Suplicação   The highest court in the Portuguese empire and therefore the supreme court for judicial disputes in colonial Brazil.

Casa de Contratación   The Board of Trade established in Spain in 1503 to organize, regulate, and develop trade with the New World.

Caudillo (Portuguese, *caudilho*)   A strong leader who wields complete power over subordinates.

Cédula   A royal edict from the Spanish monarch.

Científico   A high administrator in the government of President Porfirio Díaz of Mexico (1876–1911), infused with Positivist ideas, who believed national problems could be solved by scientific solutions. Such men were prominent during the last two decades of his administration.

Compadrio   A godparent relationship.

Composición   A Spanish legal device for claiming land through surveys.

Comunero   A participant in the Comunero Revolt that occurred in New Granada in 1781.

Congregación   The Spanish policy of concentrating Indians into villages.

Consejo de las Indias   The Council of the Indies established in Spain in 1524 to advise the monarch on American affairs.

Conseiho geral   In Portuguese America, a municipal council expanded under special circumstances to include most of the principal citizens of the municipality.

Conselho Ultramarino   The Overseas Council established in Lisbon in 1642 to advise the crown on matters relating to the empire and its administration.

Consulado   In colonial Spanish America, a guild of merchants acting as a sort of chamber of commerce.

Coronel (plural, *coroneis*)   A civilian political boss of a Brazilian municipality. The system of political control founded on the local bosses came to be known as *coronelismo*.

Corregidor   An official in colonial Spanish America who was assigned to Spanish as well as Indian communities as tax collector, police officer, magistrate, and administrator.

Creole   A white born in the Spanish American empire.

Cumbe   A settlement of runaway slaves in Spanish America.

Denuncia   Under Spanish law, the process of claiming land that does not have legally recognized owners.

Ejido   The common land held by Indian communities and used for agriculture in Mexico.

Encomendero   The person who received an *encomienda*.

Encomienda   A tribute institution used in Spanish America in the sixteenth century. The Spaniard received Indians as an entrustment, *encomienda*, to protect and to Christianize, but in return he could demand tribute including labor.

Fazenda   A large estate or plantation in Brazil.

Fazendeiro   The owner of a large estate or plantation in Brazil.

Finca   A large estate in Spanish America.

Fuero militar   A special military privilege in Spanish America that exempted officers from civil legal jurisdiction.

Gaucho   The cowboy of the Pampas.

Hacendado   A large estate in Spanish America.

Homens bons   In Portuguese, literally the "good men," those who belonged to the upper echelon of Brazilian colonial society. They voted for members of the municipal council.

Inquilino   A Chilean peasant.

Jefe   Chief or leader; boss. In Spanish America, it is often used as synonymous with *caudillo*.

Ladino   A person of mixed European and indigenous ancestry, or an Indian who adopts an Hispanic lifestyle. Used in place of mestizo in much of Central America.

Latifundia   The system of large landholdings in Latin America.

Mandamiento   A forced labor system.

Mascarada   A public festivity in which all or part of the participants wear costumes and masks.

Mazombo   In Portuguese America, a white born in the New World.

Mestizo   A person of mixed parentage. Usually it refers to a European-Indian mixture.

Mita   A forced labor system in which the Indian was required to labor for the state. It is most often associated with Indian labor in the Andean mines.

Oidor   A judge on the *audiencias* of Spanish America.

Palenque   A settlement of runaway slaves in Spanish America.

Patria chica   Literally, the small country, it refers to the immediate region with which people identify rather than the nation.

Patrón   In Spanish America, the owner or boss or one in a superior position.

Peninsular   In Spanish America, a white born in Europe who later came to the New World.

Porfiristas   Those in Mexico who supported Porfirio Díaz or his policies.

Porteño   An inhabitant of the city of Buenos Aires.

Presidencia   A subdivision of the viceroyalties of Spanish America, having a president as the chief executive officer.

Pueblo   A town, but it can also mean "people."

Quilombo   A settlement of runaway slaves in Portuguese America.

Ranchos   Squatter settlements in Venezuela.

Regidor   Municipal councilman in Spanish America.

Reinol (plural, *reinóis*)   In Portuguese America, a white born in Europe who later came to the New World.

Relaçao   The high court in Portuguese America.

Repartimiento   A labor institution in colonial Spanish America in which a royal judge made a temporary allotment of Indians for a given task.

Residencia   In both the Spanish and Portuguese American empires, a formal inquiry into the conduct of a public official at the end of his term of office.

Sambo   A person of mixed Indian and African parentage.

Senado da Câmara   In Brazil, the municipal government, in particular the town council.

Sertão   The interior, backlands, or hinterlands of Brazil. The term refers particularly to the hinterland region of northeastern Brazil.

Sesmaria   A land grant in colonial Brazil.

Soldadera   During the Mexican Revolution, a woman who was attached to a soldier. The *soldaderas* cooked for the soldiers, tended the ill and wounded, and fought.

Tenente   In Brazil, an army lieutenant. The word is often used to denote those junior army officers during the 1920s and early 1930s who favored social, economic, and political reforms.

Vecindad   Literally "neighborhood" in Spanish, but in Mexico City it can refer to a "tenement" dwelling.

Visita   In both the Spanish and Portuguese American empires, an on-the-spot administrative investigation of a public employee ordered by the monarch.

Visitador   In colonial Spanish and Portuguese America, an official in charge of making a special investigation for the monarch in the New World.

A Glossary of Concepts and Terms

Scattered throughout this text are a series of concepts and terms, some of which are defined—"reform" and "revolution," for example—and some of which are not—"capitalism," "socialism," and "Enlightenment," for example. The purpose of this glossary is to provide brief working definitions for the concepts and terms frequently encountered in the text. Definitions vary widely. They can be slippery. We have attempted to define the words in accordance with their use in the text, but we realize these definitions will neither satisfy everyone nor be universally applicable.

Capitalism An economic system characterized by private ownership and investment, economic competition, wage labor and profit incentive.
Centralism A high concentration of political power in the federal government.
Communism Communism really denotes a future society, one yet to be achieved. Societies often termed Communist are really at best in a transitional phase whose goal is a form of community living free from hierarchical controls and enjoying common property. This book uses the term within a contemporary context to mean a government ruling in

the name of the workers and peasants to best serve their ends and an economic system controlled by that government. The government owns the means of production in the name of the workers and peasants. This text distinguishes socialism from communism by the degree of state ownership, by the degree of democracy, and the existence of a plurality of political parties.

Conservatism   The term is generally associated with nineteenth-century political parties whose disposition was to preserve things much as they were, exercising caution in the acceptance of change.

Democracy   A system of government in which all or most of the citizenry participate in the decision-making process. Western democracy stresses equality of all citizens before the law, a government responsive to the majority, regular elections, civil liberties, and plural political parties.

Dependency   Dependency describes a situation in which the economic well-being, or lack of it, of one nation, colony, or area results from the consequences of decisions made elsewhere. Latin America was first dependent on the Iberian motherlands, then in the nineteenth century on England, and in the twentieth on the United States, whose decisions and policies directly influenced its economic prosperity or poverty. Obviously to the degree a nation is dependent, it will lack "independence" of action.

Development   The maximum use of a nation's potential for the greatest benefit of the largest number of inhabitants.

Elites   Those persons who occupy the highest or most eminent positions in society.

Enclave economy   An economic activity that depends on little from the host country other than low-wage labor, rather than depending on local material imports or interactions with local businesses. A classic example is the banana industry, in which local workers cut bunches of bananas that are immediately loaded onto foreign-owed ships and sent out of the country.

Enlightenment   Broadly identified with eighteenth-century Europe, the Enlightenment introduced a series of ideas associated with the forms of democracy and capitalism of the nineteenth century. Enlightenment thought stressed human social evolution and thus became a kind of philosophy of progress and perfectability. The ideas of the Enlightenment exerted a profound influence on the writing of the U.S. Constitution and on the ideology of the Latin American elites.

Federalism   In a federal political system, political power is divided and/or shared between a central government and regional or local governments.

Feudalism   Strictly speaking, this term refers to a form of social organization prevalent in Europe from the time of the dissolution of Charlemagne's empire until the rise of the absolute monarchies, roughly from the ninth to the fifteenth centuries. Its general characteristics were strict class division, private jurisdiction based on local custom, and a land-owning system in which the owner, the lord, allowed the serf to work land in return for services and/or payments. By extension, the term is used in Latin America to designate a system in which a few own the land and control the lives of the many who work the land for them. Those few enjoy comfortable lives, while the workers live in misery largely dependent on the whims of the landowners. The term today has connotations much more emotional than legal.

Growth   Growth indicates numerical accumulation in a country or region's economy and generally does not reveal who, if anyone, benefits from it.

Hegemony   Refers both to dominance, as in the United States is the hegemonic power in the hemisphere, as well as an acceptance by the majority of the role of the dominant power. A government has hegemony when the majority of the citizenry recognize the government's right to rule.

Institutions   This book's most frequently used term and its most difficult to define, "institutions" represent the recognized usages governing relations between people, an entire complex of such usages and the principles governing it, and the formal organizations supporting such a complex. Perhaps Webster's unabridged dictionary offers a more satisfactory and comprehensive definition: "A significant and persistent element (as a practice, a relationship, an organization) in the life of a culture that centers on a fundamental human need, activity, or value, occupies an enduring and cardinal position within a society, and is usually maintained and stabilized through social regulatory agencies." Examples range from patriarchal families to the military, from village social structure to land division.

Liberalism   This term is generally associated with nineteenth-century political parties whose disposition was to relax governmental control, to expand individual freedom, and to innovate.

Luso-Brazilian   This term encompasses both Portugal and Brazil. In Roman times, the area we now associate with Portugal bore the name Lusitania, the adjective being Luso.

Mercantilism   A term coined in the eighteenth century, it is a belief that the nation's economic welfare can best be ensured by governmental regulation of a nationalist character. The policy as imposed by the Iberian nations meant that the welfare of the motherlands received preferential treatment to those of the Latin American colonies, generally considered to exist for the enrichment of Spain and Portugal.

Metropolis   This term refers to that country exerting direct or indirect control over another. For Spanish America, the metropolis in the colonial period was Spain; for Brazil, Portugal. During the nineteenth century, the metropolis for Latin America was England; in the twentieth century it has been the United States.

Modernization In Latin America, modernization consisted largely of copying and adopting, rarely adapting, the styles, ideas, technology, and patterns of Northern Europe in the nineteenth century and the United States in the twentieth.

Nationalism This term refers to a group consciousness that attributes great value to the nation-state, to which total loyalty is pledged. Members of the group agree to maintain the unity, independence, and sovereignty of the nation-state as well as to pursue certain broad and mutually acceptable goals.

Nation-state This term, implying more than the area encompassed by the geographic boundaries of a country, signifies that a central authority effectively exercises political power over that entire area.

Neofeudalism *Neo,* from the Greek, signifies "new" or "recent." See the entry "feudalism."

Oligarchy These privileged few rule for their own benefit, demonstrating little or no responsibility toward the many.

Patriarchal, Patriarchy Originally this term referred to a family system and by extension social, political, and economic system in which the father or oldest male dominates. The term has since been broadened to describe social systems in which men dominate women through a variety of legal, social, and cultural mechanisms.

Patrimonialism A system in which the landowner exerts authority over his followers as one aspect of property ownership. Those living on his land fall under his control. He rules the estate at will and controls all contact with the outside world. The term describes the hacienda system.

Physiocrat Doctrine This concept originating in the eighteenth century urges society to survey scientifically its resources and, once knowing them, to exploit them. Maximum profit results from the exploitation and international sale of those resources.

Populist Political movements or governments that seem at least outwardly opposed to the status quo are in some cases termed "populist." They advocate a system appealing to and supported by large numbers of the ordinary citizens, generally the urban working class. In practice, they often provide temporary relief or benefits without actually reforming basic social structures.

Positivism This nineteenth-century ideology originated in France. Its principal philosopher was Auguste Comte. Positivism affirmed the inevitability of social innovation and progress. According to Comte, that progress was attainable through the acceptance of scientific social laws codified by Positivism.

Reform   To reform is to gradually change or modify established economic, political, or social institutions.

Revolution   Revolution denotes the sudden, forceful, and violent overturn of a previously stable society and the substitution of other institutions for those discredited.

Socialism   As used in this text, socialism denotes a democratic society in which the community owns or controls the major means of production, administering them for the benefit of all.

The Novel as History: A Reading Guide

With roots deep in the nineteenth century, the Latin American novel offers unique insights into the people and drama of the region. The increasing number of novels translated into English introduces the U.S. reading public to an exciting literature that promotes fuller understanding of Latin America. This essay suggests a few of the novels that complement and expand the major themes in *Latin America: A Concise Interpretive History.* They are splendid documents for historians.

In recent years, historians have increasingly looked to novelists as sources for a better understanding of the past. The novelists portray poverty; the hopes, triumphs, and frustrations of people; and the inequities and contributions of institutions in ways that history books cannot—or do not. They delve into a people's social world, their adaptation and rebellion. They describe people's relations with each other, with their institutions, and with their environment. They bring to life all classes and groups of society with an imagination seldom found in texts. The novelists make extremely important observations about their own societies, transcending simple description and supposedly objective analysis to reveal feeling and emotion. On one level the novel reflects the writer's world view on a topic. On another level, it is a document of, a mirror to, a period. Further and very importantly, the novels expose and sensitize their readers to Latin American viewpoints.

The historian and the novelist share much in common. Time, space, people, factual exposition, causation, and interpretation are the ingredients compounded by historians. They are also the essential components of the successful novels written by Latin Americans. A concern with "raw facts" and interpretation as well as the use of imagination link historians with novelists, certainly with the novelists recommended in this bibliographic essay.

Historians proudly cultivate their "historical imaginations" as an asset to their research and writing, the best insight into the topics they explore. It is not necessary to delve very deeply into historical manuals before discovering the high value historians place on imagination. One such beginner's manual advises the aspiring historian, "History involves the imaginative understanding of experience and its communication to an audience. It is closely related to the art of the novel, for both tell a story, the main difference laying in the amount of imaginative reconstruction of facts and personalities." Imagination is just as important to historians as it is to novelists. Indeed, without it, history could not be written.

The fundamental premise for the use of these novels as historical documents rests on the acceptance of the idea that the novelists can portray and interpret society as accurately and as validly as other intellectuals can. Of course historians should not expect, nor require, novelists to fit into their traditional modes. Novelists introduce new methods or approaches to the study of the past. Their imaginations, fortunately, enliven and enrich history and the historical process. When both the novelists and historians claim responsibility for observable data, they share a fundamental characteristic that in the long run accents their similarity. From there, both go on to shape the facts in conformity with predetermined thought patterns and with imagination. In those ways, both offer compelling views of the past.

Ignacio Manuel Altamirano, *Christmas in the Mountains* (Gainesville: University of Florida Press, 1961). *La Navidad en las Montañas* first appeared serially in Mexico in 1871. Himself an Indian born and raised in a rural folk community, Altamirano lamented the chaos and bloodshed of the first half-century of Mexico's independent life. His vision of an ideal society combining the best qualities of the traditional rural folk community with some of the best qualities of Spanish-imposed institutions illuminates *Christmas in the Mountains*. He provides a unique, articulate, and romanticized view of the folk community and the contributions it could make to national society and the nation-state. He idealizes patriarchal folk society in this novel of political solutions—or of utopia—one of the extremely rare favorable nineteenth-century discussions of that prevalent and much maligned society.

The novel relates the experiences of a young army officer who spends a Christmas in a small Mexican mountain village. In the early pages of the novel, he confesses, "I had promised myself that I would end my journey in a small village of poor, but hospitable, mountaineers who lived from the product of the soil and who enjoyed a relative well-being, thanks to their isolation from large, populous centers and to the goodness of their patriarchal customs." The only other outside influence in the village is the Roman Catholic Church, personified by a sensitive and sensible priest dedicated to the welfare of his parishioners. The idealized military and Church combine with the noble characteristics of a patriarchal folk community to create a seemingly perfect society. The symbolism of Christmas and a snow fall hangs heavily over this sometimes irritating but always fascinating novel, unquestionably one of the most important windows for a view of nineteenth-century Latin America.

Clorinda Matto de Turner, *Torn from the Nest* (New York : Oxford University Press, 1999). Matto de Turner ranks as one of the foremost female writers of nineteenth-century Latin America. This novel, *Aves sin Nido*, published in 1889, represents the first Indianist novel. It also was one of the first to note the consequences of the changes modernization imposed. Born near Cuzco, Peru, where she lived much of her life, Matto de Turner discusses the plight of Peru's Indian majority, abused, in her opinion, by the Church, the State, and large landowners. Her novel exposes that abuse and condemns it. She expressed her reasons for writing the novel as four: to call attention to the suffering of Indians, to urge the reform of backward conditions in the Peruvian interior, to suggest the progress that must be made, and to help create a Peruvian literature.

Matto de Turner saw change occurring through two media: education and the cities. The novel invests great faith in both to rescue the Indians and to develop Peru. For her, the city symbolized the civilization needed to regenerate Peru. More than one inhabitant of the remote village of Kíllac affirmed that the future lay in the city. One of the novel's principal characters remarks, "All those who have sufficient means migrate to the centers of civilization." Lima was presented in the novel as such a center. Speaking to two young Indian girls on their way to Lima, one of the leading characters of the novel declared enthusiastically,

> Oh yes, Lima! There the heart becomes educated and the mind instructed. To travel to Lima is to go to Heaven's antechamber and to see from there the throne of the Glory of the Future. They say that our beautiful capital is a fairytale city.

Fittingly, a train transports the villagers from the rural past to the urban future. The train's engineer is from the United States!

Aluísio Azevedo, A *Brazilian Tenement* (N.Y.: R. M. McBride, 1926). On the opposite side of the South American continent from Matto de Turner, Azevedo was in the process of writing and publishing one of the first major novels of urbanization, *O Cortiço* (1890), a study of Rio de Janeiro at a moment of agitated change. The novel deserves attention partly because of Azevedo's concern with social problems but mainly because of the insight he provides, a wealth of details about the routines of daily life of ordinary people.

One aspect of Rio de Janeiro was its pervasive poverty; another was the social mobility it permitted. The novel also discusses lifestyles, nationalism, social conflict, the roles of women, and race relations. Some of the novel's characters play major symbolic roles. Rita Bahiana, for example, incarnates "Brazilian character." The process of the Brazilianization of the Portuguese immigrant Jeronymo provides another set of character symbols during a period of intensifying European migration to Brazil. The period Azevedo chronicles witnessed the onset of rapid urbanization, a salient characteristic of the twentieth century.

Carlos Gagini, *Redemptions. A Costa Rican Novel* (San Diego: San Diego State University Press, 1985). The meanings derived from the symbolism saturating this short novel, originally published under the title of *El Arbol Enfermo* (1918), far outweigh in importance the rather insipid story. Gagini emphasizes the new social, economic, and political forces at work in Latin America. By 1918, Costa Rica, the locale of the novel, clearly had surrendered its economic independence and mortgaged its future to foreigners, realities that greatly disturbed nationalists like Gagini and provided a bitter backdrop for *Redemptions.* Also present in the novel is a significant new social reality: the emergence of very small urban working and middle classes. The author rather idealistically suggests the potential and benefits of their political alliance. Nationalistic apprehensions over foreign influences dominate the novel.

Much of the novel directly or indirectly centers on the differences between Anglo and Latin cultures, an old discussion in Latin America greatly enlivened by the easy U.S. victory over Spain in 1898 and the physical expansion of the United States into the Caribbean. Gagini provides insight into the conflicting emotions of the Latin Americans in a new era in which the United States emerged as the metropolis. Reflecting a well-delineated Latin American viewpoint, he stresses the spiritual qualities of the Latin Americans, contrasting them with the materialism dominant in the United States. Still, ambiguities soften the degree of Gagini's cultural dichotomy. He obviously admires the freedom, order, efficiency, and technology of the United States, just as he laments the political bankruptcy, social vices, and educational malaise of Costa Rica. He makes a great point of stressing that Costa Rica's problems not be laid at the door of the United States, at least not in their entirety. Costa Ricans must take responsibility for their own future, one in which reform, nationalism, the city, and the working and middle classes seem destined to play major roles. An understanding of Gagini's abundant use of symbolism helps the reader to appreciate the rich meanings of this novel.

Mariano Azuela, *The Underdogs* (N. Y.: A Signet Classic, 1996). *Los de Abajo* initially appeared as weekly installments in Mexico City's *El Universal*

Ilustrado in 1924 and was published as a novel four years later. The first novel of the Mexican Revolution, it reflects the deep cynicism and disillusionment felt by Azuela, who served as a doctor in the army of Pancho Villa. The protagonist of the novel, Demetrio Martínez, joins the revolution because of his hatred of the local political boss, but by the end he no longer knows why he is fighting. He is surrounded by pillaging and raping soldiers, and a variety of opportunists, who articulate the ethical ideals that all too often were not realized.

Ricardo Güiraldes, *Don Segundo Sombra* (N. Y.: A Signet Classic, 1966). Bearing the same title when first published in Argentina in 1926, this novel marks a significant passage in the national life of Argentina: the end of folk culture and the triumph of the city and "civilization." Specifically, for Argentina it marked the passing of the *gaucho,* the cowboy of the pampas, and the domination of one city, burgeoning Buenos Aires. The young protagonist grows up under the care of Don Segundo Sombra, the consummate gaucho. Upon the death of his father, the youth must abandon his cherished life as a gaucho to assume the responsibilities of a landowner, distancing himself from the everyday activities of the estate to link himself with the markets and businesses in Buenos Aires and abroad. His moving farewell to Don Segundo Sombra is, in fact, Argentina's farewell to its rural past and entrance into modernity, a highly complex break in Latin America which arouses deeply contradictory feelings. The concluding chapters with their profound emotions expose an ambivalence within Latin America about modernization. *Don Segundo Sombra* exudes poetry. It suggests the major Latin American epic.

Gregorio Lopez y Fuentes, *El Indio* (N.Y.: Frederick Ungar, 1961). The English translation bears the same title as the Spanish-language edition of 1935. In a few pages, this popular and highly symbolic Mexican novel relates the sweeping dynamic of Mexican history. The symbolic characters and events develop an allegory of race relations—and cultural dash—since the conquest. "Civilization" constantly encroaches on the Indians and the novel raises the question of what benefits, if any, the Indians receive from it. In the final, provocative part of the novel, Lopez y Fuentes seems to see the Mexican Revolution as a further enactment of the conquest. The changes it wrought benefit the "whites," not the Indians who seem destined by the changes to eventual extinction. By extension, the observations of López y Fuentes can be applied to other peoples across time throughout Latin America, giving the novel a universality in its meaning.

Graciliano Ramos, *Barren Lives* (Austin: University of Texas Press, 1992). In 1938, the Brazilians published *Vidas Sêcas,* a penetrating insight into the lives of the impoverished rural masses, the so-called rural proletariat, which possesses no land of its own. Fabiano, his wife Victoria, their two small sons, and their dog Baleia, flagellated by the drought in the dry interior of Northeastern Brazil, take refuge in an abandoned hut. The rains save them. Later, another drought and oppressive conditions start them on another journey, a cycle of migration common throughout Latin America. Fatalism, the sinew of tradition, permeates Fabiano.

This novel highlights at least two significant themes: the relationship of the ordinary people to the land and the common people as victim of institutions they did not create, cannot influence, and apparently cannot change. Those institutions and to some extent the geographical environment mold the characters of this novel, just as they shape the ordinary people of Brazil's interior. This novel is essentially a document about landowner–labor relationships. *Barren Lives* is a valuable document explaining, with details and an emotional dimension, how key Brazilian institutions work and how they affect ordinary people.

Rachel de Queiroz, *The Three Marias* (Austin: University of Texas Press, 1991). The first woman admitted to the Brazilian Academy of Letters, Queiroz wrote the mainly autobiographical *As Três Marías* in 1939. The novel details the lives of three young Marias reaching womanhood in a provincial Brazilian city, Fortazela, during the 1920s and 1930s. The three feel the frustrations of women facing inequality, educational and career restrictions, and the definition of their own sexual feelings. Through the eyes of Queiroz, the reader sees Brazil at a given moment as the women of that time did.

Ciro Alegría, *Broad and Alien Is the World* (N.Y.: Dufour, 1987). The Peruvian novelist Alegría depicts the life and disintegration of an Andean Indian community in his *El Mundo Es Ancho y Ajeno* (1941). Harmonious with their environment, rooted in their soil, the members of the Indian community are contented and well provided for until outsiders apply the "law" to deprive them of their lands, a story as old as the conquest in Latin America but one which continues up through the end of the twentieth century. Alegría contrasts the folk community with advancing capitalism and chronicles the effects of the changes on the Andean Indians. This meaty novel thus operates on the levels of a given reality and a powerful allegory.

Jorge Amado, *The Violent Land* (N.Y.: Avon Books, 1988). The first Portuguese-language edition, *Terras do sem Fim,* appeared in 1943. Basically, the ownership and use of land shaped the history of Latin America more than any other factor. It still does. Amado writes about the acquisition, use, abuse, maintenance, and loss of land. In particular, the novel focuses on the struggle of Horácio Silveira and Juca and Sinho Badaro over land whose rich soil produces the cacao tree, source of chocolate. It details the acquisition and ownership of land and all the institutions related to the struggle and possession. While it concerns only cacao lands, it could just as accurately depict sugar or coffee estates—or any other, for that matter. The story includes, among other topics, the grandeur and force of nature, the institutions surrounding the rural workers, the conflict of cultures, the roles of women, and the significance of frontiers. The conquest of the cacao lands in the search for quick wealth repeats the old incentive that propelled many to the Americas—discovery, exploration, conquest, and exploitation. It provides insight into the violence connected with the European settlement of the Western Hemisphere. In fact, the novel holds lessons pertinent for the present conquest of the Amazon or of Southern Chile.

Amado's *The Tent of Miracles* (N.Y. Avon, 1988). *A Tenda dos Milagres* (1969) is a tour de force, based loosely but unmistakably on the life of the remarkable Manuel Raimundo Querino (1851–1923), the first African-Brazilian historian. Taking as its locale the state of Bahia, once a focal point of African slavery, the novel wittily discusses the rich topic of race relations, the hypocrisies and the realities. The mature Amado amuses while he instructs his readers.

Miguel Angel Asturias, *El Señor Presidente* (Prospect Heights : Waveland Press, 1997). The roots for this Guatemalan masterpiece lie in the repressive dictatorship of Manuel Estrada Cabrera, who terrorized that nation between 1898 and 1920. Asturias began it in 1922 but the completed novel (it carries the same name in the English translation as in Spanish) only appeared in 1946. It remains the author's best novel and a major Latin American classic. Asturias won the Nobel Prize for Literature in 1967.

El Señor Presidente details Latin American authoritarianism. It illuminates the phenomenon of the *caudillo,* a major political characteristic of the region since independence. Asturias's work constitutes the definitive study of the exercise of supreme political power. The reader not only receives an understanding of how a dictatorship gains and retains power but, thanks to the powerful prose of Asturias, a "feeling" of its omnipotence and omniscience and its effects upon the population.

Carlos Fuentes, *The Death of Artemio Cruz* (N.Y.: Farrar, Strauss and Giroux, 1991). In his *La Muerte de Artemio Cruz* (1962), the eminent Mexican intellectual Carlos Fuentes confronted a question increasingly on the mind of Mexicans: "Was the Mexican Revolution dead?" Through the novel's central character, Artemio Cruz, Fuentes sweeps across the twentieth century in an effort to address that challenging question. He concludes that the Revolution died and attempts to explain why and how. In the process, the novel discusses some of the major political themes of modern Latin American history.

Cruz fought in the Revolution; later, he became a business tycoon. Through the transformations Cruz undergoes, it is possible to trace the dramatic changes of twentieth-century Mexico. One interpretation of the novel accepts Cruz as a representative of those new groups that seized power and turned the Revolution to their own advantage. Cruz himself amassed large estates despite the land reform and allied himself with foreign capital to exploit Mexico's resources. Both actions betrayed the Revolution. Thus betraying the Revolution, those groups reversed it.

Gabriel García Márquez, *One Hundred Years of Solitude* (Madison: Turtleback Books, 1998). Originally published in 1967 as *Cien Años de Soledad*, this classic is perhaps the best known Latin American novel and is the prototype of the genre of literature that García Márquez dubbed the magic of the real, and that has come to be known as magical realism. The novel follows the fortunes and failures of the Buendía family in the small town of Macondo, and through their lives tells the story of all Latin America, from discovery through the modern era. Particularly powerful are his renditions of the endless wars between Liberals and Conservatives, the impact of the North American-owned banana enclave, and the bloody repression of a labor strike that the government denies ever happened. When he accepted the Nobel Prize for Literature in 1982, he explained that Latin America's incredible reality left a novelist nowhere to go but to the fantastic; nonetheless, he maintains that every sentence has its beginning in truth.

Mario Vargas Llosa, *The War of the End of the World* (N.Y.: Avon, 1985). This lengthy but intriguing novel by a Peruvian author, originally published as *La Guerra del Fin del Mundo* in 1981, offers a fictionalized account of an important millennial movement in the interior of Brazil during the last decade of the nineteenth century. The recently established republican government perceived a threat from a folk community, Canudos, in which the millenarian movement and loyalty to the deposed monarch centered. The armed struggle between the government and the folk, brutal and prolonged, represented the official determination to "civilize" the folk and bring them within the Europeanized institutions of the modern nation-state, those favored by the elites in power. Much to the credit of Vargas Llosa, he meticulously presents both sides of that crucial and complex struggle between forces more favorable to tradition (i.e., local customs) and those desirous of modernization (i.e. Europeanization), one of the most traumatic and significant aspects of nineteenth-century Latin American history.

Manlio Argueta, *One Day of Life* (N.Y.: Vintage, 1990). The Salvadoran edition of *Un Día de la Vida* was published in 1980. Repression and rebellion permeate this novel of rural life in El Salvador during civil war. Men are absent. They fled military recruitment or the vicious death squads. Women populate this powerful novel, expressing their viewpoint of the institutions being attacked and defended and maintaining their households and communities. The novel carefully documents the brutal intrusions of official institutions into rural community life, an old but still ubiquitous Latin American reality.

Isabel Allende, *The House of the Spirits* (New York: Knopf, 1985). Allende's first novel, *La Casa de los Espíritus* (1984) became an overnight sensation as she gave a distinctly female voice to magical realism. The novel tells the story of the Trueba family through much of the twentieth century. We see the large estate of the countryside juxtaposed with the wealth and poverty that stand side by side as the city grows. The tensions between rich and poor become manifested in the political struggle between right and left that divides the family as much as society.

Though not as celebrated, Allende's *Of Love and Shadows* (New York: Knopf, 1987) is in many ways a more masterful novel than *House of the Spir-*

its. In some ways, *De Amor y de Sombra* (1985) can be seen as a sequel. The wealthy Irene Beltrán falls in love with the photographer, Francisco Leal, and as they follow the story of a girl whose fits are taken for miraculous powers, they uncover the horror of the wars waged by the government against their own people in South America.

Diamela Eltit, *The Fourth World* (Lincoln: University of Nebraska Press, 1995).   The appearance of *El Cuarto Mundo* in 1988 established Diamela Eltit as one of the most provocative voices of the new postmodern fiction of Latin America. Eltit uses the dysfunctional family as a metaphor for dysfunctional society and the fragmentation of modern reality. The book itself is told in fragments, the first narrated by a young man, and the second by his twin sister. There are echoes of García Márquez, especially in the symbolism of incest, but refracted through a distorted lens, or perhaps a clear lens viewing a distorted reality.

These novels barely scratch the surface of the lengthy list of those available in English translation. For readers of Spanish and/or Portuguese, new literary worlds await discovery. Those who want to pursue further the ways in which literature and history can be linked might begin with David T. Haberly, *Three Sad Races. Racial Identity and National Consciousness in Brazilian Literature* (N.Y.: Cambridge University Press, 1983); John S. Brushwood, *Genteel Barbarism. New Readings of Nineteenth-Century Spanish-American Novels* (Lincoln: University of Nebraska Press, 1981); and Raymond L. Williams, *The Postmodern Novel in Latin America: Politics, Culture and the Crisis of Truth* (N.Y.: St. Martin's Press, 1996). Charles W. Macune, Jr., concluding that "the novel is a unique form of historical evidence," suggests how the young historian might approach it in his "The Latin American Novel as History: An Idea for an Undergraduate Course," *Proceedings of the Pacific Coast Council on Latin American Studies*, Vol. VI (1977–79), 179–84.

Index

E

Echeverría, Esteban, 108
Economic crises, in Latin America, 227–30
Economic Societies of the Friends of the Country, 63
Economy
  British, 84
  crisis in Brazilian, 228
  crisis in Cuban, 228
  early Latin American, 30–39
  reflex, 100
Ecuador, 94
  agriculture in, 240
  slow growth of, 141
  women in, 189
Eder, George Jackson, 257
Education, 152–54
  in Argentina, 152
  in Chile, 152, 153
  in Costa Rica, 185
  in Cuba, 263
  in Guatemala, 152
  monopoly of by church, 52, 96
  in Nicaragua, 277
  as path to middle sector, 181
  in Uruguay, 186
Eisenhower, President, 262
Ejidos, 98
Elections, and democracy, 303–07
Elites, 155
  definition of, 132
  dependence of on Europe, 84
  idealism of, 90
  and move toward independence, 61
  new governments as, 305
  in New World, 62
  in post-colonial Brazil, 183
  and progress, 136
  regaining of power in Bolivia, 120–21
  revolt of, 72–77
  support of by caudillos, 112
  under Perón in Argentina, 236
El Salvador, 2
  agriculture in, 239

dictators in, 231
elections in, 306
revolution in, 299–300
and Soccer War, 298
United States in, 298–300
Eltit, Diamela, 361
Enclave economy, 301
Encomendero, 32
Encomienda, 32, 33
England
  and Falkland Islands War, 294
  industrialization of, 39
  trade with, 65
Enlightenment, 62
  legacy of, 107–12
Environment, 313, 322–24
Equiano, Olaudah, 28
Escobar, Arturo, 328
Estado Nôvo, 231
Estates, 105–06
Estenoz, Evaristo, 219
European ideas, in Latin America, 63
European intervention, fears of, 91–99
European invasions, 11–22
  Dutch, 19
  English, 19
  French, 19
  Portuguese, 11, 12, 13, 14
  Spanish, 12, 14
Export economy, 226
Export markets, and railroads, 139
Exports, reliance on, 31–32, 142

F

Falkland Islands war, 294
Family Code, 265
Farías, Valentín Gómez, 97
Fazendas, 37, 106
Federación de Mujeres Cubanas, 264–65